"Robert G. Barnwell has created a thorough, disciplin
filmmakers and producers to follow as they create brandii
strategies for themselves and their films."
                    —**Anne Parducci**, fo

Marketing, Lions Gate Entertainment

"An indispensable reference. Teaches producers what they need to know about indie
marketing and distribution, from the nuts and bolts of key art design and trailer editing
to web-based marketing such as social media, website design, email marketing and much
much more . . ."

                    —**Josh Welsh**, *President, Film Independent,*
                    Independent Spirit Awards and LA Film Festival

"Independent filmmakers face what may often seem to be overwhelming marketing and
distribution challenges. *Guerrilla Film Marketing* offers producers dozens of no and low-
cost tips, tools and templates to overcome these challenges to effectively brand, market,
promote and distribute their films."

            —**Chris Horton**, *Director, Creative Distribution Initiative, Sundance Institute*

"*Guerrilla Film Marketing* is the essential marketing guide for students and independent
filmmakers alike."

                    —**Michael Taylor**, *Former Chair of Film & Television Production, Division of*
                    Film & Television Production, USC School of Cinematic Arts

"An invaluable resource for students and professionals alike in terms of developing,
marketing and distributing a commercially successful independent film."

            —**Bradley Battersby**, *Head of Film Department, Ringling College of Art & Design*

"*Guerrilla Film Marketing* is a detailed and useful resource that can help you and your
filmmaking team handle marketing throughout the entire production and distribution
process. Don't go on set without marketing and distribution guidance and a plan."

            —**Orly Ravid**, *Founder and Co-Executive Director, The Film Collaborative*

"As Robert G. Barnwell explains, there are few things more critical to the success of an
independent film than effective branding, marketing and promotion e.g. connecting
with an audience. Should be required reading for any Producer of Marketing and
Distribution or filmmaker in the process of developing an independent film."

                    —**Jon Reiss**, *Producer of Marketing & Distribution and author of*
                    Think Outside the Box Office: The Ultimate Guide to Film
                    Distribution and Marketing for the Digital Era

"An invaluable marketing resource, *Guerrilla Film Marketing* is filled with dozens of step-
by-step instructions, checklists, tools, templates and other resources."
                    —**Kendra Ruczak**, *Editor,* Sound & Picture Magazine

Guerrilla Film Marketing

Create an irresistible brand image and build an audience of loyal and engaged fans . . .

Guerrilla Film Marketing takes readers through each step of the film branding, marketing and promotional process. Tailored specifically to low-budget independent films and filmmakers, *Guerrilla Film Marketing* offers practical and immediately implementable advice for marketing considerations across every stage of the film production process.

Written by leading film industry professional Robert G. Barnwell, *Guerrilla Film Marketing* teaches readers how to:

*   Master the fundamentals of guerrilla branding, marketing and promotion;
*   Create an integrated marketing plan and calendar based on realistic budgets and expectations;
*   Develop internet and social media marketing campaigns, including engaging studio and film websites and powerful, marketing-centric IMDb listings;
*   Assemble behind-the-scenes pictures, videos and documentaries;
*   Produce marketing materials such as key art, posters, film teasers, trailers and electronic press kits (aka "EPKs"); and
*   Maximize the marketing impact of events such as test screenings, premiers, film festivals and industry award ceremonies.

Guerrilla Film Marketing is filled with dozens of step-by-step instructions, checklists, tools, a glossary, templates and other resources. A downloadable eResource also includes a sample marketing plan and audit, a test screening questionnaire, and more.

Robert G. Barnwell is the founder and creative director of a small independent production company established to reduce the risks and increase the profitability of low-budget film projects on behalf of its investors. Previously, he worked as a strategy consultant and corporate banker providing advice and financing for such studios as 20th Century Fox, Columbia Pictures, Disney, MGM, Paramount Pictures, Universal and Warner Brothers. Robert has served as an adjunct professor at Ringling College of Art & Design and as a speaker and guest lecturer at several leading film schools, seminars and workshops.

Guerrilla Film Marketing

The Ultimate Guide to the Branding, Marketing and Promotion of Independent Films & Filmmakers

Robert G. Barnwell

Illustrated by Sandy O. Cagnan

Routledge
Taylor & Francis Group

NEW YORK AND LONDON

First published 2019
by Routledge
711 Third Avenue, New York, NY 10017

and by Routledge
2 Park Square, Milton Park, Abingdon, Oxon OX14 4RN

Routledge is an imprint of the Taylor & Francis Group, an informa business

Library of Congress Cataloging-in-Publication Data
A catalog record for this book has been applied for

ISBN: 978-1-138-91646-3 (hbk)
ISBN: 978-1-138-91645-6 (pbk)
ISBN: 978-1-138-91647-0 (ebk)

Typeset in Palatino and Futura
by Florence Production Ltd, Stoodleigh, Devon, UK

Visit the eResource: www.routledge.com/9781138916456

Dedicated to the world's aspiring and practicing filmmakers.

. . . and to the amazing women in my life.
Particularly, my wife, Jade; daughter, Kristen;
mother, Linda; and grandmother, Ruth.

CONTENTS

ACKNOWLEDGEMENTS

Even though there are many moments when it may feel like it, no one writes a book alone. Throughout my life and career, and certainly throughout the writing of this book, I've benefitted from the support, encouragement and inspiration of dozens – if not hundreds – of people.

Although we have yet to meet personally, I'd like to thank filmmakers such as Steven Spielberg, Ridley Scott, Kathryn Bigelow and Paul Greengrass for clearly demonstrating that films can be more than just thrilling entertainment . . . they can be highly educational as well.

I'd also like to thank the many accomplished filmmakers, marketing professionals, sales agents, producers' representatives, distributors, studio executives and other professionals who graciously shared their experience and insights with me. Many were also kind enough to offer testimonials and reviews (some of which are published within this book). In particular, I'd like to express my appreciation to Dan Myrick (*The Blair Witch Project*), who was also kind enough to write the book's Foreword.

With regard to the writing, editing and production of *Guerrilla Marketing for Filmmakers*, I'm particularly indebted to the patience and guidance of my friends at Routledge, including Simon Jacobs and John Makowski. And I would like to extend special thanks to my very talented and hard-working graphic designer, Sandy O. Cagnan.

In addition to those I've already mentioned, I'd also like thank my many life-long friends from Subic Bay Naval Base and the small – but critical – group of current and former members of the U.S. Rangers, Special Forces, Marine Force Recon, MARSOC Raiders, Naval Special Warfare and other military and intelligence agencies who have greatly assisted my various film projects.

And, of course, the numerous cast and crew members, past and present, of my films, including: Charles Haskins, David Rose, Travis Crane, Eric Arroyo, Jamaal Branch, Michael Richartz, Bradley Bowen, Trent Edward Arant, Stephanie Zinnes, Sean Scarfo, Ryan Blajda, Isiah Bentley, Jon Stanley, Duckenson Castel, Johua Ide, Eric Wiederecht and Jacob Centeno Healy.

Finally, I would like to thank my wife, Jade, daughter, Kristen and my grandparents, Ruth and Richard Ksiazyk. Without their limitless understanding, patience, support and love, this book might never have been possible.

FOREWORD

The publication of *Guerrilla Film Marketing: The Ultimate Guide to the Branding, Marketing & Promotion of Independent Films and Filmmakers* just so happens to coincide with the twentieth anniversary of the production and release of our film, *The Blair Witch Project*.

When my *Blair Witch* co-writer and co-director, Eduardo Sanchez, and I premiered the film at Sundance in 1999, we were coming to the end of one of the most exciting periods of independent filmmaking – a period that included Quentin Tarantino's *Reservoir Dogs*, Robert Rodriguez's *El Mariachi*, Kevin Smith's *Clerks* and Ed Burns' release of *Brothers McMullen* among many others.

Because of the success of these and similar films, the major studios rushed to create their own independent studio and distribution subsidiaries, including Warner Independent, New Line, Paramount Vantage and Miramax. Unfortunately, in the time since, the majors have largely retreated from independent films and filmmakers. Most of the subsidiaries that they were in such a hurry to create either no longer exist or haven't been active in years. (*The Blair Witch Project*'s distributor, Artisan Entertainment, was eventually acquired by Lion's Gate – one of the few large studios that continue to distribute and invest in independent films.)

Ironically, most of the major studios appear to have abandoned independent films just as a new era of independent filmmaking was beginning to dawn. Advances in digital cameras and audio recording technology; scriptwriting, budgeting, scheduling, editing and post-production software; and direct-to-consumer digital distribution channels have led to an explosion in the number and quality of low-budget indie films.

However, despite this new technology and the corresponding increased film quality, you may be surprised to discover that today's most successful independent filmmakers are rarely, if ever, those who are the "best" when it comes to employing these new tools or in their technical filmmaking skills (cinematography, lighting, direction, audio, etc.). They're talented to be sure. Highly talented. But rarely are they among the "best." Instead, successful low-budget filmmakers tend to combine a fundamental knowledge of the tools and techniques of filmmaking with a thorough knowledge of and passion for their audience and genre. And they seem to intuitively understand that branding, marketing and promotion must be integrated into every step of their film's production – from development, pre-production, principal photography and through post-production and release. This is what truly differentiates the successful filmmakers from the wannabes and the never-weres.

When done well, these filmmakers' marketing and promotional campaigns often become entertainment experiences in their own right. While promoting *The Blair Witch Project*, together with John Hegeman and his crew at Artisan Entertainment, we revamped the website to make it more interactive and to provide regular updates on the "police investigation" of the "missing" students (as well as detail on the mythology of the Blair Witch). We also created missing person posters and leaflets that we distributed on college campuses, at film festivals and to various online message boards and chat rooms. Even the IMDb entries listed our actors as *"missing, presumed dead."* The campaign quickly went viral on emerging social media platforms and with online influencers such as Harry Knowle of *Aint It Cool News* (AICN). The audience and fans became a very real part of the promotional and film experience. Many fans told us that they felt like they were a part of the story.

Because of the success of our guerrilla marketing tactics and the grassroots support from the film's many fans, *The Blair Witch Project* has become the sixth highest grossing independent film and the second most profitable of all time. And the film was able to do that despite Artisan Entertainment providing relatively little promotional support... at least by the standards of other theatrically released movies at the time.

This ability to quickly, creatively and inexpensively engage the film's core audience is the essence of *Guerrilla Film Marketing*. While large studios may employ marketing budgets of $25, $50 or $100 million or more to reach their audiences, *Guerrilla Film Marketing* allows low-budget filmmakers to employ a small group of relatively inexpensive marketing materials, promotional activities and a community of passionate and highly engaged super fans to drive film sales and rentals. The knowledge, skills and tools provided by *Guerrilla Film Marketing* can also help you and your team to attract higher-caliber cast and crew members to your film as well as to generate a greater degree of interest and attention from investors, media, managers, agents, distributors and other industry professionals.

If you're truly serious about the success of your films and your filmmaking career, I hope that you'll read and study each and every page of *Guerrilla Film Marketing*. Bookmark, highlight and write notes in the margins of important concepts, passages and pages. Download the book's many templates and tools. If you need or want more personalized help, contact Robert directly. However, whatever else you may do, be sure to embrace the challenge, creativity and empowerment that guerrilla film branding, marketing and promotion offer.

Good Luck!

Daniel Myrick, Producer & Director
Gang of Robots (www.gangofrobots.com)
Los Angeles, CA

The Blair Witch Project (1999)
Curse of the Blair Witch (1999)
An Exploration of the Blair Witch Legend (1999)
Believers (2007)
The Strand (2007)
Solstice (2008)
The Objective (2008)
Under the Bed (2016)

INTRODUCTION

"You shouldn't dream your film, you should make it!"
Steven Spielberg

The world of filmmaking is undergoing a revolution unlike any before. Not the introduction of sound. Not the introduction of color. Not the advent of home video. Nothing else compares to the impact of recent advances in digital film production and distribution.

As a result of this revolution, there has been an explosion in the number of independent films and filmmakers. Consider that the Sundance Film Festival now receives almost 20,000 film submissions each year and is able to screen less than 200. Now your guess is as good as anyone's: What percentage of all the feature and short films produced throughout the world each year are submitted to Sundance? 50%? 25%? Who knows? But whatever the number, clearly there are a lot more than 20,000 films currently being produced each year (some industry analysts estimate there are as many as 60,000 or more films produced annually).

Given the sheer number of films produced today, how can your independent film differentiate itself from the masses and win a loyal audience? That's the fundamental question that this book was written to address.

By mastering the principles and techniques described within this book and then applying them consistently, you'll find that you are able to differentiate your film (and build a loyal following) much faster and easier than you could have imagined.

That said, like filmmaking itself, film branding, marketing and promotion requires sustained effort and an investment of both time and money. And, just as importantly, it requires a clear view of the many opportunities and challenges presented in today's volatile marketplace.

THE OPPORTUNITY

Aspiring and independent filmmakers (and their investors) benefit from a number of recent developments, including:

- High-quality inexpensive camera, audio and editing systems.
- Explosion in digital distribution channels.

- Insatiable audience appetite for content.
- Ready supply of eager cast and crew members.
- Just-in-time internet-based filmmaking education, training and resources.

Taken as a whole, these developments provide independent filmmakers with the resources to produce high production value short and feature films once available to only established studios.

THE CHALLENGE

Despite these benefits, aspiring and independent filmmakers are also confronted with what may often seem like almost insurmountable challenges. In addition to the alarming increase in competing independent films discussed earlier, these challenges include:

- Major studios focusing almost exclusively on blockbusters at the expense of independent films.
- Increasing advertising and marketing expenses related to regional, national and international theatrical releases.
- Audiences' increasing reliance on high-priced "branded" actors and filmmakers in choosing films.
- High ticket and concession prices making audience attendance at movie theaters increasingly cost-prohibitive.
- Growth in competing and low-cost entertainment options/choices for audience members.
- An increasing glut of short and feature films from competing independent filmmakers available on digital distribution channels.
- Difficult-to-secure advanced distribution deals, sales and upfront payments for independent films.
- Barriers to certain digital distribution channels without the direct support of a reputable distributor or aggregator.

As a result, failure will be an unavoidable consequence for independent filmmakers without the knowledge, skills and abilities to navigate this increasingly volatile marketplace.

THE SOLUTION

Fortunately, although the future of independent filmmaking may often seem both uncertain and frightening, like a barbell, the industry has begun to stabilize around two profitable extremes.

On one side of the marketplace are the major studio films. The production budgets for studio films will range from a low of $25 million to a high of $200 million or more. The global advertising and marketing budgets (known as "print and advertising" or "p&a" expenses in industry speak) for these films will typically total 50% or more of the film's production expenses.

Given these costs, studios will allocate their investments toward fewer "blockbusters" (aka "tent pole") movies focused on proven mass-appeal genres constructed around superheroes (including Batman, Spiderman and Iron Man as well as less obvious "superheroes" such as James Bond and Jason Bourne) and relatively low-risk sequels to the studio's earlier successes.

At the other side of the marketplace are independent films that fall in a production budget range of $250,000 to $2.5 million or so (although some experienced independent production companies, such as Blumhouse Productions, have achieved success with films ranging as high as $2.5 million–$5 million). These films are typically characterized by their highly focused genre, low production and marketing costs and a reliance on profitable digital distribution channels.

Outside of these two extremes, filmmakers will find that few films within the $5 million to $25 million range can be produced profitably. First, the film budgets within this range will be too low to justify an investment in the p&a necessary to support a large theatrical release either domestically or globally. Secondly, the profit opportunity within non-theatrical distribution channels for films without the support of a large national or international p&a campaign are insufficient to both cover production costs and to reasonably compensate filmmakers and their investors.

Fortunately, feature films in the $250,000 to $2.5 million range are ideal for independent filmmakers. And, while the number of films in this budget range continue to increase dramatically, relatively few filmmakers are able to achieve the production value expected by today's audience members and properly market them in a way that builds a loyal and engaged audience. Absent both factors (production value and marketing), the vast majority of independent filmmakers and their films will fail.

Perhaps now is a good time to introduce an important reality of independent film-making: Absent a profit, every film is potentially your last. Investors will only provide filmmakers funding if they can be relatively confident that they will not only get their money back but will also earn enough profit to compensate them for the considerable risks inherent in investing in an independent film. Effective and efficient marketing of a high production value film helps to ensure that (i) your independent films will be profitable and that (ii) your future productions will have ready access to investors.

THE STRATEGY & TACTICS

While there a number of respected books that provide the tools necessary to write and produce high production value films, until now there haven't been any books, or other centralized sources of information, that provide the tools and techniques necessary to help independent filmmakers build and expand a loyal and engaged audience.

Among many other topics, this book will help you:

* Master the fundamentals of guerrilla branding, marketing and promotion.
* Create a two-page integrated marketing plan and calendar.
* Develop internet (including studio and film websites) and social media marketing campaigns.
* Assemble behind-the-scenes pictures, videos and documentaries.
* Produce marketing materials such as key art, posters, film teasers, trailers and electronic press kits (aka "EPKs").
* Craft powerful marketing-centric IMDb listings.
* Maximize the marketing impact of events such as test screenings, premiers, film festivals and industry award ceremonies.

TEN RULES OF SUCCESS

However, before exploring these many principles, techniques and tools, I'd like to share with you a collection of ten rules of success that I hope you'll keep in mind while reading this book and marketing your films:

Rule #1: Marketing is simply about making friends. All marketing is essentially an effort to develop friendships between yourself, your films and the members of your target audience. Naturally, not all of these "friendships" will be direct. Regardless, you are looking to introduce yourself and your films to strangers (create awareness and interest) who may, over time, become friends (an engaged audience you both listen to and communicate with and who, hopefully, will later rent and buy your films).

Rule #2: Own your niche or genre. Your current film is just one link in a longer chain of films. Use your past and current projects as the foundation for future film projects. If you're going to spend time and energy building an engaged audience of friends, why throw all that away to begin marketing to a completely different audience for your next film? Don't. Instead build a reputation and audience demand for films in a specific niche or genre in which you have both a passion and talent.

Rule #3: Look, sound and act like your audience expects. When you imagine James Bond, do you imagine him dressed in overalls and a straw hat? When you think of a nurse, do you imagine her dressed in a ball gown? No. At least I hope you don't. My point is that, like James Bond or any other professional, we all have expectations of what a filmmaker should look, sound and act like. Your goal as a filmmaker is to look like the best version of that expectation as possible (while remaining true to who you fundamentally are as a person and as a filmmaker). This extends to the look and feel of not only you and your films, but also of your websites, social media accounts, IMDb listings, posters and other marketing materials and activities as well.

Rule #4: Action = Results. Develop a bias toward action, starting with the first small steps. Often there is a delay between action and results. Give it time. Results will come. On the other hand, those results might not necessarily be what you had originally hoped or expected. Learn from those results and modify your actions. Wash and repeat.

Rule #5: Do what you do best – let others do the rest. Do what you do well and enjoy. Now, more than ever, you don't have to do everything yourself. Register at Elance, fiverr.com, Freelancer.com, Guru, Upwork.com and similar websites to outsource projects. You'll be surprised at how inexpensive and fast it can be to have talented professionals from around the world complete projects that neither you nor your team have the time, interest or ability to complete yourselves.

Rule #6: Be focused. French economist Vilfred Pareto discovered that roughly 80% of the results of almost any activity come from only 20% of the inputs, efforts or causes. In other words, the vast majority of your results will come from relatively few of your actions or activities. The lesson here is that you should identify those branding, marketing and promotional activities that have the greatest impact on your target audience and then focus your efforts and resources on those few activities.

Rule #7: Constant and consistent. Your marketing activities and messages must be both constant and consistently delivered to your audience to have a meaningful impact. The marketing must be consistent in terms of using familiar elements such as words, colors, typography, graphics, visuals, sounds and other elements. And then it needs to be consistent and constant in terms of delivering that familiar message to your audience on a regular and sustained basis. Consider the impact that a small trickle of water can have on rock over time. Now pick a specific market and work to deliver your message again and again.

Rule #8: Develop momentum. You only need to push particularly hard in the beginning to get your branding, marketing and promotional efforts rolling. Then, with constant and consistent activity (there are those two words again!), your efforts will gradually begin to take on a life of their own. Commit to starting strong.

Rule #9: Become a master thief. There's no reason you should ever repeat the mistakes of others. On the other hand, there is every reason you should learn from their successes. Go to school on your competition and give yourself permission to "steal" their best ideas and techniques. You might not be a major studio, but there's no reason you can't emulate (or take creative inspiration from) much of what the major studios do in terms of both production and marketing. But don't limit yourself to the film industry. "Steal" (or "borrow" if it makes you feel better) as many ideas as you can from this book and others, from people you meet, classes you've attended, stories you've heard and any other source that might provide inspiration and ideas.

Rule #10: Good enough is good enough. But how good is good enough? Ahhhh . . . that's the catch. Since most film audiences are familiar with the production quality provided by major studios, you can bet that their expectations will be high. On the other hand, the foolish pursuit of perfection will doom your film projects (as well as your marketing efforts) from the beginning. Unfortunately, knowing when good enough is good enough is more art than science.

Before closing the introduction and this list, I'd like to give you one final bonus success rule . . . and it's perhaps the most important of all:

> You are completely responsible for your success (or failure). Own it. Take responsibility and accountability. There is a sense of immense power in both understanding and accepting that you alone are ultimately responsible for the success of both your films and your filmmaking career.

Fortunately, the information contained within this book will provide you with the knowledge and tools necessary to take command of the successful branding, marketing and promotion of both your career and your films. However, only you can make the commitment to fully master and implement these tools and techniques.

GUERRILLA BRANDING, MARKETING & PROMOTION

It seems like only yesterday that Steven Spielberg, standing next to his good friend and colleague George Lucas, predicted an inevitable "implosion" of the film industry. Lucas echoed Spielberg's concerns and complained about the high costs of marketing movies and the major studios' obsession with big-budget mass-market films while ignoring niche audiences.

The inevitable implosion of the film industry Spielberg and Lucas spoke about at the University of Southern California's School of Cinematic Arts has arrived in greater force than could have been predicted. In fact, the technological and demographic pressures responsible for that implosion were well underway in the months and years leading up to their famous speech.

The greatest of these industry-altering pressures includes (i) the significant advances in low-cost film production technologies and digital video-on-demand distribution outlets (such as iTunes, Amazon, YouTube Rentals, Hulu and Netflix) coupled with (ii) the explosion in the number of entertainment alternatives available to audiences members (particularly computer gaming and social media applications available on web-enabled televisions, computers and mobile devices).

In the Introduction of this book, we discussed the resulting division of the film industry into two distinct halves. The first half is comprised of films produced by independent filmmakers for less than $2.5 million and the second group is comprised of those films typically produced by established studios for $25 million or more. We termed this separation of the film industry's business model as the "barbell strategy."

In large part, these two distinct categories of films are driven by marketing and promotional costs. A film with a production budget in excess of $2.5 to $5 million will need, almost by definition, a broad audience. In order to reach a broad audience, the studio or distributor will need to fund a national, and often global, print and broadcast advertising campaign. At a minimum, such a broad mass-market advertising campaign would require an investment of $20 million or more to be effective (the average marketing and promotional budget for major releases now averages ~$50 million according to *The Hollywood Reporter*).

As you can see, it typically makes little sense to spend $20 million plus promoting a film that costs less than $25 million to produce and which, in all likelihood, lacks the star power, production value and story elements expected from a mass audience.

FIGURE 1.1 Directors Steven Spielberg & George Lucas at the American Film Institute Life Achievement Award gala at the Dolby Theatre, Hollywood.

(Featureflash Photo Agency/Shutterstock.com)

Absent a broad advertising and promotional campaign, a film with a production budget in excess of $2.5 to $5 million will almost certainly be unable to attract a sufficient paying audience to (i) fund the film's production and marketing costs as well as (ii) provide the film's investors with an acceptable profit. On the other hand, films produced for less than $2.5 million will find it much easier to achieve profitable distribution.

GUERRILLA BRANDING, MARKETING & PROMOTION

Without access to the marketing and promotional budgets of large studios and distributors, independent filmmakers are forced to master and embrace low-cost non-traditional forms of marketing. This approach to marketing is typically referred to as "Guerrilla Marketing" in which an emphasis is placed on creativity, strategic thinking and highly focused promotional activities.

The key ingredients and characteristics of successful guerrilla marketing, include:

1. Highly targeted, primary, secondary and tertiary markets.
2. Efficient and effective use of a select number of focused no- or low-cost marketing materials, activities and channels.
3. An emphasis on inbound vs outbound marketing. In other words, rather than buying attention by spending money on outbound advertising, guerrilla marketing places an emphasis on attracting an audience into our community through low-/no-cost digital channels.
4. Integrated marketing which incorporates consistent brand messaging (as well as design elements) across marketing channels and the use of different promotional methods to mutually reinforce each other.

5. Leveraging marketing efforts, activities and materials across multiple marketing channels. Rather than producing unique content for each aspect of your marketing materials, activities and channels, you leverage content (film descriptions, cast and crew biographies, key art, teasers and trailers, electronic press kits [EPKs], etc.) across as much of your marketing and promotional campaigns as possible.

Before we move too far along on the topic of guerrilla marketing, we should agree on our terminology. For the purposes of our discussions, *marketing* is simply a broad term to describe all the activities we take (and will take) to promote ourselves and our films, including: market research, digital promotion, media relations, database marketing and, on a limited basis, advertising.

To make these marketing activities most effective, filmmakers must create a unique and powerful image of themselves and of their films in the minds of the target audience and marketplace. Developing and managing this unique image is referred to as *branding*.

The many elements that make up a film's or filmmaker's brand include: (i) the name or title of the film, studio and/or filmmaker; (ii) any taglines or slogans; (iii) colors and design elements used across the brand's marketing materials and channels; (iv) the voice, personality or character of the brand; (v) use of specific language, vocabulary and phrases; (vi) constant and consistent marketing messages; (vii) key art and other marketing imagery; (viii) the genre and target market on which the studio and filmmaker concentrate; and (ix) the quality and storylines of the studio's and filmmaker's film and promotional product portfolios.

Promotion, on the other hand, represents all of the individual and collective activities, efforts and materials designed to present the brand in a way that creates audience awareness, interest and desire in the filmmaker and their films. Promotion helps to establish and solidify the brand and, ultimately, either directly or indirectly, to increase demand for the filmmaker's movies and promotional products.

YOUR STRATEGIC & MARKETING OBJECTIVES

To maximize the efficiency and effectiveness of our branding, marketing and promotion, each filmmaker must first identify the most important strategic and marketing objectives for their films and their careers.

I think it's safe to assume that the ultimate objective of every independent filmmaker is to have an enduring career characterized by a chain of successful films. Ideally, this will be a career in which the filmmaker maintains control over the production and distribution of the films and stories they tell. After all, what is an independent filmmaker, if not "independent"?

Unfortunately, the key to achieving a long-term career in filmmaking is elusive and multifaceted. An independent filmmaker needs a loyal and engaged audience as well as ready access to talented cast and crew, managers and agents, domestic and international distributors and, of course, investors and lenders.

Although elusive, during this and subsequent chapters, we'll explore the marketing tools and techniques necessary for the independent filmmaker to develop and expand a loyal fan base of audience members, investors and other industry professionals.

Perhaps without even realizing it, we've already agreed on *our two most important marketing objectives: the development of a large and expanding base of (i) loyal audience members and (ii) supportive industry professionals, advisors and investors.*

Critical Success Factors: Fortunately, success within the entertainment business, like any other business, is typically dependent upon only a few significant determinants. These are known as the business's or industry's "Critical Success Factors." For independent filmmakers, those success factors are broadly comprised of:

1. A film and/or filmmaker worthy of promotion.
2. An engaged and loyal fan base (as demonstrated by the audience's willingness to purchase and/or rent the filmmaker's films, leave positive ratings and reviews and provide active and long-term support of the film and filmmaker).
3. Access to production and distribution resources (typically in the form of supportive industry professionals, advisors, cast and crew members and investors).
4. Ability to discourage the "wrong" audience.

While most of these factors may appear to be common sense, the fourth factor – discouraging the "wrong" audience – likely comes as somewhat of a surprise to most readers.

Consider every film distribution channel that you can think of – from theatrical release to digital video-on-demand (iTunes, YouTube Rentals, Vimeo, Netflix, etc.). Each and every one of these distribution channels has an established system for audience and professional ratings and reviews. And these reviews, usually summarized by the total number of stars out of 5, are typically placed in the most highly visible location possible . . . alongside the film's title.

Unfortunately, all the marketing in the world cannot overcome bad reviews and feedback. Given this, the first critical success factor is to have a film and/or filmmaker worthy of promotion. However, perhaps counterintuitively, the fourth and final success factor is to discourage the "wrong" audience.

As an example: The films produced by my production company, Subic Bay Films, are political-military action films. Our films tell stories that highlight little-known conflicts around the world and feature the U.S. intelligence and special operations communities. However, my team and I must keep in mind that there are American and foreign audiences who have a negative view of the U.S. intelligence agencies and the use of American military power.

Understand that human beings are social animals that tend to follow the crowd. If your film's first few (or most recent) reviews are positive, it is highly likely that the following reviews will also be positive. Unfortunately, the opposite is also true. Minimize the chances for negative feedback by dissuading those predisposed to leaving negative feedback from watching your films in the first place. The clearer your film's title, tagline, key art, description, teasers, trailers and other marketing materials, the more your audience will be able to determine if your film is really "for them" . . . or not.

That said, I recognize that getting any group of people at all to watch our films is a lot easier said than done.

Attention, Interest, Desire and Action (aka "AIDA"): To better understand the marketing challenge facing each independent film and filmmaker, consider that every audience member must be guided through four stages: Attention, Interest, Desire and Action.

First, each prospective audience member must be made *Aware* of the film's existence and availability; secondly, the audience member needs to be sufficiently *Interested* in the film that they are willing to give it some thought and consideration; third, something about the film and its marketing needs to fuel a *Desire* in the prospective audience

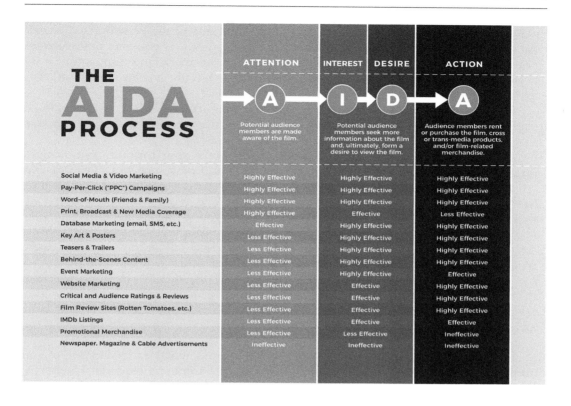

FIGURE 1.2 AIDA.

(Robert G. Barnwell/Sandy O. Cagnan)

member to see the film (for practical purposes, interest and desire can often be viewed as a single stage); and fourth, the audience member needs to be driven to take *Action* in the form of actually renting or purchasing the film and/or promotional products.

From this point forward, all of our marketing and promotional efforts will be focused on driving one or more of the "AIDA" factors. However, with a relatively small marketing and promotional budget (at least in comparison to major studio releases), *generating audience awareness will remain the single largest challenge we will face throughout our careers as independent filmmakers.*

THE MARKETING PROCESS

The secret to building an audience and driving them through the AIDA process is a proper understanding and use of each step of the marketing process.

The marketing process is essentially an endless loop in which the filmmaker (i) performs audience, market, industry and competitor research and analysis; (ii) develops a strategic marketing plan and establishes a small set of performance objectives; (iii) executes (or implements) the marketing plan; and then (iv) monitors, measures and modifies the marketing campaign to optimize its impact and results.

As an aside, I'd like to highlight part of the final step of the process: " . . . *modifies the marketing campaign to optimize its impact and results.*" At first you may not realize the power of this statement. In essence, it assumes that your marketing campaign is never perfect. This gives you permission to develop and execute an imperfect marketing and promotional campaign . . . particularly at the outset.

It's important to allow yourself the luxury of making mistakes. Much of marketing is a matter of trial and error. In the beginning of your marketing efforts, one of the most important things (if not the single most important) is to simply get started.

I encourage you to fail fast and fail forward. Make your mistakes as quickly as possible. Do it now. Learn from them, correct them and move on. As fast as possible.

Remember: It's unlikely you were anything near perfect the first time you learned to walk, swim, ride a bike or . . . shot your first film. The important thing was that you took those first steps, took off the training wheels, began to dog crawl around the pool, and filmed those first few scenes. *With regard to your marketing, just take those first steps and begin. With a little time and refinement, your marketing will pick up steam and deliver results you may never have expected.* I promise. Just keep at it.

The remainder of the book will provide you with the step-by-step tools necessary to launch your marketing in the most effective and efficient way possible while avoiding the majority of mistakes made by other independent filmmakers. In fact, just being aware and able to visualize the marketing process itself is a powerful first step.

Step One: Audience & Market Research: Having a fundamental understanding of your audience and genre as well as industry and market trends is essential to effective marketing. Ideally, you'll also be able to identify the leading independent filmmakers and films in your genre as well as the marketing and promotional elements used by your competitors. As we'll discuss later, fortunately, the film industry and industry press provide a huge amount of publicly available research and analysis on each of these issues. For the vast majority of your needs, a simple Google search will quickly provide you more than enough information to begin your marketing efforts.

Step Two: Develop Your Marketing Strategy & Budget: With a sound understanding of your audience, marketplace and competitors, the next step is to determine (i) which genre(s) and audience(s) you should focus on; (ii) how you can best appeal to your genre's audience; and (iii) what knowledge, skills, abilities and resources you offer that allow you to differentiate yourself and your films from others in the marketplace.

More specifically, during the strategic planning process you should establish:

- Strategic objectives
- Genre and target audience
- Available resources (particularly budget/financial resources)
- Brand identity and branding messages
- Marketing objectives
- Integrated marketing planning
- Marketing and content calendar
- Performance expectations and measures.

Step Three: Take Action: This is where the rubber meets the road. During Step Three we'll (i) develop our key marketing materials; (ii) deliver sustained marketing activity across all stages of film production; and (iii) distribute our marketing materials and concentrate our activities on a handful of targeted marketing channels. It is during this stage that we develop and refine our key art, websites, electronic press kits ("EPKs"), IMDb listings, social media activities, teasers and trailers, media relations, database marketing and pursue high-impact low-cost advertising.

Step Four: Monitor Results: In the business world, there is a common refrain that *"What gets measured gets done."* This is true. When a filmmaker establishes and holds himself or herself to a set of measured objectives or goals, it is far more likely that time, effort and other resources will be aligned with actions that best achieve those objectives.

In order to maximize our marketing's effectiveness and efficiency, we need to (i) identify our strategic and marketing objectives (which we did during Step Two, strategic marketing planning); (ii) establish performance metrics that measure our relative-success in achieving these objectives; and then (iii) cascade these objectives down into supporting activities and measures.

	LOW	MEDIAN	HIGH
PMD and/or Distribution Consultant(s)		35.000	75.000
Publicist		17.500	25.500
Website Design & Development	3.750	5.000	7.500
Writing & Editing Services	1.750	2.500	3.500
Graphic Design Services	1.750	2.500	3.500
Pitch Book Design & Printing	1.000	1.250	1.500
Key Art Design	2.500	3.750	5.500
Teaser & Trailer Creation (1–2 teasers; 2 trailers)	32.500	45.500	57.500
Behind-the-Scenes Photography & Videography	5.250	7.500	12.750
Electronic Press Kits (EPKs) and/or Physical Press Kits	1.500	2.750	3.750
Test Screenings	2.750	3.750	5.000
Film Festival Attendance (Fees, flights, hotels, food, etc.)	7.500	12.500	17.500
Film Market Attendance (Fees, flights, hotels, food, etc.)	5.250	7.500	12.500
Pay-Per-Click (PPC) & Banner Ad Campaigns	2.500	7.500	12.500
Promotional Merchandise	1.250	1.750	2.250
eMail Marketing Expenses (AWeber, MailChimp, etc.)	500	750	1.000
Business Cards & Stationary	250	500	750
Contingency (aka "Overages")	15.000	25.000	37.500
TOTAL MARKETING BUDGET	85.000	182.500	285.000

FIGURE 1.3 Marketing budget. (Robert G. Barnwell/Sandy O. Cagnan)

Note: The marketing budget should reflect the individual film and its target audience(s). As a result, one film's marketing mix (the choice of marketing and promotional materials, activities and channels) and, hence, budget, is likely to differ significantly from other comparable films. Therefore, the line items shown in this budget are for illustrative purposes only. Further, as any marketing professional will attest, these budget estimates are quite aggressive and do not make allowance for employing the services (e.g. of design and trailer houses) commonly used by major studios. Instead, the budget assumes judicious use of domestic and foreign freelancers as well as talented professionals already employed by the production. Obviously, the more the production team is able to do in-house, the lower these marketing and promotional expenses may become. However, as mentioned throughout this book, the audience's standards and expectations with regard to the quality of the film's marketing and promotion (as well as of the film itself) have been established by the major studios. At a certain point, without sufficient investment, the quality of the film's marketing and promotion will fail to meet these high audience standards and expectations.

For instance, one of our primary goals will be to build a large and engaged audience. Therefore, we'll need to establish *performance measures* addressing such issues as: the number of repeat and unique visitors to our website(s); the number of social media friends we have and the number of new friends; and, with regard to engagement, how many of our visitors and friends have shared our blog and social media posts or have communicated with us via website and social media comments, messages, emails and telephone calls, or sought us out during film festivals and other industry events.

To make certain that these things happen – that we have (i) a large and (ii) engaged audience – we need to have a set of *activity measures* that encourages us to make a certain number of blog posts and social media posts, and that we conduct other associated marketing activity on a regular and sustained basis.

It's surprising how powerful just having the right performance and activity measures can be in determining the ultimate success of any marketing campaign.

Step Five: Revise/Optimize: The final step is to review our performance and activities with a view to continually improving the impact of our materials and activities. You should expect your marketing materials, activities and channels to evolve continuously over the course of your filmmaking career as you master the marketing process and as new technologies and channels are developed. Again, the important point is to simply begin your marketing and promotion and to then learn and refine your campaign based upon these initial results and experiences. But first, as Nike says, you have to "Just Do It."

MARKETING ACROSS EACH STAGE OF FILM PRODUCTION

As we'll continue to emphasize, to make the greatest impact, our marketing materials, activities and content need to drive our audience's Attention, Interest, Desire and Action ("AIDA") and be aligned with each stage of our film's production. For the purposes of marketing, we break the film production process into the following five stages:

1. *Ideation/Development:* This is the stage in production when the filmmaker begins to search for an idea and the first hint of a storyline. During this stage it's important to share with your audience that you are beginning to think about ideas for a new film and invite them to make suggestions. This is a great opportunity to build audience participation and engagement. At this point, you should have a personal website (or studio website) and have established your social media platforms.

2. *Pre-Production:* During preproduction we are writing and refining our scripts, hiring cast and crew, raising funding (if necessary), securing locations, wardrobe and props, and completing other activities in advance of principal photography. At the outset of pre-production, we should have completed initial key art (we'll probably refine our key art later with the participation of our offline and online community members), registered for the film's IMDb listing, set up a dedicated website or microsite, and committed to ongoing blogging and social media activity.

3. *Production:* As we begin principal photography on our film, our audience is going to be hungry for behind-the-scenes ("BTS") pictures, videos, interviews and stories. They want to feel a part of the production and enjoy hearing about our failures as well as our successes. Consider producing a BTS documentary. Update the film's

IMDb profile and add your cast and crew to the IMDb listing. Encourage your cast and crew to regularly update their own websites and social media platforms with details of their experience on set. Consider launching a crowd-funding campaign as you have some initial footage from principal photography (or postpone crowd-funding until post-production).

4. *Post-Production:* If you haven't already, post-production is the ideal time to begin releasing your teasers and trailers. In the lead-up to the film's release, you should accelerate your media relations and distribution of news releases. Encourage your cast, crew, investors and loyal fans to pass along word of the pending release. Announce when and where the film will be appearing at film festivals and other events. Place a "preorder" button on your website and offer incentives for those who order the movie prior to release. Again, if you've not done so already, launch a crowd-funding campaign or a second follow-on campaign.

5. *Distribution:* At this point, you should have built a sizeable audience eagerly anticipating your film's release. If your film will be available on digital VOD platforms, it is absolutely critical that you encourage your audience to leave positive feedback. The first several ratings and feedback can establish (or destroy) interest and momentum. As always, continue to update your website, blog and social media. Share success stories, testimonials, endorsements and any film awards your film may have received.

One of the many benefits of cable television and digital distribution channels is that the lifetime value of a film has increased significantly. In the past, an independent film may have had a theatrical release and would then be sold and rented briefly before eventually being taken out of circulation two to three years later (due to a lack of interest and/or shelf space at local video stores such as Blockbuster or Hollywood Video). As a result, if the sales and rental proceeds from a film weren't sufficient to cover production costs and provide for a profit for its investors in the first twenty-four to thirty-six months of release, it was unlikely that they ever would. Fortunately, with the introduction of distribution channels such as digital video-on-demand, today's films are available essentially in perpetuity. Of course it helps if the storyline and production value are equally timeless.

To maximize the lifetime value of their films, it is imperative that filmmakers continue to market and promote them for as long as possible (in other words, "for as long as profitable"). However, again, for today's films, the lifetime value may very well be five years, ten years or more. Ideally, your films will produce an ongoing stream of profits . . . year after year after year. But, to do so, you need to commit to ongoing marketing and promotional support.

MARKETING MATERIALS, ACTIVITIES & CHANNELS

Throughout the remainder of the book, we'll explore the specific marketing materials, activities and channels that you must master to develop the strongest branding and promotional campaign for your films and career.

Marketing & Promotional Materials: Reflecting the integrated nature of the marketing plan, your marketing and promotional efforts will leverage several common marketing materials. These materials will appear across your marketing and promotional channels, including IMDb profiles, websites, social media accounts, sell-sheets, pitch books, electronic press kits (EPKs), press books, public releases and other marketing and promotional outlets and materials. Common marketing and promotional materials will include:

- Descriptive summaries of past, present and future film projects
- Filmmaker's professional biography as well as credit list and film reel
- Biography of regular cast and crew members (as appropriate)
- Summarized and complete film credit list
- Key art, posters and other imagery
- Teasers, trailers and film clips
- Portraits and BTS pictures, videos, interviews and documentaries featuring the filmmaker, cast and crew
- Director's statement and production notes (particularly with regard to interesting aspects of the filmmaking process such as special effects, visual effects and makeup effects)
- Reviews, quotes, testimonials and awards (if any)
- FAQ sheet(s)
- Links to associated websites and social media accounts.

Marketing & Promotional Channels: Having produced a strong portfolio of marketing materials, it's critical to make certain that they are properly distributed across multiple channels. Whether promoting a new film or your own filmmaking career, the following is a list of some of the most effective inbound and outbound marketing channels:

- Personal, studio and film website(s)
- Social media activity
- Participation on film-related blogs and forums
- IMDb profile
- Film industry unions, guilds, associations and clubs
- Film festivals, premiers and film-related events
- Existing relationships/professional network
- Direct outreach (emails, telephone calls, postcards, etc.).
- Referrals from friends and colleagues
- Print and broadcast media.

Marketing & Promotional Activities: Again, the marketing and promotional activities you select (as well as the topics/subjects of your content) will depend upon (i) your marketing objectives, (ii) the AIDA framework and (iii) where your current film stands in the production process. Here is a list of some of the most common and effective:

- Direct outreach (emails, telephone calls, postcards, etc.).
- Participation within events such as union, guild, association or club activities
- Film industry blog and forum participation
- Website development (improve website quality and increase number of pages)
- Social media activity (frequency and quality of posts/updates)
- Post new pictures and videos (on all digital media platforms)
- Consistent participation in new film projects
- Film-related travel outside of your city/region (beyond your established circle of local friends and colleagues).

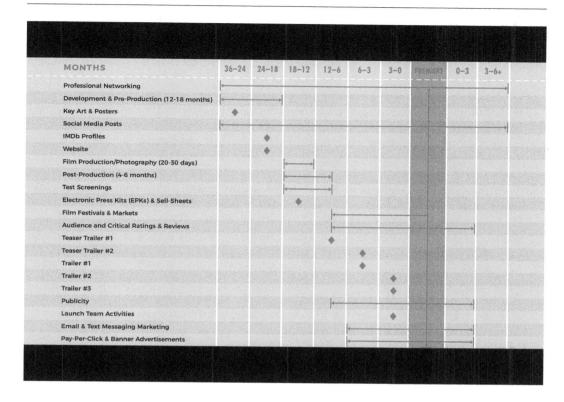

FIGURE 1.4 Marketing calendar.
(Robert G. Barnwell/Sandy O. Cagnan)

MEASURING SUCCESS

As we've discussed, in order to assess the effectiveness of your marketing campaign, each filmmaker must (i) establish a set of quantifiable strategic and marketing objectives; (ii) cascade those objectives into a collection of measurable activities; and (iii) assess the results of those activities against the filmmaker's original objectives and expectations.

(i) Establish a set of quantifiable strategic and marketing objectives: Such objectives can, and probably will, include many of the following:

1. Achieve specific projected film and promotional merchandise sales levels.
2. Achieve specific projected levels of profitability.
3. Produce and release a specific number of feature films over a given time period (twelve, twenty-four or thirty-six months).
4. Achieve a desired annual salary from your filmmaking activities.
5. Develop a community of engaged audience members and a professional network within the film industry (having established a specific number of targeted audience members and network members as well as specific objectives for the level of engagement with both your audience and network).

(ii) Supporting marketing activities: These performance measures should reflect the most important activities required to achieve your strategic and marketing objectives in the most effective and efficient ways possible. Among others, such metrics should include:

1. Frequency of social media, forum and guest-blog posts
2. Frequency of new content posted to website(s)
3. Number and frequency of public releases written and distributed
4. Number of outbound contacts (emails, telephone calls and other forms of contact initiated by you to other film industry professionals)
5. Number and frequency of film festivals, markets and other industry events attended (monthly, quarterly or annual attendance at various union, guild, association or club meetings, film festivals and other film industry events).

(iii) Measure resulting performance of your marketing activities: Such measures and metrics would include:

1. Search engine page rank for film title(s) and keywords
2. Number of inbound contacts (unsolicited emails, contact form inquiries, telephone calls, etc. from those responding to your marketing and promotional activity)
3. Number of monthly unique and repeat website "visits"
4. Number of social media fans/friends/subscribers
5. Digital, print and broadcast media coverage (interviews, quotes or mentions)
6. Personal Klout Score
7. HubSpot's Marketing Grader Score.

These are only a small representative sample of the types of performance metrics a filmmaker should establish and track. A more comprehensive list of metrics and measurement tools are provided in subsequent chapters and within the Branding, Marketing & Promotional Audit (see appendices).

PRODUCER OF MARKETING & DISTRIBUTION (PMD)

If it's not readily apparent, the successful marketing and distribution of a film now requires just as much effort and expertise as does the film's production. To meet these demands, an increasing number of filmmakers are relying on a dedicated Producer of Marketing & Distribution, or "PMD," to both manage and carefully choreograph each stage of the branding, marketing, promotional and distribution process. Responsibilities of the PMD commonly include:

1. Develop and manage the film's marketing and distribution strategy (and associated budgets) in partnership with the filmmaker and producers. It's important to recognize that every film and its audience are unique. As a result, each film demands a correspondingly unique and personalized marketing and distribution strategy based on thorough audience research.
2. Assemble and supervise the team members and freelancers required to carry out the plan, including: graphic designers, copywriters, web designers and developers, BTS photographers and videographers, publicists, sales agents, producer's reps, digital aggregators, trailer editors, marketing interns and other professionals.

3. Supervise the creation of promotional materials and activities, including: social media accounts, website, IMDb profiles, pitch sheets, key art, teasers and trailers, BTS collateral, electronic press kits, public releases, marketing events and the development of cross- or trans-media and promotional products.

4. Identify and engage with the film's audience and influencers through social media campaigns, website content, film review sites, online forums, podcasts and vidcasts, film festivals and other marketing events.

5. Recruit and choreograph the activities of the film's launch team, which will be instrumental in driving early release film ratings, reviews and promotional "buzz."

6. Serve as the principal source of contact to distribution and marketing partners such as sponsors, promotional partners, product placement firms, sales agents, producer's rep, various distribution entities, publicists, media professionals and others.

7. Oversee the selection of targeted film festivals and film markets as well as the preparation of supporting materials and activities, including applications, travel and lodging, on-site promotion, scheduling networking meetings and events (including discussion panels), private screenings, etc.

8. Supervise, in partnership with the filmmaker and producers, the creation of distribution deliverables and optimize the marketing and promotional value of individual VOD listings.

9. Coordinate pre-release marketing and promotion, including targeted advertising (such as pay-per-click [PPC] and IMDb display ads), media coverage, marketing events, intensified social media and other high-impact promotional and marketing activities.

10. In addition to helping craft the initial investment memorandum and pitch presentation materials, the PMD may also work closely with the film's Executive Producer on matters involving investor relations. This role may include activities such as helping maintain regular contact with individual investors, providing investors with monthly and/or quarterly investor reports, arranging for on-set visits, responding to individual investor concerns or comments, and leading any crowd-funding initiatives.

Unfortunately, given the complexities and rapidly evolving nature of independent film branding, marketing, promotion and distribution, the number of qualified and experienced PMDs continues to remain relatively low. However, if necessary, the role can be filled with two or three professionals with complementary knowledge and skills. Further, such professionals can be hired to work on a project or consulting basis, either full- or part-time, and either on location or on a remote working basis. As with many professionals, referrals from entertainment attorneys, sales agents, producer's reps, distributors and other filmmakers are often the best source of identifying qualified PMDs.

2

CREATING AN IRRESISTIBLE BRAND IDENTITY

Our identities as filmmakers are often strongly – and inextricably – linked to the brand of our films. *Reservoir Dogs* is Quentin Tarantino. Robert Rodriquez is *Sin City* and *From Dusk Til Dawn*. *Clerks* is Kevin Smith. *The Brothers McMullan* is Ed Burns. And, *The Blair Witch Project* is Daniel Myrick and Eduardo Sanchez. It's almost impossible to think of any of these filmmakers and not also think of their films. And vice versa.

The benefits of such an irresistible brand are considerable. A strong brand can mean the difference between a successful or failed guerrilla marketing and promotional campaign.

Proper branding clarifies your distinctiveness as a filmmaker and – when done well – makes both you and your films more familiar and memorable. When properly aligned with your genre, a brand helps generate strong and consistent demand for your films and promotional materials. It becomes easier to attach well-known cast and crew and attract investors and other industry professionals to your projects.

In developing a brand identity, we are looking to project the best image possible of ourselves and our films in the mind of our audience. But, first and foremost, that image needs to be authentic. It needs to be a genuine representation of who we truly are as individuals and as professionals.

Prior to my interest in producing films that focus on the world's lesser-known armed conflicts, I grew up at Subic Bay Naval Base in the Philippines. Although no longer active, at the time, Subic Bay was the largest U.S. military base in the world. As a high school student at Subic, I was fortunate to be able to regularly watch the Navy Special Warfare Command's SEAL Team One and Marine Force Recon teams train and refine their combat tactics.

My family have been members of the military for generations. They've served during every war and armed conflict of the twentieth century and beyond. And, during my period, I spent a brief time as a reserve member one of the U.S. Army's Reconnaissance, Surveillance and Target Acquisition (RSTA) units. This experience has driven my passion to explore the complexities of the role of special operations and intelligence services in geopolitics within my films.

When you see pictures and video of me on or off set, more likely than not I'll be wearing a hat or T-shirt featuring a special operations unit, intelligence agency or weapons manufacturer. Yes, I do this by design to reinforce my brand. But also, fundamentally,

FIGURE 2.1 Horror filmmaker, screenwriter and hard rock musician Rob Zombie maintains a relatively consistent personal brand image across his film and music projects. While the strength and consistency of Zombie's brand image may be difficult to replicate, it should serve as an aspirational model for independent filmmakers of all backgrounds and genres.

(Rob Zombie; Editorial/Fair Use)

this is who I am and what I'm most comfortable wearing. These clothes are a genuine part of who I am . . . not just my brand.

To best see what I'm talking about, I'd recommend you visit horror filmmaker Rob Zombie's IMDb profile and his website. In my mind, there is no more cohesive or unified brand in filmmaking than Rob Zombie. Consider (i) His name, Rob Z-O-M-B-I-E (born Robert Barleh Cummings); (ii) his musical stage act and stage persona as both Rob Zombie and the former front man for White Zombie; (iii) his personal appearance (and, just for fun, take a look at the design of his tattoos); (iv) his website and his digital branding; and (v) his film genre and aesthetic. Then be sure to check out his music video for "Dragula" and tell me that Rob doesn't have, if not the perfect brand, the best brand a horror filmmaker could possibly have.

Rob grew up in Haverhill, Massachusetts and was a huge fan of horror films and rock music. After graduating high school, he attended Parsons School of Design in New York City to study illustration and eventually transferred and graduated from Pratt University in Brooklyn with a degree in graphic design. After forming White Zombie with several friends, he produced and directed many of the band's music videos. Several years later, he would go on to direct such films as *Halloween* (2007), *Halloween II* (2009) and other horror films.

It's important to point out that having a strong brand doesn't mean that your films are necessarily superior (in terms of audience reception, ticket sales or industry awards). While John Carpenter, Wes Craven, George Romero and Sam Raimi are among the most recognizable names in horror, it took each of them several years and films to develop the strength of their brands as horror filmmakers. On the other hand, Rob Zombie's brand as a horror filmmaker was essentially ready-made before rolling film on his first feature.

As the example of Rob Zombie demonstrates, virtually everything we do within our marketing and promotion should be geared toward generating increased attention in – and awareness of – our films. But once we grab the attention of potential audience members, a strong and unified brand is paramount in capturing and maintaining that attention and interest.

At its core, *branding* is everything we do to solidify our reputation and to form an image of ourselves as filmmakers (and of our films) in the minds of our audience. It includes (i) the process of identifying the desired reputation or image we each want to develop in the minds of our audiences as well as (ii) the actions we take and activities we engage in to create and sustain the desired image.

In developing your own identity and brand as a filmmaker, you need to take a close look at the types of films you are most interested in. Then consider your background, personal and professional experience, education and your unique portfolio of knowledge, skills and abilities. In what ways do you compare to other filmmakers in your genre? In what ways are you different? And, most importantly, in what ways are you superior?

BRANDING: IT'S ALL RELATIVE

When thinking about your reputation and brand image, it's important to remember that your audience will constantly be measuring you and your films against the reputations and images of other filmmakers and their films.

Today's audience members are quite sophisticated. Over the course of their lives they've seen literally thousands of films and television episodes. *When a new audience member first comes across you and your films, they're naturally going to compare you to the films and filmmakers they're already familiar – and, with few exceptions, these will be the films and filmmakers from the major movie and television studios.*

So it's important that we spend the time to study the marketplace, our audience and competing major studio films and filmmakers. This research will help us best position ourselves and our films.

Specifically, we should answer the following questions:

- *What are the most popular (and well-regarded) films in my genre?*
- *Who are the most popular (and well-regarded) filmmakers in my genre?*
- *What makes these films and filmmakers unique?*
- *How are these filmmakers and films portrayed in consumer and industry media?*
- *How do these filmmakers portray themselves and their films within IMDb, their websites, electronic press kits, media interviews and other marketing materials and activities?*
- *What film festival and industry awards have these films and filmmakers won?*
- *Where did these filmmakers attend film school?*
- *With whom – and on what films – have these filmmakers worked?*
- *What is the quality and critical response to the films they've produced and directed?*

Having examined other films and filmmakers, you need to take a closer look at yourself.

- *How does your brand and the brand of your films compare with the leading films and filmmakers in your genre?*

- *How visible (or well-known) are you currently in your genre and within the marketplace?*
- *How would your audience describe you and your films?*
- *What aspects of your films and filmmaking are most appealing to your audience?*
- *How would cast, crew, investors and other industry professionals describe you and the experience of working with you?*
- *What makes you unique? In what areas are you particularly strong? In what areas are you weak?*
- *What image or brand do you want to develop and be known for? In what ways does this aspirational or hoped-for brand differ from your existing brand? What, specifically, do you need to do in order to transition your current brand to your desired brand? How, if at all, does your current IMDb profile, websites, social media platforms and other promotional material further your desired brand position and personality?*

A complicating factor in our branding is that it must speak to a relatively large and diverse market. Obviously, *we want a brand that excites film audiences. However, as important – if not more importantly – we also need a brand that appeals to potential investors and other professionals within the film industry.*

At the risk of oversimplifying matters, our audience is concerned about our genre, our personal filmmaking style and our personal image. On the other hand, industry professionals are more interested in our ability to drive a film's sales and profit levels and win festival and industry awards.

What unique attributes do you offer that makes these professional outcomes more likely than competing filmmakers within your genre?

- *With regard to sales, what do you offer that helps assure the maximum number of audience members?*
- *With regard to profitability, what makes you unique in terms of your ability to deliver a film cost-effectively and within budget?*
- *Similar to the concerns of your audience members, what distinctive filmmaking attributes do you have that optimize the opportunities for film festival and industry award nominations and wins?*
- *How do the production value and storylines of your films compare with others in the marketplace and those competing for film festival and industry awards?*

As you ask yourself these questions, consider your achievements as a filmmaker and what those achievements have meant for your audiences, investors and other participants within your films.

These are called *proof-points.*

Proof-points are essentially your past accomplishments and any other evidence that supports your brand's claims. *It's one thing to say you are a great filmmaker. It's quite another thing to be able to prove it.*

So how can you prove that you are one of the most talented independent filmmakers in your genre or have what it takes to become one of the most talented? Here are some of the most common proof-points investors, distributors, audience members and others find most credible:

1. A history of having successfully produced and directed well-regarded short and feature films.
2. Having won several film festival and/or film industry awards.
3. Having received media and industry acclaim for past film work.

4. A history of working in positions of responsibility and authority on the short and feature films of other respected filmmakers.
5. Having graduated from well-regarded film schools, programs or workshops.
6. Maintaining a highly professional attitude and image. Whether online or off, your attitude and image remain important measures by which you will continually be judged throughout your career.

If you feel that your current list of proof-points isn't as strong or impressive as you'd like, remember that you can – and should – always seek out opportunities to expand and strengthen your experience and achievements.

Periodically, throughout the year, ask yourself what proof-points you've added to your list and then commit to achieving more proof-points over the coming months and year.

BEING UNIQUELY YOU

As impressive as proof-points and accomplishments may be to your career, people don't form relationships with resumes. People form relationships with other people.

Think of Cameron, Capra, Coppola, Eastwood, Hitchcock, Kurosawa, De Palma, Scorsese, Scott (Ridley and Tony), Spielberg, Tarantino and Zemeckis. Don't hide behind a studio identity (even if it is your own studio). Your friends and fans want to get to know you. The real you.

On the other hand, there are many shades of you. You may be a brother or sister, a son or daughter, and a friend. How you are expected to act and behave, the words you use and the sides of your personality that you share with the world are often different. Regardless . . . you are still you.

In today's world, it's difficult – if not impossible – to pretend to be someone you aren't. You will be discovered. And, given the power of immediate electronic communications and social media, the fact that you are inauthentic will be quickly shared with the world.

So, first and foremost, be yourself . . . warts and all.

On the other hand, as mentioned: it's important that we are the best versions of ourselves possible. We can all use some improvement in different aspects of our lives. So don't think you're not being true to yourself if you feel the need to improve elements of your personality or the way you present yourself.

BECOMING IRRESISTIBLE

Your brand should attract people into your social media circle and make them want to engage with you and your other friends and fans. Ideally, strangers turn into followers, followers turn into fans, fans turn into audience members and audience members into advocates – recommending you and your films to their own family, friends and fans.

Although not specifically about branding or how to make yourself irresistible to fans and audience members, Robert Caldini's book, *Influence: The Psychology of Persuasion*, offers several helpful insights as we begin crafting our personal brands and films:

Authority. People tend respect authority figures. In the case of filmmaking, authority is reflected in our roles as scriptwriters, directors and producers. Authority is also reflected within our expertise as filmmakers – best demonstrated by a legacy of award-winning and financially successful films.

Social Proof. As social beings, individuals have a tendency to mirror the actions and beliefs of those they like and respect. This is why film ratings, reviews, recommendations and testimonials are so important to use when audience members select films. Social proof is further demonstrated by selection committees having chosen our work to compete in film festivals and for various industry awards.

Reciprocity. People tend to feel a sense of indebtedness when others do them a favor. If you speak well of someone, they tend to speak well of you. To take full advantage of the power of reciprocity, it is generally a good idea to do others favors and kindnesses while asking little in return. This builds goodwill that may be sought later when our film projects or careers most need support (it has the added benefit of you being perceived as a more friendly and likeable person).

Commitment & Consistency. People value consistency of behavior and commitment from others and themselves. When people commit, either orally or in writing, to an idea or goal, they are likely to honor that obligation to remain consistent with their commitment and self-image.

Scarcity. Real or perceived scarcity increases demand. Scarcity is commonly either time-bound or quantity-bound. In filmmaking, this is why deadlines, limited showings, pre-release discounts, contests, sweepstakes and other promotions are often so effective.

Liking. People respect those they like. *While likeability is difficult to define, likeable people (i) tend to be enthusiastic, optimistic and pleasant; (ii) take an interest in other people and are complimentary of others; (iii) are authentic and vulnerable; (iv) are viewed as knowledgeable and entertaining; (v) have attractive personalities and appearances (they "look" likeable); and (vi) are familiar or share traits in common with people already regarded as friends.*

As you work to create a more likeable and irresistible brand, strive to deliver the best experience possible to all first time and repeat visitors to each of your branding channels (websites, social media, etc.).

Remember that little things matter. A lot. Every single interaction someone has with you and one of your films has an effect on your brand, and that effect is either positive or negative. There is no in-between. Work to make each experience a positive one – one that they will remember and tell others about. (We'll talk more about how to do this throughout the book.)

YOUR BRAND STORY

Humans connect most closely to one another through shared stories. Great stories have the power to drive emotion and to create powerful connections between their audience and the storyteller.

Building a captivating story about yourself involves sharing the epic moments in your life that reveal your true character. Your story must present a narrative that make sense and explains how you got to be where you are now, both in life and the creation of your filmmaking career.

- *Describe the path you took to get to where you are today.*
- *What inspired you to become a filmmaker?*

- *How has your filmmaking evolved?*
- *Where are you headed as a person and as a filmmaker?*
- *How are your films and your approach to filmmaking different from others?*
- *The end of your story should summarize your brand and the aspects of your filmmaking that are unique from other filmmakers.*
- *What values do you bring to filmmaking? What problems are you trying to overcome or social contribution are you attempting to make (if any)?*

Your story needs to be true, reflect your personality and provide a sense of who you are as a filmmaker. It must also be strategic . . . remaining consistent with your chosen brand.

Within your brand story, you are the protagonist, or hero, of your own story. Tell a dramatic and engaging story that also makes you authentic and human.

As you craft your story, remember that how well you tell your story matters. Show don't tell. Use descriptive words that evoke images, emotions and action. Share the challenges, threats, losses, weaknesses and disappointments – not just your strengths, opportunities and victories. Your story should be epic with captivating moments.

Within his book, *The Seven Basic Plots: Why We Tell Stories*, Christopher Booker outlines the seven fundamental character-driven plots. To craft a strong brand story, consider using one as a simple plotline:

1. *Overcoming the Monster:* The protagonist sets out to defeat an antagonistic force that threatens the protagonist.
2. *Rebirth:* The protagonist undergoes a fundamental transformation over the course of the story.
3. *Quest:* The protagonist sets out to achieve an important objective facing several challenges along the way.
4. *Journey and return:* The protagonist goes to a strange land and, after overcoming various threats, returns with experience and self-knowledge.
5. *Rags to Riches:* The protagonist acquires success before losing it all and gaining it back upon maturing as a person.
6. *Comedy:* Light and humorous character with a happy or cheerful ending; a dramatic work in which the central motif is the triumph over adverse circumstance, resulting in a successful or happy conclusion.
7. *Tragedy:* The protagonist is a villain who falls from grace and whose death is a happy ending. Granted this one is going to be a little challenging to build a successful brand story around.

Regardless of your brand's storyline, just like our short and feature films, our brand story should have a beginning, middle and end.

During the beginning, or introduction (first act), you should set the stage for the situation, challenges and tasks you had to overcome during your filmmaking journey. The middle of the story (second act) should describe the actions you've taken to address the situation and the challenges outlined during the beginning. This section of the story should present a degree of drama and conflict. Finally, during the end (act three), you'll want to increase the tension and reach your final climax. This ending – and, in fact, the entire story – should serve to explain your brand as well as your passion and distinctiveness as a filmmaker.

The challenge of crafting a powerful brand story is magnified by the fact that it should be limited to approximately 350 words. Ideally, it should only take you two minutes to tell your story. Only two minutes in which to share your signature story. To define yourself as a filmmaker. To explain what makes you unique.

BRANDING ELEMENTS

Whatever your branding story, everything you do (and don't do) and every element that you incorporate into (or exclude from) your brand image will either reinforce or contradict your brand message.

Consider Disney Studios and the Walt Disney Company. Disney uses consistent iconography incorporated across multiple platforms, products and films. The stylized "Disney" font, the use of the Cinderella's castle as a logo, the repeated use of the Mickey Mouse ears and gloved hand, Disney's use of colors and even music: All of these factors (and many more) are used to create a particular experience across Disney's branded films and products.

Like Disney, you must be consistent – making sure that everything you communicate about yourself, your studio and your films is strategically chosen and remains the same across platforms (websites, social media, EPKs, etc.). This includes elements such as brand messages, genre and marketplace, logos, colors, typography, iconography, music, vocabulary and more.

However, unlike most major studios, you are – as an individual – a large component of the brand (not unlike Walt Disney himself). Your personal and professional brand consists of numerous influences both large and small – including such seemingly irrelevant things as your personal appearance; the clothing, jewelry and accessories you wear; the vehicles you drive; the home and neighborhood in which you live; your family, friends and acquaintances; your hobbies and personal interests; the schools you've

FIGURE 2.2 Author Robert Barnwell's personal brand is based largely on his long-term interests in foreign affairs and military special operations. His brand is, in part, illustrated by clothing preferences that include military and special operations baseball caps and T-shirts worn consistently both on set and off.

(Robert G. Barnwell)

attended; your professional experience and accomplishments; your accent and vocabulary; and, of course, your character and personality.

All of these – more or less, fairly or unfairly– will affect the way you are perceived both personally and professionally.

TOUCH-POINTS & BRANDING OUTLETS

Discipline is required to assure that your brand image is delivered consistently across every possible *"touch-point."* A touch-point is basically any method in which an individual may come into contact with you or your brand, and commonly include:

1. Direct personal interaction
2. Social media interaction (including forum participation)
3. Websites and online directories such as IMDb listings
4. Digital, print and broadcast media coverage
5. Printed marketing materials (film posters, postcards, film festival fliers, business cards, etc.)
6. Voicemail messages
7. Email and email signatures
8. Word-of-mouth, referrals, testimonials, endorsements, etc.
9. Additional marketing or promotional materials and channels.

Again, each element of your branding, marketing and promotional activities must be consistent across every possible touch-point.

This is particularly important given that (i) it is impossible to control or completely anticipate which touch-point any individual fan or audience member is likely to use and when; and (ii) it is far more effective to engage with as many prospective fans and audience members as possible across the widest variety of touch-points... including websites, social media, IMDb, emails, videos and telephone.

3

BUILDING AN ENGAGED COMMUNITY
OF FRIENDS & FANS

While a strong brand is an important tool for independent films and filmmakers, it is still only a tool. Until your audience engages (or interacts) with your brand, it will never fulfill its true potential.

An engaged audience forms a richer, more meaningful connection with a brand, they are more likely to offer positive ratings and reviews, and tend to be strong brand advocates – amplifying your message to a broader audience through social media posts, forum comments and word-of-mouth.

As a result, a small but growing number of independent filmmakers are beginning to embrace the many benefits of audience engagement.

In contrast, major studios have historically assaulted us with television and magazine advertisements and invaded our news programs with mindless interviews featuring their movies' stars. The major studios have been perfectly content to *talk at us* and to hard-sell tickets, but have shown little genuine interest in actually engaging with us (outside of prying open our wallets).

However, for independent filmmakers, audience engagement is not merely a "nice to have," engagement is increasingly a "must have." And, for the independent filmmakers who do it well, film success is far more easily achieved.

A note of caution: As film franchises become increasingly important to the financial success of major studios, the studios' interest in engaging with their audience is beginning to be piqued. Given the majors' large financial resources, it falls on independent filmmakers to stay a step ahead by increasing both the level and the innovation of our engagement. As evidence of this, look at the online communities and engagement around such blockbuster franchises as Fast & Furious, Harry Potter and Star Wars.

AUDIENCE ENGAGEMENT

Like our offline relationships, there is a broad range in the level of engagement we have with our online friends, fans, web visitors and blog readers. Not all of our relationships will be particularly deep or long-lasting.

Just managing to get a handful of strangers to become aware of and think about our films is no small accomplishment. But in reality this is the level of engagement we'll experience with the vast majority of our target audience.

Of these target audience members, several will be interested enough to watch a trailer and, perhaps, purchase or rent our films . . . never having interacted or engaged with our community in any other way. And, for major film studios, this is fine. The majors can successfully distribute a film and achieve global box offices revenues of $100 million, $200 million or more with little to no audience engagement.

However, successful independent films and filmmakers depend on their ability to form lasting and engaged relationships with members of their audience. Many of these engaged audience members will soon become enthusiastic brand advocates – recommending you and your films to their own family, friends and social media fans.

And, just as, if not even more, importantly: they will be the first to purchase or rent each of our newly released films while typically posting the most enthusiastic ratings and reviews.

THE BRAND & ENGAGEMENT EXPERIENCE

As we discussed in the previous chapter, it's vital that we manage the experience our audience has not only with our films, but across each and every touch-point – through blog and social media comments, email exchanges, personal discussions and other channels.

FIGURE 3.1 Brad Pitt welcomes fans to an exclusive fan screening of Robert Zemeckis' film *Allied* at the Village Theater in Westwood, CA.

(Kathy Hutchins/Shutterstock.com)

As with all things having to do with branding, marketing and promotion, the engagement experience should reflect our genre and our own personalities (always be authentic) as well as the personalities and tone established by our audience. As you interact with your audience online and off, you'll begin to pick up on characteristics that are unique to that community.

To create an engaged community, it's important to recognize that experiences are essentially a collection of specific sensations, feelings and emotions.

Horror films emphasize feelings of terror, fear and anxiety. Almost by definition, horror films are dark and unsettling. Action/Adventure typically emphasize locations and events that are thrilling and intense with characters exhibiting courage in the face of mortal danger. In contrast, romantic comedies are light-hearted with feelings of sexual attraction and anticipation, emotional and physical intimacy, and humor.

Whenever possible, our brand experience should also reflect these emotions and sensations.

But to create a loyal and engaged community of fans, it's critical that we also think about how our audience feel about themselves as members of our community. While people join communities for a variety of reasons, most do so to fulfill basic needs to build relationships, gain a sense of belonging, share information and common experiences, as an outlet for self-expression, to establish or reinforce social identity and/or personal status, and for entertainment.

The audience's community experience should reflect these needs, desires and expectations. And, like your films, these experiences should appeal to their base emotions and needs.

BUILDING A COMMUNITY

To build a successful community, you first need to join a community. No. That's not right. Let me correct that: To build a successful community, you first need to join *many communities*.

For example, the neighborhood, or community, in which I live and work is comprised of literally tens of thousands of homes and institutions (retail stores, post offices, hospitals, schools, etc.). My community doesn't start and end at my own driveway.

Likewise, although my website and social media accounts serve as my online "homes," they are only a small part (albeit an important part) of my overall online community. In fact, the vast majority of both my real world and virtual interactions happen outside of my physical and online homes. Similarly, your film community should be comprised of several engagement channels, including:

- Online forums
- Websites
- Blogs
- Email groups
- Social media platforms (YouTube, Facebook, LinkedIn, etc.)
- Offline conferences, film festivals and other events.

Over time, if done correctly, you'll attract an increasing number of people to your own websites and social media platforms. However, initially, you should expect to invest most of your time engaging with your audience on other popular forums, blogs and social media platforms within your genre. The people who participate in these communities have a proven interest in engaging with other community members just like you. This makes attracting loyal and active members of your own community much easier.

However, once you're active in these communities, to get people to take an interest in you, you need to make them take notice. Everything you do or say online helps build (or diminish) the interest people will take in you. So commit – from the outset – to building and posting content that is undeniably distinctive.

When working to create distinctive content, here are some questions to consider:

- *Is your viewpoint on topics of interest – as expressed within your content – the same as everyone else or do you offer a unique or contrasting point of view?*
- *Does the community have an appetite for content that they aren't getting anywhere else? How can you provide that missing content?*
- *Can you diversify the type of media (e.g. pictures, videos, blog posts) and content topics already of interest to the community?*
- *What constitutes "quality" content in your community? How can you max-out these components or characteristics of quality in your own content?*
- *Are you being deliberate about building engaging content or are you just posting information "for the hell of it"?*

When interacting with prospective audience and fan members online or off, remember to leave a trail of breadcrumbs so people can find their way back to your website, social media platforms and other points of interest. These breadcrumbs can be in the form of links provided in your email signature, business cards, forum membership biography or within the comments themselves.

Bottom line? Once people form an interest in you and what you have to say, make sure they are able to easily find their way back to your websites and social media platforms.

A note of caution: Many online marketing experts recommend that you build your own hosted and branded online forums using free or premium software (such as bbPress, PHPBB, Simple Machines Forum and vBulletin). These forums, say the experts, should be the home of your online community. However, independent films and filmmakers will find it difficult – if not impossible – to populate a forum with a minimum number of active participants. In fact, the only successful movie-specific forums I'm aware of are for characters such as Batman, Superman and Iron Man . . . and most, if not all, of these are fan sites – not studio-produced sites.

On the other hand, if your genre does not have a place for community members to meet and discuss their interests, an online forum can be incredibly powerful. However, to be clear: We're talking about a general forum for fans of the genre – not a forum focused specifically on you or your films.

In either case, understand that an unused or underused forum can do considerable damage to your brand and its credibility. Unless you can populate a forum with at least a hundred or so *highly active members*, when it comes to building your own online forum, with few exceptions, the best advice is probably *"Just don't do it"* (with apologies to Nike).

DRIVING ENGAGEMENT

It may sound obvious, but people like to engage with people and organizations that are "engaging."

To become more engaging, as we've touched on earlier, you'll first want to explore the internet to identify and join the blogs, forums, social media accounts and video channels where the people most likely to find you "engaging" are already hanging out.

Once there, avoid self-promotion. At least for now. Instead, post positive replies to the content and ideas shared by other members. Look to share interesting content of your own. Consider providing links to interesting videos, articles or other materials. Answer questions and inquiries other members of the community may have.

As you participate on these community sites, don't allow yourself to become predictable. Share content on a variety of related subjects or topics. Work to diversify the type of content you share . . . videos, photographs, articles, posts, helpful URL links, etc. Purposely mix up the channels on which you engage with your new fans: discussion forums, blogs, social media accounts, video channels, etc. Consider taking the conversations offline via telephone calls, meet-ups and other activities. Shake things up. Keep it interesting.

Engaging people are also likeable.

Among other factors, being likeable means never "flaming" others in your community. If you disagree, find a way to communicate your differing opinion without being "disagreeable." Better yet, unless someone asks you for your opinion, recognize that there are times when it's better not to offer a dissenting opinion at all.

Instead, focus on ways you can be helpful and make others feel good about themselves and their community contributions. Be enthusiastic about their comments. In your own words, regularly use phrases like: "Great comment," "Good point," "Well said," "Really helpful" and, most powerful of all, "Thank you."

With these general guidelines in mind, follow this three-step process to drive engagement:

1. *Engage:* Demonstrate that you engage with the community and value those engagements.

- Comment on the social media, video channels, blogs and forums of others.
- "Like" often and praise others for their comments and contributions.
- Repost or link to comments, blog posts and other content originally posted by others.
- Make engagement public. Mention other members of the community (by name) within your online activity.
- Post videos and pictures of you while interacting with other online friends, fans and audience/community members.

2. *Request and Encourage Engagement:* One of the easiest ways to drive engagement is to simply ask for it.

- Ask open-ended questions within social media, blog and forum posts.
- Ask for comments/feedback with regard to filmmaking, equipment, storylines or other related topics.
- Conduct polls, surveys and quizzes.

- Leverage the power of crowd-sourcing for storyline ideas, sources of hard-to-locate wardrobe and props, cast and crew members and other film-related suggestions.
- Use crowd-funding platforms (Kickstarter, Indiegogo, etc.) as a way to encourage audience participation rather than as a principal source of financing.
- Host contests, auctions and give-aways of autographed pictures, pieces of wardrobe and props and/or the opportunity for members to perform as extras within your current film project.
- Invite members of the audience and brand advocates (as well as other influential members of the community and media) to visit the film set to watch filming and have lunch with you and your cast and crew.
- Share your travel plans and let everyone know you'd like to get together while you're in their town. Consider the dates and locations of various film festivals and film-related events you may be scheduled to attend.

3. Be Everywhere: Establish a system to monitor website, social media and blog activity related to the keywords, personalities, celebrities, films and other topics associated with your genre. Don't forget to search for any mention of your own name, your studio's name and the name of your films.

- Leverage blog and social media search tools such as Google Alerts, Google blog search, Social Mention or Sprout Social.
- Participate in as many appropriate discussions as possible (making certain that you are adding value to each discussion).
- Respond to posts and comments as soon as possible. Don't allow activity and interest to wane before participating.

And, it warrants repeating: once you've participated in the conversation, make sure that you leave "breadcrumbs" for people to follow back to your website, blog and social media platforms.

Bonus Suggestions: In addition to these three steps . . .

- Ask friends in the "offline" world to engage with you in social media and other digital platforms.
- Encourage members of your community to get to know, like and speak with one another.
- Identify, interact and befriend influencers within your community.
- Take advantage of opportunities to guest-blog and co-author content with influencers.
- Make a point of regularly engaging with members who have their own strong social media following.
- Share some personal details. Encourage people to get to know and like you as a person . . . not just as a filmmaker.
- Exploit opportunities to meet members of your online community in person. Consider inviting community members to wrap parties, test screenings, premiers, film festival screenings and other events.
- Pursue opportunities to "livestream" events (screenings, premiers, etc.) to your friends and fans.

COMMUNITY-GENERATED CONTENT

As your popularity grows, an increasing amount of engagement will begin to take place on your own websites and social media platforms. At the same time, your members' comments, posts and other member-generated content will also begin to form a larger percentage of your online content.

For popular brands and personalities, it's not uncommon for a brief blog post of only 250–350 words to receive dozens of replies from community members totaling 5,000 words or more. Frequently, popular blog replies provide as much value and entertainment as the original post.

In addition to posting valuable blog and social media comments, community members often contribute a broad range of content, including:

- Ratings and reviews
- Fan art (posters and trailers)
- Story ideas
- Pictures
- Videos

- Filmmaking instructions
- News updates and gossip
- Crowd-funding contributions
- Other resources and content

While most of this content will appear on your online community platforms, your audience may also post member-generated content to such channels as: blogs (e.g. Blogger, Weebly); microblogs (e.g. Tumblr, Twitter); social networking (e.g. Facebook, MySpace); Film review sites (e.g. Yahoo! Movies, Rotten Tomatoes, IMDb, Amazon, iTunes); online industry databases (e.g. IMDb); video social media distribution channels (e.g. YouTube, Vimeo); audio and video podcasts (e.g. iTunes Podcasts); question–answer databases (e.g. Yahoo! Answers, Ask.com); wikis (e.g. Wikipedia); and fan art sites (Deviantart).

FIGURE 3.2 Launch team members are often responsible for driving a film's early success. By posting favorable ratings and reviews – to such sites as Amazon.com, iTunes.com and Rottentomatoes.com – launch team members are able to increase audience interest while improving the film's visibility and support with various distribution channels, particularly VOD. (Robert G. Barnwell/Sandy O. Cagnan)

By encouraging audience members to actively participate in conversations and to contribute content, filmmakers benefit from a supportive partnership with their many friends and fans. When engagement is more informal, conversational and participatory, it provides marketing messages with a personal quality that is hard to capture with traditional advertising. As major studios seemingly have yet to learn, audience members form a more personal connection when they are members of an interactive relationship.

LAUNCH TEAM

The ultimate form of community engagement is the launch team. A launch team is a group of 25–100 friends and fans who volunteer to help support the film's release. Members of the team are recruited from social media, email database, friends and family and other contacts. Not surprisingly, launch team members tend to be among the most engaged members of your audience and the most important members of your community.

Those who join the launch team are provided "insider" access to exclusive behind-the-scenes information, advanced access to both the rough cut and final film, discounts on film and merchandise purchases, and other incentives.

In return, the launch team provides supportive ratings, reviews and comments on web forums, social media, film review sites and distribution channels such as Amazon, iTunes, etc. The launch teams members are also encouraged to support the launch by purchasing a DVD or electronic copy of the film for themselves and friends.

A month or so prior to the film's scheduled broad release, send out an invitation and registration form to your social media, email database and friends and family. Once you've recruited the team, have them join a private Facebook group where you can interact, share ideas and coordinate and schedule activities. *A well-managed launch team is one of the fastest and most effective ways to create positive momentum for the film's premier and, ultimately, to drive film rentals and sales.*

4

MARKETABILITY VS PLAYABILITY
(or "How to Produce Niche-Dominating Blockbusters")

While there may have been a time when things were different, today good marketing virtually guarantees a bad film will only fail faster. In other words: the success of an independent film depends upon *both* quality marketing and a quality film.

The speed with which movies are now classified as either "good" or "bad" almost entirely reflects the popularity, reach, influence and immediacy of global social media. Social media friends, fans, followers and fellow community members enjoy sharing and learning about each other's film preferences and opinions. In particular, we enjoy sharing our thoughts on the film's storyline, our favorite scenes, impressive special or visual effects, the quality of acting and cinematography, and other exciting aspects of the film. At the same time, we are also anxious to share our frustration in having spent time and money on a film that leaves us disappointed.

However, regardless of whether we "love" or "hate" a film, many – if not most – of us are anxious to share our opinions on Facebook, Twitter, Renren, YouTube and other sites. We'll also post our ratings and reviews (alongside professional critics) to Rotten Tomatoes, Cinemablend, Metacritic, IMDb, iTunes, Amazon and Yahoo! Movies.

MARKETABILITY VS PLAYABILITY

Perhaps the best explanation of the relationship between marketability and playability was offered by the former co-chairman of one of the leading independent studios:

You can spend all the money in the world. If you've got a bad product, it doesn't matter.

In other words: Unless an audience finds a film entertaining (read "playable"), marketing will only lead to faster and higher levels of dissatisfaction as reflected in highly visible negative online ratings, reviews and word-of-mouth.

From a profitability perspective, depending upon the film's production and marketing budget, a major studio can occasionally recoup its negative costs (production costs) on a movie that doesn't play well with strong marketing and a good opening weekend. Once word gets out that the film is a popular and critical disappointment, the studio may have already broken even or achieved a profit.

In contrast, an independent film producer rarely has this opportunity. Without the marketing and promotional reach of a major studio, independent films cannot rely on a large promotional spend and strong opening weekend to achieve rapid profitability. Instead, an independent film often has to rely on word-of-mouth and positive reviews to gradually build its audience over weeks and months. It's not uncommon for successful independent films to have weak opening weekends or to go "straight to video" before achieving popularity and profitability.

On the other hand, a good film that is widely regarded as "playable" but isn't regarded as "marketable" also faces a serious problem: How do you drive box office sales, distribution licensing deals and VOD sales and rentals? This is the true challenge of most low-budget films. Without A-list stars, multimillion dollar special and visual effects and the support of global marketing and promotional campaigns, independents are often faced with a "marketability" challenge.

Marketability

Again, "marketability" reflects the ability of a film to attract an audience (as well as sales agents and distributors).

Fundamentally, marketability begins with a creative story developed to appeal to a specific audience. During development and preproduction, marketability can be enhanced by basing the story on a well-known underlying literary property (best-selling novels, classic books in the public domain, popular comic books, famous historical or fictional characters, etc.), or on current or historical events and trends; and the attachment of A-list actors and well-known producers, directors and other crew members.

During production and post-production, marketability will also begin to reflect the quality of the film's website, posters, teasers and trailers, IMDb and other online listings, media coverage and print and/or broadcast advertising.

Finally, once the film is completed, the marketability of the film is enhanced by festival acclaim, social media buzz and audience and film critic reviews and ratings posted to sites such as Amazon, Cinemablend, iTunes, Rotten Tomatoes and other popular review and VOD platforms.

Playability

In contrast to marketability, the playability of the film represents the extent to which the audience enjoys the film and how the film measures up against the audience's expectations. Playability is commonly attributed to the strength of the film's story, production value and its rhythm and pacing. As mentioned earlier, a film that plays well benefits from strong ratings, reviews and word-of-mouth recommendations. These factors are critical in achieving long-term sustained popularity.

Unfortunately, an audience can often sense problems in "playability" the minute they see the marketing . . . long before the film's opening. Problems in playability are often revealed in the quality of the film's teasers, trailers, key art, websites and social media as well as pre-release talk shows, TV interviews and previews of coming attractions.

However, even when pre-release marketing and promotion establishes positive audience expectations, the way the film "plays" can be subjective. For an independent film to be successful, it needs to play well with a variety of audiences, including: niche and general audience members, domestic as well as foreign audiences, sales executives, distribution executives, festival programmers and film critics.

As a result, for those of us who wish to create enduring entertainment properties, we must focus on both the film's marketability and its playability... for a variety of audiences. This involves not only branding, marketing and promotional activities, but also close attention to the film's target audience and genre, market-oriented script development, production value and mise-en-scène. Once the film is through post-production, successful producers will welcome test screenings and other opportunities to improve the film with additional pickup shots, reshoots and re-cuts as necessary.

Again, to ensure a profitable independent film – particularly if your film is intended to crossover from its target market to a broader general market – it must be marketable and playable. With indie films, you can't succeed without both.

Unfortunately, rather than achieve a successful balance, many independent filmmakers place too much emphasis on playability and not nearly enough on market-ability.

PRODUCING BLOCKBUSTERS

It is within this intersection of marketability and playability that most blockbuster franchises can be found... blockbusters such as *Avatar*, *Jurassic Park*, *Star Wars*, *Harry Potter*, *Pirates of the Caribbean* and *Toy Story*. Each of these franchises recorded over $1 billion in global box office and billions more in video games, books, apparel, DVD and VOD and other merchandise sales and rentals.

Admittedly it may be difficult to see how an independent film produced for less than $2.5 million has any relationship to blockbusters produced for $100 million or more. However, it's important to understand that the term "blockbuster" is relative. A film that costs $200 million to produce and market yet generates $250 million in sales is far from a blockbuster. When you deduct theater, distribution and other fees, it's highly unlikely such a film could even be profitable. On the other hand, a film that costs less than $2.5 million to make and market yet does over $12.5 million in sales (not including sequels and cross- or trans-media merchandise) is clearly a blockbuster.

One of the greatest sources of advice and insights into the creation of blockbuster films and entertainment was published by entertainment marketing consultant Gene Del Vecchio (2012). A widely recognized marketing and research expert with a particular emphasis on entertainment, Del Vecchio developed his principles based upon thousands of research studies and thirty years of professional experience working with such companies as The Walt Disney Company, Paramount Pictures, Starz, PBS Kids Sprout and others.

Based upon this research and experience, Del Vecchio discovered that there are broadly three categories of movie "blockbusters": (i) the *single-event blockbusters* are those that have great success, which both begins and ends with the initial film; (2) *linear-franchise blockbusters* in which the original films serve as a basis for franchise sequels; and (3) *category-franchise blockbusters* in which the original films serve as a foundation for sequels *and* cross- or trans-media products (television programs, comic books, computer games, theme park rides, Broadway plays, toys, apparel and other media and merchandise). However, regardless of the type of blockbuster discussed, most share the following eleven key success principles:

1. *Compelling Stories:* Blockbusters depend upon having a strong story with equally strong characters. Based upon his research, Del Vecchio found that

   > *Strong . . . ideas stem from having the right ingredients. These ingredients include the use of critical character archetypes and iconic characters, key plot conflicts, core emotional drivers, a character's emotional (and sometimes physical) transformations, the idea's alignment to contemporary culture and trends and even the idea's inner moral compass.*

   The importance of these issues should not be underestimated because the central story idea and characteristics will have dramatic impact on many of the script and production decisions that follow. *"The initial idea will impact the direction of the treatment and script with regard to character development, story elements, setting, era, action, and humor. Those elements, in turn, will have a dramatic impact on all the production essentials, which include casting, directing, stylization, and even editing. This will impact how it is marketed."*

2. *Relatable, Aspirational and Memorable Characters:* To a great extent, an audience experiences each film through the story's characters. In fact, the audience's emotional commitment to a movie depends upon characters whom the audience deeply cares about. These characters must be memorable and, particularly in the case of the protagonist, must be someone with whom the audience can relate and they aspire to be. Unfortunately, many films fail to create sufficiently appealing characters and, as a result, audiences do not particularly care about them, their situations or the consequences they face.

3. *Satisfy Deep Emotional Needs:* Successful films have storylines and characters that pursue a strong emotional need. Ideally, these emotional needs are fundamental human needs such as life (survival), love, social acceptance, self-esteem (confidence, respect, status, power, etc.) or self-actualization. Commonly, these emotions manifest themselves in film as bravery, courage, envy, fear, lust and romance.

   Unfortunately, both major and independent studio films commonly fail to achieve a satisfactory emotional connection with their audiences. It's critically important that the writers, director and producers ask themselves "How do we want the audience to feel?" with regard to each of the film's individual characters and scenes. And, as important, what emotions do you want the audience to feel as the movie comes to a satisfying ending and the closing credits begin to roll?

4. *Broad Audience Appeal:* Because independent filmmakers have limited marketing and promotional resources, it's imperative to focus resources on narrowly targeted primary and secondary audiences. However, at the same time, it's also important to produce films with the potential for crossover appeal to a much broader audience.

   Admittedly, this can be a difficult balance to achieve. Del Vecchio explains that

   > *There's something to be said for selecting a key audience segment and then crafting entertainment that gains their interest without having to include superficial elements in a misguided attempt to attract a broader audience. If you try to appease every audience segment, you risk watering down the emotional fulfillment for all of them. It's hard to be all things to all segments.*

5. *Aligned with Current Events and Trends:* Films also benefit from being aligned with contemporary culture, trends and events including (i) entertainment-based culture

(celebrities, music, fashion, entertainment, etc.) and (ii) current events (politics, war/terrorism, economics, religion, race, environment, etc.). The use of contemporary culture and trends can make familiar storylines feel fresh and unique.

6. *Employing the "Ever Cool" Formula:* While the importance of aligning a film with current events and trends is crucial, blockbusters should also have "timeless" appeal. Many studio executives refer to such films as "evergreen properties." Producers must consider how their films can remain fresh even as they develop the initial film. To become and stay successful, your films should (i) satisfy universal emotional needs; (ii) employ timeless themes, stories and characters; and (iii) feature strategic updates and additions (film sequels or other cross- or trans-media products) combining current entertainment and cultural trends with original story elements.

7. *Franchise-Making Elements:* With limited financial resources, independent films and filmmakers must achieve a level of marketing efficiency exceeding those of the major studios. Franchise films are particularly efficient as they are able to leverage their popularity across sequels and, often, other cross- or trans-media products.

    In addition to the other blockbuster characteristics described here, other elements crucial to the development of film franchises include: (i) a theme or story that is open-ended in that it lends itself for additional follow-on stories in film, books, comic books and other media; (ii) distinctive characters worth emulating; (iii) storylines and characters that are "playable" in that they could lend themselves to computer and board games; (iv) fanciful exotic settings and locations; and (v) unique film and genre-related iconography (wardrobe, props, locations, character design, etc.).

8. *Creation of Marketable Content ("Artistry"):* Essentially, the creation of marketable content or "artistry" reflects the significance of both playability and marketability in a film's eventual success. And, in today's world of instantaneous communications, playability is often more important that marketability: *"It's very difficult for poor and mediocre [films] to be saved by great marketing."*

    Anne Parducci, former Executive Vice President and General Manager of Marketing at Lionsgate, agrees while emphasizing that marketability should remain an essential part of the filmmaking process:

    > *I find that the most successful films and easiest to market are those where one can easily answer the following questions; Who is the film for . . . the consumer target . . . and does it deliver against that audience in terms of the genre, the story, the emotional experience, the casting, etc.? While that seems so elementary, I am always amazed by the number of films where the answer to these questions is not clear.*

    (Del Vecchio, 2012)

9. *Use Research & Analysis to Optimize Decision-Making:* As you've likely noticed, the producers of blockbusters don't often rely on gut feel. Instead, they leverage research throughout each stage of film production. This includes (i) market, audience and genre research during the development stage; (ii) small focus group testing of initial concepts, loglines (short synopses) and storylines; (iii) film screenings to assess and refine playability; (iv) market testing of film titles, key art, trailers and other marketing and promotional materials; and, finally, (v) post-release performance tracking of film sales and rental trends, professional and audience film reviews and ratings and other metrics. This post-release analysis is instrumental in developing successful sequels and other cross-media products.

10. *Ongoing Pursuit of an Idea Quest:* Finding the "right" storyline and creating the "right" script can be a considerable challenge. As Gene explains: "It takes a tremendous amount of work to generate a large number of ideas, and then more work to find the precious few that are worth pursuing. It then takes luck and time for those precious few to become blockbusters."

Fortunately, the more familiar you will become with the marketplace, your genre, target audience and recent film and entertainment trends, the more likely you are to generate and identify successful ideas.

11. *Avoid or Fix Common Execution Problems:* Beyond issues regarding marketability and production value, many films face several other common problems in achieving blockbuster status – many, if not most of which, can be addressed during the development and preproduction stages. More specifically, these problems include stories and films that audiences found boring, too slow, lacking in suspense, humor or action, were too confusing or that lacked originality. In particularly, many films fail to create sufficiently extreme characters and place them in appropriately extreme situations. Other problems included characters that were difficult to relate to or that were not sufficiently aspirational, characters that lacked sufficient differentiation from one another, and similar story and character-related issues.

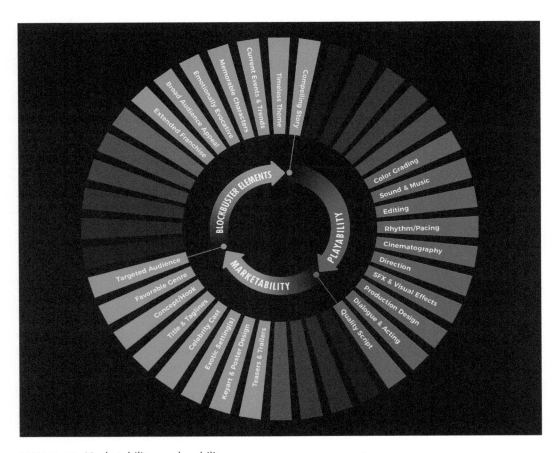

FIGURE 4.1 Marketability vs playability.

(Robert G. Barnwell/Sandy O. Cagnan)

Again, fortunately, most of these issues can – and should – be addressed during development and pre-production.

While Del Vecchio's research and suggestions are largely based on major entertainment blockbusters, his insights are just as – or even more – important to independent film producers with limited financial resources and whose success is often concentrated with – and dependent upon – a small portfolio of only one or two low-budget films.

GENRES & TARGET MARKETS

As we have discussed, the film's ability to achieve blockbuster status, in part, reflects its genre, which, in turn, is a vital component of the film's ultimate playability and marketability. In fact, in many respects, the choice of genre (or subgenre or cross-genres) largely *determines* the film's marketing, promotional and distribution strategies.

Genre is a means of classifying films together in groups according to narrative and film style, such as action-adventure, comedy, drama, horror, romance and science fiction. Each genre, in turn, can also be further classified into subgenres or can be combined with two or more genres into various hybrid or cross-genres. As an example, films within the Alien, Predator or Terminator franchises are commonly classified as horror-science fiction hybrids. Similarly, James Cameron's cross-genre film *Titanic* includes elements of the romance, drama, period and action-adventure genres.

Your choice of film genre is particularly important for a variety of marketing, promotional and creative reasons. First, our individual filmmaking experience, talents and interests tend to lend themselves best to one or two genres. Secondly, each genre presents a ready market for fans of that particular genre – albeit the demand for any specific genre tends to ebb and flow depending upon cultural and entertainment trends and fashions.

To best identify market opportunities, make it a point to regularly attend film markets and speak with sales agents and distributors – even if you don't currently have a film in development or production. You want to stay abreast of current and emerging marketplace trends: What is the current supply–demand situation within your genre(s)? Conduct an informal "gap analysis" to identify opportunities within – and across – different genres. Try to spot emerging market trends.

In addition to the state of the marketplace, you'll also want to have a detailed understanding of the entertainment habits and preferences of those within your film's target market. This includes not only details on the target audience's demographics, but also of the audience's likes and dislikes, beliefs, preferences, behaviors, viewing habits and their entertainment rental and purchase trends.

Developing a comprehensive understanding of the genres of our films is crucial to both their marketing and playability. Be a fan of your genre. Know it, own it and make it better. Every genre has its own conventions and expectations. These elements and standards are often comprised of genre-specific storylines, structures, character types, dialogue and vocabulary, settings and locations, common scenes and/or set pieces, color and lighting, wardrobe, props and other iconography.

At the same time as you work to identify your genres' essential elements, try to identify any outdated elements, clichés and other genre standards that should be ignored or abandoned. You do not want to create a "caricature" of your genre. While remaining true to your genre, you want your film to be fresh and original. To do so, consider incorporating elements and trends from other genres.

As you study your genre, concentrate on the most popular and well-respected content within your genre, including popular films, television programs, books and video games. Also develop a familiarity with the directors, authors and other creative content creators within the genre.

Begin by closely studying the films, shooting scripts and original source materials (books, articles, video games, television programs, etc.). Deconstruct and reverse engineer the films (and other cross- or trans-media entertainment) into their common elements. What genre-specific conventions were employed? What conventions or elements were missing or ignored? What was the popular and critical reception (sales figures, reviews, ratings, etc.)?

Ultimately, your choice of genre should be based on your experience, interests and passions. In many respects, your genre is a reflection of your own personality. So, in addition to questions around market supply and demand, you should also take the time to look in the mirror and ask yourself the following questions:

- *Of the movies I've produced and/or participated in the past, is there a consistent or common genre? Which genres most appeal to me?*
- *Does my existing community of audience members, colleagues, friends and family already identify me with a particular genre?*
- *With regard to my knowledge, skills, abilities, experiences and resources, which genre(s) am I best suited to?*

MARKETING-ORIENTED SCRIPT DEVELOPMENT

One of the central messages of this chapter is the necessity of thinking of marketing, playability and the audience BEFORE you choose a story and complete the script.

As suggested with regard to studying your genre, it's important to attend film markets and maintain relationships with sales agents and distributors. The information and insight they provide will be instrumental when making decisions around genre, storylines, cast attachment, budget and favorable markets and distributors. It's absolutely critical to know this information before you begin work on developing or choosing the "right" script for your film project.

Within his book and film workshops, independent film consultant, educator and author Dov Simens insists that independent filmmakers can afford nothing less than a great script:

> it starts with the script, and "good is not good enough." Your script must be great. Ideas are a dime a dozen. Everyone has one. Your job is to get the great script, which is based on a great idea. There is nothing easy about this. Don't be lazy.
>
> (Simens, 2003)

You could argue – quite correctly, in my opinion – that major studios produce blockbusters all the time with scripts that are marginal ... at best. The recent superhero and Transformers movies come immediately to mind. These films are not script- or story-driven. Instead, they are character- and visual effects-driven movies.

Unfortunately, unlike major studios, we don't have access to the millions of dollars necessary to license popular comic or toy characters and to employ a huge team of effects artists. Almost by definition, as Dov explains adamantly, low-budget films must be script- and storyline-driven. This demands a well-written and well-structured script.

Developing the Storyline

Georges Polti, a French writer (1867–1946), found that every possible storyline could be traced to one, or a combination, of only thirty-six dramatic situations. Others, including Ronald Tobias (author of *20 Master Plots*) and Christopher Booker (author of *The Seven Basic Plots: Why We Tell Stories*), have attempted to reduce these fundamental storylines even further.

By mixing and matching, the scriptwriter is able to craft an almost limitless number of plots and storylines. Some of the most common storylines include love and forbidden love, rivalry, revenge/vengeance, pursuit, rescue or escape, success and failure and quests/adventures.

However, whichever plots or cross-plots you choose, there are several story elements necessary to assure a successful film script. First, the story should focus on someone (or a small group of individuals) that the audience truly cares about. Secondly, that person (or group) must be highly motivated to achieve something the audience believes to be worthwhile. And, third, whatever it is that the protagonist is seeking must be quite difficult to achieve.

It's important to understand that the central story should focus on only one main objective. That said, in achieving that one overarching objective, scripts often benefit from the protagonist having to achieve several smaller incremental objectives on their path to the main objective. Regardless, the value of the ultimate objective must be strong enough to produce sufficient conflict to drive the story and engage the audience.

In addition to having an appealing protagonist and worthwhile goal or objective, in order that the script – and film – be most interesting and emotionally engaging, the protagonist must also face considerable obstacles on the path toward success. Ideally, the obstacles should appear to be overwhelming. And, to make matters even more interesting, there must be some dire consequence facing the protagonist if he or she fails to achieve their objective. This could be a broken heart in the case of a romantic comedy or the death of innocents in the case of an action film.

As you can see, at this point in development, we are only looking at establishing the most rudimentary general outline of our story. Ultimately, we are working toward the creation of a brief one to two sentence logline. Within twelve to twenty-five words, a well-crafted logline will establish the script's hero, the inciting incident, the hero's objective and the consequences if the hero fails to achieve the objective. The following template is a good place to start:

> When [inciting incident], a [the hero/protagonist] must [objective], or [consequences].

Before committing to your final logline (and, in fact, throughout the scriptwriting process), be conscious of your target audience and marketplace. Think about your genre and similar storylines that have already been produced. Does your proposed storyline reflect current culture or entertainment trends? What story (and other cinematic) elements can you add that leverage established and emerging entertainment trends?

Titles & Taglines

Admittedly, it seems strange to discuss the film's title and tagline before addressing the script. But the choice of a good title and tagline – even if only a working title and tagline – can provide inspiration and focus on the original story concept throughout the script development and writing process.

Strong titles tend to be memorable, genre-appropriate and reflective of the film's storyline. Titles (and taglines) should also work in harmony with the key art, teasers, trailers and other promotional materials. Some common titling conventions include titles that reflect a character's name (*James Bond, Jason Bourne, Iron Man, Spider-Man*, etc.), locations or events (*Cape Fear, Iwo Jima, Jurassic Park, Madagascar, Munich, Pearl Harbor, Philadelphia, Titanic*, etc.) and other aspects of the movie or its story such as emotions (*Rage, Misery*, etc.) and timelines (*3:10 to Yuma, 48 Hrs, Gone in 60 Seconds*, etc.).

While there are some notable exceptions, successful films tend to have short descriptive titles of one to two words. Consider films such as *Aliens, Avatar, Forrest Gump, The Godfather, Jaws, Jurassic Park, Psycho, Shrek, Star Wars, Taxi Driver, The Terminator, Titanic* and *Toy Story*. Shorter titles also lend themselves well to website URLs, social media accounts and other marketing and promotional purposes.

When considering titles, complete a Google search of potential titles. Which ones have been used before? Are the URLs, social media account names and IMDb profiles available? While titles are difficult to trademark (which is why it's not uncommon to find several films with the same title), avoid existing titles that may create audience confusion. Also, be cautious of using words in your title that may have alternative foreign meanings. This can be confusing and potentially embarrassing. Fortunately, the title of films, along with other aspects of their marketing campaign, are often changed to better reflect particular languages and cultures in the countries in which they are released.

With regard to the film's tagline, or taglines, a quick review of the logline is a good place to start. While the logline is a one to two sentence summary of the film, the tagline is a short five to fifteen word marketing phrase meant to communicate the "essence" of the movie. These differences aside, it is occasionally possible to repurpose or reword the logline as a successful tagline.

However, more likely than not, the logline will only serve as inspiration for the film's tagline or taglines (several films feature multiple taglines). As you consider alternative taglines, give strong preference to those comprised of short phrases that (i) reinforce the film's plot, tone, theme or appeal and (ii) are genre-appropriate. Successful taglines employ words that are descriptive, action-oriented and convey emotion. Consider some of the most effective and popular film taglines:

"An adventure 65 million years in the making" *Jurassic Park* (1993)

"In space no one can hear you scream" *Alien* (1979)

"Reality is a thing of the past" *The Matrix* (1999)

"Who ya gonna call?" *Ghostbusters* (1984)

"Just when you thought it was safe to go back in the water" *Jaws 2* (1978)

"You don't get 500 million friends without making a few enemies" *The Social Network* (2010)

"For Harry and Lloyd, every day is a no brainer" *Dumb and Dumber* (1994)

"The last man on Earth is not alone" *I Am Legend* (2007)

FIGURE 4.2 Many independent filmmakers and scriptwriters have found scriptwriting software, such as Final Draft and Movie Magic, particularly helpful. Not only does such software properly format the script to industry standards, but many programs also offer several writing and story development features including such tools as Final Draft's story maps and beat boards.

(Final Draft/Cast and Crew Entertainment)

Obviously, a strong title and tagline are often what first captures an audience's attention and interest in a film. As a result, the choice of title and taglines is a crucial part of the marketing campaign and can make a huge difference as to whether or not the film is financially successful.

Script Structure

Scriptwriters benefit from having a number of story structures to choose from. These structures include the traditional three-act structure as supported by Syd Field, Blake Snyder and Robert McKee; Kristen Thompson's four-act structure; Gustav Freytag's five-act structure; Frank Daniel's eight sequences; Jacob Krueger's seven-act structure; and the nine- or twelve-act structure, among others.

Personally, I prefer to use a three-act structure which I further break down into several smaller individual sequences or beats. I encourage you to adopt whatever structure you feel is most appropriate to your story, film and style of writing. However, I won't mince words here: refusing to use a structure to simply be different or because you don't like being "constrained" is just plain stupid. I don't know how else to describe it.

Human DNA is 99.9% the same across genders and race. Despite these commonalities, human beings are individuals and one person can typically recognize another – even in a huge crowd – from thousands of others. Humans can also identify differences in strangers with regard to what is "normal" or "abnormal," with fellow human beings grouped according to differences in physical presentation and mental health (I use quote marks here to acknowledge that such characterizations are commonly social constructs).

Likewise, despite using a structure to develop your script, there is no reason that your film cannot be unique. And, like the previous example, if you deviate significantly from popular story structures, your audience will likely – however subconsciously – recognize the deviation and determine whether this was "right" or "wrong."

Whichever structure you ultimately choose, at the risk of oversimplification, every script will have a beginning, middle and end as represented by the fundamental three-act structure. So it's from this perspective that we'll discuss the most common elements and attributes of a successful independent film script.

Ernest Lehman, screenwriter of *The Sound of Music, West Side Story, North by Northwest,* perhaps best summarized the three-act structure when he explained that

> *In the first act, it's who are the people and what is the situation of this whole story. The second act is the progression of that situation to a high point of conflict and great problems. And the third act is how the conflicts and problems are resolved.*
>
> (Howard and Mabley, 1993)

1. Beginning, aka "Act One" (first 25% of the script): As noted by Ernest Lehman, during the first act, the story's principal characters, their relationships, setting (location and time period) and genre should be clearly established. Relatively quickly, commonly somewhere between page 10 and page 15 of the script, the story's hero (aka "protagonist") is confronted by a significant challenge that will serve as the character's central goal or objective throughout the script. Scriptwriters refer to this challenge as the "inciting incident" or "catalyst." This inciting incident must be substantial enough for the story's hero to willingly face considerable emotional and/or physical risk. It is critical that the protagonist has a clear objective and understands the consequences of possible failure. The first act ends when the protagonist has taken action that signifies complete commitment to confronting the challenge and achieving his or her objective.

As you craft the opening of Act One, I encourage you to give considerable thought to the first scene. The film (and script) must grab the audience's attention immediately . . . and never let go. Consider opening the film with the first instance of dramatic action. Remember: backstory is boring.

2. Middle, aka "Act Two" (middle 50% of the script): The second act is commonly the weakest segment of the film and script. Over the course of the second act, the script should increase the story's pacing and tension. The protagonist must take proactive action to achieve the objective defined in the first act . . . only to be met with failure and additional obstacles. Many scriptwriters allow the protagonist to achieve a false victory before being temporarily defeated and confronting an ever-worsening situation.

At the same time, as the hero continues to struggle, the story's villain (aka "antagonist") appears to be invincible. (Note: The script's antagonist does not necessarily have to take human form, the villain could just as easily be an alien or supernatural being, cultural or societal norms, governmental regulations, a force of nature [earthquake, tidal wave, volcano, blizzard, tornado, etc.] or other threat or source of conflict.)

The second act is also where any subplots or b-stories are introduced. While there are many effective types of subplots, one of the more successful is the introduction of a different character viewpoint. Traditionally, most scripts and films follow the story of the hero. Providing a parallel viewpoint from the perspective of the antagonist (or other character) often provides more depth and richness to the film.

Regardless of whether or not you choose to incorporate one or more subplots within your script, the second act commonly concludes with the protagonist committing to an "all or nothing" – "do or die" – course of action to achieve the character's ultimate objective. This serves to transition to the film's conclusion in the final act.

3. Ending, aka "Act Three" (final 25% of the script/film): The third act features the resolution of the story and any subplots. Many filmmakers work to achieve a sense of balance, or symmetry, by having an ending that closely mirrors the opening scene. Regardless of your approach or strategy, the script's climax represents the film's most intense sequence. It is important that the climax results from the protagonist's direct actions – not from coincidence (e.g. "ex machina"). Spend considerable time developing and refining the climax and final scenes. It's critical that the emotional pay-off at the end of the film exceeds the audience's time and emotional investment in the characters and their story.

Story Elements

At various intervals throughout the scriptwriting process, you should take sufficient time to reflect on several aspects of the script; in particular, such issues and questions as:

Storyline

- ☑ Do the script and storyline reflect an understanding of the genre and market research insights?
- ☑ Was the script written to appeal to a specific target audience? Does the script contain elements that would also appeal to a broader crossover audience?
- ☑ Does the script contain trailerable moments, particularly dialogue?
- ☑ Will the story appeal to audiences across cross- or trans-media platforms such as computer games, webisodes, comic books, theme park rides, Broadway plays or other media?
- ☑ Has the script been written with the anticipated budget (and any budget constraints) in mind?
- ☑ Does the script adhere closely to the logline and through-story?
- ☑ During the first act, are the main characters, setting, inciting incident and objective properly established?
- ☑ During the second act, does the story and tension continually build? Are subplots and additional challenges/obstacles introduced?
- ☑ During the third act, does the script reach a conclusion that resolves all of the story's plot points? Does the climax represent a logical conclusion given the preceding events and actions? Does the final scene provide the audience with an emotionally satisfying conclusion?

Individual Scenes

- ☑ Does the scene have a clear purpose? Does the scene advance the story?
- ☑ Is there a "through-line" from the preceding scene(s) and to the following scene(s)?
- ☑ Does the scene generate anticipation and/or tension for the scenes that follow?
- ☑ What characters are in the scene? Does the scene advance the audience's understanding of the characters and their role in the story?
- ☑ What are each character's actions and/or objectives in the scene?
- ☑ Continuity: Where were the characters before this scene and where will they be after? Is there a continuity issue? How much time has elapsed between where they last appeared and where they will next appear?
- ☑ Are the length and pacing of the individual shots and scenes varied?

Characters

☑ Has a profile been created for each character, including information such as the character's name, nickname, sex, age, physical appearance (height, weight, skin tone, hairstyle, physical build, etc.), dress style, educational and professional background (occupation), social standing, marital status, family background, race/nationality/religion, sexual identity, preferred mode of transportation, distinguishing traits (smells, voice, skin, hair, physical disabilities, scars, distinguishing marks, tattoos, piercings, etc.), attitudes, personality traits and habits, self-perception and any unique expressions (vocabulary and gestures)?

☑ Are the characters original and complex? Or are they stereotypical?

☑ Is the nature of each character revealed through their actions as well as through dialogue?

☑ Do the characters behave realistically?

☑ Are the characters castable/attachable? In other words, will each character appeal to the type of actor required to play the role?

Dialogue

☑ Does the script rely on action to advance the story rather than expansive dialogue?

☑ Does the dialogue transition from preceding discussions, actions or scenes and help transition into those that follow?

☑ Does the dialogue advance the action and/or story?

☑ Are large blocks of exposition essential to the story? Can exposition be eliminated or broken up into smaller pieces of dialogue?

☑ Does the dialogue and action properly reflect the nature and personality of each character?

☑ Have dialect and slang been used to create more interesting language and to individualize and personify the characters?

☑ Is the dialogue clear and comprehensible to the audience?

☑ Can the actors deliver the dialogue without much difficulty? Are the words and phrases easily remembered, spoken and pronounced?

Additional Tips for Low-Budget Scriptwriting

☑ Keep the feature film script to eighty-five to ninety-five pages. As a general guideline, one script page equals 1 minute of running time. Reduce the script to its most essential and exciting elements. An 80–95 minute running time is ideal . . . a 180–195 minute running time is not.

☑ Keep the number of characters to a minimum. However, at the same time, work to include diverse characters in terms of age, sex, race, etc.

☑ Minimize the number of locations. Use single locations that feature multiple looks and uses. Moving cast and crew from one location to another creates considerable challenges and inefficiencies. Instead, secure locations that allow for multiple uses or are within only a few minutes commute from one another.

☑ Keep it simple. Simple dialogue. Simple actions. Complex dialogue and scenes will often require multiple takes for the actors and may prove equally confusing to the audience.

☑ Hire professional readers to assess your script. Also consider having your script serve as a project within a scriptwriting class.

☑ Rewrite to reduce the cost and complexity of the production (and to identify opportunities to increase production value . . . without, again, increasing cost or complexity).

☑ With regard to both scriptwriting and filmmaking, what you do is not always the primary consideration. Rather it's how. Be creative and focus on the end result. Computer-generated images and the use of miniatures and forced perspective can often substitute for more expensive vehicles, props and challenging practical effects shots.

☑ Register your treatment and script with copyright.gov and the Writers Guild of America at wga.org.

Common Problems

☒ Confusing storyline that fails to follow a focused or coherent through-story.

☒ Unbelievable storylines, situations, action, dialogue, characters, etc.

☒ A storyline and/or characters that fail to engage the audience emotionally. Often the result of a weak storyline and/or one-dimensional characters.

☒ The script with too many pages/a film with an overly long running time.

☒ Writing or editing that results in pacing inappropriate for the tone of the scene and/or story. Most commonly evidenced by slow pacing.

☒ An overreliance upon exposition – rather than action – to advance the storyline.

☒ Hero saved or story resolved by outside coincidence (aka "ex machina") rather than through the actions of the story's characters.

ELEMENTS OF PRODUCTION VALUE

As we'll continue to discuss throughout the book, *regardless of the film's budget, ultimately your audience is going to judge your film by the movies they are most familiar with. And those are, with limited exception, big-budget movies produced or distributed by the major studios. As a result, your audience is going to expect a film with qualities that rival the major studio films they are most used to viewing.*

Unfortunately, unlike low-budget independent films, large-budget films afford their producers and directors considerable resources in terms of both time and funding. In turn, these resources – when well-spent – help their producers create a higher-quality film with impressive "production values."

In essence, a film's production value represents the technical qualities derived from the methods, skills and materials used in the film's production and is essential to its ultimate playability. Among other factors, production value often reflects: the quality of the script; impressive direction, cinematography and editing; color and lighting; recognizable and talented actors; realistic visual and practical effects; production design (set design, props, etc.); wardrobe and costume; makeup and hairstyling; exotic locations; and impressive sound design. These elements are so important, that most are the subject of such prestigious awards as the Oscars (aka "Academy Awards"), BAFTAs and others.

Fortunately, despite low-budget filmmakers, by definition, having access to only limited resources, high production values can be readily achieved by (i) investing in one or two impressive "set piece" scenes and (ii) through the creative use and mastery of film technique and production management.

Production Design & Mise-en-Scène

Closely related to production value is the concept of mise-en-scène – a French term that translates to "placing on stage." While many professionals may define the term slightly differently, most professionals agree that mise-en-scène generally refers to (i) all the elements that appear on camera and (ii) the resulting impression these elements have on the audience. Mise-en-scène establishes the "essence" of what appears on the screen. Employing a broad definition, there are several areas to consider when talking about mise-en-scène:

- Direction & cinematography
  o Aspect ratio
  o Camera and actor blocking
  o Types of lenses
  o Shot types & framing
  o Camera movement (handheld, dolly, jib/crane, pan, tilt, high and aerial shots, etc.)
- Acting/cast attachment
- Color and lighting (including color grading)
- Exotic, visually interesting and story-appropriate sets and locations
- Set design/decoration/dressing
- Wardrobe, hair and makeup
- Props and vehicles
- Sound
- Special & visual effects
- Quality (including pace and rhythm) of editing
- Opening and closing title sequence

Each of these factors – individually and in combination – gives each shot (and, by extension, the entire film) a certain "look" or "feel." What the producer, screenwriter, director and cinematographer ultimately decide to include or exclude from a shot (or from the film) can make a big difference in how the audience responds and experiences the movie.

In addition to the common production elements listed previously, I'd also add such things as the film's title and tagline, posters, trailers and critical and audience reviews. While many of these may not actually appear on screen, these marketing and promotional elements all build an expectation in the audience's minds that carries over to their actual experience of the film.

As mentioned, to maximize playability, production value and mise-en-scène, the independent filmmaker must employ creative use and mastery of film technique and production management. A key component of which is the ability to recruit talented and experienced cast members and department heads, including the cinematographer, chief lighting technician, sound designer, production designer, visual effects supervisor and editor as well as casting and location managers.

TEST SCREENINGS, PICKUPS, RESHOOTS & RE-CUTS

Because independent films are resource-constrained and have investors who are understandably anxious to recapture their investments, many independent filmmakers mistakenly rush their films through post-production and into distribution.

This often proves a critical mistake as additional time in post-production conducting test screenings, pickup shots, reshoots and re-cuts can significantly improve the quality of the film and its playability.

Dan Myrick and Eduardo Sanchez used feedback from test screenings to make *The Blair Witch Project* more exciting. Similarly, Oren Peli's *Paranormal Activity* reportedly went through almost fifty test screenings in order to get things "right" – half of those screenings before being picked up by Paramount and around another twenty-five afterwards.

At the risk of stating the obvious: test screenings are effectively useless unless you are able to take advantage of the opportunity to use the findings from the questionnaires and discussions to improve your film.

When screenings are properly scheduled and budgeted, filmmakers are able to use the results for reshoots, pickup shots, re-edits and, in some cases, are able to use ADR (automatic dialogue replacement) to improve, or completely change, pieces of dialogue.

Unfortunately, while approximately 80% of major studio films incorporate such post-production improvements, independent filmmakers rarely budget the time and money for significant reshoots. And, for independent films, the ability to conduct reshoots and pickup shots is even more important to their eventual success.

As Producer Rob Cowan – producer of over thirty films, including *San Andreas* (2015) and *The Conjuring* (2013) – explains:

> *Many people look at the act of reshooting as going backwards – or trying to put a Band-Aid on something that's broken. It's the opposite in fact. It's enhancing your project with a better insight into what the film is and what the film needs. It's one of those rare chances in life where you get to reflect on where you are – take a step to the side and possibly even change course to make something better.*
>
> (Rob Cowan, 2013)

5

PITCHING & NETWORKING

William Shakespeare once wrote that "All the world's a stage, and all the men and women merely players." I can think of few instances in which this quote is more appropriate than the production of an independent film. Depending upon the situation and whom you are speaking to, you may be required to play the role of producer, director, screenwriter, fundraiser, marketing manager, publicist, salesman (or saleswoman) or any one of dozens of other roles.

A large responsibility of any one of these roles is to pitch . . . to convince others to support you and your film project. To convince them to join your film's cast or crew, to provide financing, to distribute your completed film, to provide a discount on equipment, locations or provide anyone of the thousands of other services, products or forms of support required to produce a successful film.

However, most information about pitching within the film industry is targeted at scriptwriters presenting concepts, treatments and scripts to studio development executives. Unfortunately, the process of pitching scripts (which is often more of a brief one-sided presentation) is, in many ways, quite different from the discussion-based pitches that independent filmmakers are required to deliver on an almost daily basis.

As a structured two-way conversation, the independent filmmaker's role during a pitch is more to lead rather than to dominate the discussion. And, since these discussions are interactive (involving the more or less equal participation and contribution of both participants) and involve a broad variety of objectives – both large and small – the duration of pitches can range from a single short email or telephone conversation to a series of meetings over the course of several weeks, months or, all too often, years.

PREPARATION

While pitches can take many forms, the balance of the chapter will be spent discussing how to best prepare and present some of the most challenging pitches – those to prospective distributors, production partners and investors. However, many of the insights and principles will apply equally well to pitches of all types as well as to much of your branding, marketing and promotional activities more broadly.

These challenging, yet high-value, pitches begin with the creation of a three to five page discussion guide that provides meeting details and logistics, the discussion agenda, documents key research findings, the planned responses to likely questions, and other important information.

Meeting Details: The beginning of the discussion guide should identify the date, time and location of the meeting as well as the name and a brief mini-bio of the person (or people) you are meeting, together with the name of their assistants, agents and/or representatives and their contact details. It should also include the name and a short description of their organization (if any) and a list of their past film projects and any common connections (including the names of any important colleagues, agents, representatives, spouses, children or other important people in their careers and/or personal lives) you may share with the organization and/or whomever you are meeting.

Your Goals & Objectives: Once essential meeting details have been listed, you and your team must clearly identify the primary objective of the discussion. What is that you want to achieve from this meeting? To establish a relationship for future benefit? Secure production funding? A distribution deal? Representation? Media coverage? Obtain industry or market insight? Referrals to other professionals or organizations?

Be realistic about what you can expect to achieve in any one particular meeting, particularly if it's your first meeting. While some requests are relatively easy for the other party to agree, other requests, such as for investment funding, likely require several meetings over a period of time before final agreement can be reached. In this case, the objective of an early meeting may simply be to secure one or more follow-on meetings for further discussions.

And, while it's important to have one clear objective, be prepared with a secondary objective if your meeting partners are unable to agree to your principal request. Secondary objectives may include referrals to other professionals or organizations or a more limited commitment from your meeting partner than was originally proposed (again, perhaps to take a subsequent meeting and continue discussions).

Pitch Partner's Goals & Objectives: Similarly, the second step is to anticipate the other party's objectives. Not surprisingly, the objective for most professionals and organizations within the film industry is to generate the highest fees, income or investment return possible. However, many professionals and organizations are also concerned about their ability to enhance their reputations via award nominations or other industry recognition for their work.

To meet these objectives, they'll want to learn more about your film's commercial viability, industry appeal, marketability, playability, castability, timeliness, target market and distribution strategy as well as the current progress of production and fundraising. At the same time, they'll be considering how much risk your project represents from a financial and reputational perspective.

Outline Agenda & Discussion Topics: Once you've identified your objectives and your meeting partner's objectives, it becomes easier to focus the pitch agenda on discussion topics that are mutually beneficial. Understanding the other party's objective also allows you to anticipate the decision-making criteria your pitch partner is likely to use to assess and approve your primary and secondary requests.

As you work to identify discussion topics and outline the meeting agenda, focus on those areas where your goals and objectives are most aligned (and that address the decision-making criteria the other party will likely use to approve, or deny, your request). The following represents a common pitch-meeting agenda:

1. Target market & script
    a) Marketplace
    b) Genre & target audience
    c) Script/story
2. Production & funding status
    a) Production & producers
    b) Cast & crew attachment
    c) Status of funding
3. Marketing & distribution strategy
    a) Branding, marketing & promotional strategy
    b) Sales agents & distributors
    c) Distribution strategy

It bears repeating: the discussion agenda should be customized to reflect the meeting partner and his or her objectives and decision-making criteria. While this sample pitch agenda will likely be appropriate for most meetings with distributors and investors, take advantage of the opportunity to modify this agenda in whatever way best positions you and your film project with specific individuals and organizations.

Anticipate Questions and Prepare Responses: Fortunately, having outlined the agenda, discussion topics, meeting partner's objectives and decision-making criteria, you can anticipate and prepare responses to the most likely – and most difficult – questions you'll face during the pitch.

Not surprisingly, many investors, production partners, sales agents, distributors, cast and crew members, product placement specialists and other industry professionals will have many shared questions and concerns. In particular: (i) What is the feature film experience of the filmmaker and the senior team (particularly producers and department heads)? (ii) What were the relative financial and critical success of these films? (iii) What is the current film project's target market, genre and storyline? And (iv) what is the current status of fundraising and production? If no funding is in place, does the filmmaking team have fundraising experience?

In addition to these concerns, most meeting partners will have issues that are unique to their specific businesses.

As an example, *Investors and Co-Production Partners*, particularly those with limited film industry experience, will be principally concerned with identifying and managing the risks associated with investing in your film while maximizing their potential profits. They will be most interested in the state of the film industry and market trends, your film's distribution strategy, funding requirements, production and promotional (aka "p&a") budget, and anticipated investment returns.

In contrast, *Sales Agents & Distributors* are less concerned about your investor's financial projections and profit models. Instead, they are far more interested in the film itself and associated branding, marketing and promotional strategies. During pre-production discussions, without a completed film to preview, sales agents and distributors will need look books, pre-production teasers and trailers and other supporting materials to assess the film's likely marketability and playability.

Be certain to bring as much research and supporting information – including a copy of the budget and production schedule – as necessary to answer any questions you may receive during the discussion (more details on research in the following pages).

If you've done your homework properly, you'll be in a position to (i) better position yourself, your team and your film with regard to any specific business or professional objectives they may mention and (ii) more easily mitigate any concerns they may identify.

Market & Competitor Research: One of the most fundamental, yet commonly overlooked, requirements to establish yourself as a credible professional is to demonstrate a thorough understanding of the film market, the commercial viability of your film project, and your meeting partner.

Industry, Trends and Market Statistics: As a professional filmmaker, you will be expected to know recent trends in sales, distribution, production and studio business models. This includes a knowledge of (i) the total market size for feature films and subsegments such as genres, countries or regions and distribution platforms (such as VOD); (ii) global, national and regional film viewing, rental and purchase trends; (iii) the relative popularity of your genre versus competing genres and other forms of entertainment; and (iv) demographics of your primary and secondary target markets.

Film Comparables: You also need to be familiar with recently released, in-production and in-development films within your genre, including: their production budget, film-maker or production company (or companies), producers and investors, featured cast members, distributors and theatrical and VOD performance, if available.

Meeting or Negotiating Partner: As you complete each discussion guide, list the name of each person you expect to meet, including their titles, roles, responsibilities, experience (including past employers), credit list and education. Be prepared to discuss their current and past film projects as well as the films' critical and financial performance (and, if possible, how these projects compare and contrast with your own).

An important component of your research is to identify and contact other filmmakers who the organization and/or professionals have worked with on past projects. *What were their experiences? Was the professional able to fulfill the filmmaker's expectations? Was the professional and his/her organization easy with which to work? What challenges did the filmmaker and filmmaking team experience?*

Finally, don't forget to search for any lawsuits the professional or organization may have been subject to (as well as any negative reviews or commentary posted online).

Fortunately, most of the information you need can be found using a simple internet search and such sources as (i) IMDbPro, (ii) the Motion Picture Association of America's annual Theatrical Market Statistics and other MPAA research and reports, (iii) national and regional film agencies and commissions, (iv) industry publications such as *Variety, The Hollywood Reporter,* Deadline and The Wrap and (v) stories and anecdotes collected from colleagues, film market panels, industry publications and similar sources.

Practice: Once you've completed your discussion guide and any supporting materials (discussed shortly), work on perfecting your pitch with industry colleagues whom you trust to give you honest feedback and to push you to improve. And, whenever possible, video record these practice sessions.

You may want to consider scripting out key phrases, words, research findings and other critical elements of your pitch. Make sure that your word and phrase choices reflect the language that the other party is most accustomed to. And practice speaking these scripted portions of your presentation. Unfortunately, scripted words often read much better than they sound when spoken.

While you should rehearse your pitch, it shouldn't come across as rehearsed . . . it should sound natural. However, perhaps counterintuitively, the more you know and practice your pitch, the more comfortable and natural you'll likely appear.

PRESENTATION MATERIALS & "LEAVE BEHINDS"

The pitch discussion topics, the final agenda, your meeting partner's decision-making criteria and the results of your practice sessions will determine what presentation materials and leave behinds you may need to adequately support your pitch.

Like all your marketing and promotional collateral, it's critical to produce professional-quality presentation materials customized to the reader and his or her organization. The use of low-cost photo-quality color printers allows you to print small amounts of customized presentation material and quickly revise future promotional materials. In addition to hard copies, password-protected electronic copies of these presentation materials should also be made available.

Fortunately, most of the content for your film's presentation materials will be based on creative assets you've likely already created. These include the title and tagline of the film, the logline and film synopsis, key art, storyboards, biographies of key cast and crew members, photographs of locations, wardrobe and props and pre-production teasers and trailers.

Promotional Sell-Sheet: The promotional sell-sheet is one of the most powerful pieces of marketing and promotional collateral despite also being relatively quick, simple and inexpensive to create. Printed in full-color on both sides of heavy stock high-quality paper, promotional one-sheets are easily customized and printed in small numbers in a variety of sizes (8.5 × 11 inch, A4, postcards, etc.) for specific individuals, organizations or purposes.

The facing page of the promotional one-sheet is comprised of the key art and serves, essentially, as a mini-poster of the film. The reverse side of the sheet contains a synopsis of the film, an above-the-line credit list (featured actors, producers, director, cinematographer, screenwriter, editor, etc.), logos of the production companies (and distributors if available), official website and social media URLs and other direct contact information.

The reverse side also presents an opportunity to provide additional details on the film's production, marketing and distribution strategy, pre-release ratings and reviews, testimonials, film festival laurels, film stills, BTS photographs, cast and character descriptions, technical specifications (run time, sound mix, aspect ratio, cameras, etc.) and other content of potential interest to the reader.

Project Overview (aka "Executive Summary") Page: Unlike other materials discussed in this section, the project overview page is not a stand-alone promotional asset. Instead, the project overview page will be used as an important part of various pitches and discussions as well as used as the reverse page of the project one-sheet and sent as an attachment to networking emails.

Typically, the project overview page includes the film's title, tagline, film synopsis and four to six bullets summarizing the target market, marketing and distribution strategy, production details and/or budgetary information as well as above-the-line credits and direct contact details, technical specifications and similar details.

FIGURE 5.1 Showbox's sell-sheet for director Kim Sok-Yun's film *Detective K. Showbox* is one of South Korea's largest film production, investment and distribution companies.

(Showbox Mediaplex Co., Inc.)

Pitch Book: The pitch book is essentially a twelve to twenty-six page representation of the planned pitch. The pitch book typically contains (i) the executive summary (aka "project overview") page; (ii) one to two pages detailing the film market; (iii) a four to six page overview of the project, including a summary of the film, the filmmaker and the senior team (producers, investors, featured cast, department heads, production partners, distributors, etc.); (iv) one to two pages describing the marketing and distribution strategy; and (iv) additional production, budget and funding details, depending upon the pitch and intended reader.

Like the pitch itself, the pitch book is commonly customized to the targeted reader and his/her organization. However, regardless of any changes between one version of the pitch book and another, the book must feature a dramatic description of the film and major beats. These descriptions should be reinforced with full-color photos and concepts artwork that emphasize key scenes, characters, exotic locations, wardrobe, props and other exciting film elements.

A well-written pitch book can serve multiple purposes, including its use as (i) a presentation aid to guide discussions throughout the pitch meeting; (ii) a leave behind for those who attended the meeting; (iii) support material for those who attended the pitch meeting and who may need to make their own internal presentation to superiors prior to approval; and (iv) a stand-alone presentation sent to those who the filmmaker and/or producers cannot meet with directly.

Presentation Treatment: Completed scripts are rarely provided during pitch meetings or to prospective investors, distributors or other partners. Unlike traditional script treatments that often total forty pages or more, presentation treatments are much briefer – averaging only eight to twelve pages. As a result, time-constrained executives are far more likely to read a concise presentation treatment than a traditional treatment or full script.

The presentation treatment begins with an executive summary, logline and film synopsis followed by one to three page summaries of each of the film's acts or, alternatively, a two to three sentence description of each beat or scene (most films average forty to sixty scenes). These act or scene descriptions – and, in fact, the entire treatment – should be short and punchy . . . using colorful and active words to describe each scene, character and location. Each page of the treatment must build a sense of drama and anticipation with vivid scene descriptions.

Look Books: The look book – and the images it contains – is intended to offer a visual representation of the film to allow the viewer to more accurately "see" the film prior to the completion of production. Together with any pre-production videos, the look book provides a glimpse into the film's likely production value.

Look books – whether PDF, PowerPoint or printed in glossy hardcover – are principally comprised of photographs, concept artwork, storyboards and other illustrations of major scenes, events, characters, locations, wardrobe, props and any special and visual effects. At the same, the illustrations contained within the look book should reflect the visual style and overall tone of the film through the use of color grading, lighting, framing, camera movement and other elements or visual details (such as any unique equipment or processes to be used during film production).

Promotional Videos: Like the look book, pre-production promotional videos such as teasers, trailers and test shots are intended to provide a proof of concept and illustrate how the film will look and play when completed. However, unlike static photographs and other images, promotional videos are able to give a highly accurate representation of the filmmaker's vision and completed film ... incorporating video footage, visual effects, audio, audio effects, music selection and other post-production elements.

Select shots and images that best summarize, reinforce and strengthen the film's storyline, characters, locations, atmosphere, tone and pacing. Pre-production promotional videos should also show how any novel filmmaking or post-production techniques will be used (including special effects, CGI, VFX, characters design, etc.).

Because pre-production videos and other presentation materials can easily distract the viewer from the underlying discussion, limit the number of videos shown during the meeting to no more than two or three short thirty to sixty second videos. You can always provide links to more videos and promotional materials following the meeting.

Investment Memorandum: Created in consultation with an experienced entertainment attorney and, often, an experienced accountant, the investment memorandum is a twenty to sixty page document providing a summary of the proposed investment, an overview of the film market, the filmmaker's or studio's business model, biographies of the filmmaker and key executives, synopsis of the film, production schedule, distribution strategy, financial statements and details on investment risks and mitigants.

While the investment memorandum is a sales and promotional tool, depending upon the country or region in which you plan to raise funding, the document may be subject to the oversight of multiple legal and regulatory agencies. As a result of the demands placed upon the filmmaker by such agencies, the memorandum is commonly written in an objective – almost legal and dispassionate – manner.

Unfortunately, without prior finance experience and knowledge of investment regulations and requirements, few filmmakers are in a position to create the investment memorandum without assistance. Fortunately, software templates and freelancers are available to assist in the preparation of the memorandum and accompanying financial forecasts and budgets. However, regardless of who prepares the investment memorandum, be sure to have the final version carefully reviewed by an experienced attorney and accountant before forwarding it to prospective investors.

While your accountant will be instrumental in double-checking the accuracy of your business and financial statements, your attorney will concentrate primarily on protecting your rights and confirming that your documents conform to applicable laws and regulations. Among other issues, for those within the United States, your attorney will want to confirm that you've filed copies of your treatments and scripts with the Writers Guild of America (WGA) and the U.S. Copyright Office.

However, regardless of your country of residence, your attorney will also encourage those who receive a copy of your investment memorandum (and recipients of certain of your pre-production marketing materials) to sign a non-disclosure agreement (NDA), also known as a confidentiality agreement, to protect the intellectual property associated with your film projects and production business. In addition to the NDA, your confidential materials should also include a disclosure such as the following:

This Memorandum is confidential and private. Distribution is restricted. It may not be reproduced, copied or replicated in any form including print and digital media without the express and written authorization of [name of filmmaker or production company].

This Memorandum is and at all times shall remain the exclusive property of [name of filmmaker or production company].

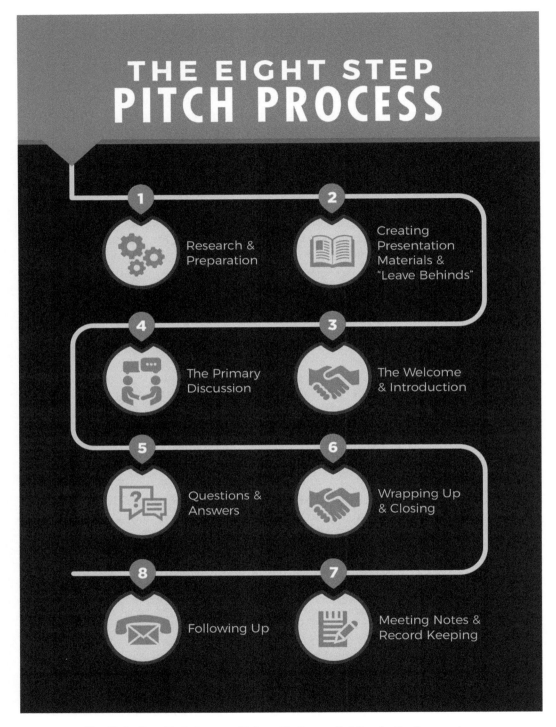

FIGURE 5.2 The Eight-Step Pitch Process (Robert G. Barnwell / Sandy O. Cagnan.)
(Robert G. Barnwell/Sandy O. Cagnan)

You are responsible for protecting the confidentiality and propriety of the information contained in this Memorandum. You will be held responsible for any damages resulting from an improper disclosure on your part.

Again, be aware that, depending upon the applicable laws and regulations, your material may require specific legal disclosures and/or require that your disclosures incorporate certain mandatory language.

ART OF THE PITCH – WELCOME & INITIAL INTRODUCTION

Start the meeting off with a friendly conversational tone. Introduce yourself and your team. Take a minute or two to get to know each other and establish a rapport. Mention any shared interests and connections such as people, colleges, neighborhoods, work experiences, hobbies, interests, associations, guilds and other organizations, and other potential commonalities.

In the absence of any notable commonalities, consider sharing an interesting personal story and/or a dramatic and unexpected fact or experience. These initial topics don't necessarily need to be film-related. Just something of interest through which you can form the basis of a personal connection.

By quickly capturing the listener's attention and creating a strong first impression, it is far more likely that your meeting partner will more closely focus on you and your message for the remainder of the discussion.

ART OF THE PITCH – PRIMARY DISCUSSION

After the welcome and initial introduction remind your meeting partner why you are having this conversation:

As I mentioned on the phone [or my earlier email], I wanted to chat with you about [casting, funding, production, distribution, etc.] of our forthcoming [genre] film, [film title.] For the past several [days/weeks/months], we've been speaking with a number of [agents, distributors, etc.] and think you'd make an excellent [partner/addition/other] to [film title]'s [production, cast, crew, distribution, etc.] team.

Then quickly describe the planned discussion agenda, encourage interruptions to guide the discussion in whatever direction they prefer, and distribute a copy of the promotional one-sheets and pitch books (hold all other pitch materials in reserve until you reach that particular point in the discussion).

Pause to allow time for your pitch partner to make any comments or questions. If none, provide a quick sixty second summary of the film before explaining how current and emerging market trends drove you to this particular genre and story. Share how these market trends and insights were, at least in part, the result of discussions you've had with sales agents, distributors and film buyers over coffee or at film markets. *The bottom line is that you must make it clear that you are a professional and well-networked filmmaker committed to producing a commercial film driven by audience and market considerations.*

This is a good point at which to show a quick fifteen to thirty second pre-production teaser or trailer. Then, using the pitch or look book as a reference, summarize each of the film's three acts and any important story beats. Identify those aspects of the film that make it unique from other films within its genre and currently available in the marketplace. Also explain how market research was incorporated into the selection of your film's genre and within script development.

Ideally, as you introduce a key scene, character, location or other interesting aspect of the film, you'll be able to provide a photograph, illustration or storyboard that best illustrates that particular element. And, by providing these pieces of support material (props, photos, screen shots, test shots, storyboards, diagrams, drawings, pitch trailers, etc.) periodically throughout the discussion you maintain the other person's focus and interest.

Before continuing with your pitch, pause a moment and allow your meeting partner to respond and ask initial questions. Again, this is a well-organized discussion, not a presentation. As much as possible, allow the other person to explore those areas that are most important to them and their team.

Fortunately, more likely than not, your meeting partner is going to want to shift the discussion from the film and its story to topics related to production progress, cast attachment, production and distribution partners (if any), marketing, promotional and distribution strategies and budget and fundraising status. By having your meeting partner introduce these topics, your transition into this stage of the pitch appears almost seamless.

While you discuss these business-oriented topics, clearly communicate (both directly and indirectly) how your meeting partner and his or her organization would add value to the film project. Be as specific as possible. Refer to successful film projects your meeting partner has participated in the past and how these projects are similar to your own.

Throughout the conversation you want to show enthusiasm for the film and its market potential as well as at the prospect of working together with your meeting partner and their organization. However, at the same time, be careful not to oversell the project. Be realistic and caution others about the competitive nature of the film market.

Although this section of the pitch is likely to be the most lengthy, it's important to be as brief as possible, avoid overly detailed explanations and limit the amount of supporting material you provide. At this point, you need only share as much detail as necessary to proceed to the next step in the process . . . which is often another meeting or pre-agreement negotiation. A good pitch doesn't run for hours and you aren't required to tell them everything. Hold some information in reserve to use in your replies to their questions and/or to discuss at future follow-up meetings.

ART OF THE PITCH – QUESTIONS & ANSWERS

As far as your meeting partner is concerned, his or her questions are likely the most important part of the pitch meeting. So allow sufficient time for questions to allow the other person to explore areas of discussion of most interest and value to them.

Because of the inherent resource constraints of low-budget filmmaking, some of the most common concerns are that the film (i) will not be completed; or, if completed, will lack (ii) sufficient production value (or "playability"); (iii) market appeal; (iv) distribution and sales; (v) critical acclaim or industry recognition (media coverage, industry awards, film festival nominations, etc.); and, finally, will result in (vi) an unacceptably low level profitability (or a loss). Not surprisingly, some of the many spoken and unspoken questions will include:

- *What is the experience of the filmmaking team? Cast? Crew? Others?*
- *How is the film unique from others within its genre and market?*
- *What is the popularity and relative marketability of any attached actors?*
- *What is the film's production status?*
- *How will the film be marketed and promoted?*
- *What is the track record of the film's sales agent and/or distributor?*
- *What is the film's distribution strategy?*
- *What is the budget? Are these funds committed/available?*

If meeting with potential investors, they'll also want to know: (i) *What type of financial returns have your films generated for past investors?* (ii) *Who has already invested in the current project?* (investors rarely like to be the first to make an investment commitment); and (iii) *Are you able to provide a professional investment memorandum with reasonable financial forecasts?*

While you would like to turn every challenging question into a supportive and positive response, don't shy away from admitting and discussing inherent risks. Acknowledge such risks as legitimate concerns and explain how you and your team plan to best reduce – although not entirely eliminate – these risks. The unfortunate fact is that the vast majority of low-budget independent films are creative and commercial disappointments.

ART OF THE PITCH – WRAPPING UP & CLOSING

Once it seems that your pitch partner has exhausted their questions or available time, bring the discussion to a conclusion. Remind them of your objective for the meeting and suggest appropriate next steps. Ask if they agree.

If an additional meeting is the logical next step, schedule the follow-up meeting now ... before the meeting concludes. If they aren't yet prepared to commit to your principal request or a next step, ask if they'll be willing to agree to a less significant request such as a referral to another professional or organization. Either way, it's critical that you project confidence in yourself and your film.

Without appearing arrogant, operate under the genuine belief that you are doing others a favor by giving them the opportunity to work with you and your team on this film project.

Conclude the discussion by making a statement similar to the following:

> Be sure to let me know if you have any additional questions. In the meantime, I'll be sure to send you a copy of [document(s) or material]. Once you've had a chance to look it over, I'll get back to you [specify timeframe] to [describe whatever next step was agreed at the end of the meeting]. Thanks again.

This statement cements the expectation that both parties will continue to have future discussions with regard to the meeting's objective. It also establishes a timeframe for completion of a series of informal commitments (to provide additional information and to place a follow-up call). Again, whenever possible, avoid leaving the pitch meeting without first creating a reason to reconnect.

TAKING NOTES & KEEPING RECORDS

While you don't need to write down every word or thought that your meeting partner shares, taking notes throughout the discussions keeps you focused and demonstrates respect for the time and insights shared by others participating in the pitch meeting.

Throughout the meeting, make note of the answers to the following types of questions:

- *Who did you meet with?*
- *What details did they share about their current and/or past projects?*
- *What are they looking for in future projects?*
- *What are their decision-making criteria?*
- *What questions did they ask?*
- *Whose names do they mention? In what context were these individuals mentioned? Are these the names of colleagues, partners, friends, other?*
- *Are there others within their organization they need to consult prior to approval or their ability to commit to any next step(s)?*
- *Are you expected to provide any contingent information or materials they may require prior to their approval or their ability to commit to any next step(s)?*
- *When and how are you expected to follow up? Alternatively, have your meeting partners committed to provide additional details or follow up?*

Also be sure to take notes during the meeting, or quickly thereafter, about anything you think might be able to help you improve future pitch meetings. For instance, (i) *At what points during your discussion did others participating in the pitch meeting show the most interest?* (ii) *When did they show the least amount of interest?* (iii) *Similarly, what pitch materials (look book, one-sheet, pitch trailers, etc.) most interested them?* (iii) *Which pitch materials least interested them?* (iv) *Were there specific points or responses to questions you struggled to communicate properly?* And (v) *Are there any other points during the discussion at which you feel you performed particularly well or particularly poorly?*

In combination with your pre-pitch discussion guide, your notes should form an accurate and fairly comprehensive record of the meeting.

FOLLOWING UP

An hour or two after the meeting, compose a short email to let those you met know that you enjoyed meeting them and that the meeting reinforced your belief that they'd be valuable project partners. In your own words, the email should read something like the following:

> [First name], Just wanted to let you know that I enjoyed meeting you [and name of any others you met with during our discussion] this [morning/afternoon/evening]. I was really impressed with [you and your team/specific idea(s)/other]. Looking forward to chatting again soon.

Note that you only need send the email to the senior-most person you met and then cc others who may also have participated in the meeting. You should also try to be as specific as possible with regard to anything they may have mentioned during the meeting and/or any special contribution to your film that they may be uniquely qualified to provide.

Within the week, to differentiate myself and my materials from others who send emails and zip-filed documents, I'll also send a priority mail envelope (I use legal-sized envelopes) containing hard copies of any pertinent promotional materials and a brief note that reads:

> [First name], I thought you might be interested in seeing [identify contents of package]. I've attached two copies in case you'd like to share a copy with [first name of other person within their organization]. Again, feel free to let me know if you have any additional questions. In the meantime, I look forward to seeing you again [specify date or timeframe].

Ideally, I like to schedule delivery of the package so that it arrives some time during the second half of the workweek. Mondays and Tuesdays are often quite busy for those in the film industry and I want to make sure that the package doesn't compete with more urgent priorities.

The following week (typically on a Wednesday or Thursday afternoon) after the package was delivered, I'll call to see if the package has been received and to confirm whatever next steps have been agreed. I'll also ask if they would like to receive electronic copies of any of the materials.

Finally, if I've not done so already, I'll make sure that I've added everyone I've pitched to a database so that I can schedule and automate periodic follow-up emails and telephone calls over the coming months to stay in touch and provide updates on the progress of the film.

In addition to proving automated reminders for any follow-up steps, the database also contains the dates, times and places we've spoken, the subjects we've discussed and any next steps or schedule follow-up meetings as well as basic details and contact information (office telephone number, email addresses, mailing address, cell phone, website URLs and social media accounts).

While this system works for me, you should create and schedule whatever follow-up process is best for you and your film. The important point is that you create a system that you will actually use and that allows you to (i) automate scheduled follow-up contact; (ii) diversify the method of contact (email, telephone, text message, direct mail, in-person meetings, etc.); and (iii) record and maintain meeting notes and other pertinent information.

NETWORKING & REFERRALS

The relationships you build prior to, during and following pitch meetings will be instrumental to the long-term success of your film production career. The most important of these relationships will be with those with whom you share a genuine bond. Essentially, you are looking to build an ever-expanding network of longer-term friends and colleagues who you both like (and, hopefully, like you) and whose businesses and careers are mutually beneficial. The strongest and most long-lasting relationships are also those that are interconnected – in which you share multiple friends, colleagues, interests and experiences in common.

As in other aspects of your life, many beneficial relationships may be short-term . . . with little real personal connection. However, these types of relationships, while far more common and often quite valuable, will rarely propel you and your filmmaking career. So it's critically important to surround yourself with the right people and organizations.

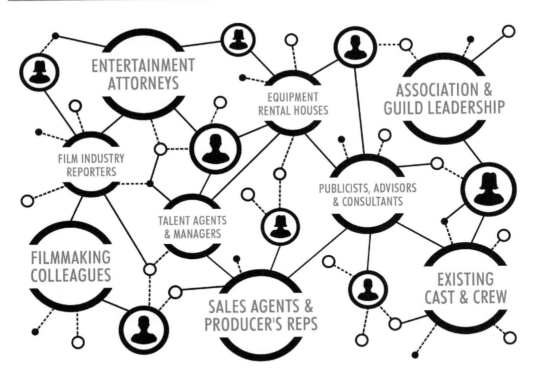

FIGURE 5.3 By concentrating your networking activities with those best-positioned within the industry, you greatly improve the quality and quantity of access to those most able to support your production company and film projects.

(Robert G. Barnwell/Sandy O. Cagnan)

Before you begin reaching out to prospective members of your network, give consideration to the current stage of your film project's production and prioritize the type of professionals most in a position to help advance you and your film to the next stage. Then make a list of the names and contact details of fifteen to thirty specific individuals for each type of professional you plan on targeting (e.g. producers, entertainment attorneys, distributors and casting managers).

You can commonly find these names and contact details by conducting a simple web search or by using IMDbPro, online directories, filmmaking forums, film commissions, fellow filmmakers and the professionals' official websites.

Once you've compiled a list of the names and contact details of targeted relationships, play detective and connect the dots . . . Who do you know who may be a close contact (friend or colleague) of your target? Take stock of your existing relationships of friends, family, colleagues and social media friends and fans. In particular, consider any "superconnectors" you may know such as producers, entertainment attorneys, film commissioners, film festival executives, sales agents and distributors and fellow filmmakers.

When asking for referrals, understand that people tend to be protective of important members of their immediate network. Reduce the risk to those who can refer you to their friends, colleagues and network by presenting yourself as an experienced professional and your project as a market-oriented commercially viable film.

I've also found that people are often more comfortable and quite generous in making introductions with members of their network who live and work outside of their own area. In other words, I'll commonly ask colleagues in Los Angeles for referrals to professionals in New York, Europe or Asia and vice versa.

Absent knowing anyone capable of providing you a referral to a specific professional, make a point of attending events where you are most likely to meet industry and media professionals . . . including those you would most like to introduce yourself to. Some of the best events for meeting industry professionals include: professional guilds, associations and related industry organization meetings; educational events such as workshops, courses and panel discussions; film school or university alumni events; film festivals, film markets and industry conferences; and connecting via social media or other online community.

Also consider hosting your own events and get togethers as well as speaking, delivering presentations, participating on panel discussions and volunteering for leadership positions with various film industry-related educational and professional organizations.

When attending any event, you must be able to quickly describe yourself, you studio or your film in ten seconds (one to two sentences). Smile, listen, ask questions and take notes. Use the other person's name. And learn how others introduce themselves, their organizations and describe the films within their portfolios.

Remember to bring plenty of business cards, postcards, promotional one-sheets and a tablet computer or other mobile device to show teasers and trailers. At the same time, in addition to expanding your network, use these interactions to collect and study other filmmakers and producers' marketing and promotional collateral (business cards, postcards, promotional one-sheets, links to websites, social media accounts, demo reels and teasers and trailers).

With these comments and suggestions in mind, the following five-step process will help improved the efficiency and effectiveness of your networking activities:

1. Set an objective for a specific number of contacts and initial networking meetings for the day, week or month: Measurable objectives provide inspiration and motivation to follow through on your networking commitments. They assist in the proper allocation of both time and effort. Measurable objectives also help you assess your performance at the end of each period and commit to additional efforts when you fall short of expectations.

In addition to the number of new contacts, establish a set of objectives for follow up to increase the bond with your new contacts. Research suggests that you need to have a minimum of five contacts with someone before a meaningful and lasting relationship can take hold.

2. Conduct advanced research and preparation: As with pitch meetings, networking success largely depends on adequate research. While a formal discussion guide is probably overkill, you should still conduct basic research into the types of professionals most in a position to help you and be able to answer such questions as: Which of these professionals are the most respected in their areas of expertise? What are their contact details? Their backgrounds? Their past film projects? Do you have any areas of shared interest or have mutual friends?

As you compile your list of targeted names, the research stage is also a great opportunity to connect via social media and LinkedIn. The more familiar you are with potential members of your network and the earlier and longer you connect (even if only on social media) and the more you have in common, the easier and less stressful it will be to begin your outreach.

3. Send a quick introductory email or message: Once you've identified people you'd like to add to your network and completed some background research, it's time to send them an introductory email. In 100 words or fewer, the email should quickly introduce you and your film project, make a connection with the recipient, explain why you are contacting them and ask for a chance to meet or have a quick telephone conversation, using language such as the following:

> [First name], I was just speaking with a friend of mine, [name of person who referred you], who suggested I introduce myself to you. I'm a producer-director working on a [genre] feature film entitled [title]. [Name of person who referred you] thought that since we both [briefly described connection or common interest] and that you [briefly describe why the person would be interested in your film project], we should [propose an quick and informal telephone conversation or meeting].

4. Keep notes of your research, copies of emails and other correspondence and a record of other relevant details: It's important to stay organized. As you expand your network and increase the number of pitch meetings, it will quickly become difficult – if not impossible – to recall significant facts and details about the many individuals and organizations within your network. So, if you haven't already, create a system that allows you to easily record your network's contact details, information on any past meetings or discussions and to place your relationship-building and follow-up processes on "auto-pilot."

While using Microsoft Access or Excel often works fine, give serious consideration to using a dedicated contact management system such as Act! Essentials, Base, Nimble, SugarCRM or Zoho. Unlike more general spreadsheet and database programs, these dedicated contact management programs allow you to maintain a database of contact names and details, track past contacts and communications, schedule follow-up tasks and reminders via email and SMS and keep notes on the progress of discussions and other details. Many of these programs also integrate with social media platforms and automated email marketing programs.

5. Maintain contact: As mentioned previously, a minimum of five contacts per individual or organization are typically required to establish a meaningful and lasting relationship. To do so I suggest scheduling a series of (i) follow-up emails two to four hours, one week, two weeks and then every four to six weeks following your initial in-person meeting and (ii) one to two additional follow-up meetings within the next twelve months.

The first email is a quick and informal thank you email sent two to four hours following your first meeting. The email should reference something specific that your contact shared during the meeting that you found insightful or fascinating. The following week, send a short email with an attachment of likely interest to your contact (the attachment should not be about you or your film but a link, article or other attachment about the contact, the contact's business or films, or some other source of interest). Mention that you recently came across the attachment and thought they might find it of interest. At the two-week point, consider asking or inviting them to get together at an industry event scheduled to take place in the next sixty to ninety days. It isn't really important whether or not they attend, it's the fact that you thought enough of them to invite them to the event or to get together during the event that is important.

Thereafter, you'll want to maintain regular positive contact with your network with an email every 4–6 weeks. These emails should have an upbeat tone and share positive progress with regard to your film project and other aspects of your personal and professional life. Periodically, perhaps every three to four months, send an invitation to meet for coffee, attend a local film festival or other film-related event, to screen a recent cut of your film or trailer, or other informal get together. At the same time, be on the lookout for other public events that you are both mutually scheduled to attend.

Likewise, you should periodically update the progress of your relationship with anyone who may have referred you to your new contact.

[First name], Many thanks for suggesting I reach out to [name]. Just wanted to let you know that we had a great [conversation/email exchange/other] and are planning on getting together sometime on [date]. I'll be sure to let you know how it goes. Again, thanks for your help . . . [name] seems like a great [describe the professional's title or business role].

Once you've had the meeting or meaningful telephone call or email exchange, be sure to write the person who referred you again to update him or her on the progress of discussions and the relationship:

[First name], Thanks again for your connecting me with [name]. As I may have mentioned previously, we were able to get together on [day or date] and had a very helpful discussion on [short list of one to three topics]. I understand why you suggested we get together; [he/she] seems like a great person and certainly knows the industry. I'll be sure to keep you updated with regard to the film project and how things go with [name].

While email is the most efficient, common and easiest form of communications to scale, understand that informal coffee meetings, telephone calls and other forms of personal contact are far more effective at establishing and maintaining meaningful lasting relationships. As a result, the more important a prospective contact may be to your long-term success, the more personalized the majority of your contacts should be.

Networking is a constant process that should begin in the earliest stages of your filmmaking career and film project. Although friendships and relationships require constant commitment and effort, by building a large and expanding network of friends and colleagues, you'll likely benefit from new friendships, higher professional visibility, increased market knowledge and insights and learn about new film projects and opportunities as well as increased access to financial and production resources and advice.

6

KEY ART & POSTERS

Together with the film's title, the most important element in the marketing and promotion of the film very well may be the key art. Commonly referred to as poster design, the key art consists of the fundamental design elements (title, tagline, images and credit block) that make up a film's poster, advertisements, website and social media banners and other marketing and promotional artwork.

If the key art – and particularly the poster – is interesting, potential audience members are far more likely to read the film's ratings and reviews and to watch the film's teasers and trailers. Assuming they like what they see, they may rent or purchase the film.

However, if the key art is weak and unappealing, potential audience members will question the quality of the story and the film. Because of this poor initial impression, most will never bother to check the ratings, reviews or watch a trailer. Game over.

So what factors differentiate good key art from poor key art? At the risk of over-simplification, good key art should accomplish the following five objectives:

1. *Informative:* The key art needs to communicate the film's title, the genre, differentiate the film from others within its genre, hint at the storyline and provide details such as the identity of the actors, producers, director and crew members as well as release dates, social media platforms and website addresses.
2. *Identify the Target Audience:* While the film's genre helps identify the target audience for a particular film, the key art can further narrow the audience by incorporating imagery that appeals to various audience demographics.

    Unfortunately, however, you'll often find that secondary or tertiary target audiences have preferences that appear to conflict with those of the primary audience. Consider the producers of a romantic comedy. The primary target audience is likely to be women between the ages of 18 and 40. However, a secondary or tertiary audience is likely to be the husbands or boyfriends of many of these women (whom many of these women will likely want to accompany them to the theaters). What can you do within the key art to help appeal to men while not alienating the women who are the film's principal demographic?
3. *Visually Engaging:* Key art must immediately capture attention and the imagination. The artwork must focus the viewer's attention on those few aspects of the foreground and background images (as well as editorial content) that best represent the film.

Successful key art typically maintains a clean design with plenty of white space that emphasizes a strong central image. The central image (and the key art more generally) should be striking, intriguing and memorable.

4. *Familiar Yet Distinct:* The design (including fonts, colors, layout, focal image, background images and other elements) should be immediately evocative of the film's genre and story (familiar). On the other hand, the design also must incorporate unique elements that help differentiate the film and storyline from other films within its genre.

5. *Brand Consistent:* A final consideration is how to tie the key art into related films and institutions. If the current film is related to a prior movie – a sequel, prequel, reboot or spin-off – the artwork must visually connect to these related works. Similarly, filmmakers may also want the key art to reflect the origins of the film with regard to source material such as a book, comic book series, video game or even producer, director or production company.

Unfortunately, achieving these objectives within the confines and constraints of key art can be particularly challenging.

RESEARCHING CURRENT DESIGN TRENDS & STANDARDS

Reflecting the significant importance and associated challenges in developing effective key art, it's essential to develop an "eye" for successful key art and movie posters.

As we've mentioned before – and as we'll continue to emphasize – since our films will compete with those from major studios, it's important to study the marketing and promotional materials of films from the majors – particularly those within our genre. Some of the best can be found out:

> The CLIO Key Art Awards
> International Movie Poster Awards, aka "IMP Awards"

In addition, I highly recommend that you bookmark and visit the sites of the leading design houses. These design houses are responsible for creating studio key art and posters (many are also award-winning website designers and produce major motion picture teasers and trailers). Some of the leading design firms include:

> Arsonal
> Art Machine – a Trailer Park Company
> Blood & Chocolate
> BLT Communications
> Cold Open
> Concept Arts
> Crew Creative
> Empire Design
> Gravillis
> Iconisus L&Y
> Ignition Creative
> Stockholm Design
> Trailer Park

Finally, I suggest that you visit the impressive fan art posted at Deviant Art. Many of the fan-designed artwork is as good – and in many cases better – than the official studio key art.

As you study the key art and posters, consider the following questions:

Q1. Are you able to deduce the film's storyline based upon the key art? How does the key art accomplish this?

Q2. What specific design elements imply the film's genre? Title? Tagline? Central image? Background images? Colors? Typography? Other?

Q3. Does the key art establish unique traits of the film that differentiate it from other films within its genre? Which elements within the key art serve as a point of differentiation (such as stars, characters, wardrobe, props, locations or other elements)?

Q4. What design elements have established themselves as popular trends? Which elements, if any, are being abandoned, appear clichéd or should otherwise be avoided?

Suggestion: Collect JPEGs and screen shots of key art – and specific design elements – that particularly appeal to you. These images will help you form and communicate your vision of your own key art with your designers.

DESIGN CONSIDERATIONS

Every aspect of the key art must be carefully considered and designed to encourage potential audience members to want to see the film. Within the confines of a single image, the key art must take the viewer through each step of the AIDA – creating Attention, Interest, Desire and Action.

Because films can have multiple targeted audiences and different elements that appeal to various audiences, major studios are increasingly creating several versions of their key art and posters. Consider the multiple versions of films in the Expendables and Fast & Furious franchises as obvious examples. Despite employing multiple versions of the key art, each is still a single image that must capture attention, provide fundamental information and drive viewers to purchase or rent the film.

As Tony Seiniger, founder of Seiniger Advertising and the creative force behind the renowned *Jaws* poster, explains:

> *Print is much more difficult than television spots and trailers because you have to pretty much focus on a single image. [And] . . . by the very nature of the single image, you have to make a choice to appeal more to one segment of the audience than others.*
>
> (Marich, 2013)

Because of the inherent limitations of the static image, the designer must carefully consider the film's target markets and use design most effectively to reflect the essence of the film (while managing audience expectations).

Successful key art uses both images and text to convey this information.

As you consider the various design elements and how the images and text should be laid out, understand that the key art will appear in a broad range of sizes and resolutions depending upon the viewing environment and technology. In fact, an ever-increasing percentage of views will be lower-resolution thumbnails displayed on mobile technology such as tablet computers and cell phones.

Given these changes in technology and viewing habits, it's critical to give consideration to the relative size and emphasis of your images as well as their "scalability" across marketing and promotional materials as well as channels. Images and other design elements of the final key art will need to be arranged and rearranged, sized and resized, depending upon its use on posters, websites, social media home pages, etc.

At the same time you give thought to scalability also consider which design elements can be potentially leveraged across any related cross- or trans-media products (such as computer games and books) and any sequels, prequels and other related franchise films.

GENRE-SPECIFIC ELEMENTS

Much of this book has sought to reinforce the importance of creating branding, promotion and marketing that reflects the genre of the films you produce. Nowhere is this more vital than within your key art, teasers and trailers.

As you study the marketing and promotional activities within your genre, you'll soon discover elements that are uniquely characteristic to your genre. These genre-specific elements often include specific vocabulary and phrases, design elements (colors, fonts and graphic elements) and iconography (images and symbols).

The following descriptions summarize some of the more common genre-specific elements. As you read through these descriptions, please keep in mind that these are only summary overviews. The research findings you compile into genre-elements for your own films and key art should be far more comprehensive:

Animated Family Films. High-chroma primary and secondary colors. Saturated reds and blues. Bright-intense colors. Emphasis on cooler colors (primarily blues) with warmer colors used as contrast to highlight text or an important image. Central image showing cute animated character(s).

Action-Adventure. Action-adventure key art places an emphasis on dark colors and gradients. They are often monochromatic. Iconography includes weapons, fire, explosions, debris, smoke and dirt. Images of characters often show dirty sweaty faces with a look of determination. A subgenre of action-adventure, superhero films, often feature red, white and blue (particularly for U.S. audiences).

Horror. Horror film key art often includes elements such as distorted faces and bodies, corpses, skulls, blood, remote and disturbing locations (buildings, forests, etc.) and dark backgrounds.

Romantic Comedies. The central image of romantic comedies almost always consists of the two romantic lead characters. The tone will be playful and romantic. Iconography includes chocolates, champagne, flowers, candlelight, heart-shaped greeting cards, ribbon-wrapped gift boxes, and urban or exotic locations. Key art typically features a white background with pastel colors such as pinks and purples.

Science Fiction. Similar to the action-adventure genre, the key art of science fiction commonly emphasizes dark backgrounds – particularly the use of blacks and dark grays. Warm colors in elements such as fire, flames and explosions are also often included and serve to accentuate specific images and create a focal point. Depending upon the storyline or subgenre, science fiction iconography includes astronomical bodies (planets, moons, etc.), spacecraft, aliens and characters in space suits.

COLOR SCHEMES

Choosing the right color combinations is crucial to creating successful key art. In fact, colors are almost as important as the text and images themselves. The choice of specific complementary and contrasting colors effects the attention, attractiveness, perception and readability of the final design.

As you consider specific colors, work to establish a color scheme by limiting the color palette to two to three dominant colors. As an example, consider the limited color palette for the key art of *Mad Max: Fury Road*, which utilizes a color scheme restricted to yellows, oranges and blues.

To study the color schemes of the key art of films within your genre, I highly recommend using Colourlovers.com. Colourlovers.com is a community in which people from around the world create and share colors, palettes and patterns, including breakdowns of the colors (complete with specific Hex and RGB color codes) for thousands of specific movie posters and key art.

While thinking about specific colors and color schemes, consider the subconscious psychological connection that people often form between colors and emotion. For example, white is commonly associated with purity, cleanliness and health; it is a good contrast to stronger darker colors. Black connotes power, sophistication, elegance and, depending upon use, can represent foreboding and the unknown. Red has the greatest emotional impact and commands attention; it represents power, passion, action and is the color of blood; in Asia, red often represents joy and luck. Blue is viewed as calm, committed, dependable, serene, stable and reliable, while greens suggest nature, purity, peace, health, harmony and prestige.

The connection between color and emotions, however, can vary significantly depending upon cultural and individual influences. It's particularly important to keep these differences in mind when considering the key art of films that may target a specific culture or country.

While researching and studying color schemes (and their psychological influence), understand that the topic of color encompasses several elements, including hues, tints, shades, tones, saturation and gradients, as well as which colors are contrasting and which are complementary.

Because of these variations in color (and the significant differences in how colors appear between print and electronic mediums), most designers select colors based on Pantone(r) guides. Pantone guides are comprised of physical color chips for thousands of colors, tints and shades. And, critically important, they specify each color by unique identification numbers through use of the Pantone Matching System, or "PMS." The use of PMS assures that key art colors are as accurately portrayed online and offline as technologically possible.

Finally, understand that your color choices will influence the ability of the key art to be easily seen and read from a distance.

When seeking to maximize readability, the designer should choose to either have light text appear against a darker background or dark text appear against a lighter-colored background. These two extremes enhance the contrast of the text fonts . . . particularly the smaller typefaces employed within (and below) the credit block.

CENTRAL, FOREGROUND AND BACKGROUND IMAGES

As you consider various key art images, understand that the central, foreground and background images must work together to (i) convey the essence of the film and its genre, (ii) suggest the storyline, (iii) establish the film's mood and atmosphere; (iv) identify the primary and secondary target audiences; and (v) create attention and visual interest.

To get started, review the script, storyboards, film footage, film stills and other imagery from the film (pay particular attention to any shots that may feature special effects, visual effects and SFX makeup). Make a note of any images that stand out . . . particularly images that are both visually striking and suggestive of the film's storyline, atmosphere, characters, genre, mood or stars.

While studying images, focus initially on the central image. This is the image that will serve as the key art's focal point. The role of the central image is to clearly communicate the film's strongest selling point . . . either the film's stars or underlying story.

Once the central image is selected, attention turns to the selection of foreground and background images. While foreground images are typically added to frame the central and background images and to provide visual depth and interest, the background images tend to highlight exotic locations, secondary characters, set piece action and other film-related elements. Background images, in particular, help establish and reinforce a strong impression of the film's production value.

Having selected the central, foreground and background images, some thought should be given to the relative size of the images in comparison to one another. The size of each image should reflect the relative importance of the various images – or subject of the images – to one another and to the film. For example, images of the stars are generally larger than those of supporting cast members. (Note: When focusing on actors and characters as components of the central image, be mindful of the characters' facial expressions, their body language and actions.)

If the film does not feature well-known stars, the key art may place an increased emphasis on other images and iconography such as specific scene or shots, exotic locations, settings, props, vehicles, colors, lighting (including moonlight and firelight), setting and other elements.

Rather than using film stills or BTS photos, the final images are usually created specifically for use in key art. These images are typically either high-definition photographs or commissioned illustrations.

Like the key art itself, the images must be of sufficient resolution to be highly "scalable" for use in relatively small thumbnails to large oversized posters (and, in some cases, billboards).

Fortunately, because of the recent introduction of relatively low cost 4k, 6k and higher digital still and video cameras, independent filmmakers are able to stage and record their own images while on set or on location.

While creating your own image is often ideal, independent filmmakers and major distributors often rely on the use of stock photography to obtain the perfect central, foreground and/or background image. The use of stock photography can provide faster and often equally powerful images.

Essentially, stock photography services provide photographs for license for particular uses. In the case of key art, permission must apply to commercial use since the images will be used for advertising and marketing purposes. The images are commonly available

ABCDEFGHIJKLMNOPQRSTUVWXYZ
1234567890@#$%&

CASTING STUNT SPECIAL VISUAL MUSIC PRODUCTION
DIRECTOR COORDINATOR EFFECTS BY EFFECTS BY SUPERVISOR DESIGNER

EDITED DIRECTOR OF EXECUTIVE ORIGINAL SCREEN DIRECTED
BY PHOTOGRAPHY PRODUCER STORY BY WRITER BY

Bee Two Font

ABCDEFGHIJKLMNOPQRSTUVWXYZ
1234567890@#$%&

CASTING STUNT SPECIAL VISUAL MUSIC PRODUCTION
DIRECTOR COORDINATOR EFFECTS BY EFFECTS BY SUPERVISOR DESIGNER

EDITED DIRECTOR OF EXECUTIVE ORIGINAL SCREEN DIRECTED
BY PHOTOGRAPHY PRODUCER STORY BY WRITER BY

SF Movie Font

ABCDEFGHIJKLMNOPQRSTUVWXYZ
1234567890@#$%&

CASTING STUNT SPECIAL VISUAL MUSIC PRODUCTION
DIRECTOR COORDINATOR EFFECTS BY EFFECTS BY SUPERVISOR DESIGNER

EDITED DIRECTOR OF EXECUTIVE ORIGINAL SCREEN DIRECTED
BY PHOTOGRAPHY PRODUCER STORY BY WRITER BY

Univers 39 Ultra Thin

ABCDEFGHIJKLMNOPQRSTUVWXYZ
1234567890@#$%&

CASTING STUNT SPECIAL VISUAL MUSIC PRODUCTION
DIRECTOR COORDINATOR EFFECTS BY EFFECTS BY SUPERVISOR DESIGNER

EDITED DIRECTOR OF EXECUTIVE ORIGINAL SCREEN DIRECTED
BY PHOTOGRAPHY PRODUCER STORY BY WRITER BY

Triple Condensed

ABCDEFGHIJKLMNOPQRSTUVWXYZ
1234567890&

CASTING STUNT SPECIAL VISUAL MUSIC PRODUCTION
DIRECTOR COORDINATOR EFFECTS BY EFFECTS BY SUPERVISOR DESIGNER

EDITED DIRECTOR OF EXECUTIVE ORIGINAL SCREEN DIRECTED
BY PHOTOGRAPHY PRODUCER STORY BY WRITER BY

Steel Tongs Font

LOGOS / BUGS

FIGURE 6.1 Credit block fonts and logos/bugs.

(Robert G. Barnwell/Sandy O. Cagnan)

for immediate online purchase and delivery. Consider using one of the following services – each of which provides thousands of images via searchable online databases:

iStock by Getty Images
Shutterstock
123RF
Fotolia

Whether you create your own images or purchase them from a stock photography service, the final images should be color-graded to reflect the film, its mood and atmosphere (and to complement, or contrast, the colors used within the branding, marketing and promotional campaign).

TITLES, TAGLINES, CREDIT BLOCKS & OTHER TEXT

In addition to creating attention and visual interest, the key art must also communicate a considerable amount of information to prospective audience members, including the film's title, tagline, stars and release dates.

The most prominent information contained in the key art is the title graphics, tagline, the names of the film's stars (commonly placed at the top or center of the key art) and the credit block. Additional details, such as film festival laurels, industry awards and professional reviews and testimonials are also commonly included.

Reflecting the importance of the film's title, design standards dictate the title of the film appear in the largest size text and in one of the most noticeable locations on the poster. As a result, the film title typically appears at the top or center of the poster in a font twice (or larger) that of the second largest sized font. The next largest font size is typically used for the film's tagline or the name of any notable stars.

Commonly placed at or near the bottom of the key art, the credit block is traditionally center or full-justified. However, despite these norms, the credit block is increasingly being incorporated as a more artistic element within the key art's design. However, these designs are often difficult to read on the smaller screens of mobile devices such as tablet computers and cell phones.

While the credit block can be longer (or shorter), most credit blocks are comprised of four to six lines with the film's ratings and the logos of the production and distribution companies appearing below. (By convention, the logos of the production companies begin at the bottom left while the logos of the distributors appears at the bottom right.)

First and Second Line: The names of the distributors (domestic and foreign) as well as the company (or companies) providing production funding are traditionally listed first. These are followed by the name of the director (or the director's production company) and the film title.

[DOMESTIC DISTRIBUTOR] AND [FOREIGN DISTRIBUTOR] IN ASSOCIATION WITH [FINANCING CO.] PRESENT A FILM BY [DIRECTOR] "[FILM TITLE]"

Third Line: The third line lists the film's stars and featured cast members, appearing as:

JOHN DOE AND JANE DOE AND JOHN SMITH

Fourth Through Final Lines: After the featured cast members, the next credits include the casting director, editor and production designer. Additional professionals are then listed whose contributions to the film were particularly notable. These additional credits often include stunt coordinator, special effects, visual effects, sound editor, sound effects and the music supervisor among others.

The final lines are comprised of the cinematographer (aka director of photographer), executive producer(s), producer, line producer, writing credits (original story and script) and, finally, the director.

When laying out the credit block, understand that the number of available credits and the relative prominence of the credit block are largely dependent upon the size of the font used and number of credit lines. The industry convention is that the font should be no larger than 25% the height of the film's title font. The lower limits of the credit block's font size are determined more by legibility and the relative importance of the information rather than any contractual requirements.

Additional Graphics & Information: Immediately below the credit block appears information such as the film's rating, release date, copyright notice and website address. In addition this area often includes the logos (aka "bugs") signifying the technology used in the production of the film, such as logos from Dolby, DTS – Digital Surround, or Panavision. If your film received state, regional or national incentives, the logo of the film commission will often appear here as well.

> While this outlines the common presentation of the credit block, each block should reflect the specific film for which it is being created (as well as any contractual obligations). Therefore, every film's credit block should be unique.

And, of course, following the film's screening and release, the key art should continually be revised to include any recently received critical acclaim such as ratings and reviews, film festival laurels and industry awards.

TYPOGRAPHY

The selection and arrangement of typefaces within key art can be as important as the use of color, images and other design elements.

The use of typography within the film's title graphics, in particular, plays a vital role in communicating details about a film such as the genre, storyline and target audience.

In addition to the title itself, the success of the title graphics and other textual elements is often determined by typographical choices such as font selection, size, color (and background color), texture, shape and any additional attached – or integrated – graphics.

When considering typography, understand that the choice of font styles (as well as considerations such as font color and texture) will directly affect the audience's perception and expectations. Because of these differences in expectations and perceptions, several font styles have become associated with particular genres. For instance, cursive or handwritten styled fonts are relatively common within romantic comedy titles, grunge fonts (or distorted fonts) are associated with horror, and strong sans serif fonts are commonly employed within action-adventure films.

Give thought to the relative importance of each piece of text and how much emphasis should be placed on that text relative to other design elements. As an example, the most important text is the title graphic. This is often followed by the tagline or the names of

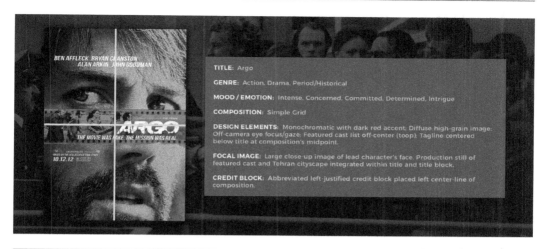

TITLE: Argo

GENRE: Action, Drama, Period/Historical

MOOD / EMOTION: Intense, Concerned, Committed, Determined, Intrigue

COMPOSITION: Simple Grid

DESIGN ELEMENTS: Monochromatic with dark red accent; Diffuse high-grain image; Off-camera eye focus/gaze; Featured cast list off-center (toop); Tagline centered below title at composition's midpoint.

FOCAL IMAGE: Large close-up image of lead character's face. Production still of featured cast and Tehran cityscape integrated within title and title block.

CREDIT BLOCK: Abbreviated left-justified credit block placed left center-line of composition.

TITLE: L'Ennemi Intime

GENRE: Action, War, Period / Historical

MOOD / EMOTION: Intense, Determined, Conflict, Mortal danger

COMPOSITION: Rule of Thirds

DESIGN ELEMENTS: Warm colors; Rugged, mountainous, rocky desert-like setting; Textures include dust and grit.

FOCAL IMAGE: Lead characters superimposed above combat scene.

CREDIT BLOCK: Center-justified at bottom center of layout.

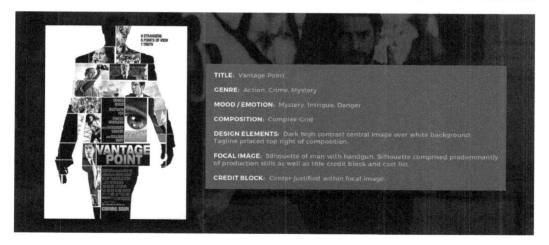

TITLE: Vantage Point

GENRE: Action, Crime, Mystery

MOOD / EMOTION: Mystery, Intrigue, Danger

COMPOSITION: Complex-Grid

DESIGN ELEMENTS: Dark high contrast central image over white background; Tagline placed top right of composition.

FOCAL IMAGE: Silhouette of man with handgun. Silhouette comprised predominantly of production stills as well as title credit block and cast list.

CREDIT BLOCK: Center-justified within focal image.

FIGURE 6.2 Key art layout 1.

(Robert G. Barnwell/Sandy O. Cagnan)

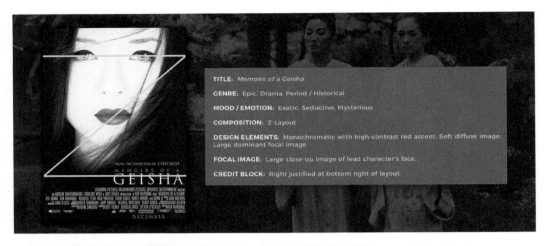

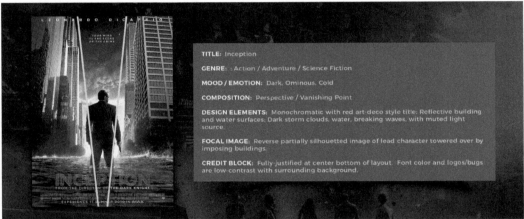

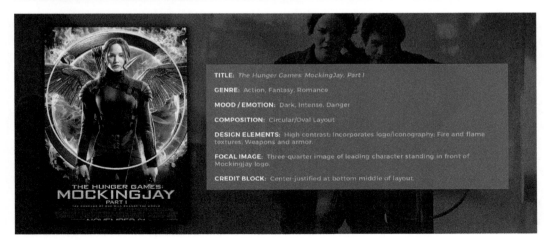

FIGURE 6.3 Key art layout 2.

(Robert G. Barnwell/Sandy O. Cagnan)

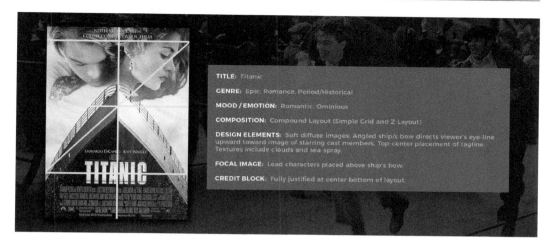

FIGURE 6.4 Key art – complex.

(Robert G. Barnwell/Sandy O. Cagnan)

any well-known stars. The size, location and prominence placed on each design element (both text and graphics) must be well-planned.

Fortunately, the availability of appropriate fonts for the title graphics, tagline and other non-credit block text is almost limitless. In contrast, *the fonts used within the credit block are commonly one of only five typefaces: (i) Bee Two, (ii) Univers 39 Ultra Thin, (iii) Triple Condensed Gothic RR Light; (iv) Steel Tongs; and (v) SF Movie Poster.*

Similarly, as discussed earlier, while the color of the fonts used for non-credit block text can also vary widely, credit block fonts are typically printed in a contrasting color of white, light gray or black (depending upon the color of the background against which the credit block will appear).

LAYOUT & COMPOSITION

Originally, key art was primarily viewed in print – commonly as posters at the local theater and as magazine and newspaper display advertisements. Over the past decade, however, consumer electronics – laptops, tablet computers and mobile telephones – have largely replaced these print outlets.

This creates new challenges for designers. Unlike prior display mediums, the new technology-oriented mediums tend to display key art in smaller dimensions . . . in some cases as little as 150 × 200 pixels (in the case of thumbnails on VOD platforms such as Amazon.com) or less.

At the same time, the wide variety of viewing technology also demands that key art must be able to scale and rescale to a wide range of orientations (landscape as well as portrait) and dimensions.

As a result, the layout, composition, relative size of – and relationship between – each design component (specifically text and images) within the key art have become more significant. By arranging the type and imagery in a logical, functional sequence, the viewer's eye is directed to the most important elements and information.

As a standard guidelines, the key art's dominant elements (such as the title and central image) should be recognizable from at least 15 feet / ~5 meters.

When composing key art, there are several graphic layouts from which to choose, including:

Grid. The grid layout aligns graphic elements with various equally sized rectangles or squares (see Figure 6.2a). Graphic elements can be aligned within the blocks or at the cross points where four neighboring blocks intersect.

Rule of Thirds. A very familiar composition to filmmakers, the rule of thirds is essentially a form of grid layout in which the artwork is divided into nine blocks by two equally spaced imaginary horizontal lines and two vertical lines (see Figure 6.2b). As with other grid layouts, graphic elements are aligned within the blocks or at the intersection of four neighboring blocks.

Circular/Oval Layout. This layout typically contains an oval shaped focal image or a focal image that is framed by an oval shape. There is typically a large block of horizontal text at the bottom (either the credit block itself or in combination with the film title) and, occasionally, text along the top that is aligned with the oval image.

"Z" Layout. Reflecting the writing and reading direction of most of the world's languages (including English), the human eye tends to travel from left to right and top to bottom. This makes the "Z" layout particularly effective for most global audiences (see Figure 6.3a).

Perspective Layout. The perspective layout is usually included as a component of a hybrid layout that uses two or more layout structures (see Figure 6.3b). Most often, it is the primary image that is laid out with perspective. The perspective layout creates a sense of depth, height and/or distance. Consider how a set of parallel railroad tracks appear to converge as they disappear into the distance. This is an example of perspective and "vanishing point."

Combination/Hybrid. Designers are not entirely constrained by standard composition. These forms of layout can be modified and combined. However, because of its effectiveness, most hybrid compositions incorporate the "Z" layout. Such designs apply the "Z" layout when aligning titles, central image and the credit block. However, the poster's central image often adheres to one of the many other layout conventions (see Figure 6.4). In fact, if you review the posters throughout this chapter, you'll notice that most of their compositions are combination, or hybrid, layouts.

During the key art's development and pre-production stages, many designers and filmmakers find it helpful to identify three to four inspirational sample posters that illustrate the overall design and any specific elements they would like to include within the final key art. In addition to identifying the most effective and dynamic imagery and text, the filmmaker and designer should also work closely to eliminate any unnecessary details. This involves exploring several alternative layouts in pursuit of the right size and placement of each element while achieving proper balance and proportion.

A word of warning: many filmmakers and designers fall into the trap of designing key art that appeals to themselves. In fact, it's unusual that anyone other than the filmmaker and designer are involved in the design process. Understand and remind yourselves that you and your designer (or design team) are not the target audience for the key art.

Instead, take every opportunity to involve your audience in the development and revision of your key art ... and in all of your promotional materials. In addition to developing more powerful promotional materials, providing website visitors and social media friends to give their opinions and suggestions helps build engagement.

If you'd like to super-charge your engagement around the development of key art and other promotional materials, consider hosting a contest for key art design and offering a monetary prize (perhaps as much or as little as $500/€500). While you may or may not use the final design, you and your designer are likely to find creative inspiration from many of the submitted designs – not just the winning design.

7

TEASERS & TRAILERS

Studios recognize that while titles, taglines, posters and favorable reviews are all critically important an audience will be reluctant spend their time and money on a film until they've first seen the trailers. Unlike other promotional materials, only trailers offer audiences an opportunity to sample the film before committing the time and money to watch it in its entirety . . . providing viewers with insight into the film's storyline and production value by showcasing carefully chosen footage and dialogue.

As a result, Hollywood regularly spends $50,000, $100,000 or more to hire trailer houses, such as Ignition, mOcean, The Refinery and Trailer Park (and their teams of editors, storyboard artists, computer animators, voice-over actors and musical composers) to produce their trailers.

Once the trailers are complete, major studios will spend several million dollars more to broadcast the trailers at movie theaters and on cable television channels, websites such as Amazon, iTunes and other popular distribution channels.

As we've discussed before, despite the independent studio's limited marketing and promotional budgets, your audience will continue to judge your film (and film marketing) based upon the standards of the major studio films with which they are most familiar. So it's important that your trailers feature the same – or similar – quality and production value.

TYPES OF TRAILERS

Although this chapter is focused on the creation of traditional trailers, the principles and suggestions apply to a variety of promotional videos. Some of the most common include the following.

Since the 1920s, *traditional trailers* have been one of the most popular forms of film advertising. Trailers include shots selected from the film based upon their ability to (i) communicate the film's storyline and (ii) highlight the film's most appealing aspects.

Reflecting the American MPAA standards, most trailers – regardless of country of origin – typically run from two to two-and-a-half minutes. However, due to evolving audience viewing habits, there is increasing pressure to keep trailers under two minute run times.

Teasers are typically produced and released before a film's principal photography has begun. Therefore, teasers often contain little (if any) actual film footage. As a result, teasers for independent films will often rely on a combination of footage specifically shot for the teaser and royalty free footage. The objective of the teaser is to simply build early audience awareness and anticipation of the film. Teasers are particularly brief – typically running for only fifteen to thirty seconds. Teasers are followed up by a main trailer campaign closer to the film's actual release date.

In contrast to teasers, an **extended trailer** can be any trailer that runs longer than the industry-accepted maximum running time of two-and-a-half minutes. As one example, some film producers and distributors are now releasing the first three to ten minutes of the film as an extended trailer – similar to what publishers have been doing for decades by releasing the first chapter of a book. This piques the viewer's interest and forces the viewer to rent or purchase the film to discover the film's conclusion.

Bonus material is typically comprised of "Making of . . . " documentaries, behind-the-scenes interviews, other BTS coverage and similar promotional footage. Unlike other types of trailers and promotional materials, there are few hard-and-fast rules with regard to the running time of individual bonus videos. While it's generally preferable to keep such videos as brief as possible, many videos run for ten to fifteen minutes or more.

A *sizzle reel* is a generic term for marketing trailers targeted at industry professionals rather than a film audience. Sizzle reels include demo reels, pre-production videos, selects, EPK videos, public relations videos and similar promotional content. Because the term encompasses a broad range of promotional videos, the ultimate running time of a sizzle reel can likewise vary widely.

Pitch (or "pre-Production") trailers are developed to market a film to prospective investors and distributors. Pitch trailers provide investors with a proof of concept, showing how the movie will be presented and how novel techniques will be used. This is often the case with movies that rely heavily on digital elements. These pre-production trailers also establish a benchmark or expectation with regard to the final look and production value of the completed film.

Since pitch trailers do not have the benefit of actual film footage, the trailer often contains stock footage and footage shot specifically for the pitch trailer. And, because pitch trailers are not for public release, pitch trailers are not subject to the same constraints of traditional trailers (such as content licensing and clearances). This provides the filmmaker with far more creative license in assembling the trailer.

Selects are a type of sizzle reel extended trailer hybrid and are often used to interest distributors, raise completion funding and to interest the media. Like traditional trailers, selects comprise the best footage and dialogue from the film. Unlike trailers, however, selects have a running time of five to fifteen minutes. Also, because they are often produced prior to completion of the film's post-production, footage and dialogue chosen for selects must often undergo post-production.

Film (or "demo") reels are essentially "pitch" trailers or "sizzle reels" crafted to support the filmmaker's career and expertise. The demo reel should remain relatively brief – ranging from forty-five to ninety seconds – and include the best footage taken from the filmmaker's past projects. In addition, some demos include a montage of the filmmaker working behind-the-scenes as well as voice-over of the filmmaker explaining certain clips and techniques.

Like any trailer, when producing a sizzle reel, pay particular attention to the use of titles, motion graphics, music, film clip selection, editing and transitions. It's also important to make certain that each reel begins and ends with a title card complete with the filmmaker's name, logo and contact details (either the filmmaker's contact details or the contact details for the filmmaker's agent or manager).

RESEARCHING CURRENT TRAILER TRENDS & STANDARDS

Before planning and assembling your trailers, first take the time to research and study current trailer standards and trends – learn the nuances, the cadence and pacing, shot selections and distinctive editing. Make a point of watching and analyzing a wide variety of film trailers across several genres.

One of the best sources for trailers is Trailer Addict – home to a database of thousands of trailers, teasers, clips and featurettes for upcoming, new and classic films. The Trailer Addict archives include trailers dating from the 1950s through today and is searchable by film, genre, actor, actress and several other parameters. Film producers and trailer editors should also be familiar with the many trailers celebrated by the Golden Trailer Awards.

In addition to Trailer Addict and the Golden Trailer Awards, one of the best sources of current trailer standards and trends are the websites of the trailer houses themselves. Some of the leading trailer houses include:

Ant Farm
Aspect Ratio
AV Squad
Buddha Jones
CARVE
Ignition
Jump Cut
Mob Scene
mOcean
The Refinery
Trailer Park
Trailerhaus GmbH
Transit
Wild Card
Mark Woollen & Associates
Workshop Creative

In addition to studying trailers from the major studios and trailer houses, it also helps to become familiar with trailer templates available from Video Blocks, Video Hive and similar services.

As you research and study particular teasers, trailers and other promotional videos, consider some of the following questions:

Q1. Are you able to determine the film's storyline and genre based upon the trailer? What elements of the trailer communicate these genre and story elements?

Q2. What elements, if any, serve to differentiate the film from similar films within its genre?

Q3. What story pattern does the trailer employ? Why do you believe the editors and producers decide on this particular story pattern?

Q4. What promotional elements are emphasized? Stars? Producers? Reviews and testimonials? Film festival awards? Other?

Q5. Which cinematic and editing principles or preferences were employed? Types of camera shots and movements? What types of transitions were used? Fades? Dissolves? Number of cuts? Shot selections? Dialogue? Action sequences? Editing speed? Music cues? Color grading?

The information and insights learned during this research and analysis stage will provide considerable help throughout the trailer production process.

TEASER & TRAILER ELEMENTS

Trailers and film posters are designed to complement each other. Like the films they promote, posters and trailers share many common conventions and elements.

In fact, many of the suggestions and considerations for the production of key art apply equally to the production of teasers and trailers. Specifically, (i) select shots and images that best summarize, reinforce and strengthen the film's tone, character and storyline; (ii) include elements that appeal to members of the primary, secondary and tertiary audiences; and (iii) be mindful of the film's genre, genre trailer elements and genre-related iconography.

The trailer, like the film's key art, must immediately grab the audience's attention, introduce the storyline and encourage viewers to see the film. However, unlike key art, which must catch our attention and give us information about a film in one still image, trailers contain moving images, music, visual and sound effects and dialogue . . . like the film itself.

Ultimately, trailers must both tell and sell the film's story. Trailers accomplish this by assembling visuals and audio that highlight the film's story and establish a sense of its tone, atmosphere, emotion and production value.

In addition to communicating a sense of the film's story and production value, trailers should also enhance the film's credibility and reputation by including audience ratings and reviews, film festival laurels, film awards, critical reviews, cast and crew runs (well-known actors, producers, directors, etc.) and the names and logos of production and distribution companies. This information is typically showcased within slides, titles, inter-titles and voice-over commentary.

Teasers and trailers typically end with the film's title, official URL address and the date of the film's public release (or an announcement that the film is "coming soon").

TRAILER PRODUCTION PROCESS

The trailer production process, like the process of filmmaking, goes through the following five stages:

Development

☑ Consider taglines in addition to the film's logline and short film summary. Together with the film's logline and synopsis, the title and tagline often suggest a through-line for subsequent teasers and trailers.

☑ During the scriptwriting process, note any specific shots, scenes and dialogue that would lend themselves well within future trailers.

Pre-Production

☑ Review script, logline, film synopsis and existing film assets. Break down clips into two categories: (i) visual film footage and (ii) sound – dialogue and sound effects. Log the time codes and location of important footage and dialogue. Consider noting corresponding page, scene and shot numbers from the film script.

☑ In addition to considering the film's storyline and genre, consider many of the film's fundamental characteristics. Does the film have unique and arresting dialogue? Cinematography? Acting performances? Production design?

☑ While reviewing and selecting film assets, make sure that the individual and collective material represents the tone of the film. Make a conscious decision with regard to the information and emotion you want the audience to experience.

☑ Select story pattern and trailer structure. Outline and storyboard the trailer using stills from the film.

☑ Allocate additional time and budget for any required post-production the trailer may require. Prepare voice-over script and audition, cast and schedule voice-over performances. Identify title and graphic requirements.

Production/Editing (aka "Trailer Assembly")

☑ Upload film footage (video and audio) into video editing software such as Avid Media Composer, Apple Final Cut Pro, Adobe Premiere or Sony Vegas Pro.

☑ Assemble a rough cut using all previously identified material. For a two minute trailer anticipate a rough cut of about three to four minutes. Continually revisit rough cuts to refine.

☑ Arrange and reassemble rough cut to adhere to story pattern, trailer structure and storyboards prepared during pre-production.

☑ Select three to five music clips. If not done previously, obtain required clearances and licensing agreements.

☑ Use the individual music (and musical transitions) to establish the trailer's rhythm and pacing. Largely dictated by music selection, most trailers average twenty to forty clips with the running time of each clip averaging two to five seconds (five to seven seconds as necessary).

☑ Create or license any additional trailer-specific footage, audio, effects or other required material.

☑ Insert titles, slides, credits, inter-credits, production and distribution company logos and voice-over audio.

Post-Production

☑ As teasers and trailers are often recreated prior to the completion of the film's principal photography and post-production, the trailer may require post-production prior to release, including color grading, visual and sound effects, automatic dialogue replacement, etc.

☑ Submit completed trailer to ratings authorities as necessary. (Note: ratings are rarely, if ever, necessary for digital distribution. However, many countries [including the United States] require ratings if the trailer is to appear on broadcast television or cable stations or will be played in theaters as a "preview." Familiarize yourself with the regulations and regulatory authorities within the countries where your trailers are expected to appear.)

FIGURE 7.1 Trailer storyboard.
(Robert G. Barnwell/Sandy O. Cagnan)

Distribution

☑ Post completed trailer(s) to official studio and film websites, social media accounts, IMDb profiles and electronic press kits (EPKs).

☑ Encourage cast, crew members and production partners (distributors, sponsors, etc.) to post trailers to their own websites and social media accounts

☑ Use social media and search engine PPC and paid placement on targeted websites to extend distribution reach.

☑ Upon VOD release, update all VOD listings so that teasers and trailers are available for viewing prior to purchase or rental.

LOGLINE & STORY PATTERNS

Before choosing a story pattern for the trailer, develop a clear understanding of the film's storyline and plot. If you haven't done so already, write a logline (short synopsis) of between twenty-five and fifty words that provides a synopsis of the story's plot and introduces the protagonist and the story's central conflict. The logline should serve as the framework around which the film's promotional materials – particularly trailers – should adhere. The logline may also determine which trailer story pattern(s) are likely to be most effective. Some of the most common trailer story patterns include:

Pattern 1. The "Character-Driven" Trailer: This pattern focuses on the film's main character(s). Although some character-driven trailers feature several characters, focusing on a single character is often simpler and more riveting. Costumes, makeup and props are often quite helpful in creating and defining dramatic characters.

Pattern 2. The "Plot-Driven" Trailer: This form – which works well with action-filled movies – requires identifying several plot points that suggest the storyline. However, when producing plot-driven trailers, it's important to reveal only limited details about the story through a few carefully selected scenes. Otherwise, viewers may conclude that they have no reason to watch the entire film. The old adage "less can be more" is especially relevant when producing a trailer.

Pattern 3. The "Trigger-Event" Trailer: In this pattern, you first need to show the world as it is – people going about their ordinary lives – and then introduce a disruptive trigger event. In a romantic comedy, this may be when the lead character first meets the love of his or her life. In a horror film, it's when the creature or other object of horror is first presented or when the first attack or killing is revealed.

Pattern 4. The "Theme-Centered" Trailer: The majority of well-written films have a central message – a theme. Many trailer houses and editors have been able to create particularly gripping trailers by focusing on these themes. Thematic trailers concentrate on such issues such as revenge, fear, courage, paranoia, justice and other themes.

Mixing & Matching: Fortunately, when it comes to using any trailer story pattern, you don't have to be a strict purist. Character-driven movie trailers may follow focused plotlines while trigger-event trailers may be built around strong themes.

TRAILER STRUCTURE

Having written the logline and chosen a pattern, the trailer and story pattern should be broken down and properly structured. Like a good script, your trailer should break down into acts. The three-act structure, as with much of storytelling, works particularly well.

During the *first act* you want to establish the storyline and introduce the viewers to the main characters, their relationships and their environment. Relatively quickly the trailer should introduce an event or incident that sets the film's plot in motion. There should be a clear goal that the main character wants to achieve or a challenge that must be overcome.

Note: As you structure and assemble the trailer, understand you have the freedom to take material from anywhere within the film and place it wherever you'd like within the structure of the trailer. The trailer doesn't have to be as linear as the film. In other words: If you find a particularly useful clip from the third act of the film that would work well in the trailer's first act (or vice versa) . . . do it.

The trailer's *second act* introduces a series of conflicts and obstacles that the film's protagonist has to overcome to achieve the ultimate objective. For dramatic and emotional effect, these conflicts must be significant and appear difficult – if not impossible – to overcome. The second act of the trailer ends as the protagonist appears defeated in his/her attempts to achieve success.

The *third act* of the trailer is often the most difficult. The action, excitement and/or humor intensify dramatically. Typically the trailer places the protagonist in a situation that will likely determine ultimate success or failure.

The challenge for the editor during the trailer's third act is that the film's ending cannot be revealed. The ending of the trailer – and of the film – must remain ambiguous. Viewers must be left in a state of heightened excitement and curiosity. If possible, use the trailer to raise questions that can only be answered by renting or purchasing the film.

As you work toward the final edit, remember to keep escalating excitement and anticipation . . . move the story forward and increase the pacing. Know the end, the theme and feeling you want to leave with your audience.

MUSIC/SOUNDTRACK – ESTABLISHING RHYTHM & TONE

The first rule of thumb for a movie trailer is to make sure it represents the tone of your movie.

Just as filmmakers commonly attribute the success of a given film to the strength of the script and casting, professional trailer editors often credit the success of the trailer (and its rhythm and tone) to the trailer's musical score and transitions. In fact, many trailer editors begin the trailer production process with music selection – finding around three pieces of music that "fit" the film's story.

Stephen Garrett – a trailer editor with more than fifteen years of experience and founder of Jump Cut and co-founder of Kinetic – explains the importance of music:

A trailer, cut well, will have a flowing motion to it, a sense that everything plays off every-thing else, and will propel the viewer through the experience of the film. Trailers build up excitement and anticipation, and a keen sense of rhythm heightens those sensations . . . [Music] literally sets the tone and the rhythm. I usually start every trailer by building my music bed, and that bed is generally composed of three music cues. Why three? Because trailers lend themselves to a three-act structure.

(Garrett, 2012)

Mark Woollen – who has created trailers for such films as Steven Spielberg's *Schindler's List* and *Lincoln* – agrees.

Directors talk about how it's all about casting for them – when they get the right actors, their jobs are easier. For us, that's true of music. Sometimes 70, 80 percent of the job can be trying to find that perfect piece.

(Kehe and Palmer, 2013)

A successful trailer is largely about its rhythm and tone, which, in turn, is established by the proper sync between sound and visuals. As result, and as echoed by both Steve and Mark, trailer production often begins by first selecting the trailer's music.

Again, the type of music you select is vital to the tone you're setting, so choose at least one reference track as early as possible. As you begin screening music, keep in mind that the completed trailer commonly employs three different pieces of music. Typically, each of the trailer's three acts will have its own bed music and the transition between one piece of music and another marks the transition between acts. While this is a common guideline, many trailers employ four, five or more pieces of music within trailers that have several changes in emotion or pacing.

Licensing Music

In the United States, ASCAP, Broadcast Music Inc (BMI) and SESAC collect license fees on behalf of songwriters, composers and music publishers and distribute them as royalties to those members whose works have been performed.

If you are using a pre-recorded song or other piece of music in your film, there are two types of licenses you need to obtain to use the music within your film or trailer:

Master Use License: The master use license provides the right to use a specific recording of a song in your film. The master use license is provided by the record label that owns the recording you would like to use within your trailer. ASCAP suggests referring to the liner notes of the music to identify the recording company. Alternatively, you can get contact information for record labels by calling ASCAP, BMI or SESAC.

If you intend to also release the music on a soundtrack album, you'll also need to negotiate soundtrack rights with the publisher and record label as you negotiate the sync and master use rights.

Synchronization License: This is the right to synchronize a song or a piece of music with the trailer's visual image. The sync license must be obtained from the copyright owner of the music, which is usually the publisher. You can find out who the publisher is by using ASCAP's Clearance Express (ACE) or at the National Music Publishers' Association "Songfile" website.

Custom Music Composition

A popular alternative to using pre-recorded music is to have music composed specifically for the trailer or film. Unlike other alternatives, a composer provides you with a greater level of flexibility – working closely with you to make various changes to the music until it's exactly "right" for your trailer.

There are two popular options to find the right music composer for your trailer: you can use a full-service audio production company that specializes in music and sound design, such as Epicsound.com; or you can hire an individual composer after screening professionals from (i) an association or service representing composers, songwriters and other recording artists (e.g. Filmmusic.net); (ii) referrals from friends, follow filmmakers and local colleges and music programs; or (iii) local job listing sites, such as Craigslist.

In contracting a composer, you'll need negotiate the composition fee based on your film budget, the amount of music required and the film composer's talent, experience **and ability.**

Purchasing Stock Music

One of my favorite sources of music are stock audio libraries. The quality and pricing of music available from audio libraries can be as good – or better – than custom composition. Some of the best music libraries include:

Audio Jungle
iStock Audio
Pond5
Premium Beat
The Beat Suite
The Music Bakery

These services are also good sources for sound effects and atmospheric music that can add significant production value. For more sources of sound effects and atmospherics, I also recommend providers such as A Sound Effect, Sound Dogs and Sound Ideas.

COPY & VOICE-OVER NARRATION

Trailers commonly start and end with slides containing the film and trailer rating, production and distribution company logos, cast run or credit block and release dates.

As noted earlier, many trailers also employ slides and voice-over to emphasize celebrity or award-winning cast and/or crew; film festival and/or industry award nominations and/or wins; excerpts from reviews; rating from sites such as Rotten Tomatoes, iTunes, Amazon, etc.

However, others rely on slides and voice-over to provide insight into the film's storyline. While this can be effective, many trailer editors caution against storyline-driven copy and voice-over. Instead, they suggest allowing the trailer to speak for itself.

Because Hollywood movies overuse copy and narration, they can look and feel tired and uninspired. They are also literally disruptive; you're watching a great image or listening to a line of dialogue, and then suddenly it's interrupted by some deep bass voice or a card full of text. Conversely, if you can cut a trailer without copy or narration, then the movie is explaining its own story organically. Showing rather than telling is always more interesting, so I try my best to avoid copy and narration whenever possible.

(Garrett, 2012)

That said, there are always exceptions to the rule. Copy and voice-over narration can be a great way to enhance an audience's understanding of a complex premise. When using slides to advance a storyline, keep the copy brief and the number of slides to three or fewer. If you need more than three slides to explain a storyline, consider replacing the slides with a narrator.

Two of the most popular sources for voice-over artists are Voice123.com and Voices.com. Either site provides native-language speaking voice-over artists from around the world.

As you screen voice-over artists, give thought to the type of voice that might best lend itself to the desired mood and tone of your trailer. There are several characteristics that should be considered, including language, the choice between a male or female voice, age, pronunciation and accent, the speed, cadence, tempo and volume of voice-over. Additionally, give thought to the vocabulary and phrasing used within the VO script. Unfortunately, some words that look perfect on paper or screen may not sound quite "right" when spoken.

THE ART OF CUTTING ("EDITING") A TRAILER

For modestly budgeted independent films, it's likely that the producers' first choice to cut the teasers and trailers will be the film's editor.

Unfortunately, the film's editor is rarely the best choice to cut teasers, trailers and other promotional video assets. The problem is that the film's editor is too familiar with the film and its storyline. In the film editor's mind – whether they realize it or not – each shot, each scene and each piece of dialogue are linked to related shots, scenes, dialogue and story elements. As a result, film editors often mistakenly cut trailers that prove highly confusing to less-informed viewers who do not benefit from the same detailed knowledge of the film.

So the first step in the process of cutting the trailer is to decide who is going to edit the trailer(s). My bias is toward hiring a dedicate trailer house or a freelance editor who has experience cutting theatrically released major studio trailers. As in similar production decisions, your final choice will represent a trade-off between quality, speed of final delivery and budget.

Once the hiring decision has been made, you and the editor should begin by viewing all of the available film assets – particularly the script and existing footage and audio clips. Take note and log any particularly interesting material such as visuals and dialogue.

As you consider dialogue, if someone in the movie says the title of the film, you should consider including it within the trailer . . . particularly if the film's title is cryptic or somewhat vague, in which case dialogue can give it context. At the same time, when reviewing dialogue, don't have characters repeat the same point unnecessarily. Keep the trailer short and tight.

I'll watch the whole movie without sound, just looking for visuals – that little head turn, that glimpse, that spark of something. Then I'll watch the movie just for dialog. I can get down to about 10 to 15 minutes and from there start crafting and making connections.

(Mark Woollen, quoted in Kehe and Palmer, 2013)

Once you have a sense of what footage you have available, select the appropriate story pattern and begin to storyboard the trailer using stills from the film – paying particular attention to the opening and ending footage. Viewers can get a feel of what type of film it will be just by seeing the first five to seven seconds of the trailer. Similarly, know the end, theme and feeling you want to leave with the viewer. Again, the first and final images are incredibly important.

At the same time, identify the film's strongest selling points. Does the film feature well-known actors? Exciting special and visual effects? Exotic locations, wardrobe or props? Critical acclaim? Box office performance? Make sure the storyboard – and final trailer – showcases those elements of the film that are likely to be particularly unique and interesting to the audience.

While considering the storyboard and associated video and audio, be aware of the common run times for various trailer elements. These are important considerations when working to targeted run time for the completed trailer:

- 5 seconds for the audience approval notification (such as the MPAA trailer rating)
- 2–4 seconds for the production company name and logo (static or animated)
- 2–4 seconds for the distribution company name and logo (static or animated)
- 2–4 seconds for the title introduction
- 2–4 seconds for the opening date
- 15–30 seconds for Act One of the trailer
- 15–30 seconds for Act Two of the trailer
- 15–30 seconds for Act Three of the trailer
- 4–7 seconds for the second title
- 2–4 seconds for the cast run or credit block
- 4–7 seconds for the release date and URL for the official website.

As you assemble the storyboard, give thought to any visuals, dialogue or any other material that are missing that you may need to create specifically for use within the trailer.

Trailers, and particularly teasers, are often released before the film's principal photography and post-production are completed. As a result, it's not unusual to schedule filming for trailer-specific footage or to include licensed stock footage for use in the trailers which may or may not appear in the final film. Likewise, many trailers will script and record – or rerecord (ADR) – dialogue that might add context and value to the trailer.

As mentioned previously, film trailers often begin with an audience approval notification from the local ratings authority, such as the Motion Picture Association of America (United States), the Ministry of Culture (France), Eiga Rinri Kanri Lankai aka "EIRIN" (Japan) and the British Board of Film Classification (UK).

If you haven't put your film and trailer through the approval process, there is no need to worry. Most independent films don't get their film reviewed by their local authorities and it is not usually necessary . . . unless the film and/or the trailer is to be theatrically released or released on broadcast or cable television.

Static or animated logos for the production studio and distribution companies typically follow the audience approval notification. However, an increasingly popular alternative is to show a series of dramatic clips and let the trailer build momentum before displaying the production studio and distribution company logos – often ten to twenty seconds into the trailer.

Having included the audience approval notification, production and distribution company logos, scheduled release date and opening title, the trailer editor will then begin to assemble the first, second and third acts of the trailer. A well-crafted trailer should be a mini-story with a traditional story arc containing a beginning, middle and end (without revealing the end of the film).

As Mike Flanagan, trailer editor and writer and director of horror films such as *Oculus* and *Ouija 2*, advises:

> *Try to keep it as true to your film as you can. If this is all people ever see of your vision, what do you want to INSIST they take away with them? Because after all, anyone will watch a trailer. For an independent, it may be the most important two minutes of their career . . .*

(Flanagan, 2008)

Referring to the storyboard and while adhering closely to the selected story pattern, begin assembling the individual shots and audio clips. Pay particular attention to the selection and order of individual shots. Only include those shots that advance the trailer's storyline and marketability. Also, because of the increased popularity of mobile technology, like our films, favor the selection of close-up and medium shots.

As you review specific shots and make final selections, consider shots and dialogue that establish the film's tone, atmosphere and emotion. However, don't allow any individual shot or piece of dialogue to run unnecessarily – the final trailer will likely include twenty to forty individual cuts.

Throughout all your marketing efforts, particularly with regard to trailers, production value remains critical. More than simply video and audio quality, production value encompasses clips that reflect camera angles, shot types (close, med, long, pan, still, motion, zoom in/out, etc.) and camera and actor movement; cinematography and lighting; special, practical and sound effects; exotic wardrobe, props and locations; musical score; storyline and acting; and editing (including shot selecting, editing pace, transitions and more).

While arranging clips and determining their individual run time, let the music guide you. The structure of your chosen tracks should be your guideline when editing. Be sure to edit your clips so that they're hitting the key musical notes and tempo. If there's a shift in the mood or tempo or your trailer, use music to emphasize those changes.

Note: Audiences have shockingly short attention spans – so keep your trailer short, sharp and to the point. Remember: "When in doubt, cut it out."

At the end of the trailer, include the film's title followed by an ending title card with the cast run, above-the-line cast and crew members, as well as any website and/or social media URLs. Finally . . . provide a slide with the release date or let the audience know that the film is "Coming soon."

Once the final edit is completed, begin work on post-production, including color grading, sound editing, visual and audio effects, etc. Post-production is also the time to assess the dialogue and completing any necessary ADR.

> *You never really know what shape a trailer will take until you start cutting it. Look at the film's assets, weigh its limitations, and then find a rhythm and structure that works best. There is no one perfect way to cut a trailer. A movie can have five different trailers, all of which take a different approach and all of which do a great job selling the product.*

(Garrett, 2012)

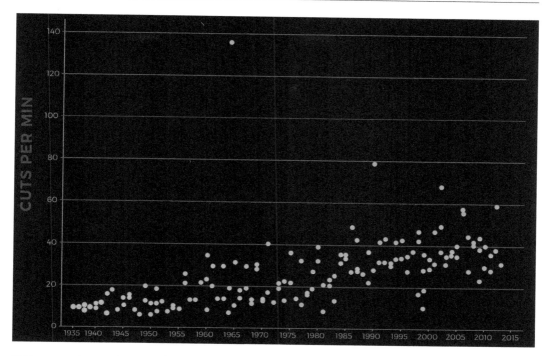

FIGURE 7.2 An analysis conducted by *WIRED* magazine reveals that the average number of cuts per minute (cpm) in trailers has increased from 12cpm during the 1950s to almost 40cpm more recently.

(*WIRED* Conde Nast)

Finally, after the public release of the trailer, make a point of reviewing of any prestigious awards or testimonials the film has received. Use this an opportunity to revise the trailer to further increase its marketability by incorporating these new awards and/or critical acclaim.

TEASER & TRAILER DISTRIBUTION

The principal objectives of trailers and teasers are the creation of audience awareness, expectations, interest, anticipation . . . and eventually film sales and rentals. Unfortunately, even the best trailers are unable to accomplish these objectives unless they are able to reach their prospective audience.

For our trailers to be a success, they must reach the highest number of targeted audience members at the right time and on the right channels.

Unlike behind-the-scenes marketing material and social media posts that are ideal for building long-term fan relationships, trailers are created – primarily – to target a more general audience and are scheduled to appear during the final weeks leading up to the film's release (ideally, intensifying during the forty-five to sixty days prior to release).

In creating a distribution and release strategy for your trailers, consider: (i) How many teasers and trailers will be included within the trailer campaign? (ii) What is the date of the film's public release? (iii) What are the film's primary, secondary and tertiary target audiences/markets? (iv) What forms of distribution – aka "windows" –

are anticipated for the film? And (v) in which countries/regions will the film be distributed?

The first question, with regard to the number of teasers and trailers included within the campaign, is particularly important. A campaign with only one trailer must be particularly careful about the timing of its release. Too soon and many viewers will forget about the film before its release. Too late and the number of viewers will likely be disconcertingly low.

Creating a campaign comprised of several teasers and trailers largely eliminates these problems. One or two teasers can be released during the second half of production (principal photography) while the release of two, three or more trailers can be carefully choreographed during post-production to coincide with the date of the film's broad release. In contrast to the single-trailer strategy, the multi-trailer strategy is far more effective at reaching and converting targeted audience members.

With regard to selecting distribution channels, most producers subscribe to the "more is better" line of thought. While it's hard to take exception to this thinking, it is a mistake to focus solely on quantity of channels over quality. The film's target audience (in large part reflecting the film's storyline and genre), distribution strategy and the specific countries or regions where the film is expected to appear are all critical considerations with regard to identifying trailer distribution channels.

Market research conducted earlier in the filmmaking process should have identified several influential personalities, periodicals, websites, audio and video podcasts and other distribution channels and online communities that appeal to your target audience. In addition to these, when considering targeted trailer distribution channels, also give thought to filming locations and the brands of wardrobe, props and vehicles that may have been showcased within your film. These companies and organizations – as well as tourist, travel or visitors bureaus – may take pride in promoting your film production's association with their locations, services or products.

Obviously, you should upload your recently released teasers and trailers to your electronic press kits (EPKs), websites, IMDb profiles and social media accounts (Facebook, YouTube, Vimeo, etc.). However, also encourage cast, crew members, production partners, friends, family and fans to do the same by embedding the film's trailers within their own websites and social media accounts.

While these suggestions will help you reach a targeted audience of friends and fans, they won't likely result in broad exposure. To reach a global mass audience, your trailers need to appear on such distribution channels as Apple iTunes, Rottentomatoes.com, IMDb.com/trailers, Movies.com, Moviefone.com, Movieclips.com (a Fandango site), MSN.com and Yahoo.com.

Many of these sites permit open trailer submissions directly from you or your distributor. Unfortunately, several (particularly iTunes and Yahoo!) strongly favor major studio films and independent films released by large global distributors. The rare self-distributed titles that are accepted by the more selective of these outlets are typically those that have won or been accepted by prestigious film festivals, have won or been nominated for industry awards, or have broad theatrical releases scheduled.

8

BEHIND-THE-SCENES PHOTOS, PRODUCTION STILLS, VIDEOS, INTERVIEWS & SPECIAL FEATURES

Behind the scenes ("BTS") content – photographs, video footage, interviews, commentary, featurettes and mini-documentaries – is among the most highly consumed and popular promotional material . . . particularly in the final weeks and days leading to the film's premiere.

As Teri Boggess, an entertainment marketing executive and former Vice President for Promotional Programming at Warner Brothers, explains, "There's an enormous

FIGURE 8.1 Perhaps the most famous production still in history, Leonardo DiCaprio and Kate Winslet appear together on James Cameron's film, *Titanic*.

(Twentieth Century Fox/Paramount Pictures/Lightstorm Entertainment)

hunger for content particularly on the Web. The public wants to know how things are shot and they want to see the stars in action" (Rubin, 2008).

Fortunately, in addition to their popularity, BTS photos and footage are also among the most easily produced forms of marketing materials. BTS can be easily and quickly recorded by a crew of dedicated photographers and videographers or directly by members of the cast and crew using smart phones, tablet computers, laptops and other mobile devices. Similarly, film stills and footage can often be taken from the day's shoot and posted immediately to websites, IMDb profiles, Facebook, YouTube and sent to email subscribers.

HIRING & SUPERVISING A BTS CREW

Although the cast and crew are commonly great sources of BTS material, the advantages of hiring a small –yet dedicated – crew of specialist unit still photographers and videographers are considerable. The knowledge, skills and experience of dedicated BTS professionals is essential in not only their ability to create great images but in their ability to navigate and work within the incredibly challenging environment of an active film set.

> There used to be different crews for BTS coverage, for home video coverage, for specialty shooting, now we have one company handle everything. You want the cast and crew to be comfortable with your crew so that there's trust, that they know when to drop the camera and move back. On some of the larger shows, it's not uncommon for a crew to come out 20–30 times.
>
> (Teri Boggess, quoted in Rubin, 2008)

As you think about hiring a dedicated crew for BTS, carefully consider their experience, portfolio and references. If your project is a union shoot, members of your BTS crew may also need to be members of an industry guild and/or union. In North America, BTS photographers and videographers should be members of the IATSE Local 600 International Cinematographers Guild in order to perform services on union productions.

Members of such guilds and unions are typically required to have – and be able to demonstrate – considerable experience, knowledge and skills. Specifically, members of these organizations (and other highly experienced BTS professionals) are often better able to:

- Coordinate with the filmmakers, sales agents, distributors and publicists to ensure the most appropriate and exciting coverage. Based upon their broad BTS experience, they are also able to capture particularly engaging images that the filmmakers, sales agents, distributors and publicists may not have otherwise expected.
- Craft a comprehensive BTS shot list and schedule based upon the film's script, shooting schedule, production meetings and location scouts. The more familiar the crew is with the script, sets and locations, the better the BTS team's shot list, schedule and plans can be with regard to selecting the most appropriate type of coverage (still, video footage, time-lapse, etc.), camera selection, camera positions, camera movement, shooting angles, lens selection, framing, etc.
- Select optimal shooting positions to capture the highest-quality images without disturbing or creating an obstacle to the film's cast and crew. Members of the team

are able to work and move through a crowded set while keeping out of the eye-line of actors, avoiding interfering with the cinematographer's set up, and remaining virtually unnoticed.

- Anticipate and accommodate changes and unforeseen opportunities as they unfold. With a team of skilled camera operators, an experienced BTS crew is typically more agile and able to move quickly, relying on a versatile selection of carefully selected equipment, including: still and video capable DSLR cameras, lightweight tripods and monopods, battery chargers, fully charged spare batteries, multiple memory cards and other easily portable gear.
- Work with the film's editor and post-production supervisor to ensure that the final stills and video footage are properly color-graded and processed to match that of final film. Depending upon their individual requirements, the BTS crew should also be able to deliver the full frame, uncropped and unprocessed images to end-users upon request.
- Keep and maintain accurate and detailed logs noting the individual photos and video footage. Log entries should include the file name or title; the date, day and time (as well as scenes numbers, when applicable) the material was recorded; a brief description of the photo or footage (and the names and titles of anyone who appears); and the identity of the individual photographer or videographer responsible for each piece of BTS content.

As a side-note: Behind-the-scenes professionals are not contractually granted photo credits. Since photographic stills and video footage created by the BTS team are produced for the purpose of marketing and promotion – and, therefore, widely disseminated to the public – they are commonly considered public domain and, therefore, clearance and credit is generally not necessary. On the other hand, the BTS team should be credited within the official film credits, IMDb, studio or film-affiliated websites and social media posts and elsewhere whenever practical.

Once they've been hired, the BTS team should quickly meet with the director, first assistant director ("First AD"), PMD, publicist, sales agent and the distributor's marketing team to discuss coverage and visual style. It's important, regardless of the genre, that the film's visual and emotional elements are reflected in the BTS coverage. To do this, the BTS crew needs to understand what makes your genre and film exciting and unique . . . and then capture coverage that highlights these aspects of the film.

For example, romantic comedy BTS should be light-hearted with coverage of people laughing and smiling. Perhaps showing the production designer preparing flowers, a candle-lit dinner or prepping bedroom scenes. You'll also want many pictures and videos of the romantic leads smiling and laughing together both on and off set. This differs from science fiction and action-adventure BTS, which are more likely to focus on cast members performing in front of a blue or green chromakey screen, the preparation and execution of various stunts, artists applying special effects makeup, and craftsmen working on unique set or production design elements.

As early as possible, the BTS crew should be provided with copies of the film script and shooting schedule and, whenever possible and appropriate, invited to production meetings and to preview sets and locations. The more familiar BTS is with the film and production, the better they will be able to (i) pre-plan their own schedule and shot lists (including interviews and cast and crew commentary) based upon the scenes scheduled to be shot that day, the type of shoot, the size of the production crew, the type of set or location and similar considerations; and (ii) identify, visualize and capture the most important shots and scenes.

It's also important that BTS study the script, shooting schedule and use these production meetings to determine what days – if any – are best to avoid. For instance, you should encourage the BTS team to avoid visits on days when you're shooting on tight interior sets or other restrictive sets and locations. On the other hand, instead of capturing traditional BTS stills and video, the crew may want to use such days to schedule interviews and commentary with cast and crew off set near base camp.

By including the BTS team in these meetings and activities, providing the team with copies of the script, shooting schedule, call-sheets and other documentation and investing the time and attention required to properly "on board" the newly hired BTS team, the film's producers and director are also sending a clear message to every member of production that BTS is a significant and valued component of the production. When BTS has been properly integrated into the production, you'll find that those on set will go out of their way to accommodate and assist the team in getting the ideal setting ups and capturing the best images possible.

Once on set, as principal photography begins, an experienced BTS team should be able to operate relatively autonomously. However, it's common practice (and a good habit) among more experienced BTS crews to first review, coordinate and confirm the day's plan with the First AD in the morning (and again over the lunch break) before filming begins. As any experienced filmmaker knows, the First AD runs the set. To the extent possible, producers and the director should make a conscious effort to establish a close and cordial working relationship between the First AD and the BTS crew.

Likewise, in addition to the First AD, the ability of the BTS team to establish a relationship with other cast and crew members is also important. Encourage everyone on the production to get to know the BTS crew . . . particularly during lunch and coffee breaks. The goal is for everyone on set to appear as comfortable as possible. As Austin Barker, Senior Vice President of Broadcast Assets at Universal Pictures, explains, "You want the interaction, that comfort level with the cast and filmmaker. You get a lot better coverage that way" (Rubin, 2008).

Let everyone know what the crew is there to accomplish and the value of BTS stills and footage. And keep your cast and crew informed by including BTS on the call-sheets. Ideally, in addition to fostering a sense of comfort with the BTS crew, you want members of the production to actually seek out the BTS team during any lulls in production. "Matt Damon was terrific on *The Bourne Ultimatum*. He would actually ask 'Where's the behind-the-scenes camera?' And he would interact with the BTS crew every day" (Austin Barker, Senior Vice President of Broadcast Assets at Universal Pictures, quoted in Rubin, 2008).

As you consider your BTS coverage and tentative BTS shot list, give some thought to the production value and design of what appears behind-the-scenes. You've likely spent weeks, if not months or years, agonizing over issues regarding your film's production design and values. However, have you considered how the production looks from behind the lens? Are you using studio-caliber equipment and other gear? Does your crew look and dress appropriately for their respective roles and responsibilities? Does your base camp and video village appear studio quality?

Obviously, you owe it to your cast, crew and audience to operate like a professional production. However, the quality of your production (including possible use of grip trucks, vans and/or trailers; camera and audio carts; on-set editing stations; craft services area, dolly set ups, camera cranes/jibs, Steadicam operators, etc.) will also be readily apparent to any audience members, industry professionals and current and prospective investors who view your BTS stills, video footage, interviews, featurettes and documentaries.

And, not surprisingly: The more your production operates and resembles that of a major studio production, the more likely you are to end up with a marketable studio-caliber film.

FILM STILLS & BTS PHOTOS

Despite the many benefits offered by video coverage (discussed in more detail later), the still image remains one of the most powerful elements of the film's marketing campaign and can be particularly effective in driving theatrical traffic, cable viewership and VOD rentals and sales.

Unfortunately, sales agents and distributors alike commonly complain about a lack of quality stills when trying to promote lower-budget indie films. Successful filmmakers recognize the value of BTS and have the foresight to know what shots producer's representatives, sales agents and distributors need to properly market and promote their films. These may be images from the film itself, studio portraits of the stars and photographs of the production crew constructing the sets, prepping individual shots and working alongside the actors.

To capture these images, the unit still photographers will often take hundreds, sometimes thousands, of photos a day. Getting this coverage means that you will have a considerable amount of material from which to (i) select the best and most powerful images and (ii) provide options for foreign markets that may prefer different images, themes and styles. As you preview the images, work closely with the BTS team, sales agents, distributors and marketing and publicity teams who often have the experience to identify which images will best "sell" your film.

Production Stills

A production still is a photograph taken of characters and action as they appear on the completed film. Production stills must look like they are from the movie and should – individually and collectively – accurately capture the essence of the story, the spirit of the producers' and director's vision and the production value of the completed film. In other words: production stills must provide viewers with a similar experience to watching the actual film.

One of the many benefits of the use of high-definition digital film cameras is that production stills can now be taken directly from film footage. Obviously, images taken directly from the film camera will most accurately represent the completed film and taking stills from the film footage potentially reduces the number of people crowding around the set, film cameras and their operators.

On the other hand, even when shooting at 6k ultra-high definition or higher-resolution, cinematic film is meant to contain a certain amount of motion blur and film grain. These are essential elements of the "film look." Unfortunately, motion blur and film grain aren't always desirable when attempting to extract the highest-quality still images. Therefore, perhaps counterintuitively, the quality of production stills is often greater when taken by dedicated unit still photographers.

To get the best coverage, the unit still photographers should be positioned as close to the film cameras as possible so that they are able to shoot every scene in detail. Depending upon how the shooting day is progressing, the director and crew should also give the photographers a few minutes to get any additional shots they need before resetting cameras or moving locations for the next shot or scene.

FIGURE 8.2 Jack Nicholson's and Tom Cruise's in-character portraits for the film, *A Few Good Men*.

(Columbia Pictures/Castle Rock Entertainment)

As discussed earlier, the script, shooting schedule and shot list are instrumental in helping the BTS crew identify and anticipate those shots and images that are most likely to explain the story and best "sell" the film. In particular, the BTS team should seek out moments when the film's stars most look and perform like stars. These include shots of love scenes, fight scenes, gun shots and explosions, vehicle chases and crashes and similarly exciting shots or scenes.

At the same time, it's necessary that the BTS team capture the supporting or contrasting image. For instance, images of the star engaged in a fight or car chase should be balanced with a set of pictures of the "bad guys" fighting or chasing the star. Likewise, consider cause and effect. If there is BTS imagery of a shoot-out or an explosion, be sure that there is also coverage of the resulting damage and any injuries. Obviously, the need to capture supporting BTS images and to consider cause and effect applies to every genre . . . not just action films.

In addition to promoting the film, the director, continuity supervisor and film crew often use production stills to capture and record details of the set, cast wardrobe, hair and makeup, props, lighting and other aspects of the shoot. The BTS team's shooting logs can also help the production crew if there are ever concerns with regard to the accuracy or completeness of their own slate and scene records.

Individual Portraits & Group Photos

Fans, media professionals and other BTS viewers are particularly attracted to photographs of the people responsible for bringing films to life. The popularity of portraits and group photos makes them important supplements to cast and crew biographies, official IMDb pages, EPKs, public releases and other marketing and promotional materials. Portraits are also a great way to introduce your friends and fans to new additions to your film's cast and crew.

In turn, the cast and crew also place considerable value on these portraits and photographs for use in their personal and professional websites, social media accounts, IMDb listings, publicity, demo reels, as casting head shots and to autograph and share with family, friends and fans. Fortunately, the film set is often the perfect opportunity for a photo shoot: the set has been "dressed" and properly lit and the actors are wearing their costumes and have had their hair done and makeup applied.

When actors aren't needed on set, encourage them to seek out the BTS team for portraits and commentary while they remain in wardrobe and have had their hair and makeup done. Also consider coordinating and scheduling two to three dedicated photo shoots where the unit stills photographer can get images of the cast in character and costume without the pressure of an immediate return call to the set.

At the same time, don't forget that every cast and crew member is part of a larger team. Encourage the cast, crew and BTS team to get photographs of the cast and crew in groups and teams. These could include group pictures of the complete cast; smaller groups comprised of the lead actors, protagonists or antagonists; and the production, camera, sound, grip, stunt, effects, makeup and hair, transportation, craft services and post-production teams. And, of course, don't forget to get pictures of the entire production (depending upon the size of your production, this may require a tall stepladder or a camera crane).

By the way: When staging group photographs, it's common to ask those with seniority – such as producers, directors, department heads and stars – to stand stage right so that

FIGURE 8.3 Oscar-winning director Kathryn Bigelow on the set of her film, *Zero Dark Thirty*. (Voltage Pictures; Editorial/Fair Use)

they appear on the left side of the frame. When captions are prepared and published in English (and most foreign languages), they will read left to right. By having those with seniority stand stage right, their names will appear first in the captioning.

In addition to their value in marketing and promoting the film, I encourage you to look at portraits and group photographs as one of many possible forms of alternative non-monetary payment to your cast, crew and other supporting professionals and service providers. Once you have a BTS crew on set, the incremental cost of providing these portraits and photographs to cast and crew members is quite negligible.

Behind-the-Scenes Photographs

In contrast to portraits and posed group photographs, true behind-the-scenes photographs are candid images that reveal the realities of making the film. The majority of BTS stills are comprised of shots of the producers, filmmaker, cast and crew going about the process of filming the movie.

And, because BTS focuses primarily on the people and personalities involved in the production, BTS photographs are most powerful when they have a sense of action and motion and incorporate medium and close-up shots revealing a wide variety of emotions and expressions of the filmmaker, director and other members of the cast and crew.

Filmmaker and/or Director: Photographs of the filmmaker and director will be featured extensively by agents, distributors and film festivals. As a result, it's important that the director make an effort to look like a "director" while on set (the key elements of the director "look" are a baseball cap, a pair of headphones and a director's viewfinder, such as the Alan Gordon Mark Vb or ARRI's PL Director's Viewfinder). Some of the more common photographs, include:

- Filmmaker or director conferring with the first assistant director (First AD)
- Director and Director of Photography (DP) framing a scene with their fingers, viewfinder, video monitor, camera lens and/or pointing off into distance
- Director and DP conferring over the shot list and/or storyboard
- Director, DP and other department heads conferring during production meeting while remaining cast and crew observe
- Director overseeing pre-production and providing cast guidance during on-set rehearsals
- Director, DP and camera operators standing next to camera set up (as a group and individually)
- Director with headphones listening to audio with audio technician.

Cast Members: Whether or not you are able to cast highly sought-after name-brand actors, the cast will feature prominently within the film's marketing and promotion. So obtaining significant coverage of the film's actors is a priority, particularly such images as:

- Assorted cast members (individually and in small groups) conferring with the director and assistant director
- Cast members getting dressed or fitted for wardrobe or having hair and makeup applied
- Cast members performing pre-production and on-set rehearsals
- Individual cast members reading or writing notes on script

FIGURE 8.4 Behind-the-scenes photograph of director Antoine Fuqua and star Bruce Willis on the O'ahu, Hawaii set of the film, *Tears of the Sun*.

(Cheyenne Enterprises/Michael Lobell Productions/Revolution Studios)

- Cast members performing on set with camera and audio crew in foreground
- Cast members conducting on-set/on-location interviews with local, national, foreign or international media
- Cast members interacting with fans, posing for pictures, signing autographs, etc.

Department Heads & Crew Members: Most of the drama and action on a film set actually occurs behind the cameras. Unfortunately, few fans and audience members have a true understanding or appreciation of the work of the production designer, prop master, costume designer, special effects supervisor, stunt coordinator and the many grips, production assistants and other crew members. To capture the considerable skill and talent required to produce a film, coverage should include:

- Camera operator(s) conferring with the director of photography over camera framing, movement or technical issues
- Audio technicians with boom poles recording featured actors as well as attaching wireless lavelier microphones to actors and as "plant" mics
- Makeup artist applying makeup (particularly SFX makeup and prosthetics) to cast members
- Stunt coordinator and/or fight choreographers supervising fights, stunts and/or practical SFX effects
- Set up and use of camera dolly, crane, Steadicam, gimbal, camera truck and/or similar equipment

FIGURE 8.5 Behind-the-scenes photograph of director Yimou Zhang on the set of his recent film, *The Great Wall*, starring Matt Damon and Tian Jing.

(Legendary East/Atlas Entertainment/China Film Group)

- Helicopter or drone crew preparing and recording aerial coverage (photographic coverage both in flight and on the ground)
- Editor, digital imaging technician ("DIT"), or other professionals working in front of monitors or mobile editing stations within the video village.

In addition to the filmmaker, director, cinematographer and cast and crew members, make a point of getting coverage of on-set guests, such as: fans; friends and family; local community members; location managers and owners; members of the print, broadcast and new media; and other set or location visitors.

In particular, have the BTS team get plenty of stills and footage of your investors with featured actors and alongside the producer, director and cinematographer. For many investors, the decision to invest in a film has as much to do with wanting to be a part of "*Hollywood*" as with an actual profit. These photographs, and the memories they have of their set visits, will play a meaningful role in raising financing for future film projects (assuming the current project breaks even or is profitable).

And, while it's important that the BTS crew focus primarily on people and personalities, don't forget to have the team capture some wide establishing shots of the set and locations as well as on-set signage, storyboards, concept artwork and any interesting pieces of wardrobe, props, equipment, vehicles and other film-related "gak."

Of course, when most people think of "behind-the-scenes," they tend to think primarily of what goes on in front and behind the camera during principal photography. However, BTS should encompass a broader definition that extends to each stage of production (development, pre-production, production, post-production and distribution) as well as what goes on beyond the set.

FIGURE 8.6 Director and cinematographer, Rain Li, appears on set alongside an ARRI Super 35 digital film camera.

(Rain Li)

In particular, the production team should get BTS coverage at events such as casting sessions, rehearsals, wrap parties, screenings, film festivals, premiers, film markets and any awards ceremonies. Event coverage should include the producers, the director, department heads and cast and crew members interacting with one another as well as with audience members, event organizers and officials, fellow filmmakers, members of the media and other friends, family, fans and celebrities.

FIGURE 8.7 Actor Mark Hamill, as Luke Skywalker, on the set of Star Wars.

(Disney and Lucasfilms; Editorial/Fair Use)

BTS VIDEO & FILM FOOTAGE

Like BTS stills, behind-the-scenes video should show the energy and excitement of independent filmmaking . . . and provide the audience with a better understanding and deeper appreciation of the people and work that went into creating the film.

In addition to capturing video footage similar to that previously suggested for behind-the-scenes photographs, encourage your BTS team to get video footage of:

- The Second Assistant Camera (AC) slating shots by calling the name of the film, the scene and take numbers and then clapping the slate (acrylic slates are perfectly fine, but there's just something about a digital time-code slate that makes the BTS of a film look particularly impressive).
- The first AD issuing commands such as "Final checks, please," "Quiet, please," "Picture is up," "Roll sound," "Roll camera," "Next set up" and similar commands.
- Director saying "action," "cut," "print," "great job" and providing other feedback or instructions to the cast and crew.
- The director and cinematographer standing over a piece of paper as they draw out a shot set up with camera blocking and lighting.
- Director and cinematographer discussing recent shots as they review footage from a field monitor and/or a camera screen.
- The crew setting up and operating their equipment during a scene (pulling focus, adjusting audio levels, adjusting a light, setting up cameras, dollies, cranes, etc.).

You'll also want b-roll of the crew members as they construct the sets and arrive in the mornings to prep, and as they strike the set at the end of each day as well as "tourist-type" shots of the areas surrounding various filming locations.

As with production stills and BTS photographs, you'll need a lot of coverage for featurettes and "Making of . . . " documentaries. The more footage and variety your team can give to the editor the better and more powerful the final video. And encourage the BTS team, particularly if they are less experienced, to hold the shot for a few seconds longer than they think they need to. Typically, video coverage and b-roll shots should run for approximately ten to thirty seconds each (longer when covering specific effects shots, scenes or other engaging subject matter).

To maximize and maintain viewer interest, the BTS crew should look for shots in which the subject is moving or is otherwise inherently interesting and exciting. To add a sense of action, keep the camera moving. Handheld shots are usually best, but hold the camera as steady as possible. Consider using a simple lightweight non-mechanical stabilizer such as a shoulder rig or Manfrotto Fig Rig (discontinued by the manufacturer but readily available pre-owned on such sites as eBay.com).

To add further interest and variety, incorporate a limited number of rack-focused and zoom shots. And mix time-lapse video with regular video footage and still photographs to give a quick and comprehensive look of interesting processes such as FX makeup, creature suit construction and stunt preparation. Consider mounting a small GoPro camera on top of a vehicle, building or other elevated vantage point to record time-lapse and b-roll footage of the entire set.

In addition to time-lapse footage, consider using screen recording software to show how the script is written and revised and pre-production completed (script breakdowns, shooting schedules, shot lists, storyboards prepared, etc.), as well as social media inter-action with fans and the completion of post-production processes, including editing,

FIGURE 8.8 Photographs of the filmmaker and cast in front of festival and awards backdrops are a common element of film marketing and promotional campaigns. On the left, Chinese Actress Du Juan arrives at the Toronto International Film Festival for her film *American Dreams in China*. (Canadapanda/Shutterstock.com). On the right, Zoe Saldana at the Los Angeles premier of *Guardians Of The Galaxy Vol. 2* held at the Dolby Theatre in Hollywood, USA.

(Tinseltown/Shutterstock.com)

visual effects, sound designs (particularly sound effects and musical score) and color grading. As with zooms, rack focus and time-lapse videos, such screen grabs and recordings can add considerably to the interest and variety of the final video.

BTS INTERVIEWS & COMMENTARY

While production photos and behinds-the-scenes stills and video footage provide the audience with a rare look inside the film and the filmmaking process, BTS interviews and commentary allow fans to hear directly about the film's production from the cast and crew. And, when combined with other BTS stills and video content, these interviews and commentary are among the most interesting and entertaining.

Not surprisingly, of those on set, the actors tend to be the most talkative and have the most experience conducting interviews. So getting good interviews and commentary from the cast is rarely an issue. On the other hand, you and your BTS team may need to work a little harder to get the director of photography, production designer, stunt coordinator, special FX coordinator, costume designers and other crew members involved. However, it's well worth the additional encouragement since their stories are often the most exciting and insightful.

In addition to working to get everyone on the production involved in video interviews and commentary, members of the BTS crew should select the most appropriate style of interview relative to the type of professional being interviewed, the subject being discussed and creative or stylistic preferences.

For instance, some of my favorite BTS interviews and commentary occur during in-the-moment or "walk-and-talk" interviews. Rather than taking place on a prepared – and often static – interview set, these interviews are recorded as people go about their work setting up cameras, lighting, reviewing storyboards, rehearsing or taking a well-deserved break. These interviews and commentary are best at capturing the feeling, emotion and action on set.

In combination with screen capture software, these types of interviews are also ideally suited to covering the work done by such professionals as digital imaging technicians, post-production supervisors, film and trailer editors, visual effects artists, color-grading professionals and music supervisors.

The second type of interview is the familiar sit-down interview. Sit-down interviews tend to be scheduled toward the end of principal photography to avoid missing discussion of any exciting developments that may occur during the final days or hours of the shoot. And, unlike the "walk-and-talk" style of interviews, the sit-down interview allows for far more control over the environment, including lighting, audio, camera blocking and surroundings.

This creative and environmental control is the result of the fact that these interviews are typically conducted on simple purpose-built sets. The sets are most commonly comprised of a black backdrop and a poster of the film in the background with folding chairs for both the host and guest(s) and, possibly, a table and plant in the mid- to foreground. Alternatively, a location can be selected that allows for the film set or location to serve as the background. This tends to be far more interesting than the standard fabric backdrop.

For the more formal sit-down interviews in particular, it's customary to provide the questions a few days in advance so that the cast and crew can prepare their responses. You may want to script a brief description of the film and suggest other specific "sound-bites" that they may find helpful to incorporate into their responses. Here are some of the most popular questions posed during sit-down interviews:

- *Tell us about the story and what it was that you found so compelling.* (Alternatively, for cast members: *What was it that first made you interested in the film and your character?*)
- *How did the story [or your character] evolve from the original script through casting, rehearsals, principal photography and final editing?*
- *How does [title of film] compare with other films on which you've worked?*
- *Have you worked with this cast or crew before? What is it like to work with [name of producer, director or other specific cast or crew member]?*
- *What was it like to work on location at [City/State/Region/Country]?*
- *What was the most interesting or challenging thing about working on this shoot?*
- *Tell us a little more about the gear you are using on set.*
- *Now that [film title] is wrapped, what's next for you? On what other projects will you be working?*
- *What advice would you give to those who want to become [film editors, cinematographers, camera operators, audio technicians, etc.]?*

During the interview, ask them to restate or rephrase the questions as a part of their answer or responses. For instance, if the interviewer or host asks *"What did you do today?,"* the cast or crew member would reply *"Today we ... "* before continuing with more details of their day. By restating the question, the editor is provided with greater flexibility in terms of the types of videos and the way in which these interviews can eventually be intercut.

Consider having many of the interviews filmed with at least one static camera placed on the interview subject only (e.g. a camera without any pans from the subject to the on-set interviewer or "two shots" or "over-the-shoulder" shots incorporating both the subject and the interviewer). This allows broadcast media outlets to have their own reporter or host act as interviewer and intercut the responses from the filmmaker,

FIGURE 8.9 Jared Leto performs an on-set interview for David Ayer's film, *Suicide Squad*. Note that the color, lighting and background graphics are purposely reflective of the film's own mood, atmosphere and colors.

(Warner Bros. Pictures/DC Comics/Atlas Entertainment)

cast or crew member. (In this case, the standard black fabric backdrop, as discussed earlier, would be far easier for an off-site reporter to visually match and intercut.) When filming with a static camera on the interview subject, it's a good idea to conduct the interview as a multi-cam shoot for more interest and flexibility in editing.

Of course, clean audio is also critical for interviews and commentary. Unfortunately, this can present a challenge when interviews are being conducted on or around a noisy film set. As a result, it's important that the BTS crew carefully select (i) interview locations, (ii) microphone placement and the (iii) use wireless lavelier mics and shotgun mics with sound blimps and windscreens to improve the clarity and quality of the audio tracks. On the other hand: Don't worry if sounds from the set work their way into the interview . . . this only adds interest and authenticity.

FEATURETTES & "MAKING OF . . . " DOCUMENTARIES

The considerable value of cast and crew portraits, production stills, BTS photos, video footage and interviews and commentary reflects both their popularity and the fact that they can both be distributed as individual stand-alone content and combined with similar content to form various featurettes, "Making of . . . " mini-documentaries and special features. And, due to the explosive growth of online video sites such as YouTube and Vimeo, the marketing and promotional impact of these videos are now approaching that of more traditional teasers and trailers.

Depending upon the amount and nature of coverage you and your BTS crew were able to capture, the resulting material can be put together and edited in an almost limitless number of combinations and possible special feature topics or storylines.

To narrow down the possibilities, Riley Hooper, a documentary filmmaker and former manager of content and community at Vimeo, has identified seven of the most popular:

1. Motive: One of the most common and interesting topics is why the filmmakers chose to make this particular film. What is important about the story? What influenced the story? How does the story and film compare and contrast with other films within its genre and previous films produced by the filmmaker?

2. People & Personalities: Use the featurette, mini-doc or other video to give the audience a sense of the many people and personalities involved in the film's production – not only on set and in a professional sense, but also during down time when people are interacting with one another informally and being themselves.

3. Equipment: Audience members are often curious about the technical aspects of filmmaking. They want to know more about the cameras, lenses, lighting, microphones, rigs and post-production equipment and techniques. And, just as interesting, have the crew explain why these specific shots or scenes were framed, lensed or otherwise shot using these specific pieces of equipment or techniques.

4. Stylistic Choices: As mentioned, every piece of equipment and technical choice should have a stylistic motivation. Everything from production design, lighting, framing, moving versus static shots and the choice of frame rates to post-production coloring and effects – all of these elements work together to create a particular mood, evoke a feeling and tell a story. This is also a great opportunity to share pre-production discussions, storyboards, production design and commentary and interviews on the preparation of the shooting script, location scouting and set construction.

5. Workflow: In addition to equipment, techniques and stylistic choices, audience members are also curious about the fundamental process of how a film is made – from development, pre-production, principal photography and post-production through distribution. In particular, explain how specific shots were staged, how practical and visual effects were produced, and how these shots, effects and scenes serve the film's story.

6. Challenges and Limitations: As any experienced filmmaker knows, low-budget independent films commonly suffer from challenges imposed by the limitations of their budgets, shooting schedules, crew size, locations and other obstacles. Fortunately, audience members are excited to learn about these many challenges and how each were overcome by the filmmakers.

7. Special Features: Think of the things that are included in the "special features" section of DVDs, including: (i) commentary from the filmmaker, director and starring cast members; (ii) music videos; (iii) teasers and trailers (as well as teasers and trailers for any forthcoming sequels or prequels); (iv) alternate endings and deleted or extended scenes; (v) out-takes and bloopers; and (vi) script, storyboards and concept artwork (set design, wardrobe, props, creatures, special and CGI effects, etc.).

As with teasers, trailers and social media videos, the total running time of special features, featurettes and "Making of . . . " mini-docs should be brief – with total run times ranging from one-and-a-half to four minutes. Whenever practical, longer video content should be broken up into two or more shorter segments.

SHARING & DISTRIBUTING BTS CONTENT

As mentioned previously, BTS content is among the most popular and highly consumed promotional material produced by a film's marketing team. However, before BTS material can be publicly distributed – and, in fact, long before a BTS team has been hired – the filmmaker and production team must address various legal and contractual issues.

The film's producers should include BTS clearance as a component of the cast's and crew's employment agreements and contracts. Such agreements must grant the production company permission to record and disseminate their images for the purposes of marketing and promotion. Similarly, individual cast and crew agreements should provide permission (and detail any restrictions) to distribute official BTS and any BTS they may create on their own.

In the case of cast members, some (particularly those considered A-list stars) may negotiate a clause in their contracts that allows them to preview all such material and "kill" any images of themselves which they do not approve. This is an important consideration and may affect just how quickly some BTS coverage can be released (or whether or not certain coverage can be released at all).

Once the BTS stills and video footage have been selected and cleared, the material is posted to the film's EPK, website, social media platforms, IMDb profiles and are provided to the sales agent, distributors and publicists for the press and adverting campaign. Among many other outlets, behind-the-scenes coverage is commonly featured on such broadcast programs as *Entertainment Tonight*, *Access Hollywood*, *CNN Showbiz Today* and *E! Entertainment Channel*.

To help target specific distribution outlets, during pre-production, create a database on each cast and crew member to include: (i) where each was born; (ii) where they live and have lived in the past; and (iii) where they went to film school, college or university; (iv) what clubs and organizations they belong to; and (v) films and broadcast programs on which they have worked. The film's PMD and publicist can then use this information to target relevant local news, industry organizations and university or film school media outlets.

Another valuable source of distribution are the members of the production team themselves. Capture plenty of BTS coverage of each cast and crew member and then encourage them to share it on their own websites and social media accounts. Production stills and BTS photographs can also be given to the actors to autograph and send to their many fans. To help the cast and crew in better distributing BTS coverage, set up a board in base camp with select picture-quality prints of two to three dozen images from the prior day's shoot and provide links where these images and related footage can be downloaded.

As coverage is reviewed, particularly video footage, members of the production team should pay particular attention to any positive comments that one member of the cast or crew may make about another. Together with BTS interviews, commentary, production stills, film footage and BTS photos and video, these testimonials can serve as valuable additions to a cast or crew member's reel or video portfolio.

Not surprisingly, the more interesting, exciting and better-quality your behind-the-scenes still and video footage, the more likely your content is to be broadly distributed . . . and to go viral.

9

IMDB – MARKETING & PROMOTION

A subsidiary of Amazon.com, IMDb is the world's most popular and authoritative source for movie, TV and celebrity content with more than 250 million unique monthly visitors. IMDb offers a searchable database of 200 million data items including more than 5 million movies, TV and entertainment programs and more than 7.5 million cast and crew members (and film-related companies and organizations).

Audience members have come to rely on the information IMDb provides – including local movie showtimes, ticketing, trailers, critic and user reviews, personalized recommendations, photo galleries, entertainment news, quotes, trivia, box office data, editorial feature sections and a universal watchlist – to help choose which films they want to watch and where to watch them.

In addition to IMDb's audience-focused site, IMDbPro is a subscription version of IMDb designed exclusively for professionals who work in the entertainment industry. Among its many services, IMDbPro provides an industry database of millions of cast, crew and film-related organizations, production status listings for film and television projects, an archive of industry insider news (from such sources as Box Office Mojo, *Variety*, *The Hollywood Reporter*, Deadline, The Wrap, etc.) among other information and tools.

FILM LISTINGS

Most audience members, and many industry professionals, begin using IMDb by performing a title search for a specific film. Having arrived at the proper film profile, the typical visitor will quickly scan the film's user rating (based on a scale between 1 and 10), Metascore and key art before reading the film summary and viewing the trailer(s) and other videos and images.

Assuming that the visitor likes what they see, IMDb provides links at the bottom of each listing to find local showtimes and to rent or purchase the video from IMDb's parent, Amazon.com. In addition, visitors can save the film to their IMDb watchlist, click the share buttons to post the page to their Facebook or Twitter accounts, email a link to the film page to a friend or post their own rating and review of the film.

To increase the likelihood that a visitor will purchase a ticket or a copy of your film, it's critical that the filmmaker and marketing team fully optimize each film listing in

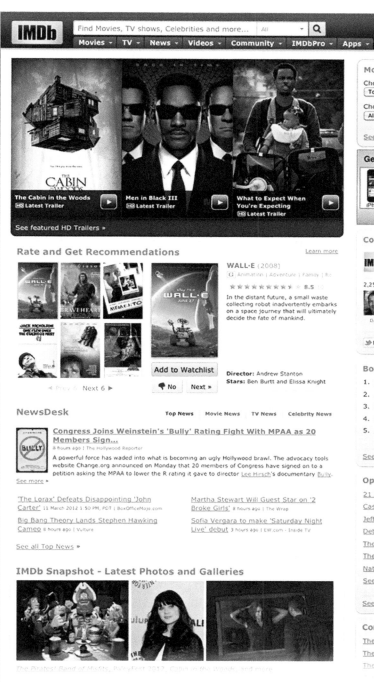

FIGURE 9.1 IMDb home page.

(IMDb/Amazon.com)

the studio's archive and slate (many listings are posted during development and early pre-production). By properly optimizing each film listing, the films also benefit from an increased opportunity to be showcased in the *"People who liked this also liked . . . "* suggestions of competing films within the genre.

Tips and suggestions for optimizing IMDb listings and profiles are provided later in the chapter, but, at a minimum, each film listing must include such details as the title, tagline, key art/poster, a short film summary, the release year, running time, genre classification, filming locations, technical specifications (run time, sound mix, aspect ratio, negative format, cinematographic process, etc.), a full listing of the distributors, producers, production companies and cast and crew as well as a link to the film's and studio's official sites.

To add a film to the IMDb directory, the film must meet what the service terms "general public interest" criteria. To meet the criteria, the film should meet at least one of the following standards: (i) have, or be scheduled to have, a theatrical release, (ii) be broadcast on regional, national or international television, (iii) have been released via VOD or have DVDs available to the general public, (iv) been accepted and shown at a film festival or (v) the film was produced by a famous artist or person of interest.

General public interest does not include films that were produced and distributed (i) on an internet page, (ii) for public viewing via the web, (iii) for a film course, university or workshop, (iv) for a local business or institution for internal use or (v) for private home use or local consumption for friends and/or family.

Once you've had your first film approved and posted, you'll find that posting further film listings is much easier. However, IMDb can be quite stringent in determining that each film (particularly the first film posted by a filmmaker or studio) meets its criteria. One of the easiest work-arounds is to simply list your film on Withoutabox.com – IMDb and Amazon.com's online film festival submission service. After your film has been posted to Withoutabox.com (registration is free), you can create IMDb title pages in just one step using the existing information from your Withoutabox project page.

FILMMAKER PROFILE

As a filmmaker, your two most powerful personal branding and marketing channels are your IMDb profile and your website. Therefore, visitors to either channel should be able to readily identify your brand message and those attributes that distinguish you as a filmmaker (aka your unique selling propositions, or "USPs"). As with other aspects of your branding, marketing and promotion, whenever possible, each component of your IMDb profile needs to support a highly focused image and brand message.

The first step in preparing your IMDb profile is to register and subscribe to IMDbPro. The subscription can be paid monthly or annually and should be considered an essential expense as long as you remain in the film industry. Should you ever cancel your IMDbPro account, your IMDb profile will remain active (as long as you have at least one entry in your "Filmography" section) although your pictures, videos and resume may be deleted.

Once you've registered from IMDbPro, check to see if your name has already been used by any other IMDb users. Whenever possible, your name should be unique. Users shouldn't be confused when trying to identify you and your profile.

If your name has already been taken, consider changing your listing by adding a middle initial or middle name; removing your middle initial or middle name; substituting the first initial of your first name (instead of spelling out your full first name); using an alternative spelling of your first, middle or last name; or, in what may be viewed as an extreme case, change your name and use a pseudonym.

Whatever name you use (and/or any changes you may make to your IMDb name), ideally it should be the same as used on your websites, social media accounts and all other public materials. Given this fact, the name you choose should be unique (so as to avoid confusion with other professionals, films or organizations) and available on IMDb, possible website URLs, social media accounts and other platforms.

Having completed registration and secured your IMDb name, you'll need to craft a well-written biography that both (i) communicates your knowledge, skills and experience as a filmmaker and, hopefully, (ii) allows readers to form a personal connection. The following template is a good place to start:

[Name] is a [location]-based filmmaker known for [his/her] [describe your distinct attributes as a filmmaker, also known as your unique selling proposition or "USP"] and films such as [list of well-known film projects]. [First name] is a graduate of [university/college/film school/film workshop] [(city, state, country)] where [he/she] received a [associate/baccalaureate/Master's/certificate] in [subject].

Growing up in [hometown/region], [first name] developed an intense interest in [describe your film interests] and, in particular, [films such as . . . /the works of . . .].

More recently, [first name] has been involved in a number of film and entertainment projects, including [identify/describe projects . . .] winning such awards as [list awards]. [He/She] is currently [describe current/future film-related projects or plans].

In addition to filmmaking, [first name] has a strong interest in [list unique hobbies, philanthropic causes and/or other interests].

This template allows you to strategically spotlight your USPs and brand message while providing readers several opportunities to form a connection with you based upon your background and interests. The importance of the reader being able to identify with you as a person, as well as a professional, cannot be overstated. It's not enough that people respect your abilities, they need to *like you and want to work with you (or to purchase or rent your films).*

Not surprisingly, one of the most well-crafted and complete IMDb profiles is that of director and producer Steven Spielberg. Created with the support of a team of publicists and other creative professionals, the amount and quality of supporting information (particularly photos and video footage) is impressive. I strongly encourage you to review Steven Spielberg's IMDb profile as well as the IMDb profiles of four to six of your favorite filmmakers for more inspiration.

When completing your film profile and listings for your production company and films, follow Steven Spielberg's example and make each as comprehensive as possible. IMDb is essentially a search engine (similar to Google and YouTube) in which results are driven largely by relevance and popularity. By including as much information as possible, you'll maximize the number of people driven to your IMDb listings and increase the number of links throughout the site.

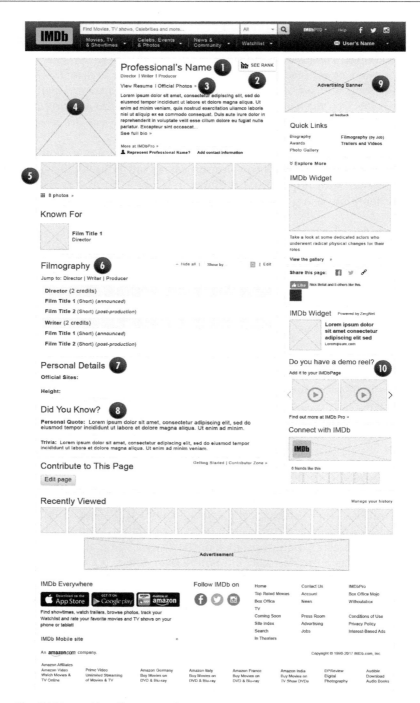

FIGURE 9.2 The IMDb profile offers considerable opportunities to promote the filmmaker. The key components of the IMDb profile include (1) the filmmaker's name; (2) IMDB STARmeter ranking; (3) biography; (4) portrait; (5) photo album; (6) filmography, i.e. credit list; (7) personal details; (8) quotes and trivia; (9) optional banner advertising; and (10) the filmmaker's demo reel.

(Robert G. Barnwell/Sandy O. Cagnan)

STUDIO OR PRODUCTION COMPANY PROFILE

Unlike film listings and filmmaker profiles, studio and production company listings are of far more interest and use to industry professionals than audience members. As a result, the description of your studio or production company should focus on aspects of you and your business that are of most interest to such professionals and organizations. Consider the following template as an example:

> *Based in [city, state/Region, country], [studio name] was established to produce independent films that [purpose]. Working with a talented and experienced group of investors, distributors and other industry professionals, [studio] develops, produces and distributes [describe business model, approach to filmmaking or list titles of past, current and future film projects].*
>
> *[Studio name] was founded during [year] by [name] – a [location]-based filmmaker known for [his/her] [USP]. [First name] is a graduate of [list any film schools, universities or colleges from which you've graduated/completed]. Growing up in [hometown/region], [first name] developed an intense interest in [describe your film interests] and, in particular, [films such as . . . /the works of . . .].*
>
> *More recently, [first name] has been involved in a number of film and entertainment projects, including [identify/describe projects]. [He/She] is currently [describe current/future film-related projects or plans].*

Notice how the studio description quickly changes the focus from the broader studio organization to the filmmaker. For the independent filmmaker, the studio and the individual and collective brands of its film portfolio should revolve around the film-maker's personal brand. In fact, many branding experts make a strong case for the independent studio to carry the filmmaker's name, e.g. Jane Smith Studios or John Smith Productions. This is particularly the case when the filmmaker has won prestigious awards and has earned a degree of visibility and respect within the industry. (On the other hand, for beginning filmmakers without an established track record, a studio name that sounds more established and "corporate" may prove beneficial.)

However, as mentioned previously, regardless of how you choose to name your studio, the studio description – and particularly the first paragraph – should clearly identify your studio's business model, genre focus and any other relevant aspects of your business that differentiate it positively from others in the industry and marketplace.

CAST & CREW PROFILES

If you're lucky, you've been able to attach a few well-known actors and highly experienced department heads to your film. However, more likely than not, reflecting the financial constraints of the low-budget independent film, most – if not all – of your cast and crew will have relatively little experience and only a few film entries within their individual IMDb profiles.

For the majority of those cast and crew members without a professionally prepared IMDb bio and profile, I strongly encourage you to have a member of your marketing team conduct a brief five to ten minute interview with each member of the production team and then prepare personalized biographies.

Don't leave the preparation of the biography and IMDb profile to the individual cast or crew members. If you do, despite their promises and best intentions, you'll be disappointed to find that few of your cast and crew will actually complete a quality profile.

When well-crafted, these cast and crew profiles will provide valuable back links to your own films, studio and filmmaker profiles and listings.

Fortunately, many of the same principles and tactics suggested for the filmmaker's, studio's and individual film's IMDb listings apply to cast and crew members, including a well-written biography, professional portrait, BTS photos and videos, a complete filmography and personal details (such as biographical information and links to official sites).

Throughout film production, be sure to work with the BTS video and photography teams to assure that every member of the cast and crew receives proper coverage. Particularly in the case of highly experienced professionals with extensive credit lists, you and your team should commit to producing marketing and promotional materials (including BTS) that are noticeably superior to those of other films that may appear on your cast's and crew's IMDb profiles.

Finally, as you work on these cast and crew profiles, don't overlook casting directors, production accountants, lawyers and legal assistants, catering, location, transportation, minor supporting cast members, production assistants and anyone else who may have participated in the production or administration of the film.

OPTIMIZING IMDB PROFILES & LISTINGS

To differentiate your profiles and listings from competing filmmakers, films and studio listings, IMDb provides several opportunities for you to optimize your listings.

These optimization opportunities include the use of vanity IMDb URLs and the ability to post personal details, behind-the-scenes photos and film stills, teasers and trailers, film clips, key art, frequently asked questions (FAQs), trivia, quotes, copies of print and broadcast media coverage and links to your blog, websites, social media accounts. Essentially, you'll want to make sure that every page you publish is complete and that you take advantage of every opportunity IMDb provides to strengthen your filmmaking, studio and film brands.

Beyond assuring that your listings are complete, *optimization involves the selection of those keywords, key phrases, images, videos and other content that most appeal to your target audience members.* As with other aspects of your branding, marketing and promotion, be conscious of how this information and content (particularly photos, trailers, film clips and artwork) will appear to readers and viewers on the relatively small screens of cell phones, tablets and other mobile devices.

A final key component of optimization involves activities that drive traffic to your listings, such as: posting your customized IMDb URLs on your websites, social media platforms, email signatures, EPKs, public releases, articles, postcards, letterhead and business cards. Also encourage cast and crew members, agents, distributors, friends, family and fans to post and/or share your IMDb links and consider the use of pay-per-click campaigns (discussed later in this book) to drive further traffic to your IMDb profiles and listings.

When pages have been well-optimized, your IMDb profiles and listings will have higher numbers of page views and greater degrees of audience engagement as evidenced by the number and quality of user reviews and film ratings; message board posts; teaser, trailer and film clip views; visitor watchlist additions; and the volume and consistency of content shares via email and social media.

FIGURE 9.3 IMDb Pro dropdown menu.
(Robert G. Barnwell/Sandy O. Cagnan)

The increased popularity of your profiles and listings (as evidenced by the number of page views) results in two additional consequences: First, the sum total of these page views forms the foundations of the IMDb's STARmeter, MOVIEmeter and COMPANY meter rankings. This forms a "virtuous cycle" in which a greater number of page views results in higher meter rankings that, in turn, result in more page views.

Secondly, IMDb listings are often prioritized in the search results of Google, Bing, Yahoo! and other search engines. As your listings and profiles increase in popularity on IMDb, they will often increase in ranking and visibility among the search engines – driving yet more traffic volume and a higher level of awareness among audience members and industry professionals.

MAXIMIZING USE OF IMDBPRO

For those committed to successfully marketing their films and filmmaking careers, a subscription to IMDbPro is essential. The membership-based service includes comprehensive information and tools that are designed to help filmmakers achieve success throughout their careers and each stage of film production. There's a database of detailed contact and representation information for cast and crew members from around the world, comprehensive and expanded industry data from a variety of trade publications, a casting service, tools to improve and optimize your IMDb profiles and so much more.

In particular, once you've subscribed, fully complete the items within the *"My Page"* menu item, particularly *"My Profile," "Resume," "Photos,"* and *"Demo Reel."* Much of this information will be used to automatically populate your public IMDb profiles and listings, including your biography, filmography, portrait photo and other personal and professional details.

However, your resume, credit list, demo reel and contact details will also be made available to industry professionals such as investors, distributors, film festival committee members, prospective cast and crew members and others. Therefore, your IMDbPRo profile is critical in establishing your credibility as a successful filmmaker and industry professional.

Double-check that the information contained in your IMDb profile and resume reads well and is accurate. Likewise, make certain that you post a short thirty second version of your film reel with contact details on title cards at the beginning and end of the reel. Contact details on your IMDbPro profile, resume and demo reel should include your website URLs, social media platforms, email and physical addresses and telephone numbers as well as contact details for selective representatives (such as attorneys, agents, managers, studio or public relations professionals).

Once completed, your IMDbPro profile will join a comprehensive database of over 6 million other professionals. In addition to promoting your own filmmaking career and projects, the IMDbPro database serves as a comprehensive directory of highly talented and experienced professionals and companies, including: actors, cinematographers, distributors, producers, investors, casting directors, publicists, special and visual effects studios and professionals, camera rental houses, sound stages, post-production facilities, location services, film commissions, sales agents and other professionals and organizations.

The IMDbPro database allows you to screen professionals and companies by filmography and/or past clients, geographic location, industry experience, guild affiliation, awards and nominations, IMDb STARmeter or COMPANYmeter rankings and any shared connections you may have with others within the IMDbPro directory.

In fact, for many filmmakers, IMDbPro's database and Pro Casting feature have proven indispensable in casting the right actors for their films. By searching specific skill sets, previous experiences and other criteria, filmmakers and casting professionals are able to rapidly compile a list of prospective actors. As Richard Hicks, casting director (credits include *Gravity*, *Zero Dark Thirty*, *Game Change*), explains, "IMDbPro is probably the single most helpful tool in the tool box when I'm casting one of the leads in a movie" (Thompson, 2014).

Apart from its extensive database of professionals and organizations, IMDbPro also includes a vast database of upcoming movie and television show titles. The service provides extensive details on existing film titles as well as movies in development, pre-production, production, post-production and forthcoming releases (as well as television programs).

This information is invaluable in compiling "film comps" (aka "comparables") and conducting marketing research on a specific film title's genre, budget, awards, producers and/or production companies, distributors, casting directors, cinematographer, director, scriptwriter(s), visual and special effects supervisors, filming locations, theatrical/box office performance, actors, etc.

For market research purposes, IMDbPro is also a centralized source for industry news. Throughout the day, the site is updated to provide the latest entertainment news from such publications and sources as Box Office Mojo, *Variety*, *The Hollywood Reporter*, Deadline, The Wrap, etc. These sources – and others – provide information on recent distribution deals, domestic and international box office performance, profiles of industry professionals and organizations, global entertainment business trends and indicators, and other news.

Similarly, IMDb and IMDbPro also allow you to study and research trends in key art design, titles, taglines and descriptions, trailers and teasers, BTS content, biographies, film descriptions and other marketing and promotional trends.

ADVERTISING ON IMDB

Reflecting its status as the world's most popular source for film and celebrity content, IMDb has become a highly popular advertising outlet for studio films. The popularity of IMDb among studio advertisers reflects the site's ability to reach a variety of highly targeted audiences.

IMDb offers a broad range of display and rich media advertisements, including wraps, enhanced title pages, promoted videos, pre-roll video and promoted editorial content. These advertisements are able to target specific genres, locations and sections of site to maximize their promotional impact. In addition, IMDb's advertising team is able to work closely with advertisers to create customized advertisements and promotional campaigns.

Unfortunately, advertising with IMDb often requires a budget of $50,000 USD or greater. However, depending upon the nature of your film and its distribution potential, unlike other paid advertising and promotional alternatives, the higher advertising expenses associated with IMDb are often quite cost-effective.

Whether or not you choose to advertise with IMDb, it's essential that every filmmaker recognizes the importance of IMDb's role in branding, marketing and promotion and work to have a comprehensive and powerful IMDb presence as early in their careers and film production process as possible.

10

SOCIAL MEDIA & VIDEO MARKETING PLATFORMS

Social media – like all your branding, marketing and promotional activities – is fundamentally about relationships: the people who like, friend, follow and subscribe to you and your channels. In fact, as audience attention spans continue to get shorter, social media – which provides instantaneous connection – is perhaps the single most efficient and effective way for filmmakers to establish and manage relationships with their audience.

At little to no direct cost, well-executed social media campaigns expand brand awareness, reach and loyalty with new and existing audience members. And, reflecting the ability to easily target audiences as well as the variety of content media which social media supports, filmmakers and PMDs are able to create highly customized and personalized experiences for friends, fans, followers and subscribers.

As a result of these many benefits, social media has the potential to significantly reduce the cost of marketing, promotion and distribution while increasing film sales and rentals. However, to achieve these benefits it's imperative that your social media activity be properly aligned and integrated with your other marketing activities. Sue Kroll, President of Marketing and Distribution at Warner Bros. Pictures, explains, "If the combination of things is not right . . . it's not going to matter. You have to get the whole mix of it right, and [social media] alone is not enough" (Kapko, 2014)

SOCIAL MEDIA STRATEGY

Reflecting its importance and visibility within the overall marketing and promotional strategy, social media activity must be closely aligned with other marketing channels. This alignment requires consistency with regard to images, colors, keywords and phrases, messaging and content. By leveraging and integrating activities across marketing and promotional channels, the impact of your marketing activities is far greater.

Not surprisingly, an effective social media campaign requires a combination of strategic thought and dedication. Fortunately, the amount of time required to support such a campaign can be significantly reduced by developing a social media content plan and publishing calendar using the following five steps:

Step 1. Establish Objectives

To fully realize the many benefits of social media, it's important to identify your objectives and allow for these objectives to evolve alongside your career and your films' production schedules (development, preproduction, principal photography, release and post-release).

While far from an exhaustive list, among many other objectives, you can use social media and associated relationships to:

1. Enhance the brand visibility and awareness of your films
2. Gain insights into target audiences
3. Increase the total number of audience contact points
4. Create and expand a fan following and engagement
5. Crowd-source storyline, script development, partial financing and production
6. Increase the number and quality of reviews, ratings, recommendations and word-of-mouth.
7. Drive film and merchandise sales and rentals
8. Monitor the activity and performance of fellow filmmakers and studios
9. Identify and network with industry professionals
10. Improve search engine optimization and website page rankings.

However, as you build your social media following in an attempt to realize these many benefits, understand that it's often the quality of your social media friends, fans and subscribers that's important . . . not necessarily the quantity.

Step 2. Know Your Audience

Monitor what your friends, fans, subscribers and target audience are saying on social media and the types of content they find most engaging. *What topics and types of content do they share with their own fans, friends and viewers? What topics and types of content do they most activity comment or share? What other social media personalities and accounts do they visit and subscribe?*

Similarly, follow and subscribe to popular social media personalities and organizations within filmmaking and your genre. In particular, be certain to follow the major studios, independent studios and production companies, fellow filmmakers, your cast and crew members, industry trade publications, industry professionals and other influencers as well as your own friends, fans and audience members.

In particular, it's helpful to know: *How active are these other filmmakers and studios on social media? Does social media appear to be an integral part of their marketing and promotional strategy? What content seems to best work for them? Specifically, which content tends to receive the most views, comments, likes and shares? Alternatively, are there promising topics that these professionals and organizations aren't adequately covering or being covered utilizing lower-quality media or formats? What is the typical length of their posts or videos? How often do they post or update their content? Are you able to identify common words, phrases and types of media (such as photos and videos) they use to drive views and engagement?*

In addition to those people and organizations you already know, you can use various free and low-cost services (such as Buzzsumo, Fanpage Karma, LikeAlyzer and Klear) to identify, analyze and connect with other popular film-related professionals and organizations on social media.

FIFTEEN POPULAR SOCIAL MEDIA POST TOPICS

Although there are hundreds if not thousands of possible social media topics, the following is a list of 15 of the more popular topics which you should consider incorporating into your social media:

1. Announce the progress of your current film project, including the beginning or completion of pre-production, filming, or post-production.
2. Publicly thank individuals who recently agreed to join your film project (producer, director, star, department head and/or other cast or crew members).
3. Request suggestions on film equipment and techniques; grip and other equipment rental houses; post-production facilities and professionals; references to any necessary department heads, cast or crew members; suggestions and opinions on prospective shooting locations; and/or other film-related products and services.
4. Crowd-source opinions on possible movie titles, key art, websites and other aspects of your branding, marketing and promotional campaigns.
5. In advance of your film's global premier, announce the film's release date, solicit volunteers for your launch group and encourage others to leave favorable reviews to Amazon, iTunes, Rotten Tomatoes and other sites.
6. Ask if anyone can (i) introduce you to someone (or film or organization) you'd like to meet with and/or partner; and/or (ii) suggest who you should meet while visiting a particular city or attending a particular event.
7. Invite friends, fans, followers, viewers, subscribers and others to get together with you at an upcoming film festival, film market, screening, premier, convention, conference, workshop, panel discussion or similar event.
8. Record video commentary or post updates from an event (film festival, film market, convention, workshop, panel discussion etc.), your film set or other event or location of interest.
9. Share photographs or videos of you while on set, location, meeting a celebrity filmmaker or posing with fans while attending a film festival, awards program or other film-related event.
10. Repost an interesting video or post from a filmmaking colleague, friend, fan or subscriber or share a link to an interesting industry or business article, statistic or other information from *The Hollywood Reporter*, *Variety*, or other respected publication or industry source.
11. Congratulate a friend, fan, fellow filmmaker, current or former department head, or cast or crew member on a recent accomplishment.
12. Share an interesting experience or discussion you've had with a friend, fan, fellow filmmaker, department head or other cast or crew member.
13. Let everyone know of a newly posted item of interest on your website (such as the release of a new teaser, trailer, poster mobile app, film-branded computer game, soundtrack, promotional merchandise etc.).
14. Be real. Give your social media fans and friends a glimpse into your personal life. Share photos of you while on vacation, moving into a new home or apartment, standing alongside your new car or with family and friends during your birthday or the holidays.
15. Thank someone for commenting on one of your social media posts and, if appropriate, provide additional information or a more detailed comment in response.

Step 3. Social Media Topics & Content Mix

As you develop an understanding of your audience's social media preferences and the content provided by other filmmakers and studios, you'll better your ability to align your own marketing objectives and audience content preferences with the subjects, topics and types of content you share on social media.

You'll want to focus your social media content plan on a relatively small number of popular topics and content formats. Ideally, in addition to their popularity, these formats will make content creation relatively easy for both you and your team so that you can provide your audience with a regular and timely stream of content.

As a filmmaker, most of your content should be highly visual and concentrate on the magic of movie making, including such topics as: (i) a director's journal or production diary; (ii) BTS, film stills and clips; (iii) teasers and trailers; (iv) sneak peak of your film (such as the first five to ten minutes of your film); (v) an introduction to key cast and crew members and/or production partners; and (vi) fan profiles.

In addition to these topics, some of the more interesting and engaging posts include those that comment on recent industry news. The release of a highly anticipated studio film or trailer, the struggles (or success) of a particular film project or studio, the death or retirement of a respected director, producer or actor, the recent achievement of a fellow low-budget filmmaker or details on an industry event you've recently attended (or plan on attending).

And don't forget to include occasional posts and videos that promote your own film's premier, film festival showings and theatrical or online sales and rental promotions. However, to avoid alienating your audience, be sure to keep your marketing and promotion low-key. Ideally, direct promotional content should represent no more than 5–10% of your social media activity.

Yes, audiences realize you have a film to sell and expect a degree of self-promotion, but they still want to feel they are forming a connection and relationship with the real you. This means that your social media posts should be in a conversational tone and reflect your personality. And make a point of sharing aspects of your personal life (to the extent you feel comfortable) including photographs and videos of you at home, on vacation, with friends and family as well as posts announcing new developments in your life (changes in relationship status, a recent move, pet adoption, new car purchase, etc.) and discussing any charities or causes you may support.

Finally, if – or rather when – you struggle for content ideas, publish posts asking your fans, friends, viewers and subscribers for suggestions on the types of content they'd most enjoy. Services such as BuzzSumo, Digg, Google Trends, Social Mention and Moz Content can also help you identify trending topics and content that your audience may be interested in. And don't hesitate to share material (and your own comments) on content posted by your friends, fans and subscribers as well as other filmmakers, studios and sources.

In addition to identifying appropriate social media subjects and topics, experiment with different types of content. Ideally, your social media activity should be comprised of a variety of interactive and rich media formats. These are likely to include text-only posts, photographs, video, PDFs, PowerPoint slideshows, audio and video podcasts, etc. As you experiment with different content formats, consider which are easiest for you and your team to create and easiest for your audience to consume and share with their own friends, fans and subscribers.

Step 4. Select Social Media Channels

The fourth step is to select the appropriate social media platforms on which to engage. Focus on those channels most popular with your target audience, which best leverage the types of content and media most suited to your audience and your marketing and promotional objectives, and those that you enjoy and are most likely to use consistently. These platforms and channels may include microblogs, photosharing, videosharing, podcast or vidcast platforms. Some of the most popular include Facebook, Flickr, iTunes Podcasts, IMDb Message Boards, Instagram, LinkedIn, Pinterest, Slideshare, Tumblr, Twitter, Vimeo and YouTube.

Of these, which social media networks will work best for you? Which networks will have the most responsive, engaged and largest audience for your material? Which networks offer or specialize in the types of content that you enjoy most and are best suited? Which social media channels would you most enjoy using? Least enjoy? *It doesn't help to engage on a platform that you don't like or aren't particularly skilled in. Instead, encourage other members of your team who might enjoy and do a better job with these social media activities and platforms.*

As you look to further narrow your list of potential social media channels, prioritize those platforms that (i) your target audience is already using and (ii) that allow you to exploit the power of visual images such as pictures and videos (Facebook, YouTube, Vimeo, Flickr, Pinterest, etc.). Ideally, these platforms are also mutually supportive. For instance, if you post a trailer or other video to YouTube, you want to be able to promote it on your other social media platforms by blogging about it, tweeting about it and by adding it to your Facebook page.

Despite the value of a strong social media presence, you must be careful not to spread yourself too thin on social media. Instead, pick a few different social media platforms and focus on those channels. Being successful on one or two channels is far more beneficial than having weak or modest popularity on a large number of platforms. If you overwhelm yourself by trying to use too many social media and marketing channels, the quality of your content and value of your other branding, marketing and promotional activities will inevitably suffer.

Only once you've achieved success on two or three channels should you begin considering expanding your social media reach to other platforms and channels.

Step 5. Create a Publishing Calendar

To maximize the benefits of social media activity, you should post on a frequent and consistent basis – you want to become a valued part of the regular social media habits of your audience and post at sufficiently regular intervals that your audience can look forward to – and anticipate – updated content.

On the other hand: posting too frequently can alienate your audience and detract from other filmmaking and marketing priorities. Just how frequently you post will depend on your audience, the social media channels you choose to employ, the particular stage your film stands in production and any time constraints you and your team may encounter.

An easy solution to achieving and maintaining a proper balance in frequency and consistency is to create a social media calendar. You should keep this simple. The calendar need only include the dates and times you intend to post as well as the topic and type of content. Then, once every three to four months, sit down and update your social media calendar.

As you schedule your posts, remember to gradually increase the intensity and frequency of your activity as you approach your film's release date. If the film's production schedule or anticipated premier date change, make corresponding adjustments to your marketing calendar and social media activity.

Another important consideration are the times and days of the week you post fresh content. Keep in mind that your new posts and content will compete with newly posted content from other people and organizations. To reduce this competition, consider posting your content during off-peak hours (early in the morning and later in the day) and on weekends and holidays. (Important: It's likely that your audience is comprised of people who live in different cities, regions, countries, continents and time zones ... keep this in mind as you plan your schedule.)

When preparing your social media calendar, be careful how you plan to allocate your time. Your social media activity, while important, can easily detract from other priorities. One helpful suggestion is to prepare several social media posts in advance. These posts can then be scheduled for release over an extended period of time on your Facebook, YouTube, Twitter, Instagram, Pinterest, LinkedIn and other social media platforms using a service such as Hootsuite.com, Buffer.com, Postplanner.com, or Sproutsocial.com.

Many of these services also provide additional tools designed to help you better manage your social network activity, engage your audiences, identify trending topics by audience and keyword, measure the results of your social media activity to determine which posts (and which type of posts) perform best.

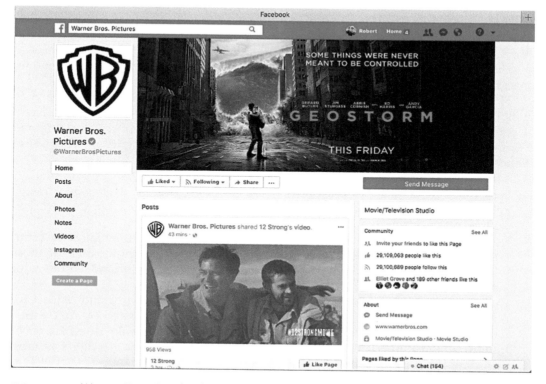

FIGURE 10.1 Warner Bros. Facebook page.

(Warner Bros. and Facebook; Editorial/Fair Use)

MICROBLOGGING & FACEBOOK

Of the many various types of social media activity, microblogging on platforms such as Facebook, Twitter and LinkedIn is now the most popular form of social engagement. Posts on these platforms are commonly comprised of short sentence fragments and links to or attachments of videos, images and websites. And, because microblog posts consist of quickly digestible content, filmmakers find that it is far easier to interact and engage with their audience in real time.

Given their significant popularity and the immediacy of engagement, microblogs provide filmmakers access to large populations of existing and potential friends, fans and audience members. Of all microblogging channels, Facebook has the largest number of monthly users (~2 billion) and incorporates the greatest variety of content. As a result, filmmakers are able to create rich social experiences, build lasting relationships and provide their friends and fans with exclusive information, updates, events, promotions and contests.

When establishing their accounts, Facebook users may create a personal "profile" and establish "pages" for their studios and films. In most respects, the nature of profiles and pages are quite similar. However, organizational pages do offer certain benefits for a filmmaker's studios and films over personal profiles. These benefits include the use of Facebook tabs, apps and offers that allow you to add a button on your page for visitors and fans to purchase or rent your film (use "create offer" to provide a promotional discount), contact you, register or subscribe for exclusive updates, create and promote an event, watch an introductory "about you" video or download a promotional app or game.

Facebook pages also allow you an unlimited number of fans (pages are limited to 5,000 friends), provide search engine optimization by being indexed by Google and other search engines, access to Facebook advertising and other promotional services (e.g. promoted and boosted posts) and they allow you to "pin" particularly important posts to the top of your wall.

Having set up your accounts, before you begin posting, I'd recommend that you first build out your list of friends and fans. The greater number of readers and viewers of your posts, the more impact your posts are likely to have on your marketing and promotional efforts. A few of the most effective ways to quickly build out your list of friends, fans and followers include:

1. Send friend requests to your existing network, including your family, personal friends and anyone you may have met attending film school and workshops, or worked with as cast or crew members of past films.
2. Selectively send friend requests to filmmakers and others you may know by reputation but have yet to meet personally . . . in particular, you're looking for those who are well-connected within the world of independent film and within your genre.
3. Examine the friend or fan list of those who have accepted your friend request for other people and organizations who you'd like to reach out to and connect with.
4. Participate in several Facebook interest groups. There are literally dozens – if not hundreds – of film-related Facebook groups. I've participated in several groups, including those focused on low-budget filmmaking, distribution, practical effects, visual effects, film school specific groups (USC, UCLA, AFI, etc.), state and regional filmmaking groups, film festivals and cast and crew "call" groups among others.

As your friend list grows into the hundreds (and, perhaps, thousands), you'll begin to receive requests from other people who want to add you to their list of friends. Likewise, as your friend lists expands, more people will begin to discover, like and fan your studio and film Facebook pages.

To manage the increasing number of friends, pages, profiles and groups with which you engage, consider creating one or more Facebook "lists" to sort and categorize people, organizations, brands, groups and others into similar groups. Facebook creates a type of newsfeed for each of these lists, which simplifies following the posts and discussions of certain groups of people and conversations. You can also subscribe to the lists of other users.

Once you've built out a list of a hundred or so friends (which you should be able to do relatively easily within twenty-four to forty-eight hours if you follow the approach outlined above), it's time to begin posting and engaging with your audience.

Your posts will appear on your profile or page's wall (the main section of your profile or page's home page) and will be published on the newsfeeds of your friends and fans. Unfortunately, like other microblogging platforms, once posted, the popularity of your Facebook posts will quickly decline as they compete with more recently published posts from other Facebook profiles and pages. As these new posts are published in the newsfeeds of your friends and fans, your earlier posts will appear lower and lower in their feeds until they effectively disappear from view.

As a result, Facebook posts must capture attention and encourage immediate engagement. To create posts that accomplish these goals, you should incorporate many – if not each – of the following guidelines:

1. Include an attention-getting image or video thumbnail. These images should be brand-appropriate, reflect the topic of the post and be visually interesting to maximize engagement. As you select and edit your images for posting, it's helpful to keep in mind that Facebook desktop newsfeed images appear at 470 × 245 pixels while images on mobile newsfeed: 560 × 292 pixels.

2. Limit your post to fifty words (200 characters) or fewer. Shorter posts receive significantly more likes, shares and comments. Why? Briefer content is far more inviting, easily consumed, integrates better across multiple social media platforms and is often quicker and easier to create.

3. Post during non-peak times. Because your posts compete with the posts of others, you want to avoid posting content during peak times. This means releasing content on Saturdays, Sundays and weekday evenings. These non-peak posting hours maximize the number of the newsfeeds to which your updates are posted and your posts' visibility.

4. Post on an established schedule. The general consensus among internet marketers is that five to ten posts per week (one to four times per day) posted during non-peak times is ideal. Not surprisingly: the more often you post, particularly at times when your content competes with fewer posts from others, the more likely your friends, fans and followers are to notice and engage with your posts.

5. Include a call-to-action. While post readership is valuable unto itself, the value of your post and readership is increased when you include a call-to-action that drives readers to like, share, comment, friend or fan, click on a URL, subscribe to your mailing list, attend an event, take advantage of a promotional offer, enter a contest or sweepstakes, rent or purchase your film or other action.

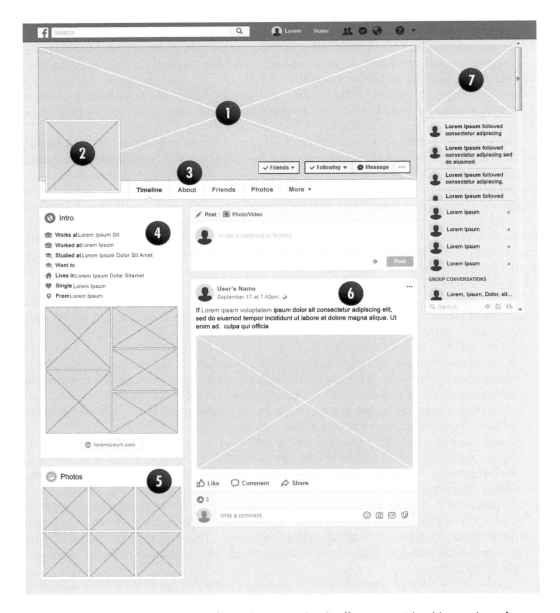

FIGURE 10.2 While familiar to most filmmakers, Facebook offers a considerable number of opportunities to optimize Pages and Profiles. These include (1) the banner; (2) portrait; (3) details contained within the "About" section; (4) intro; (5) photographs and videos; (6) timeline/wall, which contains the user's posts as well as PPC and banner ads; and (7) right-hand column containing PPC and banner ads as well as list of contacts and other details.

(Robert G. Barnwell/Sandy O. Cagnan)

6. Include a link. Links can allow readers to learn more about the topic of a specific post, access or download alternative content media or formats, or better enable readers to complete any call-to-action contained within the post.
7. Optimize your page posts with a paid "boost" to increase reach. From time to time, particularly for posts that may be exceptionally interesting or of promotional value, pay to "boost" a post. Boosting increases your posts' visibility within the newsfeeds of highly targeted fans and friends of fans within certain demographics or geographic locations. In addition to their effectiveness, page post boosts are currently the least expensive form of marketing Facebook offers.

In addition to these suggestions, you'll find that your posts have greater newsfeed visibility when the Facebook algorithm determines that your friends, fans and followers are actively engaged with your content. Facebook continually scans the engagement of individual users to improve and prioritize the types of posts and content provided in their newsfeeds. Naturally, an individual's past history of engagement is one of the best determinants of the type of content they'll most enjoy in the future.

If you follow the guidelines provided earlier, you should see a significant improvement in visibility and engagement. However, you should also develop a habit of interacting with their audience. Begin by reading, liking, commenting and sharing the content of your friends, fans and followers. Respond and thank them for their comments. Communicate with them directly via Facebook Messages and Chat. Again, the more you engage with your audience, the more they will engage with you. And, the more they engage with you, the better the placement and visibility Facebook will provide your posts within their newsfeeds.

To make sure your Facebook activity is achieving your engagement and business objectives, it's important to regularly analyze the performance of your Facebook profile and page activity. For pages, Facebook provides the Page Insights tool to let you know what type of content your audience likes best and which segments of your audience are most engaged. Page Insights details your activity's likes, audience reach and relative engagement. Page Insights also provides information regarding your audience's age, gender and geographic location.

Unfortunately, Facebook doesn't provide an equally useful analytical tool for personal profiles. Fortunately, by consistently monitoring the number or likes, comments, shares and friends your personal profile and posts receive, you'll be able to determine the relative success of your Facebook activity and identify areas for potential improvement. Alternatively, filmmakers can also use one or more non-affiliated Facebook services (Wolfram Alpha and Sproutsocial.com are two such services) to analyze their personal profiles and their profile's performance in greater detail.

VIDEO MARKETING (YOUTUBE AND VIMEO)

As we enter the second decade of the new millennium, video now represents half of all web traffic. And social media posts that include video tend to receive more views, likes, votes, comments and shares. Like independent filmmaking itself, the explosion in the popularity of video-based social media content is a reflection of video's superior entertainment attributes as well as a combination of global technological advancements, including the popularity (and quality) of inexpensive HD cameras, video editing software and high-speed internet access.

While almost every country and language has its own social videosharing sites, globally, video marketing is dominated by two platforms: YouTube and Vimeo. And, the larger each site has become, the more its popularity has attracted new users to the platform.

YouTube's community is comprised of more than 1.5 billion users who collectively watch hundreds of millions of hours of content a day. On an individual basis, the average YouTube visitor watches thirty minutes of videos each and every day. As a result, YouTube has become the world's second largest search engine (after its parent, Google) with more than 3 billion searches per month. With its large size and numerous marketing and promotional opportunities, YouTube offers filmmakers unparalleled audience access. And, since YouTube is owned by Google, YouTube videos receive favorable search result placement.

Unfortunately, YouTube's large size makes competition among videos and channels quite intense. In contrast to YouTube, the second largest video platform, Vimeo, has a much smaller community, with 45 million registered users and 250 million monthly viewers. However, despite its smaller size, a large percentage of Vimeo's community is comprised of creative professionals (such as filmmakers and other visual artists). As a result, video content on Vimeo is generally of higher production value and its users tend to be more active and engaged than users of competing video platforms.

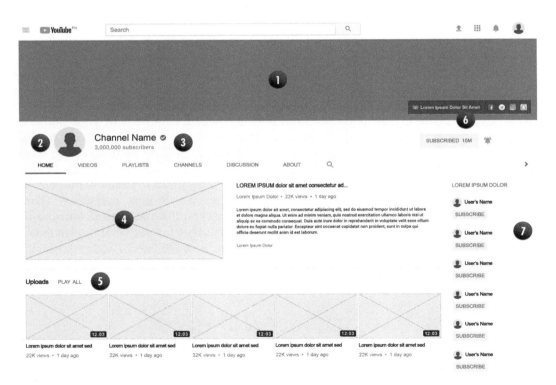

FIGURE 10.3 As with other social media platforms, YouTube offers several opportunities to optimize channels. These opportunities include: (1) the channel banner; (2) channel icon; (3) channel name; (4) introductory or welcome video; and (5) customizable playlist sections and also details on (6) the total number of channel subscribers and (7) related video channels.

(Robert G. Barnwell/Sandy O. Cagnan)

Additionally, Vimeo offers password protection options that allow filmmakers to upload private screeners for media professionals, distributors and other industry professionals.

Vimeo's smaller niche audience, however, is somewhat of a double-edged sword. On the one hand: Vimeo's smaller community and the nature of its niche audience result in an audience that is easier to reach and which is generally more engaged. On the other hand: outside of creative professionals, you'll likely find that few of your film's targeted audience members are active Vimeo users. With fewer targeted audience members – combined with the relative lack of promotional opportunities when compared with YouTube – Vimeo is less effective as a marketing and promotional platform.

Despite the popularity and longer lifespan of video content on platforms such as YouTube and Vimeo, videos require more time and effort to plan, record, edit and release than most other forms of social media content. More disconcerting is that much of this time and effort may be wasted on the majority of viewers. Research studies suggest that, on average, more than half of all viewers abandon videos within their first sixty seconds.

In order to achieve the many benefits available to video marketers – while managing the additional time demands and high abandonment rates – filmmakers should carefully consider (1) the topics of the videos posted to their channel, (2) the length or duration of their individual videos, (3) the structure and elements contained within each video, (4) the details provided and features enabled during the video upload process and (5) the release schedule.

1. Topics of Videos Posted to Your Channel

The topics of the first half dozen or so videos you post to your channel will have a large impact on establishing viewer expectations and momentum for your video marketing activities. As a result, these initial videos should include (i) demo reels, (ii) teasers and trailers, (iii) film clips, (iv) behind-the-scenes videos (including interviews with cast and crew members and coverage of exciting stunts, visual effects and interesting wardrobe, props and locations) and (iv) events such as test screenings, film festivals and premiers (don't forget to record quotes and reactions from audience members).

Once these videos are posted, the topics of additional videos should be a reflection of your target market (both potential audience members and industry professionals), your brand and the brand of your films and studio, and your marketing and promotional objectives.

However, regardless of the specific topics you eventually choose, as always, provide viewers with the opportunity to get to know you. Post videos of you on vacation, moving into a new home or apartment or new office or studio space, and introduce viewers to your new car, computer, filmmaking gear, pet, day job or new relationship (depending on just how much personal life you are comfortable sharing or feel is appropriate).

In addition to these videos, many filmmakers and video personalities have begun posting channel trailers. A well-crafted channel trailer should explain more about you, your studio and your films and why viewers should subscribe to your channel. Include clips from your past films and explain your path as a filmmaker . . . where you've been and where you're headed. Don't forget to include shots of you on set, behind the camera and consulting with cast and crew members. At the end of the channel trailer remember to invite viewers to subscribe to your channel.

2. Duration of Individual Videos

As mentioned, video content suffers a significant abandonment rate during the video's first few minutes. At the same time, online viewing habits show a clear preference for quick and easily digestible content. As a result, filmmakers should focus 80–90% of their channel's video library on those videos with run times ranging between one and three minutes.

To determine a more precise ideal running time for your videos, consider the following questions: *Which of your channel's videos receive the most views, likes and comments? What is the average length of these videos? What about the videos of competing studios or filmmakers? Where and under what circumstances are your videos being viewed? Are they being viewed on weekends when viewers have an abundance of available leisure time? Alternatively, are the videos being viewed during the work or school week when viewers are under increased time pressures? Are your videos being streamed and viewed on televisions, home computers, laptops, tablets, smart phones or other mobile devices? What is the purpose or objective of each video? What is the impact of these various considerations on the ideal length of video for you and your audience?*

Admittedly, there will be occasions, such as with "Making of . . ." documentaries and BTS interviews, when you may want to consider posting a few longer videos of five to fifteen minutes. However, even then there may be advantages in breaking some of these videos into smaller segments and publishing them within a subject-specific playlist. By dividing a single long-form video into a series of smaller videos, you will also benefit from an increased number of videos within your channel's library and, quite likely, increased viewership and engagement.

3. Standard Video Structure & Elements

While some videos, such as teasers, trailers and film clips, have their own format or structure, most successful videos on YouTube and Vimeo are structured more like episodic television than film. This means that most videos posted to a given channel will have standard title conventions, opening and closing credits, run time, music and sound effects and other branding and structural elements.

Begin with your channel's visual branding, titles and thematic bed music – all of which must remain relatively consistent across the majority of your channel's videos. In addition to establishing your visual and audio branding, it's important that the opening credits and introduction confirm that the video contains the content indicated within its title and description.

Once the opening title sequence and introduction are concluded, the video should quickly transition to the main content. While the fundamentals of filmmaking continue to apply to short-form videos, the episodic nature, limited duration of such videos and the small screens on which they are likely to be viewed create their own demands and constraints. This means that the videos should:

1. Remain consistent in terms of organizational structure as well as topics, wardrobe, locations and branding elements.
2. Emphasize a steady tripod-mounted medium and close-up shots (minimize or avoid handheld shots).
3. Include the use of lower-thirds, voice-over narration and on-screen text (such as bullets and pull-quotes overlays) to quickly convey and reinforce important points presented within the video.

4. Include a call-to-action during both the video's first and final thirty seconds. To increase the likelihood that viewers will complete your call-to-action, use YouTube annotations to add layered text and hotlink overlays within your videos.

During the conclusion of the video, thank viewers for watching, let them know what to expect in the next video and invite them to like, favorite, share, comment or subscribe to your channel. As with the beginning, the video should end with the channel's standard branding elements and theme music as well as outro-graphics (which should include addresses to your website and other social media accounts).

4. Video Upload Details & Enabled Features

Not to be confused with the registration details you provided when registering your channel, every time you upload a video to YouTube you'll need to provide such details as the video's title, a brief description of the video (be sure to include hotlilnked URLs to your website and other social media channels, email address and other contact details) and keyword tags appropriate to the video's topic, and you will need to select an appropriate category and video thumbnail.

You'll also have the opportunity to enable or disable certain YouTube features. For instance, for most – if not all – of your videos, you'll want to enable public viewing, comments, comment voting, video responses, ratings, syndication (which permits viewing on mobile devices and enabled televisions) and embedding.

Note: A significant percentage of YouTube and Vimeo videos are embedded and viewed on other social media sites . . . and within online articles, forums, websites, etc. By enabling the embedding option, you allow others to spread your content to their own website viewers, social media friends and fans and video channel subscribers – providing your videos with more views and your viewers with greater access across multiple platforms. Likewise, embedding videos on your own websites and blog posts further increases your video viewers and subscribers while also improving organic page results within search engines such as Google.

As you complete the video upload process, consider using an automated tool such as Speechpad.com to transcribe your videos and provide closed captions. By enabling the closed caption feature and uploading a transcript that includes relevant keywords (and correspondingly disabling YouTube's automatic transcription tool), your search engine rankings are vastly improved . . . thereby increasing visits and views of both your video and channel.

In addition to search engine rankings, YouTube uses the keywords contained within your video's titles, descriptions and tags to recommend your video to users who watch similar content. These recommended videos are entitled "Suggested Videos" and appear on the right side of the screen. YouTube's suggested videos typically include content from a number of different channels and, unfortunately, often serve to draw viewers away from your channel and videos. There are two solutions:

1. First, you can simply deselect "Suggested Videos" so that viewers are not encouraged to leave your channel for competing videos or channels.
2. Second, you can include one or two nonsense words (such as "zifflitis," "filmitia" or "psyfilm") in all of your video tags. Your videos will continue to be showcased within other users' suggested videos based on common keywords and tags. However, your videos will dominate the suggested videos alongside your own videos which all share the common nonsense word(s).

You should also consider grouping your related videos into playlists (using unique titles, descriptions and tags). When videos are included within a playlist, YouTube highlights the other videos contained within your playlist within "Suggested Videos" and automatically plays each successive playlist video... improving the likelihood that viewers will continue watching your videos rather than clicking away to competing videos and channels.

5. Video Release Schedule

Plan on launching your channel with five to ten videos and then release new videos individually on a regular basis . . . perhaps once or twice a month. Whatever you decide, select a routine publishing schedule and let your viewers know what days of the month they can expect new releases (if they subscribe to your channel, YouTube will notify them whenever you post a new video).

In addition to strengthening fan relationships, frequently publishing newer videos provides your videos and your channel with more favorable placement within the YouTube and Google search results. Newer videos also receive higher-priority placement within YouTube's suggested and related video sections.

However, unlike other social media platforms such as microblogs, specific release dates (days of the week and time of day) are less of a concern. Rather than discovering your video as a result of a newsfeed such as that on Facebook or Twitter, those who find and view your videos on YouTube will likely do so as a result of either a specific search or from an update resulting from having subscribed to your channel.

If you read and follow these recommendations, your YouTube and video marketing results will be better than those of the vast majority of other independent filmmakers and low-budget films within your genre. However, to increase the performance of your video marketing even further, it's necessary to continually monitor the performance of your videos and channel using YouTube Analytics.

For instance, YouTube Analytic's "Views Report" provides insight into the overall performance of your YouTube channel as well as individual videos. Among other details and datapoints, the views report lets you know:

1. How many people clicked play on your videos (each click is known as a "view" whether or not the viewer watched the entire video).
2. The total cumulative minutes that all viewers have viewed your videos and/or specific videos.
3. Average view duration: Are people watching the entire video or are they clicking away (and, if so, at which point are they clicking away)?
4. The gender and geographic locations of your viewers.
5. The sites on which your videos are being viewed (whether that be YouTube or other sites on which your videos may be embedded).
6. Traffic sources: Are your viewers discovering your videos on search engines? Referred by other websites or social media platforms? Pay-per-click ("PPC") campaigns? Or from YouTube itself (either through searches, playlists, suggested videos or channel pages)?
7. Viewing devices: YouTube Analytics can let you know how many of your views are being watched on computers, mobile phones, tablets, gaming consoles and other devices.

Maximizing the number of views is just one part – albeit an important part – of building a successful YouTube Channel. You'll also want to be mindful of the type

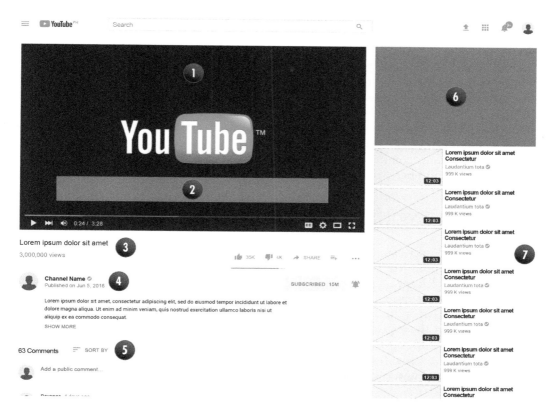

FIGURE 10.4 As with the YouTube channel, each of YouTube's video pages also offers a number of optimization and promotional opportunities. These include (1) the video thumbnail; (2) pay-per-click overlays; (3) video title; (4) channel name and video description; (5) viewer and subscriber comments; (6) advertising and pay-per-click banners; and (7) recommended videos. Note that, in addition to overlays and banners, YouTube advertising and/or pay-per-click promotion can also appear as short video commercials and within the user's video search results.

(Robert G. Barnwell/Sandy O. Cagnan)

of engagement your videos are generating– both positively and negatively. YouTube tracks and analyzes this data within its "Engagement Report," which provides such details as:

1. The number of people who have subscribed and unsubscribed
2. The number of likes and dislikes
3. The number of comments that each video receives
4. The number of video shares
5. Details on the click-through and close rates for any annotation or calls-to-action you've added to your videos.

In addition to views and engagement reports, YouTube allows you to analyze the data in graph form to better compare your channel's and video's performance. The graphs include line, pie, bar and bubble charts that can compare up to twenty-five different datapoints. Charts can be displayed with datapoints in daily, weekly or monthly increments. Similarly, YouTube also allows users to view and analyze performance using interactive maps. By hovering the mouse over certain countries, YouTube displays detailed data for viewers from that specific nation.

As you seek for incremental improvement, pay particular attention to those factors that YouTube's algorithm uses to rank videos within its search and recommended video listings. These factors includes such elements as: keywords, tags, title, description, thumbnails, transcript, channel authority (total channel views, subscribers, etc.), video views, video retention (i.e. bounce rate), average time on channel, community activity (number of shares, favorites, comments, etc.), number and ratio of video thumbs up to thumbs down, and the number of back links to the video.

OPTIMIZING YOUR SOCIAL MEDIA ACCOUNTS

To a greater or lesser extent, every popular social media platform provides its users the opportunity to optimize their accounts and, often, posted content. In addition to the benefits to the account owner, such optimization makes it easier for other users to find the content and accounts that they are likely to find most appealing.

The first step in optimizing your accounts is to take full advantage of the opportunities provided within the registration and administration pages. Some of the most obvious opportunities include optimizing (i) the name of your account, (ii) the account description, (iii) registration details, (iv) individualized account design elements and (v) the title of your posts, videos and other content.

Channel or Account Name

Ideally, the name of your social media accounts will each be the same as your website URL and IMDb vanity URL extension. If you intend to maintain separate social media accounts for your studio and film titles, the name of these social media accounts should likewise be the same as their website and IMDb URLs.

If these social media account names are unavailable, consider adding a descriptive word such as "studio," "productions" or "movie." Alternatively, you may be able include a significant keyword or keyword combination as a part of the account name.

However, regardless of what name you eventually select, account names should be uniform across social media platforms and be brief ... ideally, twenty characters or fewer.

Channel or Account Description

Your account will also provide an opportunity to post a description of you and your account. In the majority of cases, the description will be closely based on the professional biography, studio, or film summaries created for your website, IMDb profile and other marketing materials.

However, one important difference from your standard bio and summaries is the need to provide readers some detail on the types of subjects and content that they can expect from your account or channel. While not necessary, you may also want to consider providing a general idea of how frequently – or infrequently – you intend to post content.

Another important difference is the necessity of including links to your websites, IMDb profiles and other social media platforms or accounts you may use within the description. These links serve as a vital source of new websites visits, friends, fans and subscribers. Recently, as noted above, many filmmakers have also been uploading or embedding a welcome video that serves as a type of trailer for the account. In addition to providing an overview of what visitors can expect from your social media account, the welcome video's end credits, like your account description, contain addresses to your websites and other social media accounts.

As you draft your social media description, be conscious of the fact that there is often a word or character limit to the length of your description. For instance, YouTube's channel description offers a generous 5,000 character limit (~800 words). However, whatever the limit, only the first two sentences will likely be featured prominently on search engine results and social media platform specific searches. This means that you must carefully consider not only what to include within your description but also where in your description you decide to include certain higher-priority information.

Registration Details

Beyond the standard professional, studio and film summaries included within account descriptions, many social media platforms, including Facebook, encourage users to post other details about themselves. These include details on your past work and educational experience, the places you've lived and worked, the names of family members and other relationships, important life events and personal details such as contact information, birthday, political and religious affiliation, relationship status, etc. Among other benefits, these additional details help people form a more personal connection with you and your filmmaking.

While not every social media platform has a dedicated registration space for keyword tags, you can often add a list of ten to fifteen unique keywords and key phrases to the bottom of your profile or channel description. In addition to making it easier for users to locate your account and content, keyword and key phrase tags help the platform to better recommend your posts to readers or viewers of related content. (FYI: It's not necessary to tag your name or the name of your studio or films as these will often appear throughout the remainder of your account profile, registration details and content posts.)

In addition to keyword tags, many platforms (such as YouTube) allow you to identify and list accounts or channels similar to your own. The social media site's administrators, in turn, will use this list to recommend and refer visitors, fans, followers and subscribers of those channels to your own account or channel.

Before completing your registration details, double-check that type of account you've selected (particularly in the case of Facebook) is appropriate. Is this a personal account or an organizational account? Likewise, most social media platforms also provide an opportunity to further categorize your account by interest or type such as entertainment, film, television, etc. If you select film as your category, YouTube also allows you to list the genre of your film, including action and adventure, comedy, crime, fantasy, horror, independent, mystery and suspense, thrillers, etc.

Design Elements

Recognizing the increasing role of social media to many companies and organizations, most social media platforms allow you to customize your account to create a strong brand image using design themes, background colors, photos and similar design elements.

One of the first things visitors to your account will see is your banner picture and avatar image. The banner image is the large image that typically appears at the top of your account's home page. Facebook refers to the banner as the "Cover Picture" while YouTube refers to it as "Channel Art." For your personal accounts, choose an image that strikes a balance between personal and professional. For studio-specific or film-specific accounts, use images that incorporate your studio logo and key art as appropriate.

In contrast, your account's avatar – which Facebook refers to as the "Profile Picture" and YouTube refers to as the "Channel Icon" – is a smaller image that appears next to your individual posts. While it's important to consider how both your banner image and avatar will appear on smaller screens of laptop computers, tablets and cell phones, this is a particular concern with regard to avatar images. On YouTube it may appear in as few as 98 × 98 pixels, while on Facebook your avatar may be displayed as small as 32 × 32 pixels.

Obviously, with such limited screen space, whatever photos or graphics are used must be easily recognizable and able to sufficiently communicate your brand without the detail afforded by larger images. Not surprisingly, key art and other graphics that contain a combination of images and words rarely work well. Instead, consider using your studio logo or a close-up portrait photo as your avatar. If you struggle for ideas or images, consider working with a graphic designer to have layouts prepared for each of your social media accounts so that they reflect a consistent design across platforms and, in particular, with your website.

Finally, many social media platforms now allow you to upload "skins" that effectively serve to customize the user's entire home page. Among other design elements, skins commonly include customer banners and avatars, background colors, button and text colors (and fonts), and other header, footer and side column elements. Unfortunately, several social media platforms limit the use of skins to organizations and higher-fee accounts.

Title of Posts, Videos or Other Content

Particularly in the case of videos, it's critical that you write creative, compelling and informative content titles. A well-written title should describe the content of your post or video by incorporating (i) keywords and key phrases, (ii) a promise (*"Learn More About . . . ," "How to . . . ,"* etc.), (iii) specificity (numbers and time such as a Top 10 list) and/or (iv) the identity of the target audience (filmmakers, horror fans, etc.).

For microblog posts, consider the first five words of the post . . . in many ways, the first few words serve as the title of the post. In fact, consider publishing the first two to five words in all caps to draw additional attention to your posts.

Filmmakers and other internet marketers have found a number of titles and words that consistently generate increased views and engagement. Some of these words and phrases include: *top 10, review, testimonial, secrets, tips, tricks, how to, DIY*, etc. Descriptive words and phrases such as *most popular, best, new, recently released, coming soon, exclusive, highly rated* and *award winning* have also proven popular.

As you consider the topic, description and titles of your content, never underestimate the level of fan interest in learning more about the magic of filmmaking and seeing what goes on behind the scenes. Notice that many of these popular title words and phrases (such as *secrets, tricks, how to* and *DIY*) provide a direct or implied promise to reveal a little of that filmmaking magic.

Regardless of the title you choose, restrict it to sixty-five characters or fewer so that the title won't be clipped – or "truncated" – within the search engine or social media platform's search results.

GETTING MORE VIEWS, LIKES, COMMENTS, SHARES, FRIENDS, FANS & SUBSCRIBERS

Ultimately, the quality of your social media engagement is far more important than the quantity of engagement. On the other hand, the more people discover and interact with your social media content, the more effective your branding, marketing and promotional activities are likely to be. Fortunately, there are five relatively simple methods that have proven particularly useful in increasing the engagement of your social media content.

The first and easiest way to get more views, likes, comments, shares, friends, fans and subscribers is to simply post attention-getting content that people enjoy. And, the more you know your audience and the types of content they are already consuming and posting themselves, the better the quality your own content should become. (Hint: If haven't done so already, go back and answer the questions posed within the second step of social media strategy development, "Know Your Audience.")

At the risk of stating the obvious (yet again), the second method is to simply ask for engagement. Encourage your visitors to like, share, friend, fan, subscribe and to leave reviews and comments. Begin by asking those who already know and like you (family, friends, fans, cast and crew members and audience members) to kindly post favorable initial ratings, reviews and comments. These first favorable ratings, reviews and feedback will establish a powerful tone for successive comments. Again, be sure to put your best foot forward by soliciting favorable comments from those who already enjoy and respect your work as a filmmaker.

The third method is to model the behavior you are seeking. This is something we've discussed before and is just another way of saying that if you want people to view, like, share, friend, fan, subscribe, review and comment, you often need to first comment, engage and interact directly with them, their posts and their accounts. In other words: The more you engage with your audience, the more likely they are to engage with you.

Use services such as Hootsuite, Buffer and Google Alerts to monitor and reply to anyone who has recently shared your content or mentioned you in social media or elsewhere online. And be sure to respond and thank those who have left responses, comments or posted messages to any of your posts or accounts.

The fourth method is to pursue opportunities to increase your reach. Not surprisingly, the more people who come into contact with you and your content, the more views, likes, comments, shares, friends, fans and subscribers you are likely to have.

Some of the most popular methods of extending your reach and visibility include: (i) cross promotion with other filmmakers, studios or influencers who have similar audiences to your own; (ii) making guest appearances on popular video channels, podcasts and "vidcasts"; (iii) joining film and genre-related social media groups; and (iv) leaving track-back links (contact details and hotlinks to your website, IMDb profile and/or social media accounts) within your online comments, reviews, email signatures and other marketing and promotional materials.

If you've not done so already, use plug-ins such as Social Media Feather, Ultimate Social Media and Share Icons, and Sociable to add social media sharing, follow and like buttons to your websites (website plug-ins are discussed in more detail within Chapter 11, Dedicated Film & Filmmaker Websites). Similarly, look for opportunities to include hotlinks and social media buttons throughout your social media profiles, email signatures, IMDb profiles and other online and offline marketing and promotional materials.

Next make sure that you announce or share important content posted on one platform with the friends, fans and subscribers on your other social media platforms. Distribution services are able to automatically and simultaneously distribute video and other content across multiple social media channels. At the same time, consider sending an email to announce new videos or other important content to your email database and encourage your cast, crew, friends and family to do the same (as well as with their own social media friends, fans and subscribers).

And fifth, consider using pay-per-click ("PPC") to expand your reach. Many social media platforms, including both Facebook and YouTube (through Google AdWords), allow you to run PPC ads that only charge a fee if and when someone clicks a hotlink embedded within the ad or views the video. One of the key advantages of PPC advertising is that advertisers can control who sees the ad by targeting their audience using such factors as: keywords and phrase, viewing history (related content), location, language, age, gender, income, education, political affiliation, entertainment interests and those who are fans, friends or subscribers of similar or competing pages, profiles or channels (depending upon the specific social media PPC platform). Advertisers can also set account spending limits that establish a bid amount per click and a limit on daily and total spending.

To maximize the performance of your PPC campaigns, each advertisement should have a clear objective, a strong call-to-action with a compelling offer, an attractive image and be targeted to a carefully defined audience. Results can be further improved by employing multiple ads targeted at different audiences and rotating these ads every one to two weeks. Facebook and YouTube also offer comprehensive analytics to help you monitor the performance of your ads and campaigns so that you can quickly revise them as needed.

Warning: Never buy views, likes, comments or subscribers. Purchasing views or other forms of engagement (likes, ratings, reviews, comments, etc.) is a violation of the terms of service of every major social media platform. Break this rule and there's a very good chance you'll find that the platform's administrators ban your account.

Three of the common themes of this chapter, the book and the entire branding, marketing and promotional process are the importance of (i) knowing your audience and (ii) continually revising and improving your marketing and promotional activities based upon (iii) regular monitoring and assessment of the performance of your marketing activities using the analytic tools provided by each social media platform as well as services such as Google Social Reports within Google Analytics, Brand24, Brandwatch, Social Mention and Klout.

However, assuming you've committed to the first two (knowing your audience and ongoing improvement) as you analyze the performance of your social media strategy, don't get too hung up on the absolute numbers of your views, likes, shares, fans, friends and subscribers – particularly during the beginning of your social media campaign. Instead, focus on your activity . . . the number, frequency and quality of your posted content and audience engagement.

- *Do the numbers suggest that your social media activity and performance are better or worse than last week, last month or last year? How much better or worse are they?*

- *On an absolute, relative and directional basis, how do the numbers compare to other independent filmmakers and studios?*
- *What is the impact of your social media activity? Have you added important new members to your professional network or audience? Increased the rate of film or merchandise sales or rentals? Secured new opportunities, projects or investors?*
- *How can you improve the performance and impact of your social media campaign? Are you encouraging readers and viewers to visit your website? To subscribe to your email database? To purchase or rent your film on its premier date? Are your friends and fans engaged? Sharing your content? Commenting on your posts?*

Again, social media is fundamentally about relationships and your ability to create highly customized and personalized experiences for your friends, fans, followers and subscribers. Over time, as your social media engagement expands and improves, social media will become the most efficient and effective way to establish and manage relationships with your audience.

11

DEDICATED FILM & FILMMAKER WEBSITES

A filmmaker's website and social media activity are increasingly vital in achieving long-term success within the film industry. Your website – or websites – can differentiate you from competing filmmakers while assisting in the promotion and distribution of your films and merchandise directly to fans.

Reflecting the marketing efficiency and effectiveness of websites, many filmmakers choose to develop two categories of sites: (i) a filmmaker- and/or studio-specific site focused on content of interest to investors and other industry professionals; and (ii) official film sites for each of the filmmaker's – or studio's – films that have been designed and developed primarily for the benefit of audience members, media professionals, sales agents and distributors.

Admittedly a single all-encompassing site is far easier and faster to both launch and manage. However, combining a filmmaker- or studio-specific site with individual film-specific sites results in an online marketing campaign with more focus and impact on specific audiences (and objectives) than a single site.

Regardless of whether you choose one or multiple sites, your websites should serve as the hub of your branding, marketing and promotional activities. Ideally, providing visitors with insights both into you and your production studio, your film projects and the many talented filmmakers, cast and crew members with whom you've worked on past projects. Many websites also feature password-protected areas for confidential material for investors as well as cast and crew members.

Despite the many benefits of official film websites, major studios are increasingly dismissive of the value of official websites. Katie Kahn, Head of Digital Promotion at Paramount Pictures UK, explains, "Social media is where conversations naturally take place, while official websites require users to be driven to them. Official sites are a one-way conversation with film fans; social media is a dialogue" (Gray, 2014).

Unfortunately, this increasingly common view among the major studios ignore new web 2.0 and 3.0 functionality that effectively link social media and website communications into a network of interconnectivity and interactivity.

The studio's perspective on dedicated film websites (as opposed to studio websites) and social media activity also ignores the fact that studios don't, as a general rule, use social media to engage in interactive two-way discussions with fans. Instead, most studios use social media to blast marketing messages at their audiences.

For independent filmmakers and more enlightened studios, the inclusion of a dedicated movie website (with its own distinct URL) in a marketing campaign has provided fans with greater accessibility to material in two ways:

1. Websites are generally created weeks – and occasionally months – in advance of the film's theatrical premier. As a result, audience members and fans have access to information and content at a much earlier stage, well before many studios fund concerted poster and trailer campaigns.
2. Dedicated film websites provide fans with content that is rarely available otherwise, including: bonus materials such as downloadable screensavers and wallpaper backgrounds; behind-the-scenes pictures, footage, interviews and "Making of . . . " documentaries; online fan merchandise, pre-release ticket or VOD sales and rentals; contests and sweepstakes; and more.

Working together, your websites and social media activity are able to provide a variety of media-rich content that would be difficult to replicate on any one platform.

GETTING STARTED

To get started, first register the URLs (aka "domain names") for (i) your name, (ii) the name of your studio and (iii) each of your past, current and future film projects. (With regard to future film projects, check the availability of URLs for movie titles of films you have in development. If you can't get the URL for the film's working title, strongly consider other titles.)

Whenever possible, the domain names should be identical to your listings within IMDb. And, importantly, you'll want to get ".com" URLs (which are viewed as more credible). Remember: the URLs will appear on essentially all of your marketing materials (as well as your email addresses) – be certain that every URL is the best available.

Second, you'll want to select a host through which your websites will be accessed through the web host's computer servers. While I use and recommend Bluehost.com, there are several quality global providers including Arvixe, DreamHost and GoDaddy among many others.

Third, choose and upload a content management system (CMS) on which to base your website. While it can be tempting to build your website from scratch with your own CMS, it is far better to use existing open source platforms. The most popular, and one of the easiest to use, is WordPress; however, also consider the possible benefits of alternative CMS such as Drupal, Joomla and Magento (particularly for sites with e-commerce applications).

Regardless of your choice of CMS, each is easily set up and will provide essentially all of the functionality you're likely to need. In addition, each of these CMS options features numerous optional plug-ins that will increase the effectiveness of your online branding, marketing and promotional efforts.

STANFORD WEB CREDIBILITY GUIDELINES

Before proceeding to a discussion on website design and development, it's important to understand that the majority of websites suffer a bounce rate of 30–60% – meaning that a large number of website visitors will leave most websites without ever having navigated beyond the page on which they arrived.

According to various research studies, the majority of visitors will make their decision about whether or not to click away from your site within the first seven to ten seconds of their having arrived on the site. Alarmingly, some research suggests visitors form an initial opinion of your site in as little as fifty milliseconds. During those few seconds (or milliseconds), a visitor will quickly make assumptions about (i) the quality of the site and (ii) relevance to whatever they are searching.

Perhaps the most insightful and respected study into website credibility and retention was completed, and is regularly updated, by Stanford University's Persuasive Technology Lab (credibility.stanford.edu).

Here are some of the most important lessons from Stanford's findings as they apply to most websites, including those of filmmakers, movie studios and films:

Design your site so it looks professional and is appropriate for your purpose: People quickly evaluate a site based solely on visual design. Visitors have an expectation of what a site should look like reflecting its purpose. As a result, when designing your sites, pay particular attention to the layout, typography, images and content of other movie studio and film websites.

Make your site easy to use – and useful: Visitors expect sites to be easy to navigate and to be able to access the information they want with a minimum number of clicks. Many filmmakers forget to consider the visitor's perspective (WIIFM – "What's In It for Me?") and, instead, focus only on their own objectives. Without sufficient focus on the user and the site's ease of use, the site will suffer a high bounce rate and will witness few repeat visitors.

Use restraint with any promotional content (e.g. ads, offers): Users are annoyed when being subjected to numerous ads. Further, promotional content often competes or conflicts with the most important objectives of your site and individual web pages. The focus should always be concentrated on your films, studio and filmmaking.

Show that there's a real person or organization behind your site: Particularly within the world of independent film, fans want to get to know – and feel a sense of relationship with – the filmmakers responsible for the films they enjoy. Be sure to post first-person stories and photographs of you on set and at events with well-known actors and other filmmakers. Engage with friends and fans both online and offline

Highlight your expertise and the expertise of your cast and crew: A filmmaker's website should highlight a variety of "proof-points" when it comes to the film's and filmmaker's credibility. As we've discussed before, these proof-points can come from any number of sources, including: film schools or workshops you've attended, any film festivals or industry awards you or your films may have won, the name of other filmmakers and films on which you've worked, etc.

Update your site's content often (at least show it's been reviewed recently): People assign more credibility to websites that have been recently updated or reviewed. While visitors realize that dedicated movie websites are relatively static, visitors continue to expect that a filmmaker's and the filmmaker's studio website will be updated at least once or twice a month.

Avoid errors of all types, no matter how small they seem and make it easy to verify the accuracy of the information on your site: In addition to fact-checking and repairing broken links, pay particular attention to eliminating spelling, grammatical and other related mistakes. Such mistakes undermine the site's (and your) credibility and image.

Make it easy to contact you: The Stanford research reveals that a simple way to boost your site's credibility is by making your contact information clear and, in addition to a contact form, including a direct phone number, physical address and email address. While some filmmakers may be reluctant to provide such public information, most filmmakers find that their contact information is rarely abused.

CASE STUDY: B-REEL

Can you tell us a little more about B-Reel and how it was founded?

B-Reel was formed in 1999 in Stockholm, Sweden by five friends: Anders Wahlquist, Fredrik Heinig, Johannes Åhlund, Pelle Nilsson and Petter Westlund. From the beginning, B-Reel has worked across concept development and production – whether it's a digital product, a documentary film series or a brand platform, one team takes the project from idea to execution, in close partnership with our clients.

Today, we're proud to say that B-Reel has more than 170 designers, writers, producers and developers across six offices.

B-Reel served to design and develop Warner Brothers' and Alfonso Cuarón's Gravity website. What were the original objectives and expectations for the site?

As mentioned, Warner Bros. came to us with the exciting prospect of creating an online experience for Alfonso Cuarón's magnificent movie *Gravity*. We explored with the Studio and filmmakers what thoughts they had for the website, their marketing objectives, and closely examined the film, script and other creative content for inspiration.

continued . . .

More than anything else, Gravity is about being lost in the immensity of space. With that in mind, we decided the best way to complement the film was not to "gamify" the web experience, but rather to recreate the feeling of being utterly alone in the infinite.

We agreed on the idea of recreating the film's visceral feelings of panic and awe through an interactive exploratory experience. To do this, we needed to turn the user into the star of the experience, giving each visitor an insight into what it really feels like to float freely in the vastness of space.

While keeping in bounds of the film's marketing guidelines and working within a limited time table (we completed the site in only ten weeks), I'm immensely proud of the site and all that the B-Reel team accomplished in partnership with Warner and the filmmakers.

Amazingly, the production value responsible for the film's many Academy, BAFTA and Golden Globe awards appears to have been seamlessly carried over to the website.

Beautiful, clean, functional design was our goal with the site. We wanted the imagery and the environment to be the focus. While the biggest creative accomplishments with this site fall into a more technical category, the real beauty in the experience is a balance between performance, load time, pay-off and a realistic look and feel.

To do this, we created a space environment with the main locations from the movie like the ISS and the Hubble. The goal was for the user to feel as if they were space-walking from a first-person perspective, lost and alone in the vastness of space.

For that reason, we created a special feature we termed "Space Walk" which allowed visitors to navigate between the locations and featured sound design and camera moves to highlight moments of both fear and wonder.

Another cool viral tool we created to promote the film is the Helmet Cam. With Helmet Cam the user activates a camera in their EVA suit helmet that allows them to take photos from anywhere in the experience. This highlights the dynamic nature of our experience and creates endless unique pieces of content as each user captures their own perspective of space and shares with friends.

In creating the site and the experience of Space Walk, one of the greatest advantages in this project became one of our main challenges on the technical side: We were fortunate enough to receive the actual 3D models used in the film itself! Of course, that meant having to deal with the large number and crazy file size of the models.

An incredible amount of skill and time were required to recreate the beautiful imagery from the movie: post processing effects, free cameras, debris that looks like thousands of pieces made of merged chunks, and the realtime intro.

Based on your experience with Warner Brothers and other studios, what suggestions would you give to independent filmmakers when it comes to the design and development of their films' websites?

Regardless of whether or not the site is for a major studio or an independent film, the first step should always be to agree on the site's objectives and audience. This isn't always as straightforward as it might sound since a site's objectives and target audience tend to evolve over the various stages of the film's production.

For instance, during preproduction, filmmakers are unlikely to have teasers or trailers and will certainly not have production stills or film clips. Similarly, preproduction is too early to begin promoting ticket sales. In contrast, during post-production, the website should – at the very least – feature teasers, trailers, behind-the-scenes content, film stills and clips, and a downloadable electronic press kit. Some sites will include purchase or rental preorders and, perhaps, a digital clock counting down the days, hours and minutes until the film's release date.

If you consider the *Gravity* website, we were brought in to design and develop the site just prior to the film's theatrical release. As a result, the site's principal objectives were to drive ticket sales and media coverage . . . as well as to support the studio's industry award campaigns. And, since we were so close to release, we were blessed (and perhaps a little cursed) to have had a considerable amount of potential content assets from which to choose.

However, regardless of the stage of production, it's incredibly important that the site be an extension of the film itself in terms of its visuals, audio, interactivity and visitor experience.

WEBSITE DESIGN

As revealed within Stanford University's research, website visitors quickly assess the credibility and appropriateness of a website based upon its design. If the website doesn't look quite like what the visitor expects, there's a high probability that the visitor will immediately click away from the site.

Therefore, before considering final website designs, study the websites of the major and "mini-major" studios, websites for recently released major studio films and the websites of accomplished filmmakers such as Michael Bay, Werner Herzog, David Lynch and Oliver Stone.

As you become more familiar with the current design trends and standards for film-related websites, you should begin to form a written or mental list of the design attributes and types of content you'd like to include within your own site.

However, remember that your websites must integrate the design elements and "look" established by your other marketing channels and assets . . . leveraging similar colors, typestyles, layouts and images.

Page Layout

Website design is also a critical component of the website visitor's overall user experience (aka "UX"). The visitor's experience – either good or bad – largely reflects the usefulness, usability, navigability and accessibility of the website and its content.

Reflecting the critical significance of the overall user experience, UX is particularly important when planning web page and content layout. User experience considerations will largely determine how information is presented on the page and how naturally the visitor's eye moves across the page and its content.

As a reminder, most of the world's written languages are read from top to bottom and from left to right. Because of this, as confirmed by numerous eye tracking, heat mapping and click mapping studies, UX is improved when the layout follows the natural eye movement of the vast majority of website visitors.

These studies have also revealed – due primarily to these tendencies – that the most commonly viewed and clicked areas of a web page form an "F" or "E" pattern. The visitor's eye tracks along the top of the website first and scans the header navigation bar and page title from left to right. The visitor then continues viewing the site down left side of the page and moves to the right when presented with subtitles, subheads, listed items, bold, colored or italicized text, bullet-pointed text, images or other points of interest.

Since the left side of the website tends to receive the most attention, you need to be quite strategic about the content placed along the left side of the site. Do you want

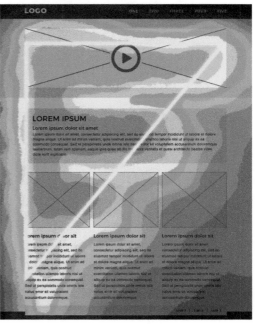

FIGURE 11.1 Heat maps track and visualize visitors' mouse or eye movement across a web page. Reflecting the reading patterns of most of the world's languages, visitors tend to view web pages from top to bottom and from left to right . . . forming an "F" or "E" pattern. As a result, website administrators should attempt to place the page's most important elements within these areas.

(Robert G. Barnwell/Sandy O. Cagnan)

to emphasize various calls-to-action? If so, then you should place a side column on the left side of the site with the wider primary content column to the right. Do you want to emphasize the primary content of each page? In that case, the side bar should be placed to the right side of the site pages.

Equally important, you need to be deliberate about those items that attract the eye from the left column to the right. We touched upon these items before: titles, subtitles, subheads, bullet-pointed text, images or other points of interest. Because visitors tend to "scan" rather than "read" pages, the ability to break up the text and add items of visual interest is essential. And, because of this tendency to scan, those items that draw the interest from the left side of the page should be carefully chosen to make the greatest impact on the site visitor.

With regard to layout and structure, other studies have revealed that (i) left-justified text tends to be easier to read and more visually interesting; (ii) a single primary content column is preferable to two or three columns; (iii) any side columns should be no larger than half the width of the primary content column; and (iv) headers (including logo, tagline, navigation or menu bar, search box, etc.) should be as small as possible to maximize available above-the-fold content (i.e. the content that can be viewed without having to scroll further down the screen).

Navigation

It's important that visitors be able to navigate your sites intuitively. Intuitive navigation incorporates website standards with which visitors are already well-familiar. In most cases this means providing the primary navigation in a horizontal menu bar along the top of the site. Secondary navigation options are commonly provided as drop-down menus beneath individual primary navigation items, within a sidebar and within the footer.

In addition to being intuitive, visitors should find the process of navigating the site and finding the pages in which they are most interested as simple as possible. This means limiting the navigation bar to five to seven items and limiting the drop-down menu selections to three to five for each primary navigation menu item. Simple navigation also means being able to access any page on the site within no more than three clicks – regardless of where you land on the website.

The ability to quickly access information with simple navigation requires that the total number of pages within a site be limited – often ranging from a static five to seven page site to as many as seventy-five pages. Unfortunately, any more pages and the site may quickly become cluttered, confusing and difficult to navigate.

Many sites also repeat the navigation menu within the site's footer to reduce the need for users to unnecessarily scroll to the top of the site. Footers are also a good location to include such information as copyright notices and privacy policies as well as links to related sites, social media, IMDb profiles and links to subscribe to email updates, register for upcoming events and to purchase or rent tickets or copies of your films.

Colors

When selecting colors for use within your websites, choose colors strategically. Proper color selection both maximizes site readability and reinforces your brand image.

Currently, website designers favor using a predominantly neutral color palette (whites, light grays and light tans) with small splashes of color for headlines, important editorial and graphic content, and to accentuate calls-to-action and branding. In addition to helping direct visitors to the site's most important content, this use of color projects an elegant, clean and more timeless appearance.

It is also important to use a color palette that complements your studio logo and your films' key art, and remains consistent with your other marketing materials.

Typography

The proper selection of fonts (and font sizes) enhances a site's readability and its visual interest. The accepted standard is to choose one typeface for headlines and subheadings and a different font for body copy.

Sans serif fonts (those without the little lines at the end of the strokes of characters and numbers) are particularly well-suited for titles, headings, subheadings and particularly small type (any type less than twelve pixels). In fact, almost two-thirds of websites use sans serif typefaces for both headlines and body copy, the most popular of which are Arial, Lucida Grande and Helvetica.

When selecting fonts and designing your site, there are some standards with regard to type that should be adhered to: With regard to font size, the accepted standards are that headlines should range in size from twenty-two to twenty-eight pixels, subheads should range between sixteen and twenty-four pixels, and body copy should range from twelve to sixteen pixels.

Depending upon the width and size of the body font's characters (numbers, letters, symbols and spaces), the number of characters per line should range from fifty-five to seventy-five which typically translates to an average of around fifteen words per line.

Finally, as with other design considerations, keep in mind that people will be viewing your website on a variety of desktop and mobile devices. Be certain to choose fonts that are easy to read across a variety of devices and web browsers.

Additional Design Tips

In addition to those design elements already discussed, the following are important website design and development considerations:

Eliminate Page Clutter: Make certain that pages don't have several competing calls-to-action or other visual clutter that would draw the visitor's eyes away from the most important parts of the page. Streamline each page and remove unrelated, duplicative or unnecessary editorial content, graphics, photographs, embedded videos, etc.

Embrace White Space: Web visitors consider white space more inviting, visually interesting, easier to navigate and less intimidating than a dense page of text. As a result, it's important to break up text and content with subheads, subtitles, bullet points and provide sufficient spacing between lines and paragraphs. By achieving a balance between white space and on-page content, the page layout is more likely to keep users focused and engaged with the site and its content.

Respect the Page Fold: While the admonishment to eliminate all scrolling is outdated, below the fold scrolling should be limited. A good rule of thumb is to have no more content below the fold than appears above the fold. If additional scrolling is required, consider breaking up the content into two pages or more. Also, remember to favor placement of the most important information and calls-to-action above the fold.

Design Every Page as a Landing Page: Most search engines rank and list websites by individual pages rather than by the site's home page. As a result, website visitors are just as likely – or may be more likely – to enter your website through a page other than the home page. Therefore, it's important to design each page so that the site's key information and important calls-to-action are properly highlighted on every page.

WEBSITE TEMPLATES VS CUSTOM-DEVELOPED SITES

Of the two alternatives (using a website template or having a site custom-developed), I highly suggest that you study – and consider purchasing – the site templates available from providers such as Templatemonster.com and Themeforest.com. In addition to providing additional design inspiration, you'll find that templates are – in almost all respects – superior to custom-developed sites.

Website templates provide Cascading Style Sheets (CSS) with consistent and complementary page layouts, typography and color schemes – all of which are highly customizable. The designers and developers have produced each template design to leverage and maximize user experience standards. Further, the templates have been tested and optimized to work for specific content management systems such as WordPress, Joomla, Drupal and Magento.

The highly customizable nature of site templates (and available plug-ins) presents a difficult argument for the considerable expense associated with custom sites. That said, major studios regularly spend tens and hundreds of thousands of dollars for custom websites that deliver exciting and dynamic visitor experiences. B-Reel's design and development of Warner Brothers' *Gravity* website is an excellent example of a custom site that could only be accomplished by a global team of highly talented animators, designers and developers.

Whether or not you decide to purchase a site template or choose to develop a custom site, the site must employ a "responsive" design. Responsive design technology automatically adapts and optimizes the site to the browser size of whatever device is being used by the website visitor (whether that be desktop, internet-enabled television, laptop, tablet or other mobile device). Responsive designs improve the UX for every visitor – translating into lower bounce rates and higher conversion rates.

CALLS-TO-ACTION

A call-to-action (aka "CTA") is a banner, button or other graphic or text that prompts website visitors to take an action... typically by clicking a link.

Every web page should have multiple calls-to-action including links to the filmmaker's IMDb profile, social media pages, the contact page and other relevant sites as well as encouraging visitors to register for email updates.

However, despite employing multiple CTAs, only one or two calls-to-actions should be the focus of any given page. And, ideally, those CTAs that appear most prominently should reflect – or be related to – the specific objective, or subject, of the individual page on which they appear.

For example, on the "Press Room" or "Media" page of your website, the two primary CTAs should be to encourage media professionals to download a copy of the electronic press kit and/or complete the contact form to request an interview. Similarly, on the

"About" page, you'll want visitors to view or download copies of your credit list, demo reel, behind-the-scenes material or film trailers.

As you consider the types of CTAs to post on each page, recognize that some calls-to-action require less commitment than others. Clicking a link to visit a related page or view a short video, for instance, requires less commitment than pulling out a credit card and purchasing a copy of your film or film-related merchandise. As a result, provide a select number of calls-to-action that visitors can choose from based upon interest and whatever commitment level they are most comfortable with.

In addition to the many CTAs already discussed, common CTAs also often include:

- View another website page or watch an embedded video
- Register or subscribe to email list
- Like, share, reply or comment on a post
- Rate, rank or review your films on VOD platforms and film review sites
- Like, friend or fan social media
- Preorder, purchase or rent film
- Order film-related merchandise.

An important concept to understand and embrace with regard to CTAs is the idea of "conversion rate." Essentially, a conversion rate is the percentage of a website or page's visitors who actually complete a call-to-action.

In attempting to improve a call-to-action's conversion rate, there are a number of factors that need to be considered: *Are the benefits of the CTA to the website visitor clear, meaningful and of interest? Are the calls-to-action obvious to the visitor? In other words, does the website visitor see and understand the call-to-action? How easily and quickly can the visitor complete the call-to-action?*

In addition to these considerations, think about how you can eliminate or reduce the steps or hurdles your visitors may experience in taking action. Use contrasting colors to draw attention to CTAs (and reserve use of these colors only to highlight CTAs). Encourage visitors to spread the word. Tell them how. Post social media sharing and email buttons and calls-to-action throughout your website, including each page and at the end of each article.

Finally, consider the location in which various CTAs are placed. Calls-to-action can be placed in the navigation bar, footer, side columns and within the web page and multi-media content itself. The most important calls-to-action should be placed prominently above the page fold (i.e. the area that is viewable on the screen without having to scroll).

One of the more prominent locations is the side column, which is ideal for showcasing adverts and banners for email subscription, discounted pre-release film rental or purchase, merchandise discount, event announcement, adverts for marketing partner, teasers or trailers, bonus material and similar announcements or calls-to-action.

However, of all the placement options, the navigation bar is the most highly viewed section of any website and the most effective CTA placement. As a result, reserve placement on the navigation bar for only the most important call-to-action such as a menu item or button for email registration or to preorder or purchase a ticket or copy of your most recent film.

Despite the fact that they are regarded as an annoyance to many visitors, pop-ups have also proven incredibly effective. To reduce the annoyance, consider pop-up alternatives such as Leadpage's Welcome Gate(tm) and other CMS plug-ins like Slide In, Optin Footer, LeadBoxes, etc.

WEBSITE CONTENT

Your website will need to serve a multitude of purposes and potential visitors, including long-term fans, potential audience members, existing and prospective investors, sales agents, distributors and cast and crew members. The type of content you post to your website should reflect each visitor's individual objectives, expectations and desires as well as whether or not they are first time or repeat visitors to your site.

That said, do not introduce too many topics or visitors will be confused as to the website's purpose. Identify specific themes and related topics. Obviously, some pages will appeal more to one category of visitor than others – be aware of this and make an effort to regularly produce content for each category of visitor.

Remember: All content – and every page – should have a purpose. Consider the following questions:

Q1. What is the #1 objective of the website and each individual page?

Q2. What types of visitors are likely to visit each page?

Q3. What do I want my visitors to do or click on this page?

Q4. What items on the page might distract visitors from achieving the objective?

As you reflect on the purpose and content of each page it may prove helpful to identify a specific keyword or phrase for each web page. Use those keywords or phrases to focus the content as well as within the page URL, file name of any images, page titles, headings and subheadings.

For on-page copy – and most downloadable editorial content (credit lists, cast and crew biographies, production notes, public releases, etc.) – it's best to keep copy short and simple (aka "KISS"). As your English teacher likely taught you, focus on the page topic's "Who, What, Why, When, Where and How." Also, if you're not familiar with it already, learn more about the "inverted pyramid" strategy of writing in which the topic is summarized in the first paragraph and subsequent sentences and paragraphs provide increasing levels of detail.

After having drafted your on-page copy content, read it to yourself out loud. How does it sound? Generally, content sounds better when you use simple language in a conversational tone. Infuse your writing with personality and talk to your audience in the first person whenever appropriate (i.e. using "you," "we," "me," "us," etc.). And, to "punch up" your writing, make it more engaging and exciting by using active words and phrases.

It's helpful to understand that although native English speakers typically read at an average speed of 250 words per minute, the use of fewer (and relatively simple) words tends to promote better rhythm and understanding. As a guideline, try to vary the length of sentences and paragraphs. Each sentence should range from five to fifteen words while paragraphs should comprise only two to four sentences each (with the word count of each paragraph averaging thirty-five to seventy words). If you restrict yourself to an average of three to five paragraphs per web page, the resulting page word count should fall somewhere between 250 and 500 words.

Reading rhythm, comprehension and retention are further improved when you write for scanners rather than readers. Scanability is enhanced when you write short sentences and paragraphs; use titles, headings, subheads, bullet points and lists to break up text; include a limited number of graphics (photos, illustrations, embedded video, etc.) to

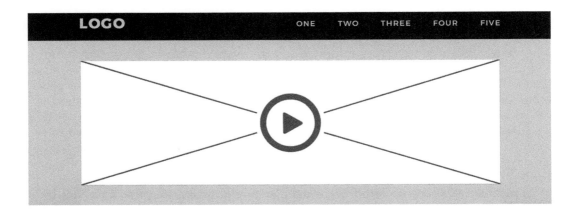

LOREM IPSUM

Lorem ipsum dolor sit amet

Lorem ipsum dolor sit amet, consectetur adipiscing elit, sed do eiusmod tempor incididunt ut labore et dolore magna aliqua. Ut enim ad minim veniam, quis nostrud exercitation ullamco laboris nisi ut aliquip ex ea commodo consequat. Sed ut perspiciatis unde omnis iste natus error sit voluptatem accusantium doloremque laudantium, totam rem aperiam, eaque ipsa quae ab illo inventore veritatis et quasi architecto beatae vitae dicta sunt explicabo.

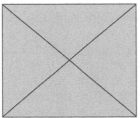  

Lorem ipsum dolor sit

Lorem ipsum dolor sit amet, consectetur adipiscing elit, sed do eiusmod tempor incididunt ut labore et dolore magna aliqua. Ut enim ad minim veniam, quis nostrud exercitation ullamco laboris nisi ut aliquip ex ea commodo consequat. Sed ut perspiciatis unde omnis iste natus error sit voluptatem accusantium doloremque.

Lorem ipsum dolor sit

Lorem ipsum dolor sit amet, consectetur adipiscing elit, sed do eiusmod tempor incididunt ut labore et dolore magna aliqua. Ut enim ad minim veniam, quis nostrud exercitation ullamco laboris nisi ut aliquip ex ea commodo consequat. Sed ut perspiciatis unde omnis iste natus error sit voluptatem accusantium doloremque.

Lorem ipsum dolor sit

Lorem ipsum dolor sit amet, consectetur adipiscing elit, sed do eiusmod tempor incididunt ut labore et dolore magna aliqua. Ut enim ad minim veniam, quis nostrud exercitation ullamco laboris nisi ut aliquip ex ea commodo consequat. Sed ut perspiciatis unde omnis iste natus error sit voluptatem accusantium doloremque.

Link 1 | Link 2 | Link 3

FIGURE 11.2 The website's home page is designed to clearly communicate the site's brand and direct the viewer to the most important content. This home page, based on UX studies, places a banner with a static graphic, slider or video beneath the navigation menu with a large text box and three columns immediately below. The text box and columns direct the visitor to those areas of the site of greatest value to filmmaker and/or visitors.

(Robert G. Barnwell/Sandy O. Cagnan)

support text; and use bold, italics, all caps and colored text sparingly. (Caution: Don't use underlining unless it's to designate a hotlink.)

In addition to page copy and other text-based content, the website should feature multi-media and interactive elements, including: embedded media content (audio and/or video); downloadable pictures, videos, presentations and other files; external links to related sites and social media accounts; e-commerce capability to support film purchases, rentals and movie-related merchandise orders; and other multi-media and interactive content.

While most of the website's editorial and multi-media content will be original, also consider (i) sharing stories from your cast, crew and fans; (ii) reuse past content created for other purposes or marketing campaigns; and (iii) archiving content created by other professionals and organizations (with permission).

However, regardless of the content's origins and influence, successful content should be entertaining and offer a reason to return to the site in the future. It should also be consistent in terms of frequency of new content, topics and subjects covered, and voice, tone and personality. As many web professionals will tell you: Content is king.

HOME PAGE

The home page is typically the first page that most visitors will see during their visit to your site. The impression that the home page makes on the visitor will largely determine if the visitor will continue to explore the remainder of your site or not.

Essentially, the home page has two primary objectives:

1. *Serve as the Ultimate Brand Statement:* The home page should verify that visitors have arrived at the "right" site. It should quickly identify you, your studio and your films and leverage the same design elements (and messages) as your other branding, marketing and promotional campaign materials.
2. *Preview and Showcase the Site's Most Important Content:* Leveraging the navigation bar and other prominent on-page cues, the home page should quickly direct visitors to the site's most important content and calls-to-action.

A successful home page accomplishes these objectives by incorporating many of the following elements: (i) a website title, logo and, often, a tagline; (ii) a simple navigation, or "menu," bar; (iii) an interesting and attention-getting header; (iv) one or more prominent images or videos; and (v) effective calls-to-action encouraging visitors to explore the website, register for email updates, to contact you directly, etc.

Visually, the home page of an official dedicated film website is predominantly comprised of a large background image. Website designers and developers have several choices in terms of how the images are displayed – either a single static image, a collection of several images contained in an automated "slider," or an HTML5 trailer or other video. In addition to the visual elements, film-related sites often include atmospheric sound or bed music.

The home page should also include several prominent credibility devices, including film festival laurels, film industry awards, reviews and testimonials, pictures of you with famous actors or filmmakers and similar content.

Again, the home page should have a focused message. Don't dilute your message or distract your website visitors with an overwhelming amount of information or too many choices. Use short messaging and get quickly to the point.

LOGO　　　　ONE　TWO　THREE　FOUR　FIVE

Home > Breadcrumb # 1 > Breadcrumb # 2 > Breadcrumb # 3

LOREM IPSUM

Lorem ipsum dolor sit amet

Lorem ipsum dolor sit amet, consectetur adipiscing elit, sed do eiusmod tempor incididunt ut labore et dolore magna aliqua. Ut enim ad minim veniam, quis nostrud exercitation ullamco laboris nisi ut aliquip ex ea commodo consequat. Sed ut perspiciatis unde omnis iste natus error sit voluptatem accusantium doloremque laudantium, totam rem aperiam, eaque ipsa quae ab illo inventore veritatis et quasi architecto beatae vitae dicta sunt explicabo.

- At vero eos et accusamus et iusto odio dignissimos
- Ducimus qui blanditiis praesentium
- Voluptatum deleniti atque corrupti quos
- Dolores et quas molestias
- Excepturi sint occaecati cupiditate

Sed ut perspiciatis unde omnis iste natus error sit voluptatem accusantium doloremque laudantium, totam rem aperiam, eaque ipsa quae ab illo inventore veritatis et quasi architecto beatae vitae dicta sunt explicabo. Nemo enim ipsam voluptatem quia voluptas sit aspernatur aut odit aut fugit, sed quia consequuntur magni dolores eos qui ratione voluptatem sequi nesciunt. Neque porro quisquam est, qui dolorem ipsum quia dolor sit amet, consectetur, adipisci velit, sed quia non numquam eius modi tempora incidunt ut labore et dolore magnam aliquam quaerat voluptatem.

Ut enim ad minima veniam, quis nostrum exercitationem ullam corporis suscipit laboriosam, nisi ut aliquid ex ea commodi consequatur? Quis autem vel eum iure reprehenderit qui in ea voluptate velit esse quam nihil molestiae consequatur, vel illum qui dolorem eum fugiat quo voluptas nulla pariatur

LOREM IPSUM

Lorem ipsum dolor sit amet

Nam libero tempore, cum soluta nobis est eligendi optio cumque nihil impedit quo minus id quod maxime placeat facere possimus, omnis voluptas assumenda est, omnis dolor repellendus. Temporibus autem quibusdam et aut officiis debitis aut rerum necessitatibus saepe eveniet ut et voluptates repudiandae sint et molestiae non recusandae. Itaque earum rerum hic tenetur a sapiente delectus, ut aut reiciendis voluptatibus maiores alias consequatur aut perferendis doloribus asperiores repellat.

Nemo enim ipsam voluptatem quia voluptas sit aspernatur aut odit aut fugit, sed quia consequuntur magni dolores eos qui ratione voluptatem sequi nesciunt. Neque porro quisquam est, qui dolorem ipsum quia dolor sit amet, consectetur, adipisci velit.

Lorem Ipsum Dolor

Lorem ipsum dolor sit amet, consectetur adipiscing elit, sed do eiusmod tempor.

Lorem ipsum dolor sit

Incididunt ut labore et dolore magna aliqua. Ut enim ad minim veniam.

Your Name

Email Address

SUBMIT

Submenu Heading

Link One
Link Two
Link Three
Link Four
Link Five

ORDER NOW

or, take a tour

Link 1 | Link 2 | Link 3

FIGURE 11.3 The website subpages contain the site's main content. These may include "About" pages, "Press Rooms," "Films" and other such pages. Again, based on UX studies, this wireframe provides a large left-hand column to accommodate the page's main content and a smaller right-hand column for email registration banners, film rental or purchase banners, a list of most recently posted or most popular content, and other calls-to-action or internal links.

(Robert G. Barnwell/Sandy O. Cagnan)

ABOUT PAGE

After the home page, the second most highly viewed page is the "About" page. Not surprisingly, visitors want to learn about you as both a person *and* as a filmmaker.

As a result, the About page should reflect your personality and explain your career path as a filmmaker. The biography should convince readers that you are a talented professional and someone they'd enjoy working alongside and whose films they'd enjoy viewing.

The content of the About page is based on the biography (or biographies) that you prepared earlier within the "Your Brand Story" section of Chapter 2 and for your IMDb profile. And, like your brand story and IMDb biography, in addition to being factual, your About page should reflect your personality and be written in a style that appeals to your target audience.

As with other aspects of your marketing and promotional activity, the About page should provide credibility and social proof of your expertise. Mention current and past film festival and industry award nominations and wins. Post excerpts of favorable print and video film reviews, testimonials or endorsements. Demonstrate that you are well-connected within the industry by providing pictures of you with – and quotes about you from – other well-known and well-respected filmmakers.

The About page should also contain several downloadable files, including your credit list, resume and professional biography. You may also want to post a short welcome or introductory video explaining your passion for filmmaking as well a demo reel with clips of past projects, trailers or other related videos.

FILM PROJECTS PAGE

The film projects page presents an overview of the various short and feature films you've completed as well as film projects that you may have in development or pre-production.

The page's first paragraph should be a brief overview of your films. Specifically, you should explain what makes your films and filmmaking unique (genre, signature elements, mood, atmosphere, pacing, etc.) and identify any unifying themes. These unique and unifying film attributes should be the same (or similar) as those you've included in your filmmaking biography and IMDb profile.

The subsequent paragraphs are comprised of the film's title and date of release in bold followed by a brief one to two paragraph descriptions of each film (approximately seventy-five words per description). Each film entry is typically preceded by a thumbnail of the respective film's poster (approximate dimensions of 150 × 200 pixels).

In addition to key art and film descriptions, also consider including (i) a list of any film festival or industry awards a film may have received; (ii) particularly impressive quotes or testimonials; (iii) embedded clips and/or trailers; and/or (iv) your title, role and responsibilities on each movie.

Note: During development, pre-production and principal photography, maintaining film details on a single studio and/or filmmaker website is acceptable (if not preferable). However, as the film approaches ninety days prior to release, it is advisable to give serious consideration to launching a dedicated film website hosted on its own URL.

PRESS ROOM

The purpose of the press room, or media center, is to welcome members of the media and direct them to the EPK and other content of interest (photographs, teasers and trailers, archive of past media coverage, etc.).

While the press rooms of many film-related sites feature little more than a menu of available media-related content, a better tactic is to include a welcome paragraph and invitation to contact you for background, quotes or interviews. At some point within the on-page copy, you should also prepare a short list (two to three) of the topics you enjoy – and on which you are most prepared – to speak.

The press room is also the page where your electronic press kit (EPK) should be posted and available for download (in its entirety as well as by individual component files). In addition to inviting members of the media to contact you directly, the press room (and EPK) should contain elements such as:

1. Contact information and form for media inquiries
2. Archive of press releases
3. Links and/or copies of past print, audio and/or video media coverage
4. Video interview(s) with the filmmaker answering the FAQ questions
5. Copies of past media coverage (print and/or broadcast)
6. Archive of public releases
7. Quotable Q&A sheet
8. Archive of past print, broadcast and internet media coverage
9. Invitation for media to contact you with regard to specific topics
10. Contact form.

CONTACT PAGE

Like its name suggests, the contact page is where users come to connect directly with you. In addition to enhancing engagement with audience and fans, direct visitor contact often results in increased media coverage, improved recruitment of talented cast and crew members and greater interest from sales agents and distributors.

The focal point of each contact page should be the contact form itself. As with other website features and functions, there are a number of contact plug-ins for each of the leading contact managements systems. Some of the most popular include: Contact Form, Fast Secure Contact Forms, JetPack's Contact Form Module and Ninja Forms.

Regardless of which plug-in or contact form you choose, it's critical that you spend the time to make the process of contacting you as simple as possible. For instance, research has proven that the more information you request in your form, the fewer people will actually complete the form. So take care to limit the information you require to the minimum necessary. Eliminating unnecessary form fields can significantly increase the conversion rate of your contact form.

If there is additional information that you'd like to collect, consider attempting to collect it from subsequent contact at some point in the future.

In addition to reducing the number of required form fields, there are several elements you can build into your contact forms that will improve completion rates. These include:

1. Provide ghost text in fields to let users know what should go there. You can even hint at formatting with the ghost text. For example ghost text for phone numbers

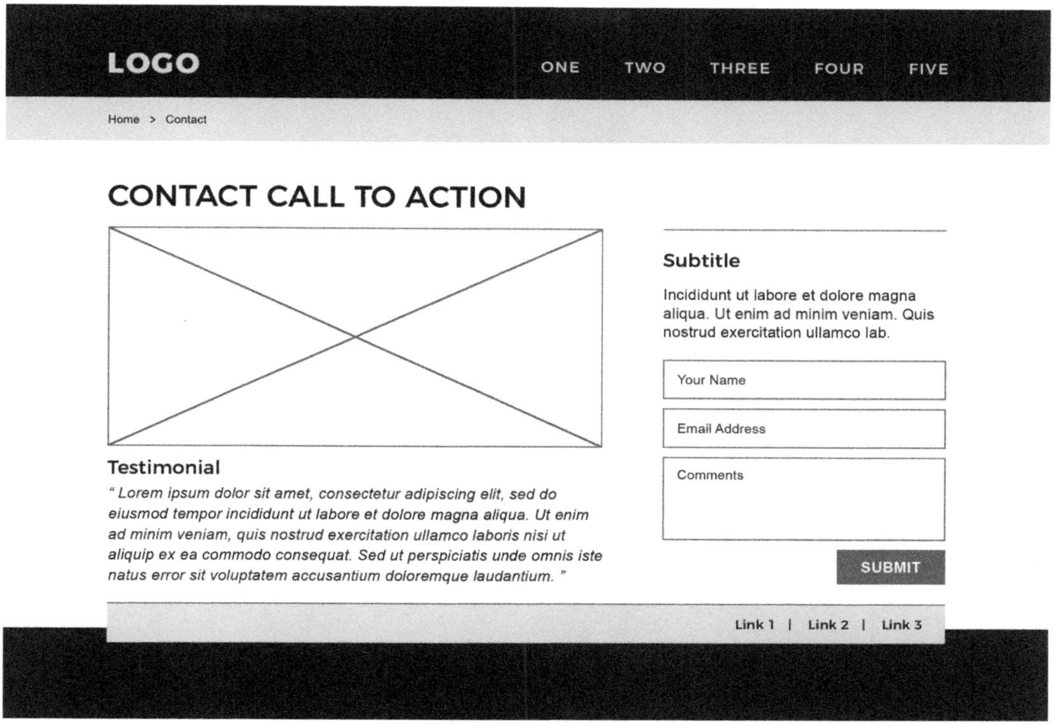

FIGURE 11.4 The website's contact page is one of the site's most valuable calls-to-action. The contact page depicted here is optimized to generate the greatest response rate. This includes the use of a prominent headline, supporting photograph or video, a respected testimonial or quote and a subtitle and brief paragraph encouraging contact. Further, the contact form requires visitors to complete only three fields.

(Robert G. Barnwell/Sandy O. Cagnan)

that use the (xxx) xxx-xxxx example will encourage users to complete the form in that style.

2. Set the tab order to allow the user to move quickly and sequentially through the fields by using a tab key.
3. Field focus and highlighting: Let users know where they are in the contact form. Highlight the respective field where the user is expected to input information.
4. In-line validation is another way you can reduce friction. Some Javascripts can let users know if they have a malformed email address *before* they submit their inquiry.

Once the contact form has been completed and submitted, use an auto-responder to thank the visitor for contacting you and to provide details on when they can expect a reply.

In addition to the contact form, provide as many alternative methods of contact as possible. Encourage visitors to contact you using whatever method is most convenient – and comfortable – for them. While that may be the contact form, other visitors may prefer to contact you by telephone, email, social media or via a related website. Also consider providing contact details for your talent manager, agent, press agent or film distributor.

FIGURE 11.5 Email registration banner.

(Robert G. Barnwell/Sandy O. Cagnan)

Finally, while many contact pages offer little more than contact details and the contact form itself, others have found it beneficial to include page copy or a brief video encouraging visitors to contact you. Such invitations commonly contain a brief explanation of the benefits of contacting you directly and the types of contacts you most welcome.

EMAIL REGISTRATION

One of the most valuable – and most commonly overlooked – opportunities available to film marketers is the email database. By encouraging visitors to subscribe, filmmakers are able to enhance their relationship and engagement with subscribers while improving film and merchandise sales.

In turn, your fans receive exclusive access to production updates, special events (premiers and film festivals), pre-release film purchases, rentals and merchandise discounts available only to subscribers.

As with contact forms, to improve registration rates, registration forms should have the fewest numbers of fields possible. For email subscriptions, one field requiring only an email address is ideal. Also be certain to post email registration buttons in the navigation bar, footer, side column, landing pages and at the end of any posts.

To further increase registration rates, consider having visitors register to download or receive various types of material such as a full copy of the EPK, screensavers and wallpaper backgrounds, or special discounts on film purchases, rentals and merchandise.

The creation of registration or subscription forms is relatively easy when using one of a number of well-respected CMS plug-ins from providers such as MailChimp, AWeber, Constant Contact and GetResponse. These services also provide no- or low-cost database and email management services once visitors have registered.

As with the contact form, when a visitor completes and submits the email registration form, use an auto-responder to thank your visitor for their registration and let them know how frequently they can expect to receive email updates.

COMMENTS ON WEB-BASED BLOGS

For more than a decade it has been accepted wisdom that independent filmmakers must maintain a blog on their websites to build audience engagement and increase their fan base.

Unfortunately, web-based blogs have found it notoriously difficult to build and sustain readership. And the time demands required to regularly churn out well-written and engaging blog content are equally challenging. As a result of such challenges, bloggers quickly become disenchanted . . . with the vast majority of new blogs abandoned within only a few months.

The ineffectiveness and inefficiency associated with web-based blogs result in significant opportunity costs. The time and resources consumed by blogging could – in almost every instance – be better allocated toward other marketing or filmmaking activities.

The reality is that microblogging platforms such as Facebook, Twitter and Weibo are much better at engaging with fans then web-based blogs. These microblogs offer immediacy, require less time, are less structured and less formal, briefer and easier to consume, and offer ready access to friends and fans.

SEARCH ENGINE OPTIMIZATION

With more than 60,000 estimated new short and feature films being released throughout the world each year, it shouldn't be surprising that few visitors will discover our films and websites using a blind search on Google, Bing, Yahoo! or other search engine. Instead, most of our website visitors will have already been familiar with us through social media activity, media coverage or other channels.

In addition to the overwhelming number of competing film-related sites, search engines such as Google continue to revise their search algorithms to make it difficult to manipulate page rankings. So those who think they can use "gray" or "black hat" off-site search engine optimization (SEO) techniques (those that are viewed as unethical or are unauthorized by the leading search engines) to increase their search engine rankings and visibility will be quite disappointed.

But that doesn't mean that there are no other worthwhile methods and techniques to build our search engine visibility and rankings. By properly optimizing our websites, it becomes easier for existing friends and fans to find us online and for new fans and audience members to discover us.

When conducting searches on search directories or engines such as Google, most users read the title and description of the first three listings, then the title and a small part of the description of the next few results. As users scroll down the page, they read fewer and fewer links. For marketing and SEO purposes, being able to have your site's pages listed as one of these first half dozen or so listings can be quite significant.

While each the search engine and directory have their own proprietary algorithms to determine how web pages rank relative to others, the majority use some combination of the following four elements: (i) the number and quality of inbound links to your site and site pages; (ii) the relevant keywords and key phrases contained on your website and web pages; (iii) the number and "quality" of pages contained within the website; and (iv) the frequency with which the website is updated.

For the purposes of SEO, these elements are often categorized as being either on-site or off-site optimization factors.

On-Page/On-Site Optimization

On-site factors are largely comprised of the quality and content of keywords and phrases as they appear within the website's on-page content and meta data.

Keywords and phrases should include your name, the name of your studio, the titles of your films (past, current and future film projects) and film genres as well as any applicable words or phrases that reflect the topic of a given page. Don't forget to add any exotic locations, famous actors, characters or interesting props, wardrobe or vehicles that may appear in your film as well as any relevant events, holidays, partner organizations, etc.

Tools such as Google's Keyword Tool, Marketsamurai.com and Wordtracker.com can also help you select additional keywords and phrases that should appear within your site's content and meta data.

A note of caution: some search engines and directories, such as Google, will penalize the search ranking of your site and pages if they feel you are using too many keywords in your copy to drive SEO. This is termed "keyword stuffing." Most search engines and directories like to see keyword density of no greater than 2–5% of your on-page copy and multi-media content. Keywordensity.com is a helpful tool that analyzes your content to avoid keyword stuffing.

In addition to quality and relevance of your on-site content, each page of your website should include meta titles and meta descriptions. These titles and descriptions are those that appear on Google and other search engines when people conduct a search for particular terms or phrases. So it's important that you do all that you can to make certain that titles and descriptions are well-written, contain keywords and prompt readers to click on your web page link.

When using WordPress, or other popular content management systems, your site will provide access to an administration area. Once you've logged onto this administration section of your CMS, you simply visit the individual site pages within the administration section to provide meta titles, descriptions and tags.

While completing the areas for meta information, pay particular attention to the meta page titles, descriptions, headings (H1, H2, H3 tags), meta keywords and tags, and image tags and descriptions.

It's helpful to understand that most search engines and directories restrict your listing titles and descriptions to a certain number of characters. For instance, Google displays up to a maximum of seventy characters for page titles and no more than 160 characters of the description. Keep these restrictions in mind when crafting your meta titles and descriptions.

Another tool to improve on-site SEO is the inclusion of an XML sitemap CMS plug-in such as Google XML Sitemaps, XML Sitemap and All in One Webmaster. XML sitemaps alert search engines and directories to new or revised content that, in turn, ensures that the content is rapidly indexed and revised by the search engines.

Off-Page/Off-Site Optimization

Although not as easily or quickly optimized, off-page factors have the greatest impact on search results and page rankings. These factors include: the number of inbound links from external sites, the relevance of inbound external linking pages, the relative page rank value of these external linking pages and the number of clicks and activity these links – and links from the search engines and directories themselves – receive.

The problem with off-page SEO is that these factors are largely a reflection of (i) time and (ii) the quality and relevance of your site's content. Search engines and directories continually work to refine their algorithms to make it challenging to manipulate off-page results. As a result, in my opinion, it's best to largely ignore off-site SEO in favor of the creation of popular films and content.

On the other hand, despite my advice to largely ignore off-site SEO, I would suggest that you use analytic tools such as Google Webmaster Tools to identify the total number and specific websites that are linking to your site. Tracking these trends will help you determine – not only your off-site SEO progress but – the relative popularity of your site and its content.

While it's difficult to manipulate off-page SEO, search rankings ... in a manner of speaking ... can be bought. Most search engines and directories – including Google, Yahoo! and Bing – offer pay-per-click (aka "PPC") advertising. PPC advertising places your listings near the top of each search page. In return, you are required to pay (typically through a bidding process) a certain amount of money per visit, or "click." Search engine marketing programs, such as Google's AdWords PPC program, allow you to focus on which users you wish to target, where the ads appear (geographically by zip codes, countries, etc.), keywords/phrases and establish per-click bids and daily budget limits. As a result of PPC's effectiveness, 25% of all Google search clicks are now comprised of PPC listings.

FIGURE 11.6 Google search results page detailing the placement of pay-per-click listings (in yellow) relative to organic search results (in blue).

(Robert G. Barnwell/Sandy O. Cagnan)

Until your website and web pages begin to regularly rank among the top listings of search engine and directories, PPC is often an intelligent investment to improve search visibility.

PROMOTING YOUR WEBSITE CONTENT

In addition to search engine optimization and pay-per-click, there are a number of other methods of promoting your websites, web pages and content.

The most important method is to prominently display your websites' URLs on your key art, trailers, social media accounts, IMDb profile, professional biography, resume, credit list, business cards, letterhead, promotional postcards and anything else associated with the branding, marketing or promotion of your films, studio or filmmaking career.

Figure 11.7 Google analytics.

(Robert G. Barnwell/Sandy O. Cagnan)

It's also important to "cross promote" recent website content by posting updates and summaries (with track-back links) to social media, forums and other internet communities, and within your emails and email signatures. Be sure to also encourage family, friends, fans, cast, crew and other influencers to share and post links to your website content to their own social media accounts and websites.

Also work to optimize your website for content sharing: (i) provide internal links to related site content; (ii) create and post a "Most Popular . . . " (pages/content/posts/ articles, etc.) graphic within your sites side column; (iii) at the beginning or end of each page's editorial content, include "Email," "Print," "Share," "Like," "Favorite" and "Post" buttons to make it easier for – and to remind – visitors to promote and share your website content.

Finally, remember to enable comments on your web page content and be certain to respond to those comments. The more you engage with your audience and visitors around web content, the more likely they are to promote both you and your content.

WEB ANALYTICS

Once completed, it's imperative that we monitor our digital media and promotional sites to make sure that they are performing adequately (and identify areas for improvement). Here are some of the key website performance metrics available from Google Analytics and similar website performance apps:

- Number of total vs unique visitors
- Organic vs paid traffic
- Search engine rankings (site & pages)
- SEO keyword rankings
- Number of inbound links
- Traffic sources/referral sites

- Entry and exit pages
- Bounce rate
- Page views per visit
- Average time on site
- Most/least popular pages
- Conversion rates

By tracking these – and similar – web metrics over time, you'll quickly learn how to identify and make the right changes to improve the website's performance, increase user satisfaction and experience and maximize conversion rates with regard to email subscription registration, film-related merchandise sales and movie purchases and rentals.

In addition to monitoring website performance, you should also test the results of your digital marketing efforts using HubSpot's Marketing Grader and Klout. Hubspot's Marketing Grader assigns a grade based upon an analysis of your website and social media activity and offers specific suggestions for improvement. Klout, on the other hand, is a measure of your online influence, reputation and "reach." Like HubSpot's Marketing Grader, Klout assigns you a score and provides recommendations for improvement.

By the way, the use of Google Analytics, HubSpot's Marketing Grader and the Klout Score are entirely free.

And while numbers are great, keep in mind that you only need a handful of the "right" people to see your digital marketing and promotional efforts. Consider the impact if either Steven Spielberg or Megan Ellison were the only one to ever read your website and social media accounts . . . and then decided to support your next film project? In this case, it might only take one visitor to cement your entire filmmaking career.

Again, numbers are great . . . but concentrate on the impact of your efforts on your career and filmmaking.

12

ELECTRONIC PRESS KITS (EPKs) & PRESS BOOKS

The electronic press kit (EPK) is a significant component of the marketing and promotional campaigns of your feature film projects. In addition to their role in media relations, EPKs also play a role in the success of film festival applications and, in some measure, can determine which films ultimately win awards.

Essentially, an EPK is an electronic file (typically in PDF form) that contains the important marketing and promotional details of the film, the film's cast and crew and URLs or "hotlinks" to additional supporting information such as photographs, key art, trailers, film clips, video interviews, press releases, past media coverage and similar files.

In contrast to physical press kits, EPKs are produced and distributed on websites, memory sticks, DVDs and similar storage devices so that all the information can be provided in one convenient media while minimizing – and often eliminating – the need for external hotlinks.

A successful press kit – whether print or electronic – must highlight those aspects of the film most likely to appeal to your audiences as well as the audiences of targeted media outlets. The point of a good press kit is not only to present a summary of the film and the bios of cast and crew members but also to tell the story of the film's development and production as well as the many successes and challenges that led to its successful production.

For instance, among the considerable information contained within the production notes of the EPK for James Cameron's film *Titanic*, the EPK provided details of the size and depth of the pool in which Titanic was filmed in Rosarito, Mexico, how the model of the Titanic was constructed and how the ship's movements and waves were created.

As James Cameron, Paramount and Universal did with the EPK of *Titanic*, we also need to identify and focus on those aspects and features of our films that most appeal to their audiences (e.g. locations, stars, special effects, creature designs, etc.).

When strategically crafted and designed, the EPK is able to serve several significant roles. During pre-production and principal photography, the role of EPKs often includes:

- Fundraising and investor relations
- Supporting crowd-funding initiatives
- Attracting cast and crew members

- Obtaining interest from sales agents
- Fueling pre-release film sales and rentals
- Generating pre-release media coverage
- Building community and engagement
- Clarifying and solidifying vision during pre-production and production.

Similarly, during post-production and distribution, the role of EPKs will include:

- Generating media coverage
- Attracting film festivals and strengthening film festival applications
- Attracting domestic and foreign distributors
- Increasing film sales and rentals
- Generating film-related merchandise sales
- Expanding the community and fueling additional engagement.

COMMON EPK ELEMENTS

To maximize the EPK's ability to fulfill these many roles, filmmakers must carefully consider and select each piece of material to be included in the press kit. And, while many of the components of the EPK will remain unchanged, you may choose to include more or less depending upon who you are sending the EPK to and for what purpose.

Some of the many items traditionally found in the more successful EPKs are:

1. Cover letter personalized to recipient
2. Logline and short (thirty-five to fifty word), medium (~100 word) and long (~250 word) film summaries
3. Director's statement
4. Production notes
5. Biographies of filmmakers, key cast and crew with brief list of credits and awards, if any, for each
6. Credit list with technical production details including running time, aspect ratio, sound quality, shooting format, year of production, locations, etc.
7. Print, audio and/or video cast and crew interviews
8. "Making of ... " documentary
9. FAQ/question and answer sheet
10. Key art/poster (JPEG)
11. Film title/logo (JPEG)
12. Teasers, trailers and film clips
13. Film stills, BTS and other pictures of notable film elements such as: practical effects, special effects, locations, vehicles, weapons and/or other wardrobe and props (JPEG)
14. Storyboard frames and concept artwork (JPEG)
15. List of awards and copies of film festival laurels (JPEG)
16. Copies of current and/or relevant past press releases
17. Archive/copies of print and/or broadcast media coverage
18. Critical reviews and/or second-party endorsements
19. Websites, social media and IMDb links
20. The title and logo (JPEG) of the company that is distributing the film
21. Contact information (consider adding your agent and/or manager's contact info as well).

Notice the many commonalities of the individual components of the EPK (particularly key art, film synopsis, teasers and trailers, cast and crew bios, production stills and BTS pics, videos and interviews) with the materials and content contained within your other marketing platforms such as your websites, IMDb listings and many other marketing platforms.

This economy of effort – leveraging activity across multiple channels – is the essence of successful independent guerrilla film marketing.

Because these elements will be leveraged across websites, IMDb profiles, social media accounts and other marketing and promotional channels, it is imperative that each and every piece be well-written and well-edited.

Understandably, not all filmmakers are going to feel comfortable with the quality of their writing or copy-editing. If not, I highly advise you to work with professionals from Fiverr.com and/or Upwork.com or other online service to help write, refine and edit your marketing and promotional materials. Carelessly written website and marketing copy will damage the credibility of your film.

FIGURE 12.1 EPKs and press books. Samples of press kits and press books are readily available online as well as for purchase online from sites such as eBay.

(Robert G. Barnwell/Sandy O. Cagnan)

COVER LETTER

The first piece of EPK material that the recipient sees should be the cover letter. In many respects, the cover letter may be the most important document in the EPK.

Within the confines of a single page, the cover letter must briefly achieve three important objectives: (i) introduce the film to the reader; (ii) explain why the recipient has received the EPK and the nature of your request; and (iii) state the benefits of reviewing the additional EPK material in more detail.

The challenge is to provide enough details to pique the recipient's interest while keeping the letter as brief as possible. The secret to both maximizing the reader's interest and maintaining brevity is to personalize the cover letter to each recipient and to customize the contents of each EPK to the individual (or type of individual) it is being sent to.

The following provides a paragraph-by-paragraph template on which you can base your cover letters. Notice that the first paragraph is customized depending upon whether or not you have an existing relationship with the recipient.

First Paragraph

The first paragraph serves to introduce you, the film and outline the reason you've contacted the recipient.

Cold contact – No prior relationship:

> I wanted to quickly introduce myself to you and provide you with a copy of the EPK for our recent film, [film title]. As the producer-director, I'm particularly proud of the film and am confident that you'll find it to be [a great addition to the Sundance Film Festival/a great addition to your distribution catalog/Other].

Warm contact – Prior relationship or discussion:

> I just wanted to quickly let you know that I really enjoyed speaking with you on [date and date] and discussing [subject]. Also, as promised, I'm attaching a copy of the EPK for our recent film [film title]. As the producer-director, I'm particularly proud of the film and am confident that you'll find it to be [a great addition to the Sundance Film Festival/a great addition to your distribution catalog/Other].

Warm Contact – Network referral:

> I was just speaking with [name] of [relationship/professional title and film or organization], who encouraged me to reach out to you about our recent film, [film title]. As the producer-director, I'm particularly proud of the film and am confident that you'll find it to be [a great addition to the Sundance Film Festival/a great addition to your distribution catalog/Other].

Second Paragraph

The second paragraph provides a brief two to three sentence summary of the film.

> [Film title] is an exciting [or other descriptive word] [genre]-film. [Insert one to two sentence film synopsis/summary.]

Third Paragraph

The third paragraph serves to describe the key contents of EPK as well as any hotlinks for teasers, trailers or a sneak preview of the film (and any required passwords).

> Within the enclosed press kit, I've included several pieces of interesting content regarding the development and production of [film title]. In particular, I think you'll enjoy watching the film's trailers and film clips. If you like what you see, let me know and I can send you a link and password for a preview of the film.

Closing Paragraph

Restate request and invite them to learn more about the film via the website and to contact you with any questions. Mention a specific date you will follow up via telephone and invite recipient to contact you if another day and time is more convenient.

> I hope [film title] proves a strong candidate for [acceptance/distribution/other] with [specific name of film festival or other recipient organization]. If you should have any questions with regard to the film or our desire to [detail nature of request], please do not hesitate to contact me via cell phone at [cell phone number] or via email at [email address]. If I don't hear from you beforehand, I'll plan on following up with you during the week of [date]. In the meantime, many thanks for your consideration and support.

Following the final paragraph, include a signature block and personally sign each cover letter. Keep in mind that the person who signs the cover letter should also be the person who you've designated as the film's press contact. Also be sure that this same contact information is provided on each piece of material within the EPK.

FILMMAKER'S OR DIRECTOR'S STATEMENT

The filmmaker's or director's statement is a five paragraph note explaining why the film and its storyline were important to the filmmaker and what he/she hoped to achieve.

Like the cover letter, the director's statement should be written in a first-person conversational tone. And, ideally, the statement will bridge the filmmaker's personal history and personality with the film's story. More specifically, the director's statement should address several topics within the following paragraphs:

First Paragraph

During the first paragraph, you should explain your enthusiasm for the story and its origins. It's particularly effective if you can tie something from your personal experience to the desire to bring this particular story to life. Why did you feel compelled to write the screenplay and produce the film? What was your inspiration? Did the story remind you of any films or books that have made a particular impact on you? A personal, family or professional experience?

Second Paragraph

Within the second paragraph, you should begin by briefly sharing the central through-story of the film. This is often the short film summary or a slightly edited version of your short film summary (around thirty-five words). Having explained the through-story, explain how the film is unique from other films in its genre. What did you want to achieve from both a story and technical perspective that would make the film distinctive? Whenever possible, attempt to tie the film's distinctiveness to the thoughts you expressed in paragraph one.

Third & Fourth Paragraphs

With regard to the third and fourth paragraphs, most director's statements discuss one of three general subjects:

1. *Themes:* Is there a moral or underlying social message the film is attempting to communicate? What personal and social impact do you hope the film will accomplish? Discuss the conflicts addressed by the characters, some of the decisions they make in the film and how they relate to the film's underlying theme or values.
2. *Overcoming Challenges:* Identify the problems and challenges you, your cast and crew experienced in bringing the story/film to life. Were these challenges story-related? Budget-related? Technical? How did you overcome these problems?
3. *Technical Objectives:* From a technical point of view, many directors choose to discuss the "look" or "feel" they were trying to achieve. How was this goal reflected in the performances? Cinematic style? Special and visual effects? And other technical aspects of the filmmaking?

Fifth Paragraph

During the final paragraph, you should comment on the results of the film relative to the goals and objectives as outlined in paragraphs three and four. Naturally, the expectation is going to be that you are proud of the cast, crew and resulting film. But try to point to specific elements that you believe helped you achieve or support the objectives from the previous two paragraphs.

Finally, come to a strong close. The final sentence of director's statements are often either (i) a call-to-action to watch and enjoy the film, (ii) a meaningful quote (possibly of a character from the film) as it relates to the theme and underlying story; or (iii) a statement that ties to the thoughts expressed within the first paragraph (bringing the entire statement full-circle to its final conclusion).

While I hope this structure is helpful, I also hope that you'll feel comfortable in abandoning it if you have another structure or topics that are more appropriate. Be true to yourself and your film (and true to your film's and the EPK's audience). What do you think the reader will be most interested in hearing about?

PRODUCTION NOTES

The production notes form the largest component of the EPK and provide the reader with a more comprehensive understanding of the film and insights into its production. Essentially, when well-written, the production notes read as an extended-article (3,000–5,000 words) focused on the adventures of producing the film.

Like the director's statement, the production notes describe the origins of the project and the many motivations of the filmmakers, cast and crew. However, unlike the director's statement, the production notes take the reader through the film's entire journey – from development through post-production. And, instead of a single page, production notes range from five pages to as many as forty or more.

In addition to page length, another difference between the director's statement and the production notes is that the production notes are written in the third person rather than the first person. To get the best feel for the tone and content of successful production notes, read the EPKs and production notes posted on the studio and film festival websites (EPKs and press kits are also available for purchase on eBay.com).

As you'll discover, the majority of production notes provide a brief one to three page introduction before being divided into subtitled sections covering such topics as (i) development (scriptwriting, storyboarding, location scouting, character, costume and prop design, etc.); (ii) cast and crew attachment; (iii) on-set and on-location experiences (production); and (iv) any special or visual effects.

Periodically, the production notes should include quotes from cast and crew members as well as interesting facts and figures related to the story and film production.

Unfortunately, particularly in the case of low-budget independent films, many production notes lack interest. They're boring. They're often written without passion while suggesting that the film production proceeded flawlessly from beginning to end.

Instead, well-written production notes communicate a passion for the film and the filmmaking process. They embrace the challenges encountered during production and sharing how these obstacles were overcome. In short, they have personality.

As David Fincher mentioned when discussing his film *The Social Network*,

> I always find the stuff that makes me intrigued about how movies get made was when you hear people talk about how they didn't get what they wanted, but it ended up being more interesting. I find that's the most valuable learning stuff.
>
> (Aint it Cool News, 2011)

CAST & CREW BIOS

The production notes typically end with several pages of cast and crew bios. For major studio productions, these bios focus only on the filmmakers, featured cast and above-the-line crew members. For independent films with smaller cast and crew numbers, it often makes sense to include bios for most of those involved in production – not just a select few.

In the majority of cases, each bio should be a single paragraph of approximately 150 words. The bio, written in the third person, should identify each cast and crew member by name (check and double-check spelling!), their role or character and their filmmaking or acting experience. Also seek out opportunities to connect with readers by mentioning such facts as where the person currently lives, where they grew up, where they attended school, outside interests and other interesting aspects of their lives.

While the following example can serve as a template, be cautious about using the template for too many cast and crew members and from repeating the same sentences and phrases from one bio to the next. Depending upon the number of cast and crew members, it will be understandably difficult – if not impossible – to completely eliminate repetition. However, work to make each bio as unique and distinct as possible.

> Jane Smith, A.C.E. served as the director of photographer on [film title]. This is Jane's first film as DP. Prior to [film title], she was best-known for her work as second unit director and camera operator for such films as [list film titles]. Raised in Boston, Jane completed film school at Emerson College's Los Angeles campus and later completed the DGA's prestigious Assistant Director Training Program. She has produced and directed several short films which have gone on to win [list awards]. When not on set, Jane enjoys [list interesting hobbies].

Although I've suggested that bios should be brief (ideally one paragraph), the length of the bio should reflect each individual's experience, accomplishments and relative celebrity. Starring actors and well-respected crew members, particularly if they are an industry "name," will naturally merit a longer bio than others on set.

And, as another quick aside: Although I have – and will continue – to emphasize the importance of leveraging marketing materials across marketing and promotional channels, EPK bios may not necessarily be the same as those bios each individual has posted to their own websites, social media platforms or IMDb profiles. Instead, the EPK bios should reflect the biography of each cast and crew member as they apply to your film, its genre and its distinct storyline. So don't hesitate to edit and modify any existing bios your cast and crew provide (with permission, of course).

FAQ SHEETS

The frequently asked questions ("FAQ") sheet provides you an opportunity to create ready-made quotes for the print, broadcast and electronic media while answering questions that most appeal to your audience and fans (as well as potential investors, distributors, agents, managers, employers and cast and crew members).

The current trend among film publicists and studio publicity departments is to create FAQ sheets comprised of approximately ten questions. As you would expect, many – if not most – of the questions are tailored specifically to the individual films and genre. On the other hand, there are several relatively common questions that filmmakers and publicists should considering including:

1. *What were the origins behind the story for [film title]?*
2. *What elements of the story or script proved particularly challenging in bringing it to life on screen?*
3. *How is [film title] distinct from other successful [genre] films such as [list three popular films within your genre]?*
4. *[Name] is well known for [his/her] work on [television, film or web series], what did [his/her] experience bring to the production of [film title]?*
5. *What has been the initial reaction so far from test and festival screenings?*
6. *So what's next for the filmmakers, cast and crew? Can we expect a sequel?*

Again, these are fairly common questions and you should consider including a few within your own Q&A sheet. But whatever you choose, make sure the questions are those that most interest your reader and reflect best on you and your film.

Having decided on the final ten questions, you'll provide a response, in quotations, within one to two paragraphs (each paragraph should be no more than four to five sentences each). Write each response in a natural conversational tone. Again, ideally, your responses will be used to quote you in various print, broadcast and electronic

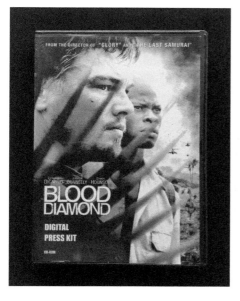

FIGURE 12.2 A CD-based EPK for Warner Bros.' film *Blood Diamond*. While EPKs can take many forms and can be distributed across a variety of digital channels, this EPK, with enclosed press book, remains common.

(Robert G. Barnwell)

media. So make sure that each response is written in your own voice, reflects your personality and the personality of the film.

In addition to the FAQ sheet, you may want to consider filming yourself being interviewed using the same questions as the FAQ. In this case, whomever you've hired to conduct the interview must remain off screen from you and their audio track must remain separate from your own track. If done correctly, members of the broadcast media can then use the video interview as recorded, or they can replace the original interviewer with a recording of their own host or newscaster asking the same questions . . . essentially appearing to show them conducting their own interview of you.

DESIGNING & FORMATTING THE EPK

EPK menus for DVDs and other media can also be created using any one of a number of popular programs, including Adobe Encore, Adobe Premiere, Adobe Photoshop, Apple iDVD, Windows DVD Maker and many others. In addition to these programs, there are a number of free tools to create DVD menus for your EPK available online.

Regardless of the program or tools you use, most filmmakers will find the creation of EPK menus relatively easy. For those unfamiliar with the menu creation process, you'll find many helpful step-by-step instructions on YouTube and the websites of the individual software companies.

Another alternative to creating an EPK menu in-house is to use one of the many well-designed menu templates available from such providers as ActiveDen (a member of the Envato Marketplace).

Regardless of how you choose to create the menu, the EPK menu page should feature the film's key art in the background with the navigation or menu bar in the foreground.

Again, colors, font selection and other design elements should reflect the branding choices made in the design of the film's key art, website and other marketing materials.

With regard to the EPK material, in addition to being viewable directly from the DVD or other media, much of the EPK content should be downloadable. This means providing EPK users with the option of downloading PDF, JPEG and high-definition MP4 files of the EPK's director's statement, production notes, storyboards, photographs, teasers and trailers and other materials.

Similarly, when it comes to DVDs, cases and covers, they can each be designed and full-color printed (i) in-house on either a standard color laser printer or a dedicated color DVD printer (by manufacturers such as Primera, Rimage and Epson) or (ii) printed using any one of a number of short-run digital printing services such as Discmakers.com, Groovehouse.com, MediaExpress or Mixonic.com.

PHYSICAL PRESS KITS

Since the introduction of EPKs in the 1970s, EPKs have established themselves as the standard for press kits. However, while their role may have been diminished, physical press kits continue to be important as discussion guides and "leave behinds" during in-person meetings with potential investors, industry professionals, members of the media and film festival committee members.

Today's physical press kits are presented within a two-flap folder large enough to accommodate fifty to seventy-five pages of standard 8.5″ × 11″ or A4 documents. The left flap should have die cuts to insert a business card with the right side flap having die cuts to accommodate a mini-DVD copy of the EPK. Facing outward from the left flap are the (i) cover letter followed by (ii) the director's statement, (iii) a copy of the key art (with partial credit list and the film's technical details printed on the reverse) and (iv) FAQ sheet. The right flap begins with (v) cover sheet, (vi) the extended end credits, (vii) the production notes and (viii) the cast and crew bios. All four of these final elements are stapled together as a single unit. Following these production materials, additional items such as past press releases, press coverage, BTS and film stills, storyboard frames and other printed material may be included.

Because EPKs have largely replaced physical press kits, it is best to only print press kits in limited quantities and only as required. With regard to presentation folders, these should be produced in heavy stock and be either a solid-color or a full-color reproduction of your key art using economical digital printing technology. Impressive solid-color presentation folders can be easily found online or at your local Staples or Office Max (in North America) while full-color printed presentation folders can be economically sourced from online providers such as Vistaprint.com in quantities as low as 100.

In terms of cover letters, the director's statement, production notes and other printed matter, these should be printed only as needed using high-quality paper on a full-color office laser printer. By printing materials only as needed, the press kit materials can be customized to the recipient and regularly updated whenever necessary. Current high photo-quality color office printers range in price from $250 USD to $1,500 USD or more.

PRESS BOOKS

In addition to press kits, many studios also produce physical press books. These press books feature several high-quality photographs and a limited amount of text . . . usually short excerpts from the director's statement and production notes.

Major studios will occasionally produce press books as large hardcover editions in support of films nominated for prestigious industry awards such as the BAFTAs, Independent Spirit Awards and Oscars. However, most are printed as glossy four-page or six-page self-cover bi-folds or tri-folds. While these can be printed on high-end color office printers, most filmmakers will likely need to have press books printed at an online provider such as Vistaprint.com.

FIGURE 12.3 A simple tabloid fold-over four-page press book for Universal Pictures' *Jurassic Park III*.

(Robert G. Barnwell)

Press books have the advantage of being quite impressive and easier to navigate given their smaller page count when compared to a full press kit. Fortunately, despite the lower page count, press books can be used during meetings as well as to support campaigns for film festival and industry awards.

DISTRIBUTING YOUR EPK & MATERIALS

At the risk of stating the obvious, in addition to the nature and quality of the materials, the ultimate impact of your EPK will depend largely on getting copies into the right people's – and organization's – hands.

Broadly, there are three categories of EPK distribution you'll want to leverage:

Online: As mentioned previously, many elements of the EPK – including key art, teasers and trailers, storyboards, BTS stills and video and others – will appear throughout and across your marketing and promotional channels.

Consider distributing the EPK and individual EPK materials via: (i) your websites and social media platforms; (ii) the websites and social media platforms of your cast and crew; (iii) the websites and social media platforms of your sales agent and distributors; (iv) the websites of any supporting businesses or organizations (non-profits and any companies who have featured product placements); (v) links on the IMDb profiles of the filmmakers and official film profile; and (vi) links within the email signatures of your personal and official studio accounts.

Direct Contact: Throughout the development, production and distribution of your film, you'll discover a number of professionals and organizations in a position to further your film's success. In these cases, you'll want to contact these people with copies of your EPK or press kits. This includes people and organizations such as: film festival committee members; sales agents and distributors; existing and prospective investors; local, regional, foreign and international print and broadcast media personalities; bloggers and vloggers; and others.

In-Person Meetings: Physical press kits are a valuable visual reference and "leave behind" for meetings with investors, sales agents, distributors and other industry professionals. However, it's also important to have copies of the EPK and press kits when attending film festivals and film markets such as the American Film Market, Marché du Film, European Film Market and CineMart. Rather than handing them out to everyone you come into contact with at these events, only provide copies to those that expressly ask for one and those people who you feel would be a perfectly good professional match.

Reflecting *the importance and power of repetition, consistency and constancy*, the EPK (and individual EPK components) should be incorporated into – and across – all of your digital marketing and promotional channels, including your IMDb profile, website(s) and social media accounts.

By creating a well-designed and crafted EPK, you'll find that you easily differentiate your projects (and yourself) from competing films in the marketplace and film festivals. Professional-quality EPKs will also serve in your efforts to raise film financing and generate print and broadcast media attention for your films.

13

MEDIA RELATIONS & PUBLIC RELEASES

Few things are able to project your message and cement credibility faster than media coverage from local, national and international newspapers, magazines, radio and broadcast television or from "new media" outlets such as subject-specific websites ("webhubs"), popular blogs, online forums, online newspapers and magazines, audio podcasts, vidcasts, YouTube channels and more.

Unlike other marketing and promotional material – through which you claim your own and your own films' greatness – media coverage essentially provides second- and third-party support and validation of the quality of your films and your expertise as a filmmaker. Media coverage is also a highly effective no- or low-cost channel to increase brand recognition and drive increased ticket, film and merchandise sales.

In addition to these many benefits, media coverage often leads to still more media coverage. Even local news coverage is commonly internationally syndicated via global news services such as the Associated Press and United Press International . . . generating rapid momentum and multiplying your coverage.

Unfortunately, despite the explosion in the number of online and offline media outlets, as a result of email, press release distribution services and other inexpensive media outreach tools, it can be harder than ever to break through the noise to get the attention of a reporter, writer, broadcaster or news director.

The solution is to take a personalized and targeted approach in building media relationships to gradually gaining coverage and slowly climbing the ladder from local and niche media to larger national and international media coverage. With the right strategy and a little effort, the hurdles to achieving successful media coverage can be overcome relatively quickly.

LAYING THE GROUNDWORK

Before we begin developing our media strategy and implementing an outreach plan, we need to make certain that we've laid the proper groundwork. The first question we need to ask ourselves and our filmmaking team is *"Are we ready to pursue media coverage?"*

FIGURE 13.1 A collection of global film industry publications as distributed at the Cannes Film Festival, France.

(Denis Makarenko/Shutterstock.com)

Take a quick moment to think about the perspective of the news director of a global news program. Before contacting us, the news director would likely visit our website and perform basic online research. What would he or she find? Would it create sufficient credibility and interest in our filmmaking to encourage the program to take the next step: to call or email us with an interview request? And, assuming that they do decide to interview us for a forthcoming article or broadcast episode, consider many of these same questions from the perspective of the media organization's own readers, viewers or listeners.

While it may not be necessary to have a completed EPK at this point, depending upon your goals or objectives, at the very least you should have (i) a credible website containing (ia) short biographies and portraits of the filmmaker, cast and crew, (ib) key art and (ic) film logline and short description; (ii) complete IMDb profiles and film listings; and (iii) an active social media presence.

In addition, if you have it, consider posting an archive of any past media coverage; film stills and BTS photos; an FAQ sheet with a list of questions and ready-made quotable responses; and any pre-recorded audio and video interviews to your website's press or media page.

Once you've launched a media-friendly website and had the opportunity to become engaged in social media, your efforts at media outreach will be more productive.

DEVELOPING A MEDIA STRATEGY

While almost any media coverage is likely to increase the recognition and appreciation of our filmmaking, studio and films' brands, the benefits of media coverage are considerably greater when combined with a well-developed media strategy.

Specifically, you and your team need to make thoughtful decisions with regard to questions such as: (i) *What goals or objectives are your media efforts attempting to achieve?* (ii) *Which media outlets (and, more importantly, which audiences) are most likely to help you to achieve these goals?* And (iii) *which topics or storylines are most likely to both appeal to these targeted media outlets AND help you to achieve your media goals?*

Expect your answers to change as you progress through the production process.

For instance, during script development and pre-production, you may be focused on appealing to investors and industry professionals, including casting directors, talent agents and managers, and potential cast and crew members. Media coverage during this stage should be targeted at trade publications and other film industry related outlets such as IndieWire, *Variety, The Hollywood Reporter*, Filmmaker Magazine or MovieMaker Magazine and related websites, podcasts and other channels.

On the other hand, during principal photography, post-production and the lead-up to the film's release, you'll likely change focus to increasing the number of active fans and prospective audience members. Media coverage during this stage should target media outlets specific to your film's genre as well as broad local, regional, national and global media outlets.

BUILDING MEDIA RELATIONSHIPS

Once you've formed a basic idea of your media strategy and have established a professional web and social media presence), you'll want to begin building relationships with members of the media who may be interested in covering you and your films.

One of the first and easiest steps is to list yourself in various directories that the media frequently use to identify people and professionals for their stories. Some of the most popular directories include Haro, Profnet and NewsCertified Exchange.

In addition to allowing you to post a brief description about yourself, your studio and your films, many of these directory services also send out periodic emails notifying subscribers of reporters in search of people with your expertise.

Unfortunately, while such directories and emails offer an easy and obvious first step in your efforts to begin building media relationships, you'll inevitably be disappointed by the lack of resulting coverage if they are your sole source of media outreach.

Instead, such directory listings and email services should be coupled with highly targeted direct contact with specific writers, hosts or radio, television, video or social media personalities.

The process of direct outreach should begin with the assembly of a list of targeted members of the press and media. You'll want to focus on those organizations, writers and reporters whose subject matter and audiences will benefit most by having you as a resource. To identify such media organizations and professionals, refer to such print and online directories as:

Bacon's Media Directories
Bacon's MediaList Online

Broadcasting & Cable Yearbook
Burrelle's Media Directory
Standard Periodical directory
Ulrich's Periodicals Directory
Media Finder
National Directory of Magazines
Television and Radio Directory

Note: If you are based outside of North America, consult with the research librarian at a library near you for a list of more appropriate national, geographic or language-relevant directories and services.

As you conduct your research, don't focus solely on traditional media outlets. Again, today's media includes such outlets as blogs, forums, websites, podcasts, vidcasts, video channels and social media personalities as well as the newsletters and websites of various associations and other organizations. Expand your research by conducting Google searches and services such as the Oxbridge Directory of Newsletters and the Directory of Associations.

While conducting your research, make note of any outlet that you think might be appropriate in the immediate or distant future. Such media outlets may serve the film industry or your film's target audience. Regardless, initially, you'll want to identify no more than two dozen or so media organizations that you'll want to concentrate your initial outreach activities on. And, whenever possible, try to develop a relationship with at least two professionals from each organization.

Keep in mind that the smaller and more narrowly focused the media outlet and its audience, the more success you are likely to have in terms of building lasting and meaningful relationships. These media outlets are often run by just two or three people who are often more receptive to establishing new relationships than many of their colleagues from larger national or international media organizations.

And, as your coverage grows with these local and specialty media outlets, you'll find it easier (although never altogether "easy") to get national and global digital, print and broadcast coverage.

While researching media outlets, irrespective of their relative size, be certain to visit their websites and consider their audience. What topics and subjects have they covered in the past? Identify frequent writers, contributing editors and the managing editor (often the same as the publisher) – particularly those that cover topics and subjects that may relate to you and your films.

After you've identified and researched appropriate media outlets, begin thinking of the best way to reach out to each organization. Do you know anyone who works there now or in the recent past? Anyone who has recently been covered by the organization? If you don't have anyone who can introduce you to an influential member of the organization's team, consider:

- Complimenting a reporter via Twitter, Facebook or the media organization's website on a story he or she recently published.
- Responding regularly to posts they've written either on their blog, the organization's site or a popular subject matter forum.
- Writing a positive post or comment on your own website, blog or social media account highlighting a story of theirs (and email them the link to the post).
- Congratulating them on their birthdays, or other personal news they post.

Once you've taken any one of these initial steps, use it as an excuse to follow up with a short emails to the reporter. Three or four sentences total. And devote lots of thought and time to the email subject line. Your email is much more likely to get read by busy reporters if it has an interesting subject line and is short and to the point.

Initially, you want to establish yourself only as a resource. Offer to provide background information and express a willingness to refer the writer to your colleagues and other professionals who they can also interview for quotes and background. However, don't pitch any ideas or send a press release. At least not yet. Instead, just focus on building a professional – and friendly – relationship.

Having begun interacting with targeted media professionals, work to sustain regular contact and build the relationship. Invite them out for coffee or to join you on location or on set, to a coming film festival, screening, premier or other event. By meeting in person, the relationship is able to become more meaningful as you each get to know one another better (remember to ask the reporter a lot of questions about their lives and their work . . . a relationship should not be entirely one-sided).

GENERATING & PITCHING IDEAS

Ideally, you should plan on establishing an ongoing relationship with a reporter several weeks in advance of pitching a story idea or public release. However, while it's important to build your relationships over time, don't wait too long to begin to pitch them on an interesting storyline, or you might lose the opportunity. Timing is imperative.

By now, since you've been researching and studying what each reporter and media outlet publishes and shares, you should have a good understanding of the types of things that interest them on a professional and personal level. Use this insight to develop pitches that meet three criteria:

Criteria #1. The topic must be appropriate and of interest to the specific media outlet and audience being pitched: Editors, producers and journalists ultimately decide what will be delivered to *their* audience. Specifically, they want to know:

- *Is the story idea or public release interesting to their subscribers, readers, viewers or listeners? Does the story have a local angle, human interest or other connection to the organization and its audience?*
- *How does your story or release compare relative to other topics, subjects and public release submissions the organization has published or may be considering publishing?*
- *Is it timely? Explain why the subject should be of interest to this media outlet and its audience now? Is the story or release tied to current events? A coming holiday? An anniversary of an important date? Other timely event or activity?*

Criteria #2: You, your studio, your film(s) and/or your cast and crew members must be relevant to the story: Assuming that the proposed story or release is appropriate and of interest to their organization and audience, media professionals will want to know how you are relevant to the story.

- *Has the pitch or public release been written in such a way that you, your studio and films are an obvious part of the storyline?*
- *Can your film's or studio's performance be appropriately compared and contrasted with industry trends, other filmmakers and films that may be relevant to the proposed story?*

- *Are you able to offer any particularly useful insights, data, case studies, anecdotes or relationships that would help the journalist with his or her article or broadcast?*

Criteria #3: The story or release, if published, must serve your marketing strategy: Before pitching a specific story or writing a particular public release, carefully consider your marketing and promotional strategy as well as your media, production, distribution, business and financial goals and objectives. Consider the following questions:

- *What stage of production are you at? What types of media coverage would be most helpful at this stage of production?*
- *Is the targeted media organization and its audience appropriate for your current media goals and objectives?*
- *Does the proposed storyline or release contain specific content or calls-to-action (direct or implied) that best advance your media strategy's goals and objectives?*
- *Is the pitch or public release timed to correspond with other marketing, promotional or media campaigns?*

With these suggestions in mind, the following is a list of ten of the most popular types of story ideas and public releases currently published by traditional and new media editors: (i) current events; (ii) celebrity news; (iii) holidays and anniversaries; (iv) fashion and popular trends; (v) exotic locations; (vi) emerging camera, film, distribution or similar technologies; (vii) how-to tips ("DIY"); (viii) human interest or exposés related to your film's storyline; (ix) top 10 lists; and (x) film industry trends.

Again, it's important that your story ideas and public releases be as interesting and relevant as possible to the subscribers, readers, viewers and listeners of your targeted media channels. Obviously, the more you can leverage popular topics such as these, the more success your media outreach and public relations efforts are likely to achieve.

Once you have a storyline or public release that meets these three criteria and have established some relationships, it's time to begin pitching your media contacts. Begin by sending a short personalized email that (i) references any earlier discussions you may have had with the recipient, (ii) describes your story idea or the topic of your public release and (iii) explains how – and when – you intend to follow up. For example,

> It was great chatting with you on [social media channel] about [subject]. Based on our conversation, I'd like to see if you and your audience might be interested in learning more about [topic]. [Briefly describe the topic and angle in one to two sentences.] Feel free to email or call me back at XXX.XXX.XXXX. If I don't hear back by [time/schedule/timeframe], I'll be sure to reach out to you with a quick call.

When pitching a storyline, pitch only one media outlet at any one time. It is important that you not email multiple pitches of the same story idea to more than one organization. However, if you've not heard back from the reporter or have been unable to reach him or her within the timeframe mentioned within your email, send a short follow-up email to let them know you intend to send the pitch to other outlets unless you hear from them in a day or two. (Note: This doesn't apply to public releases that, by their very definition, are distributed to multiple media outlets simultaneously.)

If your pitch is successful and your story or release is eventually published, offer occasional ideas you think would make for interesting articles or stories (particularly if the follow-up story has little or nothing to do with you, your studio or your film).

Depending upon the media outlet, many, if not most, of their stories are links in a long-running chain of similar stories.

On the other hand, if your story pitch doesn't result in media coverage, don't give up. Like every business, media outlets have both busy and slow periods. Be patient. Sometimes success is just a matter of reaching out to the right person at the right time.

PREPARING FOR BROADCAST AND PRINT INTERVIEWS

If done well, the pitch will result in a story in which you are included. While a public release (discussed in more detail later in this chapter) may be republished almost entirely as originally written, a successfully pitched story is hoped to result in an interview – or series of interviews.

Once a reporter contacts you regarding your story and a possible interview, respond as quickly as possible. Confirm the day, date and time as well as if you'll be speaking via telephone or meeting at the studio or other location. Also ask if the interview or discussion are meant for attribution or merely background.

If the reporter needs a quote or interview from you that day, say "yes" and ask if the reporter will give you a sense of the questions or quotes they need for the story. Then offer to call them back in thirty to forty-five minutes. Use this time to compose yourself and prepare some thoughtful sound-bites and responses to the reporter's questions. And, whatever else you may do, be certain to call the reporter back at the scheduled time.

Fortunately, reporters and hosts will typically provide you several days of advanced notice regarding a potential interview. Use this time to forward them a copy of your EPK and a list of suggested interview questions. While reporters are likely to have their own questions, many hosts will use many, if not all, of the questions you provide within your list.

If the reporter or host has their own questions (and they usually will have at least a few), they'll commonly agree to share the questions with you in advance so you can prepare your responses. From their perspective, both they and their audience benefit from the best possible responses to their questions.

Regardless of whether or not the reporter agrees to provide you with the questions in advance, be certain to research the reporter or host before the scheduled interview. Pay particular attention to articles and interviews they've done in the past. Are there common themes, subjects, topics or interview questions? How long (in word count or in minutes and seconds) are the quotes or guests' responses? Use this insight to anticipate, prepare and rehearse your own responses to likely questions in advance.

When preparing responses to questions, be certain to cover the fundamental details of who, what, when, where, why and how. But just as importantly, make your sound-bites and quotes stand out. As you craft your responses, use exciting and emotionally evocative analogies, examples, datapoints and action words and phrases.

At the same time, consider your own goals and objectives. What is it that you want or need to communicate? Identify three key messages that you want to deliver throughout the interview. *Can you incorporate these into generic responses that will fit different types of questions? How can you consistently communicate these three messages without being obviously repetitive?* As important as it is to repeat your key messages, however, don't avoid the reporter's questions. Make sure that your responses directly answer the questions that you've been asked.

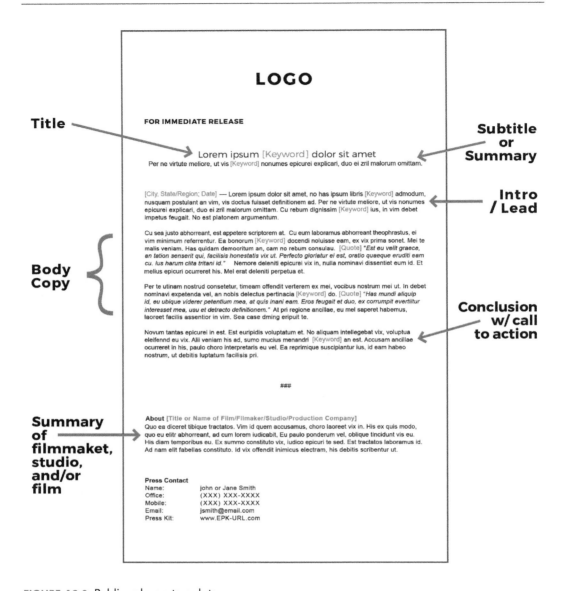

FIGURE 13.2 Public release template.

(Robert G. Barnwell/Sandy O. Cagnan)

It's also important to avoid concentrating only on your own experiences. Make a point of mentioning other well-known and well-respected filmmakers and their films. By making these celebrity references, you and your films will benefit from credibility by association.

Print Interviews: If you're being interviewed for a print or online story, be prepared to allow the reporter to lead the interview. And speak slowly so the reporter has time to take notes and mentally process what you're saying. Explain things chronologically if possible. Otherwise, consider providing information from most-to-least important. Again, work to prepare your responses to anticipated questions in advance.

Toward the end of the discussion, ask the reporter if there is any information that they'd like you to verify, clarify or expand upon. Keep in mind that you are being interviewed because you are an expert on the subject of your film, filmmaking or the industry. What you might think is common knowledge may not be to the reporter.

Broadcast Interviews: If, on the other hand, you are participating in a broadcast interview (on radio or on screen), make certain that you familiarize yourself with the program on which you are scheduled to appear. Get a feel for the host's personality and rhythm. During the interview, remember to smile. Talk to the host like a good friend. Use their name. Appear as if you have known each other for years. Be familiar, comfortable and confident.

When appearing on screen, be conscious of your clothing and accessories. Solid fabrics and colors work best on camera. Avoid clothing with patterns. Also consider your hair color and skin tone when choosing the color of your clothing. And, in addition to smiling, remember to lean forward slightly (10–15 degrees), which will make you appear more alert and athletic.

If you are appearing on a call-in broadcast program, arrange for three to four friends to call in with previously prepared questions. And keep your responses and sound-bites short. Ideally to less than twenty to thirty seconds. If the caller or host wants to know more, allow them to pose a follow-up question.

Finally, when the print or broadcast interview is complete, send an email or note a day later to thank the reporter for his or her time and express how much you enjoyed participating in the interview.

If you haven't done so already, use this follow-up email or note as an opportunity to get a release date for when the interview or article is expected to appear. Once you have a release date, pre-write emails and posts to promote the interview or article on your website, social media channels and other outlets. And, after the article or episode has been published or broadcast, seek permission to reprint or republish the interview and/or footage on your website's media or press page (and post to your social media accounts).

WRITING PRESS/NEWS/PUBLIC RELEASES

Press releases are an essential element of any public relations strategy. In addition to the many benefits of media coverage already discussed (second- and third-party validation, expanded brand recognition and increased ticket, film and merchandise sales), because public releases are often republished as originally written, releases give you unprecedented control over your story and message.

Public releases, however, can only achieve these benefits if they are written and structured properly. First, public releases need to be compelling and of clear interest to both the media organization and its own audience. Second, public releases need to be written in a neutral fact-based tone. Inform don't promote. The use of obvious sales language and hype will result in immediate rejection by credible media organizations. And, third, the release must be structured properly.

While there are an almost limitless number of possible release topics, the structure of public releases are relatively uniform, containing the following elements: (i) a published release schedule; (ii) a title and, occasionally, a subtitle; (iii) an opening or introductory paragraph; (iv) body copy; (v) concluding paragraph; (vi) contact information; (vii) filmmaker, studio and/or film description; and (viii) any supplemental information.

Each element of the public release has a specific purpose or objective.

Release Schedule

The release schedule informs the media of when the release is available for publication.

"For Immediate Release" informs the editor that the information is to be made available immediately. Immediate release is typically used when the information contained in the release is urgent or pertains to a topic that has happened or will happen in the very near future.

"For Release On [Date]" is used when sending a news release in advance of the date you want the information distributed. A release that you wish republished on the same day, or day prior, to your film's theatrical premier is a good example of an advanced-scheduled release.

"Release at Will" is used when time is not a critical factor in the release of the information. Since there is no time sensitive data and the release is not associated with any specific date or event, the media organization is free to republish the release at a time of its convenience.

Headline

The headline is the single most critical component of a public release. Your headline is the first, and often only, impression you will make on a prospective public release reader. On average, eight out of ten people will read your headline copy, but only two out of ten will go on to read the remainder of the release. It's crucial that the headline captures the reader's attention and drives them to read the remainder of the release.

Study the headlines from competing studio PR campaigns and magazine articles. You'll discover that the best headlines tend to be those that are descriptive, compelling and attention-getting. Such headlines tend to use action verbs, clear understandable language and contain keywords and key phrases.

Successful headlines are also short and simple. Google and many other search engines will only display the first sixty characters or fewer of the headline so work to keep headlines to one sentence and try to limit them to eighty characters or fewer. If you feel this eighty-character limit is too restrictive, consider the use of a subtitle. Regardless, both the headline and subtitle should be brief and published in bold type using a font that is larger than the body text. Title words should be capitalized with the exception of prepositions ("a," "an," "the," etc.) or any words of three characters or fewer.

Lead (First) Paragraph

The lead paragraph begins with the location and date of the story and transitions into an engaging summary of the story's most important points. In fact, if readers only read the first paragraph they should understand the story as well as the relevance of the story to themselves and/or their own readers. Again, assume that they will only read the first sentence and, perhaps, scan the remaining release.

Like the headline and subtitle, the first sentence of the lead paragraph, in particular, must capture the reader's attention and persuade the reader to continue reading. Reflecting the importance of these two elements, many publicists suggest spending as much as half your time developing and refining the release's title and lead paragraph.

Body Copy (Paragraphs 2, 3, 4 . . .)

The body of the press release is comprised of two to three paragraphs following the lead. These paragraphs transition from the general information provided in the introductory paragraph and expand into more specific details.

This approach is essentially the same "inverted pyramid" that journalists use to structure their own articles. The benefits of the inverted pyramid are three-fold: (i) the resulting release, since it is written to the same standards as used by the media, can be republished as submitted . . . without further revision or edit; (ii) the media, and their own readers, can quickly understand the story having read only the title and first paragraph; and (iii) the structure further assists in navigating readers through each successive detail through to the final concluding paragraph.

In addition to adhering to the inverted pyramid structure, the release should also feature attention-getting quotes, dramatic statistics or facts, interesting examples, stories or anecdotes and other elements that support, reinforce and expand upon your storyline. Two or three quotes, in particular, are effective at shaping your core messages and making them more compelling. Quotes also give a human element to the release . . . allowing the media and their readers to form a connection with you by hearing from you in your own "voice."

As you outline and write the key details within the release, don't forget to place yourself and your film(s) into the story. At the same time, consider tying yourself and your films to more prominent filmmakers, studios, films and events. This adds credibility to you and your project even though few readers may have ever heard of you before having read the article. By forwarding a copy of your release or resulting articles to those higher-profile filmmakers and industry professionals mentioned within your release, you also provide yourself an opportunity to build new relationships and expand your professional network.

Concluding Paragraph

The final concluding paragraph serves to summarize the preceding content and should contain a call-to-action. And, like the first sentence of the lead paragraph, the final sentence of the concluding paragraph is particularly important. The final sentence establishes the most lasting impression and should reinforce the release's main point. Following the conclusion of the final paragraph, double or triple space and mark the end of the release with three hash-marks (###).

Contact Information

Below the concluding paragraph hash-marks, a contact block should appear with the name, email address and telephone number of the contact person. Also consider including studio and film website URLs, social media links and possibly a link and password for a preview of your film.

Biography, Studio Description or Film Synopsis

End with a short three to four sentence paragraph describing your filmmaking career, studio, or film. If you are filing a joint press release with another organization – such as a promotional sponsor, co-production company or distributor – include a brief summary of the partner organization as well . . . along with a link to your home page.

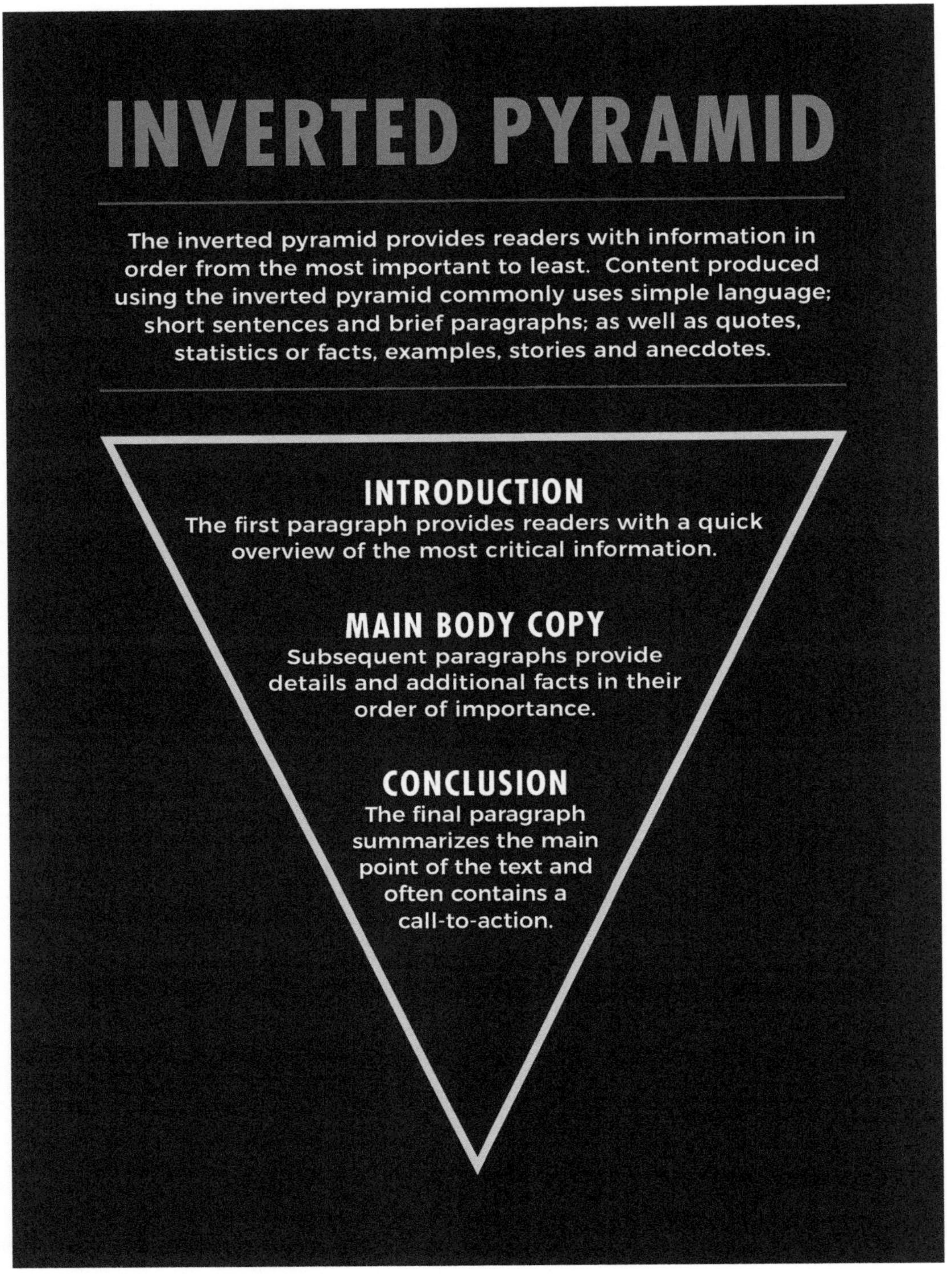

FIGURE 13.3 Inverted pyramid.

(Robert G. Barnwell/Sandy O. Cagnan)

Double-check to ensure the first sentence accurately and clearly describes you, your studio and/or your film(s) in a way that could easily be directly republished by a reporter or editor.

Supporting Information

Whether the release will be republished in print or online, reporters prefer releases and articles accompanied by photographs, illustrations and embedded multi-media content. Such supporting information typically includes an electronic press kit with key art, high-resolution photographs of the filmmaker, key cast and crew members, film stills, BTS photos and video and related materials.

Make certain that supplemental materials are converted to popular file formats such as PDF, JPEG, PNG and MP4 before attaching to your email or electronic release submission. Attachments (including photographs) should not exceed 25MB in total or should be zipped so they can be emailed. In addition to the attachments, consider providing a URL within the public release to your website's press room where additional information (such as the EPK) can also be downloaded.

PR Writing, Structuring & Formatting Guidelines

One of the most significant advantages of public releases is that they are commonly republished word-for-word. However, this requires that each release be written, structured and formatted to the same standards as those used by both traditional and new media.

Since most U.S. publications adhere to *The Associated Press Stylebook*, you'll have more success if your press release is written to AP standards. *The Associated Press Stylebook*, updated annually, is a guide for proper grammar and punctuation; styles for capitalization, abbreviation, spelling and numerals; and in-text attribution format. Once completed, hire a professional to edit your release and confirm that it conforms to AP standards (or other appropriate standard if you are targeting media outlets outside of the United States).

In addition to the AP style, the release should be written in the third-person using an active voice and easily understood language. Every element and every sentence within the public release is meant to get the reader to read the following sentence and paragraph. So work to eliminate or replace any word or phrase that threatens to disrupt readability and flow.

As with most good writing, shorter is usually better. If you have a topic that requires more than 500 words, find a way to divide the topic in half and write two separate public releases. Likewise, keep your sentences and paragraphs short; a paragraph should be no more than three to four sentences. Long blocks of text commonly frustrate readers, so consider using bullets to break up the text when appropriate.

Finally, if you are using an electronic release distribution service, the service's online program will typically format your release. Otherwise, there is a standard public release format that most journalists require, which includes:

- The page should be formatted with 1.5–2 inch margins (4–5 centimeters) around each side.
- Copy should be left-aligned and double-spaced using 12 point font such as Times New Roman, Arial or Verdana (the headline and subtitle should use 14–16 point font).

- Each paragraph should use block formatting (i.e. double-spacing between paragraphs and *not* indenting the first sentence of each paragraph).

If your release requires more than two pages, type " –MORE–" at the bottom of the first page. And, as you come to the bottom of the first page, be certain that you not split a paragraph between pages. Each paragraph should end on the same page on which it began. Once the concluding paragraph is complete, double- or triple-space and then type " –END– ."

Proofreading

Great press releases (like most marketing and promotional copy) aren't written – they're rewritten. Give yourself permission to write a rough first draft of your press release. It's alright. Just get it on paper. Then take time to add additional details, rewrite and edit. If you're still unhappy with the results, consider hiring a virtual writer or editor to rewrite the release for you.

However, regardless of whether or not you write the release yourself, it's important that you carefully proofread your press release – and let a few other people proofread it as well – before distribution. Even a single mistake can diminish your credibility and result in your release being tossed aside.

Begin the proofreading process by printing out the release. Do not read it on screen. Read the release carefully and then reread it again out loud. *How does the copy flow? Are there proper transitions from paragraph to paragraph and from thought to thought? Does it contain ordinary and easily understood words?* The release should avoid (i) clichés, special characters, bold, italics, exclamation points, words that appear in all caps and other formatting that emphasizes text; (ii) abbreviated words and industry jargon; (iii) HTML or embedded multi-media elements (including email addresses); as well as (iv) first-person perspective and the passive voice.

As mentioned previously, it's also important to remember that the release should be written to inform the reader rather than to promote. So avoid promotional language or words that appear to overly hype your filmmaking career, studio or films. Instead, the release should focus on the facts and substantive content.

After these first two read throughs, read the release a third time backwards, from the last word of the final paragraph to the first word of the introduction. During this reading focus primarily on spelling, grammar and paragraph structure.

Then, once you are happy with the revised release, have at least three other people read it. One person who has some familiarity or expertise in the release's topic and someone else who is unfamiliar with the subject. Finally, third, hire an experienced editor to review the release to make any necessary corrections and offer possible suggestions for a final round of improvement.

PUBLIC RELEASE DISTRIBUTION

Once the public release has been written, proofread and revised, it's time to distribute the release and make sure it finds its way into the right hands. There are four common methods of effective release distribution:

1. Free or Low-Cost Release Distribution Services: The first step in distribution should be the use of a public release distribution service (such as PR.com, PRNewswire.com and PRLog.org) that will distribute the release to thousands of potential media outlets (press, broadcast media and websites) as well as such services as Lexis-Nexis, Northern Light, Google News, Associated Press, U.S. News Online and hundreds of other global news services.

In addition to distributing the public release itself, many services publish a summary description of your release, detail on your PR firm (if you've employed one), a link to your organization's website, an email link to your point-of-contact, multi-media attachments in support of your release and archives of your past public releases and resulting media coverage.

2. Direct Distribution: The next step is to submit the release directly to media outlets (i) with whom you have already established a relationship and/or (ii) who have some special connection with the release. If you haven't already, have your film's cast and crew fill out a form listing birthplace, hometown, colleges attended, past media coverage, etc. Use this information to reach out to local hometown, university or other newspapers and broadcast news stations covering those areas. If cast and crew have been covered in the news in the past, contact the members of the media who conducted those original interviews.

3. Website Archives: Post your releases and any resulting media coverage to your website's press or media room. Remember: your website is your digital home. It's where you want everyone to eventually visit. Make certain that visitors can find all of your most important content . . . particularly past releases and media coverage.

4. Social Media and Email Subscribers: Finally, promote your public releases and resulting media coverage on your social media platforms. Include links and cite interesting quotes or facts from the release. When properly written, your press releases contain information of very real value to your fans. So don't let your PR work go undiscovered. Make sure you post to your Facebook, Twitter and other social media accounts as well as sending announcements and copies to those who've subscribed to your email list.

In addition to these channels, there are a few other things to consider to maximize the impact of your public release campaign. For instance, whenever possible, distribute your releases early in the morning and at least seven days prior to the date you'd most like the media to publish your release. When sending releases to specific members of the media, be sure to follow up by phone or email during the late morning or early afternoon.

And, like other marketing and promotional activities, consistency remains important. Plan on writing a release every sixty days (or even more frequently). As the number and frequency of published releases increase, you'll likely find that the effort required to obtain media inquiries and coverage will actually decrease.

One of the easiest and most effective ways to determine the relative effectiveness and impact of your public release and media strategy is the use of Google Alerts to track your media and internet coverage. Once you set up your account, Google Alerts will send you periodic emails to update you whenever your name is mentioned virtually anywhere on the web (including the major social media platforms).

As you monitor the effectiveness of your public release campaign, pay particular attention to (i) the number of times your release has been reprinted or posted; (ii) the number of media mentions and/or quotes; (iii) results or trends related to film sales and rentals, website visits, social media activity, film-related merchandise sales and other trends immediately before and after the distribution of specific public releases and any resulting media coverage.

When properly planned and developed, a sustained media outreach program provides your films with the opportunity to reach a tremendously large audience of readers, listeners or viewers. And well-implemented media-relations initiatives are able to do so without the expense associated with traditional advertising programs. The resulting cost-effective coverage serves to expand your studio's audience and increase film-related sales and profits – particularly when successfully integrated with other powerful marketing and promotional campaigns.

14

EVENT MARKETING: SCREENINGS, FESTIVALS, FILM MARKETS & OTHER EVENTS

Unlike most other branding, marketing and promotional activities, the strength of event marketing does not come from its ability to reach broad audiences of tens of thousands of friends and fans. Instead, events – such as wrap parties, film festivals, awards ceremonies, film markets, premiers and screenings – provide filmmakers the opportunity to interact, meet and reconnect directly with fans, influencers, sales agents, producer's representatives, distributors, co-producers, investors, product placement consultants and other potential members of your professional network and audience.

In addition to meeting face-to-face with fans and industry professionals, many events provide filmmakers with the opportunity to promote their films through film festival nominations and industry awards. Such nominations and awards can significantly increase awareness and interest in your film as well as your studio, career and any film projects you may have in development. Of course, events are also the ideal venue from which to identify and recruit members of your launch team, who will be instrumental in promoting your film premier through social media posts, reviews, ratings and word-of-mouth.

It's also important to note that the people you meet, as well as the workshops, seminars, panel discussions and sessions you attend, are also critical sources of insights into current and emerging filmmaking and industry trends, including: changes in demand for specific genres; scheduled releases of forthcoming films; identification and production status of various projects-in-development with fellow filmmakers and studios; and new marketing and promotional ideas.

EVENT MARKETING

Not surprisingly, there are literally hundreds – if not thousands – of events (and types of events) filmmakers can use to market their films. For the sake of simplicity, at this point in our discussion, we'll categorize these events into two broad groups: self-hosted events and external events (those events hosted by other filmmakers and film organizations).

Self-Hosted Events

Although considerably more demanding in terms of both time and financial resources, self-hosted events provide filmmakers with complete control over the topic, location, schedule and audience. Examples of such events include: investor events, launch parties, wrap parties, test screenings, private screenings, charity fundraisers and smaller more intimate events such as house parties, dinners, etc.

When planning any event, begin by establishing two objectives: First, *what do you and your team want to accomplish as a result of the event?* And, second, *how will your guests or attendees benefit from attending?* The more clearly you define these two objectives, the more likely you are to be to identify the most appropriate type of event to host and the more effective will be your planning and coordination.

These objectives will also be instrumental in generating a list of targeted attendees to invite. Consider the types of people who would most enjoy and benefit from the event and, at the same time, are in the best position to help you meet your own objectives. This, in turn, will provide a rough estimate of the number of likely attendees and, ultimately, the size of the event.

Once you've identified the most appropriate target audience, consider both the schedule and venue. You want the event to be as accessible to as many attendees as possible. *Will your proposed schedule conflict with other events or activities? What days and times are particularly convenient? Is the venue easily accessible with regard to local hotels, transportation (highways, subways, train stations, bus routes and/or airports) and convenient parking? Does the venue offer suitable access to food and drinks, restrooms and access to equipment such as film projectors, screens and audio systems if necessary? Cellular and public WiFi access?*

When considering locations to host your screenings, you'll want to achieve a balance between cost, convenience and quality. Some of the most popular locations or venues include: hotel meeting rooms, conference centers, film schools, local colleges, post-production facilities and community centers.

Having established (i) the event's objectives, (ii) the type of event, (iii) the number and type of attendees; (iv) the schedule; and (v) venue, you'll begin to form a rough estimate of the event's likely budget. In addition to these costs, you'll want to consider additional expenses, such as:

- Event marketing and promotion
- Event room rental
- Airfare and/or other travel
- Food and beverages
- On-site branding and signage
- Event staffing
- Equipment (projector, screen, etc.)
- Presentation materials
- Swag bags/promotional merchandise

An important, but often overlooked, logistical consideration is the number and type of staff required. As the filmmaker, your primary job is to engage and interact with your guests. You should not be working the door, serving food and beverages, or cleaning up inevitable spills (although, depending on the event, you may need to pitch in to help set up and clean up before and after the event). In particular, consider the staff required for check-in, to operate AV equipment, provide audience and guest support and to capture photos and videos of the event, attendees, cast and crew members, fans and other guests.

You'll want to make sure the event is as impressive as possible while remaining within budget. If necessary, consider incorporating a co-sponsor and co-host to offset expenses and increase reach. Depending upon the popularity of the event, you may also want to think about possibly selling tickets.

In the weeks and days leading up to the event, confirm details and logistics with the hotels and/or venues. It's particularly important to do this again forty-eight hours prior to the meeting. If anything is amiss, two days typically provides sufficient time to rectify the problem. Any later and it may be too late.

Shortly after you arrive and begin preparing for the day's event, take an inventory of equipment, table and seating, food and beverage service, signage and marketing, promotional and presentation materials. Have an audio-visual technician from the venue work with members of your staff to verify that equipment (including lighting, microphones, speakers, projectors, etc.) are functioning and that staff both understand and are comfortable with their operation. As an important precaution, make sure that your staff equipment operators have direct numbers to the venue's AV department and technicians.

Remember that your events must form lasting and powerful impressions. In addition to the quality of the event itself, consider setting up locations at the venue that serve as photo or "selfie stations." These include traditional film backdrops, large film posters on easels and opportunities to get pictures with interesting props, members of the cast wearing wardrobe, and film vehicles or set pieces.

Once the scheduled time and audience have arrived, thank everyone for attending and describe the nature and goals of the event. Provide attendees with passwords to the venue's WiFi system. And, as time and circumstances allow, introduce guests to one another and to other members of your production team. Encourage the photographer and videographer to record any event presentations and audience members congregating and talking among themselves. And finally, tell members of the audience what they can do to best help you and your film.

Attending the Events of Others

While self-hosted events present filmmakers a number of benefits, particularly with regard to control, few filmmakers have the time and budget to promote their films exclusively through self-hosted events. External events, in addition to typically being more cost and time efficient, provide filmmakers and PMDs with a large number and variety of events, the opportunity to win awards and achieve recognition for their films and accomplishments, to increase their network of professional relationships and benefit from the increased visibility and prestige that many of these events and organizations provide.

International film festivals, film markets, awards ceremonies and conferences such as the Academy of Motion Picture's Oscar Awards, British Academy Film Awards, American Film Market, CineMart, Hong Kong International Film and Television Market and Comi-Con International. These large and often highly prestigious events tend to attract the most well-regarded industry professionals and require less planning and investment than self-hosted events.

As you consider various events, don't become fixated solely on festivals, markets and awards. Various industry organizations, including associations, guilds, film schools, film commissions and trade publications, host regular meetings, workshops, summits and annual conferences. For instance, *Variety* hosts an annual Entertainment Marketing Summit, the Producer's Guild of America presents a series of "Produced By . . . " events, *The Hollywood Reporter* hosts an annual Women in Entertainment Breakfast (by invitation) and the Directors Guild of America hosts a series of discussions with accomplished feature film directors.

To find out more about film events near you, consult the calendar of events of regional, national and international trade publications and organizations. You can also discover smaller local film organizations and get togethers on such sites as Meetup.com and Facebook. These smaller events, although often less prestigious, are ideal in forging longer-term relationships during your film's development and pre-production. Many of the people you meet will become some of your first launch team members and will make important introductions and referrals to others in the local film community.

Depending upon where you live (as well as your budget and schedule), you may find it surprisingly easy to attend two, three or more film-related events each week ... particularly if you live and work in the Los Angeles area.

Regardless of the type of event you plan to host or attend, there are a few ways to help you maximize the value of any event you host or attend:

First, be sure to come prepared. Make sure that you bring more than enough business cards, postcards, mini-posters, pitch or sales sheets and physical or electronic press kits. And don't forget to bring your laptop or tablet computer, smart phone, extra batteries and charging devices. You'll want to be able to show teasers, trailers and film clips upon request. You'll also want your smart phone or a convenient camera to capture photographs with celebrities, fans, friends and family as well as to record testimonials, endorsements and video posts.

Second, know who you want to meet and where you are most likely to meet them (at the event, venue or hotel lobby, opening night gala, etc.). Don't leave this to chance: whenever appropriate, invite those you'd like to meet to the event and schedule a time to get together. These may be agents, reps, distributors, potential cast or crew, members of the media, your fans or others who you would like to meet and may be prove helpful.

Third, network efficiently. Typically, particularly if the event is relatively large and you have many people you'd like to meet, work to keep conversations short while networking – no more than five minutes. Not only will this provide you the opportunity to meet the greatest number of people, it will also keep you from monopolizing the time of those you meet.

Begin by introducing yourself and asking a simple – yet relevant – question such as: *Did you attend the event last year? What other events have you attended recently? How do you know so-and-so? What do/did you think about such and such?* Hand them a business card with your name, title, name of your studio or production company, website URL, email and telephone numbers to reach you both during and after business hours (ideally one of these numbers should be a cellular number). And be sure to ask for their business card as well. Write notes on the back of their cards on how you met, the subjects you discussed and details of any promised follow up. Keep a few pens and a notebook close at hand for those without business cards.

And be sure to also take advantage of the opportunity to collect marketing and promotional collateral from other films and filmmakers in attendance. Not only will you learn new marketing and promotional ideas but you'll also gain insight into how best to position yourself relative to other films and filmmakers in the marketplace.

PROMOTING EVENTS

How you choose to promote (and how intensely you promote) an event has a lot to do with the nature of the event itself, including the extent of your financial investment to host or attend the event, its size, its relative prestige, its location and the importance of your objective(s) in attending the event. And remember: It can be just as important to promote events you may not be hosting but will be attending, such as festivals, film markets and awards ceremonies.

If you have a public calendar posted on your website, you can begin promotion by updating it with the details of each new event you intend to host or attend. You'll also need to incorporate the event into your marketing calendar. Among other activities, the marketing calendar should establish a targeted number of social media posts, group emails and other promotional activities to be completed each day or week in the weeks and months leading up to the event.

If you are attending an external event – such as a festival – the organizers have likely already prepared shareable event-specific promotional graphics and designs. On the other hand, if you are promoting an event of your own, you'll want to create your own promotional graphics and visual elements. These graphics will be used to produce banner ads for websites and social media platforms. The banner ads should clearly communicate the benefits people will derive from attending the event; create a sense of urgency, special offer or incentive to register now; and provide a link to register. You may also want to consider incorporating pictures and videos of past events and a map – and perhaps a photograph – of the actual event venue or location.

As with other marketing and promotional campaigns, it's important to incorporate a multiple number of touches across a variety of marketing channels, including social media and website updates. In addition, be sure to send a series of "Save the Date" and reminder emails to your contact database with an "Add to Calendar" button for Google calendars or Outlook. And encourage other members of your team, coop partners or sponsors and audience to also post details of the event.

FIGURE 14.1 A private screening held at the Soho House West Hollywood's well-appointed screening room.

(Soho House; Editorial/Fair Use)

For particularly important people and personalities – such as influencers and celebrities, reach out directly by telephone, email or social media message to encourage them to attend and arrange to get together. You may want to think about offering them free or highly discounted tickets to encourage them to attend.

Don't overlook the need to continue promotion during and after the event. Among other activities, send out email reminders of any planned on-site get togethers, private meet-up, or after-parties. Work to integrate the event into social media by live-streaming, posting comments, pictures and videos live from the event using an event-specific hashtag. At the very least, set aside thirty minutes twice a day to send and respond to emails and post social media updates.

By providing regular updates from the event, including the films, speakers and the people you meet, you'll both (i) encourage others at the event to seek you out and (ii) encourage those who were unable to attend to make a point of attending the next event so they don't miss out on the excitement.

LAUNCH PARTIES, SET VISITS & WRAP PARTIES

As with other marketing and promotional activities, event marketing should begin long before the film's premier – with the film's launch party (if not sooner). Not only are the cast and crew instrumental in the film's production, they are also among the most important marketing promotional representatives of the film. So it's critical that you use the launch party, set visits and wrap party to establish, communicate and encourage the many ways they can support the promotion of the film both as individuals and as a team.

In addition to their promotional value, these events are often the first opportunity that the cast, crew, production team and investors are able to meet and get to know one another. From the point of view of the producer and director, you'll want the launch party, in particular, restricted to those on the cast and crew who will be working closely on the film's production over the coming days and weeks. Ideally, when well-planned and executed, the launch party will foster a sense of togetherness and team spirit that carry over to the film set. Understandably, it's difficult to establish a team environment if the launch party is open too broadly beyond the immediate cast and crew.

As a result, you'll want to keep the launch party guest list limited to members of the cast and crew. The venue should be relatively private and closed to the public and media (particularly if you'll have any A-list celebrity actors in attendance). Ideally, the venue should also offer plenty of space for people to break off on their own to have conversations without having to shout to be heard over the sound of the band, music or crowd. Host drinks for at least two to three hours and establish a hard closing time (12:00–1:00AM work well).

Typically, the launch party is held two days before production begins. The following day is commonly a light day with a mid-morning start to allow the hardest-partiers a chance to recover from the prior night's festivities. The day also allows the cast to read through and rehearse the week's coming performances; for the crew and production team to complete last-minute issues with regard to locations, sets, wardrobe, props or equipment; and an opportunity for the director and cinematographer to finalize the shot planning, actor and camera blocking, etc.

Set visits, although commonly less structured than launch and wrap parties, can be no less important. Set visits are typically reserved for only the most important guests, including investors, sales agents, members of the media, super-fans and, perhaps, one or two colleagues, friends or family members. Ideally, set visits are limited to only five to ten people per day so as not to unduly burden the set and production. In fact, it is for this reason that set visits are typically prohibited during the first and last week of filming (which admittedly is going to be a problem for those attempting a ten-day shoot) as well as during morning hours.

Set visits should be coordinated and hosted by a member of the production team who will give guests a tour of the set, make introductions to the director, cast and crew members, and attend to them as they watch the action from an out-of-the-way but not-too-distant location. Mid-day set visits are often preferred and allow visitors to eat lunch and interact with the cast and crew.

When planning the wrap party, refer to the earlier launch party invitation list and then add any subsequent additions to the cast (including extras), crew and others on the final credit list (include post-production professionals if they live or work nearby). If your cast and crew have traveled far and wide for the production, you may want to schedule the wrap party for the final evening of production before people disband and fly to their respective homes. In most respects, the wrap party is not unlike launch parties. However, one nice touch is to give out humorous awards to members of the cast and crew for innocent mistakes or interesting personality traits exhibited on set.

With any luck, your cast and crew will remember your production fondly, will do all that they can to promote its release and will join you again on subsequent film projects.

TEST SCREENINGS

As noted in Chapter 4, because independent films are resource constrained and have investors who are understandably anxious to recapture their investments, many independent filmmakers mistakenly rush their films through post-production and into distribution – rarely budgeting the time and money for test screenings, reshoots, pickup shots and re-edits. Unfortunately, not only do screenings and additional post-production often spell the difference between commercial success and failure, but also members of the test screening audience, much like cast and crew members, are often your film's earliest and strongest supporters.

Given the significant potential value of screenings, let's explore the three types of recommended audiences and screenings: (i) the first comprises both niche and general audience members; (ii) the second is hosted for technical experts – those familiar with cinematography, sound, practical and computer effects, etc.; and, finally, (iii) third, private screenings for cast, crew, investors, producers, sales agents, distributors and others with a professional interest in the film.

From a logistical point of view, I recommend hosting two screenings per evening. The first screening of the evening for general audience members and the second later screening comprised of technical professionals.

For general audience screenings, each screening should have an audience of twenty-five to fifty participants split roughly in half – with the first half comprising carefully selected members of your target audience and the second half, a broader audience demographic. This second half should be as diverse as possible, with a wide age range, evenly split between male and female, multiple races, cultures, nationalities and socio-economic backgrounds, and with varying movie tastes.

Note: Professional test screening companies will often recruit as many as 100–250 audience members per screening. However, for independent filmmakers, not only is enlisting such large audiences difficult and often cost-prohibitive, but it is almost impossible to elicit an interactive and meaningful post-screening discussion from such a cumbersome group.

Technical screenings would be comprised of an audience of five to ten film school professors and students, professional filmmakers, screenwriters and other technical production and post-production professionals (cinematographers, sound engineers, special and visual effects supervisors, etc.). Unlike some members of the larger general audience screenings, members of the technical screening rarely need prodding to provide input and suggestions. Technical professionals often build and expand upon one another's comments. Therefore, you'll likely find that it's far easier to maintain an interactive and informative discussion with such technical audiences than with a more general audience.

I also suggest video recording the audience during both the screening and post-screening discussion. In combination with your written notes, the video provides an opportunity for you and your production team to revisit the audience's reactions, comments and insights. The video captures valuable nuance that is often lost when reactions and spoken comments are summarized only in writing.

Ultimately, the purpose of the early screenings is to help identify opportunities for improvement while the subsequent screenings confirm that the problems – and any other issues – have been adequately addressed. Once you've identified and rectified one set of problem areas, the next screening will identify a whole new set of problem areas that the prior issues overshadowed. This could go on indefinitely. However, a series of two to three general audience screenings and technical screenings should be sufficient to address the film's most significant issues. On the other hand, if you're still unsatisfied with the film after this initial group of screenings, continue to do as many more as you feel you need.

Wait to schedule any screenings until you've completed a fine cut of the film (final stage before "locking" the film) with temp music, preliminary sound mix, special effects, color grading and other post-production work. The idea is for the audience to identify issues that you and your crew may not already be aware of. If the screened movie is largely a work-in-process, the audience comments will likely point to aspects of the film that you are already well-aware of and have planned to address with further post-pro.

To assure proper turnout, confirm attendance with each audience member the day or night before the scheduled screening date – by both telephone and email, if possible. *Despite everyone's best intentions, there will always be no-shows, so it's a good idea to modestly overbook to assure your targeted attendance.* You may also want to prepare a contact list of six to eight alternates . . . just in case.

If you haven't already done so, get the name, telephone number and email address of everyone who attends. These are potentially the first fans of your film, and if they like the film or at least liked you and enjoyed the experience, they can be useful champions later in the process. In addition, use the contact information to assure that you do not accidently invite the same test audience members to more than one screening. It's important that each audience is unique and that thoughts and comments from one screening do not influence other screenings.

Pre-Screening Comments

Make sure that you and your team arrive well in advance of the scheduled screening. Before the audience arrives, (i) double-check that the projector or disk player and speakers are operating correctly; (ii) set up a folding table or two with food and drinks; (iii) locate the nearest restrooms and make certain they are unlocked and clean; and (iv) place the survey questionnaires and pens or pencils on each audience seat.

As the audience arrives, welcome each and introduce them to any members of the film crew and cast that may be in attendance as well as fellow audience members. Bring along copies of BTS photos and select props and wardrobe for audience members to view and discuss.

If you don't already know your audience members by name, you may want to have them wear color-coded name-tags. One color for members of your target audience and another color for general audience members.

A few minutes after the scheduled screening time, be sure to let everyone know the location of food and drinks and the restrooms. Explain the purpose and value of their contribution as well as the run time of the film, anticipated time to complete the questionnaire and discussions and what time they can expect to leave. Ask that they limit their discussions with one another until after the film and questionnaire are completed. Finally, thank the audience for attending, welcome the cast, crew and special guests (who are typically seated in the front row), turn down the lights and roll the film.

Questionnaires & Discussion

As the end credits begin to roll, just before turning up the lights, begin distributing forms for people to complete once the screening is complete. Remind everyone that the forms are anonymous and to please complete the forms before discussing what they thought with anyone. Make it clear that you want their candid opinion and need to learn what they both liked most and liked least about the film.

The questionnaire (a sample of which is provided in the appendices) will ask the audience member to answer questions regarding the story, characters, music, pacing and ending as well as how much they liked – or disliked – individual scenes and shots, before finally asking them to share general demographic information about themselves. As you can see, it's important to not only establish whether or not they enjoyed the film but for them to identify their feelings regarding specific aspects of the film.

When everyone has filled out and submitted their questionnaires, it's time to begin the discussion. Start the discussion by asking general questions to allow issues to come up naturally . . . without guidance. During these general questions, encourage everyone to participate while allowing individual participants sufficient time to get comfortable and "open up."

Once the audience has responded to the general questions, introduce specific questions and concerns which you and your editor may have with regard to this initial cut of the film. However, as you direct the discussion, be very careful not to provide guidance on the types of answers or responses you may expect... at least initially. If you have a specific concern, first ask an open-ended question such as *"How did you feel about the film's ending?"* Once everyone has had a chance to comment, then you can feel free to ask a more pointed question such as *"You didn't feel the climax was too obvious?"*

If you have considerable concerns with regard to specific aspects of the film, it might make sense to ask the audience to focus on these concerns or issues at the outset – prior to playing that evening's screening. You may even want to provide audience members with a small notecard containing specific issues with which you may be concerned.

As you direct the discussion, recognize that some participants will be more engaged than others. Those that talk the most will have a tendency to shape the direction of the discussions and influence the other participant's responses. If a small group of vocal participants reach a consensus around a particular point, ask if anyone else has a differing opinion. Finally, be sure to identify quieter members of the group and ask them for their opinions.

As any statistician will tell you, the small screening audiences will not provide statistically sound results. Many filmmakers may also be alarmed to discover that, after the discussions have ended and the questionnaires reviewed, what was said during the discussions often conflicts with what participants had previously written on their forms. Despite these contrasting opinions, holistically, the questionnaires and discussions (i) give filmmakers an idea of how well the film plays to an audience as well as (ii) that audience's opinion on various topics. It also provides (iii) an opportunity for filmmakers to see how audiences react to specific moments in the film.

At least one filmmaker, Quentin Tarantino, relies almost exclusively on observation of the test audience reaction to the screenings of his films. Fred Raskin – who served as editor for both *The Hateful Eight* (2015) and *Django Unchained* (2012) as well as an editorial assistant on both *Kill Bill* films (2003 and 2004) – describes Tarantino's screening process:

> *We do a number of screenings, first for Quentin's director friends, and then later for a recruited audience or two. Quentin doesn't do comment cards, nor does he care about numerical scores. The screening process is all about feeling the energy of the audience – where are they laughing, where are they not laughing when we thought they would be, where are we feeling them getting restless, where have we traumatized them and, of course, where are they most engaged with the movie? The adjustments we make following a screening are much more about reacting to the audience's energy than to their specific comments, although without question, an insightful remark during a post-screening chat will not go ignored if it resonates with us.*
> (Fred Raskin, Editor *The Hateful Eight* (2015),
> quoted in Hemphill, 2015)

It's important to note that – when well planned and executed – screenings are a great opportunity to build on your fan base and to recruit members of your film's launch team.

Based on the results of the audience and technical screenings, consider selective reshoots, additional post-production work and re-edits of the film. Once you are satisfied with the final film, you'll want to (i) arrange one or more private screenings for cast, crew, investors, producers, sales agents, distributors and others with a professional interest in the film; and (ii) work closely with your production team (including PMD, sales agent and/or producer's rep) to develop a film festival and promotional strategy.

Note: There are a number of services now offering online test screenings of feature films and trailers, including: iScreeningRoom.com, National Research Group, Rentrak, MarketCast, Screen Engine/ASI, PSB Research and Vibetrak. Among the benefits of such services, many allow you to test your film with highly targeted demographic groups from various regions throughout the world. On the other hand, among the downsides of such online services is the fact that it is difficult – if not impossible – to gauge the "feel" for the way a film plays with a live test audience.

FILM FESTIVALS

Film festivals are an important outlet for each filmmaker and independent production company to increase awareness and credibility with colleagues, agents, managers, distributors and investors (as well as future cast and crew members). In addition, many film sales will be completed at first-tier film festivals. Some festivals also have their own

FIGURE 14.2 Evening at the Palais des Festivals at the International Film Festival de Cannes, France.

(Featureflash Photo Agency/Shutterstock.com)

cable channels or licenses that provide for distribution to nominated films. So be prepared.

Determine your primary and secondary goals of entering into film festivals. These goals could include recognition, awards and cash prizes; media coverage and reviews; the opportunity to meet and network with prospective investors, sales agents, reps and distributors; and intelligence on the latest marketing, distribution and production trends. With almost 5,000 film festivals around the world, chances are good that there are several that will meet your needs and objectives.

While your strategic objectives are certainly the most important festival selection criteria, you'll also want to consider the festival's prestige, relative competitiveness, schedule and location, and budgetary considerations, such as entry fees, transportation, lodging, food and the cost of festival passes. Make a list of those film festivals that most align with these goals, note the entrée fees and deadlines and assess your resources (particularly with regard to time and budget) to determine the number of festivals to which you can submit, market, promote and attend.

This talk of strategic objectives and budget notwithstanding, when all is said and done, not surprisingly, most filmmakers (and their investors, cast, crew and sales agents) hope to show their films at one or more of the world's most prestigious festivals. These festivals typically include:

1. Festival de Cannes (Cannes, France)
2. Sundance Film Festival (Park City, UT)
3. Toronto International Film Festival (Canada)

4. South by Southwest (Austin, TX)
5. Venice Film Festival (Italy)
6. Berlin International Film Festival (Germany)
7. International Film Festival Rotterdam (Netherlands)
8. Tribeca Film Festival (New York, NY)
9. Busan International Film Festival (South Korea)
10. Hong Kong International Film Festival (China)
11. BFI London Film Festival (England)
12. Edinburgh International Film Festival (Scotland)
13. Telluride Film Festival (Telluride, CO)
14. Melbourne International Film Festival (Australia)
15. Dubai International Film Festival (United Arab Emirates).

In addition to these and other of the world's most twenty-five to fifty prestigious "first-tier" festivals, there are a number of other highly regarded second-tier and specialist film festivals such as Hot Docs (Toronto, Canada) and Visions de Reel (Nyon, Switzerland)

FIGURE 14.3
People attend the Tribeca Film Festival premier of *Genius* at BMCC Tribeca PAC in New York City.

(Miro Vrlik/Shutterstock.com)

for documentary films; horror film festivals such as Screamfest (Hollywood, CA) and Toronto After Dark (Toronto, Canada); family and children's film festivals such as the International Family Film Festival (Los Angeles, CA); and gay and lesbian film festivals such as Outfest, the Los Angeles Gay and Lesbian Film Festival (Los Angeles, CA).

Such second-tier and specialty film festivals aside, there are those who rightly point out that, to a large degree, the marketing and promotional benefits of attending – and perhaps even winning – any of the many less regarded film festivals just isn't worth the effort. On the other hand, smaller festivals allow you to perfect your presentation skills and get comfortable in front of an audience before screening at larger more prestigious festivals. It's also a good idea to screen at festivals in the cities and hometowns of major investors (assuming any live outside of an area with a major first or second-tier festival). This gives investors an opportunity to proudly showcase the film to their many local colleagues, friends and family.

Not surprisingly, the competition among films at first- and second-tier film festivals is intense. As just one example: Sundance now receives more than 15,000 applications for fewer than 250 screenings. Obviously, the higher the quality and production value of your film, the better its chances of being accepted. However, there are other ways in which to further improve your chances of selection:

1. *Apply Early:* Most festivals have a "rolling acceptance" that gives preference to early applicants.
2. *Attachment:* Casting is also important, even for film festivals. If your film features well-known domestic or international film, television, sports or other entertainment personalities, your film's nomination application will be greatly improved.
3. *Prior Festival Experience:* Similarly, most festival committees give precedence to filmmakers – particularly screenwriters, producers and directors – who have screened at the festival (or other prestigious festival) previously.
4. *Preferred Genres and Films:* Although rarely acknowledged, many film festival committees have distinct preferences in terms of the genres and types of films they nominate. Those with films that align with such preferences will naturally be advantaged over those that don't.

Another important admissions consideration is the status of your film's official premier. Most of the first-tier festivals require that films are submitted with the understanding that, if accepted, the festival screening will serve as the film's "world premier." Therefore, never show your film using the term "premier" until you have an official festival premier. Instead, call any showings a "sneak preview" or "private showing" or other term. But never the "premier."

Audit your letters of agreement, contracts and licensing to make sure all is complete (particularly with regard to music). Review submission requirements and make certain that, in addition to agreements and licensing, you have all required submission materials and are prepared to submit the film in the proper format. Read each festival's instructions carefully and create a checklist of required materials . . . again, for each festival. Typical application requirements include:

- Title and tagline
- Category/genre
- Logline (20–40 words)
- Film summary (100–200 words)
- Principal cast and crew listing
- Key art
- Stills/pictures
- Running time in minutes
- Releases and clearances

Keep detailed and accurate electronic records of submissions, requirements, key dates and festival contacts/organizers. The process of festival submissions (as well as managing and tracking submission dates, submission materials and admissions status) has been vastly improved with the use of Withoutabox. The platform provides filmmakers a database of over 2,500 film festivals on five continents and the ability to electronically submit their films to almost 1,000 film festivals worldwide. In turn, Withoutabox allows festivals to market their event to almost 500,000 registered film-makers, accept electronic submission fees and automatically notify filmmakers of acceptance into their festivals. As a result, many festivals, including such first-tier festivals as Sundance and Toronto, now prefer to receive applications through Withoutabox rather than direct submissions.

Unfortunately, as mentioned previously, the competition among films for the leading first-tier festivals is intense. However, festival committees have found that the majority of submissions are plagued by one or more of the following problems: incomplete applications (including missing or improper clearances), weak script, casting non-film actors (correspondingly weak acting), bad sound, inadequate post-production and editing and weak marketing and promotion.

An experienced production team and thorough pre-production process will help avoid many of these issues. However, it remains helpful to regularly review your material to identify any weaknesses and opportunity for improvement. If necessary, reshoot problematic scenes, film helpful pickup or insert shots, and, perhaps, re-cut the film. Fortunately, if worst-comes-to-worst, you can often retitle the improved film and resubmit to many of the same festivals that may have rejected your film the prior season.

Once your film has been accepted, ask the festival how many tickets you will be provided. In addition to yourself and contingent of cast, crew and other professionals (publicist, lawyer, etc.), have enough tickets in reserve to accommodate sales agents and buyers. If you've been accepted to a first-tier film festival, give serious consideration to hiring a publicist and other professionals (such as a producer's representative and/or a sales agent). Bring actors and key crew members whenever possible (particularly those responsible for cinematography, CGI, special effects, stunts, etc.). And invite repre-sentatives from any promotional or production partners to attend.

If you haven't already been contacted by the festival's publicist and head of marketing, introduce yourself and ask ways in which you can best help promote the festival and your film's screening. Quickly update your website calendar with the date, time and location of the festival screening and email invitations to your database of friends and fans. You'll also want to be prepared to promote your screening at the festival. Enlist a small team to post fliers with screening details and location, handout postcards and promotional items (such as posters, mini-posters, postcards, sales or pitch sheets, business cards, hats, T-shirts, wristband and other promotional materials).

When the time for your screening has finally arrived, keep the introduction short. Thank everyone for attending; remember to thank your cast, crew and the rest of your production team (many of whom, hopefully, have been positioned in the front row); ask that everyone turn off their cell phones; and then encourage them to enjoy the film.

Once the film ends and the lights come up, thank everyone again for attending and ask them to stick around for the Q&A. To help facilitate the Q&A, ask a member of your team or the festival staff to pick audience members to ask questions. Few things are more embarrassing than asking for questions and then hearing nothing but silence in response. To make sure that this doesn't happen to you, arrange for friends to attend your screenings and provide them with a few questions. And practice your answers.

FIGURE 14.4 Sha Yi, Zhang Yi, Wang Qianyuan and Yuan Wenkang attend *The Golden Era* premier during the Venice Film Festival, Italy.

(taniavolobueva/Shutterstock.com)

When responding to questions, make a point of repeating the question before answering. Not everyone will have heard the question and this provides a few extra seconds to formulate your response.

Here are some of the most common Q&A questions you can expect to hear following a festival screening:

Q1. *Where did you get the idea for the film?*

Q2. *Where did you get the idea for specific scenes in the film?*

Q3. *How did you execute specific shots or effects?*

Q4. *Who are your filmmaking influences?*

Q5. *What were the most difficult aspects of the film?*

Q6. *Where did you shoot the film?*

Q7. *How long did it take to shoot?*

Q8. *What equipment did you use?*

Q9. *How much was the budget?*

Q10. *How did you raise the funding?*

Q11. *What is your follow-up film?*

Following your screening and the Q&A, encourage the audience to tell their friends about the film – particularly if there is a second screening scheduled. Make a point of sticking around to circulate among the crowd and introduce yourself. And work to obtain video testimonials and photographs of yourself with members of the audience.

Obviously, your first priority will be the success of your film's screening. However, it's also important to get out among the festival crowd, meet as many people as possible and take in screenings of other films. Which films will be screening? Who would you like to meet? Where do people hang out? You should be able to meet many people in the hotel lobbies and at nearby restaurants, coffee shops, cafes and bars. Festivals occasionally post lists of the major parties, including the opening night gala, on their websites. If you contact festival organizers early enough, you might be able to get an early invite to some of the more exclusive parties and events (publicists are also a good source of invitations).

In addition to parties, workshops and other festival events, you'll want to attend the films of other filmmakers . . . particularly those with similar genres and production budgets to your own film. Pay close attention to the opening and closing credits. In particular, make note of the production companies and executive producers of each film. With few exceptions, these are the companies and professionals who financed the film and that likely finance similar independent films. Of course, if there were elements of the film you particularly liked (script, cast members, SFX makeup, CGI, color grading, editing, etc.) you may also want to take note of the professionals responsible for those elements as well.

Once the screening has ended and you've completed your notes, stick around afterwards to chat. Introduce yourself to the other filmmakers and their production teams. Congratulate them on the film screening and let them know what aspects particularly impressed you.

Depending upon the quality of your film and festival promotional strategy (and networking skills), a successful festival season should result in a number of awards, new relationships and increased market recognition.

AWARDS CEREMONIES & OTHER INDUSTRY EVENTS

As important as film festivals can be in creating buzz and recognition for independent films and filmmakers, even the most prestigious festivals have a difficult time competing with the considerable media coverage and recognition afforded by award ceremonies such as the Academy of Motion Pictures Arts and Sciences' Academy Awards (aka "Oscars"), the British Academy Film Awards (BAFTAs), Independent Spirit Awards and International Film Critics Award (Fédération Internationale de la Presse Cinématographique).

Winners (and nominees) of such awards commonly witness a significant increase in theatrical and VOD sales and rentals. Not surprisingly, the largest increases are often afforded to lower-budget films that audiences may have previously had limited knowledge of prior to their nominations. Not only do these smaller films benefit from increased exposure, but award nominations also afford such films with enhanced credibility and industry validation. And nomination for an award often leads to a theatrical release or re-release of these films. Finally, filmmakers who receive such nominations and awards often find it easier (although never altogether easy) to raise funding and distribution for follow-on films.

FIGURE 14.5
The Oscars (aka "The Academy Awards") at the Kodak Theater in Los Angeles, CA.

(egd/Shutterstock.com)

Unfortunately, despite the considerable benefits of industry awards and nominations, the cost of an awards campaign can be considerable. For instance, the cost of a "Best Picture" Oscar campaign commonly ranges from $7.5 to $15 million dollars. Approximately half of these expenses are associated with advertisements placed in trade publications, websites and other venues. The remaining campaign expenditures include DVD mailings and online screeners, private screenings for voting members of the awards organization, campaign and public relations consultants, and the cost of tickets, hotels, travel, dress clothing and other expenses associated with attending the event itself.

As a result, many smaller studios and filmmakers find that they are insufficiently resourced to mount a successful campaign for such premier awards. Fortunately, in addition to these highly prestigious awards, as with film festivals, there are a number of other industry awards organizations for regionally produced and genre-specific feature films as well as awards presented by various guilds and associations such as the Art Directors Guild, Directors Guild of America, Producers Guild of America and the Screen

FIGURE 14.6
Director Kathryn Bigelow at the Directors Guild of America Awards at the Century Plaza Hotel. She won Best Feature Film Director award for *The Hurt Locker*.

(Jaguar PS/Shutterstock.com)

FIGURE 14.7 Marc Schauer, Laura Linney, George Clooney and Sarah Larson at the Governor's Ball after-party for the Annual Academy Award's Oscars Ceremony.

(Everett Collection/Shutterstock.com)

Actors Guild in North America. Many of these awards, particularly guild- and union-associated awards, are highly prestigious in and of themselves (and can lead to nominations to larger awards ceremonies).

Regardless of which awards nominations you may choose to pursue, in addition to campaign costs, each filmmaker must consider the individual nomination qualifications. Some awards qualifications restrict consideration to only those films that have been screened at specific film festivals, members of particular guilds or associations or to films financed and shot in particular territories or countries. Among the largest and most prestigious awards ceremonies (such as the Oscars and BAFTAs), in addition to other nomination qualifications, films must have first been theatrically released for a minimum period of time and showings. In the case of the Academy Awards, among other possibilities, this requirement may be met by scheduling a "four wall" release (see Chapter 16).

FILM MARKETS

While it's impossible to know the precise number, many industry analysts estimate that more than 20,000 feature films are produced around the world each year. And, of those, the Sundance Film Festival now receives more than 6,000 feature film submissions. In addition to the acclaim associated with first-tier film festivals such as Berlin, Cannes, Sundance, Tribeca and Toronto, acceptance greatly improves a film's chances for distribution.

In recent years, ~75% of those films accepted to Sundance received distribution with such deals reportedly averaging ~$2.0 million each. And, even for those films that don't receive distribution at the time of their festival screening, based on their acceptance to a tier-one film festival, most films and filmmakers are then able to hire leading sales agents and producer's reps and will later achieve successful distribution.

However, given the state of intense competition among films in the festival circuit, even many commercially viable films fail to generate the attention they would have otherwise deserved from festival committees. As a result, with the exception of a few award-winning films from the world's leading festivals, the majority of filmmakers and their representatives rely on film markets to promote, screen and sell their films. Some of the leading film markets include:

1. American Film Market (Santa Monica, CA)
2. Berlin International Film Festival and European Film Market (Germany)
3. Busan International Film Festival and Asian Film Market (South Korea)
4. Cannes International Film Festival and Marché du Film (France)
5. Cinequest Film Festival (San Jose, CA)
6. Hong Kong International Film and TV Market (China)
7. Independent Filmmaker Project (IFP) Week (New York, NY)
8. Japan Content Showcase/TIFFCOM (Tokyo, Japan)
9. Marché International des Programmes de Communications (Cannes, France)
10. Rotterdam Film Festival and CineMart (Netherlands).

As you may have noticed, many of these film markets are hosted alongside leading film festivals. And, although not formal film markets per se, several leading film festivals such as the AFI Festival, Raindance Film Festival (London, UK), South by Southwest/SXSW, Sundance, Toronto International Film Festival, Tribeca and Venice have also

FIGURE 14.8 The world's largest and most renowned film market is the American Film Market, held late in each year in Santa Monica, CA. (American Film Market)

become important film markets unto themselves. Like the top film markets, each of these festivals offers attendees the opportunity to meet the industry's leading sales agents, producer's reps and distribution executives.

However, unlike film festivals, film markets are structured specifically for the purposes of putting film buyers and sellers together to sell and license films for theatrical, broadcast and other distribution channels. As a result, particularly for filmmakers without an agent and/or producer's rep, the leading film markets can be a great place to perform fundamental market research and to meet and network with such professionals.

When attending any given market for the first time, it's a good idea to make plans to go with people you "know" who are already experienced with that particular market. Ideally, you'll be able to attend with a distribution consultant, publicist or other industry professional who is able to make important introductions. On the other hand, don't be afraid to attend the market with people you may not have had the opportunity to meet with in real life. These may be fellow filmmakers you regularly exchange posts and messages with on social media, via email, text message or via the telephone. The important thing is that you do what you can to find people who will agree to show you around and, ideally, introduce you to the types of professionals you want and need to meet.

Fortunately, although these types of relationships are helpful, you don't need established contacts and relationships to make the markets worthwhile. Take the opportunity to introduce yourself and your project to sales agents and reps on the market floor, in the hotel lobby and at parties and other after-hour events. Understandably, sales agents and reps are attending the market to sell and license films that they are already representing. This is their first priority. So, while they may not have a lot of time to talk about your project, they'll usually be open to a quick summary of your film and – if they like what they see and hear – will often encourage you to send more materials (and perhaps arrange a meeting) at some point following the market.

Not surprisingly, you'll find agents and reps have more interest if you are able to attach industry "names" to the film project. Obviously, your film will be perceived as having a higher value if you are able to attach name actors. However, also work to include "name" producers, directors, department heads, editors, post-production professionals and others to the film. Remember that there are different levels of "names." Some of these names, although unknown by the viewing public, may be that of other members of your production team with an established history of market and critical success.

Again, sales agents will be pressed for time, so don't expect that they'll have time or interest in previewing a full screening of your film at the market. However, bring your laptop or tablet in the event that they'd like to see a quick teaser, trailer or clip. And, as always, have plenty of business cards, pitch sheets and press kits close at hand.

In addition to any films you may have in production, be prepared to discuss three or four development projects. If you meet an agent or rep who may not be interested in your current films, you'll have more projects of potential interest that may be a better fit with agent, rep and his or her team.

On the other hand, if you have a completed film on offer at the market, you'll probably want to take a step back and let your sales agent or producer's representative take the lead. They have the experience and relationships that you and your team often lack and are often better able to market your film as a component of their larger film slate. Again, stand back and let them do their jobs. If your sales team schedules any private screenings for distributors and feel that your attendance will be helpful, they'll be sure to let you know. Otherwise, much like you did before you had a film on offer, use the opportunity to explore the market, reconnect with colleagues and learn more about any emerging domestic and international distribution trends.

OTHER SELF-HOSTED & "HYBRID" EVENTS

In addition to production-related events, such as launch parties, wrap parties and screenings, there are a variety of other self-hosted and co-hosted events that filmmakers should consider, including such events as premiers, charity events, dedicated launch team events, independent movie marathons (involving the rental of a local theater to show three related films over a weekend evening) and more.

In particular, many filmmakers have achieved success by "piggy-backing" off large festivals, film markets and awards ceremonies by hosting their own (i) welcome event the evening before the official kick-off of the main event; (ii) individual break-out sessions, luncheons or cocktail parties during the event; (iii) private screenings of your film or that of a special celebrity guest; and (iv) a closing or wrap-up event during the final night of the event (or a breakfast the following morning).

By "piggy-backing" off of larger and often more prestigious events, your event often benefits from (i) lower marketing and promotion expenses, (ii) an ability to attract higher-profile professionals who are already on site and in attendance, and (iii) the associated prestige, credibility and recognition of the primary event.

Finally, if you have plans to travel to a large city where several members of your filmmaking network live and work (Los Angeles, New York, London, etc.) consider inviting several for an informal meet-up over dinner, drinks or, perhaps a private screening.

CONVENTIONS, CONFERENCES & EXHIBITIONS

As many studios and filmmakers have discovered, most famously with events such as Comi-Con International in San Diego, there are almost a limitless number of non-film related conventions, conferences and exhibitions that allow you to promote your film directly to your target audience.

Not entirely surprisingly, there are conventions and conferences for almost any interest, including fans of horror, romance science fiction, anime, manga and others. In addition to Comi-Con International, there are conferences such as Comiket in Tokyo, Japan for those interested in comic-book characters; gaming conventions such as Gamescom in Cologne, Germany; Tokyo Game Show in Chiba, Japan; and PAX East and West in the United States. And films such as *Fast & Furious*, *James Bond*, *Mad Max* and others have had success exhibiting featured cars and trucks at various car shows

FIGURE 14.9
Lionsgate film booth featuring the *Hunger Games Mockingjay* artwork at San Diego Comi-Con, the annual pop culture and fandom convention in San Diego, CA.

(Lauren Elisabeth/ Shutterstock.com)

FIGURE 14.10 The Netflix booth at the Sao Paulo Comi-Con Experience, the annual pop culture and fandom convention in Brazil.

(Beto Chagas/Shutterstock.com)

including the Frankfurt Motor Show, Auto Shanghai, North American International Auto Show and the Specialty Equipment Manufacturers Association ("SEMA") show in Las Vegas. Films that feature particularly exotic or travel-friendly locations have also exhibited at various travel and vacation conventions – often with the support of travel-related product placement and co-sponsors.

When selecting event marketing opportunities, consider each event's title and theme, the anticipated number and demographic of attendees, location, exhibitor list and a detailed description and schedule of sessions, panels, seminars, keynote discussions and social events. Read event coverage and review photographs and videos from prior years.

Focus on how best to entertain visitors and the creation of a unique and noteworthy experience. The booth or exhibit space should be a reflection of your film and genre as well as the conference and its audience. The exhibit must also be interactive and visually exciting. Among other design possibilities, consider having two to three screens playing film clips as well teasers, trailers, BTS videos and similar content. Establish "selfie stations" where visitors can take photos of themselves in front of a large film poster, cast portraits, with wardrobe and props or alongside any of the film's actors who may be in attendance.

Again, few other promotional venues or activities allow you to interact directly with members of your audience. Unfortunately, this access can come at considerable cost. Exhibit spaces typically run in the thousands of dollars and reflects only one-third (or less) of the total cost. Other expenses include the design and construction of the booth or exhibition space, signage, promotional handouts (including promotional merchandise and giveaways), booth staffing, pre-event marketing and promotion, transportation of

FIGURE 14.11 Auto shows, much like Comi-Con and cosplay events, have proven particularly effective for many films and production companies.

On the left, a selection of cars from the Fast & Furious franchise are on display at the Detroit AutoRama. (Steve Lagreca/Shutterstock.com). On the right, a Land Rover Defender featured within the recent James Bond film, *Spectre*, is on display at a convention in Frankfurt, Germany. (VanderWolf Images/Shutterstock.com)

wardrobe and/or props and travel and hotel expenses. Fortunately, conferences and conventions are the ideal opportunity to share the spotlight with existing product placement and coop partners. Not only do such partners offset many of the costs, the services and products they promote often drive significant traffic to your exhibit.

In addition to the promotional advice offered earlier in the chapter, you'll want to advertise within the official convention or conference guide and position staff and supporters throughout the convention center and pass out fliers, postcards or invitations for attendees to visit your booth. Throughout your advertisements and promotional materials, post a URL where attendees can register for your official email list in return for a promotional T-shirt, autographed mini-poster or other incentive ... but only if first they stop by the booth for the secret password. This will serve to drive increased traffic to your event space.

If the film has already been released, record video testimonials and reviews of the film. Also encourage attendees to provide online ratings and reviews. You may want to set up one or two computer stations so that attendees can leave online feedback immediately at the booth.

Regardless, be sure to post updates of the event on social media periodically throughout the day, including mini-blog posts, photographs and videos. And make a point of passing along interesting content from other exhibits and exhibitors that is likely to be of interest to your audience. On the final day of the event, post a few "wrap-up" comments that provide interesting summaries of the event and your team's experiences.

PANEL DISCUSSIONS

The first experience most filmmakers have with panel discussions is with the panel that follows their film's official premier. These panel discussions commonly include the executive producer, producer, director, screenwriter and starring actors and the discussion focuses on a topic with which they are intimately familiar ... their film.

If you are participating in a panel following your film's premier, you'll find that the moderator's and audience's questions will largely mirror those you received following screenings of your film at film festivals, such as: *Where did you get the idea for the film? How did you execute specific shots or effects? What where the most difficult aspects of the film? What equipment did you use? How much was the budget? What is your follow-up film?*

FIGURE 14.12 Fast & Furious actors Vin Diesel, Jordana Brewster, Michelle Rodriguez and Paul Walker attend a "Fast & Furious" press conference in Mexico City.

(Miguel Campos/Shutterstock.com)

However, as their visibility – and the visibility of their films – increase, successful filmmakers will begin to receive invitations to participate on other panel discussions at film festivals, markets, union, guild and association events, and at film schools. Instead of their own films, filmmakers will be expected to speak knowledgeably on such topics as low-budget production techniques, fundraising and investor relations, marketing and promotion, distribution and fundraising.

Shortly after you've been invited to participate on a panel discussion, the panel moderator will likely schedule a conference call with you and the other panelists. During this call, the moderator will share such information as:

- *Panel Info:* The title of the panel, date, time and location as well as a brief description of the panel and how it fits into any larger event of which it may be a component. An introduction of your fellow panelists, including their names and professional backgrounds.
- *Audience:* Audience demographics and estimated size so panelists can bring the appropriate number of handouts (if applicable) and better tailor their contributions and content.
- *Questions:* A good moderator will share the questions he or she intends to ask to each panelist in advance. Again, this provides each panelist the ability to better craft their responses and contribution to the discussion.
- *Panel Format and Instructions:* Panelists will be provided guidance with regard to the duration of the panel and the ideal length or duration of panelist responses, and given information such as room set up, audio-visual resources and whether or not any video or audio recording (or transcripts) of the panel will be made or permitted.

Following the prep call you should have a better understanding with regard to your role and why you were invited to participate. *What specific perspective does the moderator hope you can add?* Look at the other panelists. *What can you contribute that they can't, and vice versa?*

The more you know what is expected of you and how you can best contribute, the easier it will be prepare a short one or two page summary of talking points, stories, anecdotes, examples, quotes, statistics and other information that will resonate with your audience. When thinking about the type of anecdotes and sound-bites you want to share, remember that your role as a panelist is to entertain . . . not only inform. So work to keep your sound-bites short, focused and memorable.

Likewise, use the information you learned during the prep call to craft a self-introduction or brief biography specifically for the panel discussion and its audience. The self-introduction should be brief but long enough to provide an adequate overview of your experience and differentiate you from the other panelists. Two to three sentences is usually sufficient. Be sure to get a copy of your introduction to the panel moderator at least a week beforehand.

Once you arrive at the venue for the discussion, seek out your panelists to say a quick "hello." This is meant to be an opportunity to relax, get to know each other and build a rapport that will, hopefully, be obvious on stage. Think of the panel as a friendly conversation in front of several dozen or more of your closest friends. Relax and have fun.

Fortunately, as mentioned previously, a good moderator will have provided panelists with the questions well in advance so they are able to prepare thoughtful responses. So work to reduce the most complex and technical issues to something plain, simple and short for your audience. Refer to the talking points and other supporting information included within your notes. Once you've answered the question, feel free to build on earlier comments or to make an interesting change to the direction of the conversation.

FIGURE 14.13 Kathryn Bigelow, James Cameron, Lee Daniels and Pete Docter participate on the directors' panel at the Santa Barbara Film Festival in Santa Barbara, CA.

(aspen rock/Shutterstock.com)

But be mindful of keeping things brief and within the timeframe your moderator has suggested.

On the other hand, if the moderator directs a question to you that is not a good fit for you given your limited experience or knowledge, it's fine to pass the question on to one of your fellow panelists.

Remember that you are participating on a panel "discussion." A good panel is interactive and dynamic. Listen to what your fellow panelists have to say and refer to any particularly interesting or informative points they may have made. Again, the discussion shouldn't just be between the moderator and panelists, but among the other panelists as well. In fact, look for opportunities where you can build – or extend – on a point introduced by one or more other panelists. And, if there are areas in which you can politely and respectfully disagree, do so. Audiences enjoy hearing opposing viewpoints. This makes for a more fluid and engaging panel discussion.

Obviously, as a member of the panel, more often than not you'll be listening to the moderator and other panelists rather than speaking. Nevertheless, you'll be sitting front and center of the audience and will remain the subject of attention. So never look bored or glance at your phone or watch. Instead, focus on the moderator and each panelist as they speak. Smile. Shake your head in agreement. Take notes. During the open question and answer period, look intently at members of the audience as they pose their questions.

You'll know that you've done well when (i) audience members are listening attentively and taking notes during your panel comments; (ii) you receive a particularly large number of questions relative to other panelists during the panel's Q&A session; (iii) many people queue up to meet you after the panel to speak and exchange business cards; (iv) attendees post positive comments on your performance to the event's tweet stream or using the event's hashtag; and (v) your panel comments are quoted or referenced by traditional and/or new media outlets.

POST-EVENT FOLLOW-UP

Once home, follow-up with your connections. Begin by entering their business cards, contact information and a brief description of any notable details on your discussions within your contact database. Whenever possible, you'll want to send the first follow-up email within two to three days of the end of the event while you and the event are still fresh in their minds. Then send a second follow-up a week or two later. If appropriate, make plans to reconnect.

Obviously not every event you attend or host will prove as worthwhile as you'd originally expected. In assessing the value or performance of an event (and whether or not an event is worth hosting or attending again in the future), consider the total number of people who registered for the event, the actual number of people in attendance, the number and nature of the people added to your network, traditional or new media coverage you or your film may have received, increases in social media and website activity (Livestream views, social media posts, website visits, etc.) and similar measures.

On the other hand: It's not always easy to measure the value and performance of any one event – particularly in the immediate hours and days that follow. You may meet someone whose importance to your film's and studio's success isn't clear until several weeks or months after the event. Or you may learn a piece of information that only proves valuable further along in your film's production or distribution.

15

HIGH-IMPACT LOW-COST ADVERTISING & PROMOTION

The business models of studios within the independent film industry combined with the economics of advertising present a considerable challenge when attempting to financially justify the use of advertising to promote independent films.

Major studio films typically receive 50% of the proceeds from box office, VOD and other sales and rentals. Independent films, on the other hand, which often have to rely on sales agents and unaffiliated distributors, typically receive 15–25% (or less) of box office proceeds, 35–50% of VOD sales and rentals and 10–35% of foreign territory, broadcast and many other sales and licensing agreements, net of fees and expenses.

The problem with receiving such a small percentage of the sales and rental gross is compounded when you consider the relatively low prices of theater tickets and film sales and rentals. This means that, for every $15.00 USD ticket or film sold, the filmmaker will only gross $3.75 or less (again, depending upon distribution channel and associated fees and expenses).

Clearly, given the challenging economics of independent film production and distribution, advertising is rarely cost-efficient. This lack of efficiency is compounded by the fact that the success of any individual advertising campaign can never be guaranteed, requiring the use of multiple advertising and promotional activities that further increase budgetary and scheduling costs.

However, advertising can make sense if and when the independent filmmaker is able to both (i) significantly decrease the expense of reaching the film's target audience *and*, at the same time, (ii) increase the rate of response from those audience members.

The following advertising activities and channels – when combined with the branding, marketing and promotional elements discussed in previous chapters – are particularly well-suited to guerrilla marketing and promotional campaigns.

RELATIONSHIP MARKETING

Relationship marketing focuses on audience loyalty and long-term audience engagement rather than shorter-term goals like customer acquisition and individual sales. The goal of relationship marketing is to create strong customer connections to a filmmaker, studio or film franchise brand. Ideally, these are relationships that lead to greater audience engagement, more consistent audience experience, higher film ratings and more positive reviews, and increased sales, rentals and merchandise sales.

Relationship marketing involves creating easy two-way communications between customers and the filmmaker, studio or film's brand. The principles of relationship marketing incorporate many of the branding, marketing and promotional elements already discussed . . . particularly with regard to building a community of engaged friends and fans.

In addition to its focus on the establishment of long-term engaged relationships as a key objective, relationship marketing is also distinguished by the personalized nature of each interaction. Relationship marketing is comprised of email, text message, telephone, postcards and one-on-one interactions in which the messages are addressed to an individual, using their name, contact details and possibly additional personal information that are specific to each recipient.

As well as using the recipient's name and other personal details, your interactions should be in a friendly informal tone and not overtly self-promotional. Share your personal experiences during preproduction, on the film set, during postproduction and with meeting friends and fans. Forming lasting relationships is easier when your fans feel you are opening a window into your experiences with the filmmaking, marketing and distribution process.

The ultimate form of relationship marketing is one-to-one marketing in which you and your team reach out to individual audience members directly via personalized telephone calls, emails, notecards and in-person meetings. Although difficult to scale, these one-on-one interactions form the strongest bonds between you, your film and your audience.

DATABASE DIRECT MARKETING

The success of your relationship marketing depends – in large part – upon the ability to maintain a large and ever-expanding database of interested audience members.

Ideally, the database should include audience members' names (first and last), contact information (email, cell phone number and physical address), demographic information and film viewing and entertainment habits. Marketing and promotional campaigns can then be created which target potential audience members within highly specific areas or territories, particular demographic segments, and those with common interests, traits and other characteristics.

Unfortunately, generating a database with this level of detail can often be difficult. Audience members are frequently reluctant to provide such personal detail, either because (i) it can be frustrating and time-consuming to provide and/or (ii) because people are rightly suspicious of how their personal information will ultimately be used. As a result, compiling a useful database of audience members will remain a challenging component of the direct database marketing process.

To partially address this challenge, there are, broadly, four types of database lists and methods of compiling a marketing database:

- The first is known as the *house list* in which interested audience members have registered to participate in the database. This is usually done via forms provided on websites, landing pages and social media pages.

FIGURE 15.1 Customer relationship management (CRM) software and services, such as GoldMine, allow filmmakers to better manage relationships and interactions with fans and members of the filmmaker's and production company's professional network.

(Goldmine)

- The second is the *compiled list* in which you and your team add names and contact details from sources such as print and online directories, social media friends and fans and from your cast's and crew's own list of personal and professional contacts.
- The third is the *partner list*, in which you are provided a list of names and contact information from marketing partners and any other affiliated organizations. Like the purchased list, it's important to determine any constraints on your use of the provided partner list.
- Finally, fourth is the *purchased list* in which a database of potential audience members is purchased or rented from organizations such as associations, print and e-publications and other organizations such as marketing list brokers.

Not surprisingly, database marketing presupposes that you will be using a database software or cloud-based system through which to manage and maintain your direct marketing campaigns. Some of the most popular systems include AWeber, Constant Contact, iContact Pro, Mailchimp, Robly and Salesforce.

Ultimately, your choice of database marketing system will reflect (i) the various types of campaigns (email, text message, telephone, snail mail, social media, etc.) the system is capable of supporting; (ii) compatibility with specific online apps and files provided by list brokers and/or marketing partners; and (iii) any one-time set-up and regular ongoing expenses.

While the use of database marketing software makes marketing to your audience relatively easy, be careful not to overwhelm your audience. Many marketers have found that contacting their subscribers more than twice a week quickly becomes an annoyance. On the other hand, those who contact their database subscribers less than twice a month discover they are quickly forgotten. As you monitor your performance metrics (particularly with regard to unsubscribe rates relative to conversion rates) you'll soon discover the most successful contact frequency for you and your audience.

CONTESTS, GIVEAWAYS & SWEEPSTAKES

The unspoken challenge in direct marketing (such as email, text message, postcard and one-to-one marketing) is in building an ever-expanding database of interested fans and audience members. Fortunately, one of the easiest and most effective ways to build your audience "house list" is to regularly run contests, giveaways and sweepstakes.

In addition to building and expanding your audience database, online contests are also able to support: (i) market research via contests that involves a brief survey as a part of the entry process; (ii) user-generated content through photo, video and key art contests; (iii) enhanced "buzz" associated with particularly interesting contests and contests that feature a public voting component; and (iv) strengthened relationships and audience engagement.

Of the various contest options available, a basic enter-to-win sweepstakes often provides the best option for those just starting out with contests or without a large established audience database. However, regardless of the type of contest, sweepstakes or giveaway you choose, there are a handful of factors that will help assure success.

First, make sure that the contest's title, description and associated images are as enticing and exciting as possible. As we've discussed throughout the branding, marketing and promotional process, be sure to select keywords and images that most appeal to your target audience. You may only have a split-second to capture their attention. So make every word, image and design element count.

Second, make sure that any and all methods you use to promote your contest (including landing pages) such as banner ads, social media posts or promotional emails include key details such as a description of the contest, the method of entry, start date and deadlines and any specific calls-to-action.

Third, consider the contest prize or other incentive. Not surprisingly, the higher the perceived value of the incentive, the greater the buzz the contest will generate, the larger the number of people likely to enter and the more information or details entrants will likely be willing to share about themselves.

Common incentives include (i) exclusive behind-the-scenes information unavailable to the general public; (ii) promotional merchandise such as stickers, decals, hats and T-shirts; (iii) autographed postcards, photographs, scripts, director's slates, props or wardrobe; (iv) an opportunity to attend the film's premier or to appear as an extra in the film (or its sequel); and similar incentives.

To enter, people are encouraged to register via a landing page form on your website (although you can also host your contest on almost any one, or more, of your social media accounts). And, once your contest is live, be sure to promote it throughout your marketing network, including your website, social media accounts, email lists and other outlets. Depending upon the nature of the contest and its expected promotional impact, you may also want to consider the use of paid social media advertising.

Even after your contest is over, you can use it to promote your business further. Here are a few suggestions on how to leverage your contest and keep your entrants engaged with your film and studio:

1. Profile winner(s) on your blog and share on Facebook, Twitter and other social networks.
2. Create a video showing you choosing the winner to create excitement.
3. Send a personalized follow-up email to contest entrants to convert them into sales.
4. Share your plans for future contests to keep your entrants hooked.

A quick note of caution: Like other types of advertising and promotion, before you start a contest, be sure to first familiarize yourself with your country's, state's or territory's regulations. In the United States, every state has its own contest laws, so it's necessary to become familiar with these regulations to make certain your promotion is legal.

EMAIL MARKETING

Email marketing is one of the staples of independent film marketing in general and relationship and database marketing in particular.

Email marketing allows you to communicate your message immediately to a global audience – irrespective of country borders or time zones. Your messages can be sent to an entire database or highly personalized messages can be sent to very specific audience members. An additional benefit is that emails can contain a broad variety of multi-media files and external links . . . making it easy for your friends and fans to download, share and post to their social media platforms.

As a benefit to email subscribers, subscribers should be the first to receive updates on the film and much of the information should be exclusive to subscribers only. Such email content often includes: behind-the-scenes photos, videos and interviews as well as announcements regarding forthcoming film festival appearances, screenings or premier dates, contests and sweepstakes, and similar special events.

To maximize your email marketing campaign's success, there are only a handful of guidelines that you really need to follow:

1. *Match the Audience to the Message:* It should be obvious, but focused messages should be sent to targeted audiences, and messages with broad appeal should be sent to a broader audience. For instance, if your film is appearing at a local film festival, you'll want to send email invitations to those who live in the same area as the festival. On the other hand, if one of your featured actors just completed an interesting behind-the-scenes interview, you'll likely want to share the video with all your subscribers. In other words: the message determines the audience (and vice versa).
2. *The Email Should Be Familiar:* You want your audience to both look forward to and recognize your emails. To help your audience quickly distinguish your emails from others competing for their attention, make sure that (i) the sender's email address contains a familiar name from your team as well as the name of your studio or film title within the email address, and (ii) keep the design of your emails consistent across each email you send (particularly with regard to email letterhead, email signature and any embedded images or videos).
3. *Create Interesting Subject Lines:* Even when recipients are familiar with you and your emails, they may be reluctant to open your email unless they find the subject line enticing. Most successful subject lines contain fewer than ten words and a combination of action-oriented keywords of interest to your audience.
4. *Keep It Simple and Repeatable:* Ideally, if your email campaigns are to be a success, they need to be easy for you and your team to create and send . . . and for your

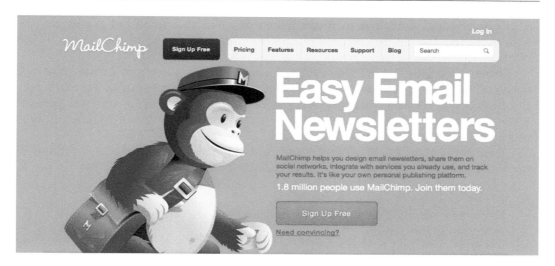

FIGURE 15.2 Email marketing software and services, such as MailChimp, provide film marketers with the ability to conduct frequent, highly customizable and inexpensive email campaigns with their audience.

subscribers to consume. Like most marketing and promotional copy, this means short sentences and paragraphs punctuated with numbered lists or bullet points. Embedded images and videos can also make emails more interesting and engaging; however, be careful that images and videos load quickly and do not clutter the page.

Unfortunately, no matter how well they may be written and designed, your emails can't promote your film if they are misidentified as spam. In fact, studies suggest that as much as 20–25% of legitimate emails are incorrectly classified as spam. To avoid spam filters and email firewalls, send marketing emails only to those who have registered to receive them, make certain that your return email address is not associated with an IP address known for sending unsolicited bulk emails, and ask subscribers to add your address to their address book.

To make sure that your emails are avoiding spam filters and having the targeted promotional impact, continuously monitor delivery, open, click-through and conversion rates. In particular, closely observe unsubscribe rates. To avoid excessive "unsubscribes" make certain that recipients find each and every email both interesting and entertaining . . . and that you achieve that elusive balance between emailing too frequently and not often enough.

POSTCARDS

As the popularity and use of email marketing have increased, the corresponding use of direct mail (such as postcards) has declined. With fewer competing pieces of direct mail being sent, the effectiveness of direct mail – including the use of postcards – continues to increase.

And, despite the fact that direct mailings are some of the most expensive methods of promotion (on a per-target basis), postcards are also among the most effective.

This effectiveness is further increased when directed at a small but highly targeted group of fans and audience members with whom you already have an established relationship.

When preparing a postcard mailing campaign remember that quality counts in terms of the mailing list, card design and offer. Carefully select your target market and the mailing list. Because postcards can be printed in short runs of 100 or fewer, consider using multiple card designs and multiple postcard mailings to appeal to different types of audience members and fans.

Despite the many possible types of postcard designs and potential types of recipients, the most highly effective postcard designs employ the following elements:

- A clear bold headline
- Key art or graphic that support the headline and message
- Attention-getting color
- Subheads that lead into any text
- The copy
- Film title and credit block
- Call-to-action
- Contact information.

While most of your postcard campaigns will likely feature postcards with specific marketing messages, don't forget to print several blank postcards for personal one-to-one marketing purposes. Encourage members of your cast and crew to use these blank postcards to send personal hand-written and addressed messages to their own list of friends, family and followers. Also be sure to send personalized postcards to attendees of screenings and other events.

One simple way to improve the performance of postcard mailing campaigns is to individually sign each card. In fact, the value of a postcard can be significantly increased if the postcard features (i) a photograph of one of the members of the cast or the film's key art and (ii) includes an autograph of the cast member featured within the photograph or poster.

Finally, when scheduling a postcard campaign, remember that, unlike email and text message marketing campaigns, postcards can require a month or more to have the cards designed, printed, addressed, posted and delivered to your audience. However, with proper planning and expectations, postcard marketing can be among the most effective advertising mediums available – particularly when targeting a small and highly focused audience (such as existing friends and fans).

SHORT MESSAGE SERVICE ("SMS")/TEXT MESSAGES

Among all advertising and promotional activities, none command more recipient attention than text messages. In fact, various studies suggest that almost 95% of marketing text messages are read as compared with ~10% of marketing emails. And the majority of these text messages are read within four minutes of their receipt.

Because of the immediacy of text messages, SMS lends itself particularly well to (i) announcing pending film releases; (ii) forwarding discount coupons for the purchase or rental of films or film merchandise; (iii) surveying audience members; (iv) announcing contests and sweepstakes; (v) alerting audience members to upcoming film festivals, premiers, screenings, local meet-ups and other special events; and (vi) sending reminders to those already registered for forthcoming events.

When selecting an SMS marketing service or application, concentrate your search for those that are able to:

1. Send messages to all mobile carriers within your country or region
2. Support auto-responders and scheduled messages
3. Collect customer data via text
4. Customize the content and sequence of the messages you send when people opt-in or opt-out of your lists
5. Create personalized "mail-merge" text messages

Some of the most popular SMS marketing services include SUMOTEXT, Ez Texting, Trumpia, SlickText and ProTexting and computer and smart phone based apps such as MightyText and Clearstream.

The two distinct components of an SMS marketing campaign are the keyword and the shortcode. Here's an example:

Text "FILM" to 654321 to receive exclusive updates!

"FILM" is the keyword. When audience members decide to opt-in to your text list, they'll place the keyword into the body of the message. They will then forward to the message to the "654321" shortcode.

Once you've received the audience member's opt-in, you should send an automated response thanking them for joining your SMS list. Other ways to "opt-in" customers are to let them check a box on an order form or submit their phone number online. Before adding them to a campaign, you'll have to confirm their participation with another message: i.e. *"Text "YES" to receive exclusive updates on [Film Title]."*

After you've compiled a sufficient number of SMS opt-ins and begun to prepare your SMS marketing campaign, keep in mind that text marketing messages are limited to only 160 plain text characters and, at the present time, cannot contain images. To avoid using too many of your allotted characters on links, use a URL shortener such as Bitly or Google's URL shortener tool. Also take advantage of the opportunity to send messages with links to pictures, videos and voice messages.

When scheduling your text messages, the best time to send your messages is typically late afternoon or early evening during the mid-week (Tuesdays, Wednesdays and Thursdays). Like other marketing campaigns, text message marketing often benefits from opportunistic promotions leveraging holidays and other special dates. Regardless of the schedule you eventually choose, restrict your text campaign to two to three text messages per month. Any more and you risk alienating your audience.

To amplify your message and expand your opt-in list, ask recipients to share messages with other interested friends and promote registration on your website pages, social media platforms, email, business cards, direct mail and other advertising and promotional campaigns.

PERSONAL ONE-TO-ONE MARKETING

There is no doubt that the strongest form of marketing is personal one-to-one marketing in which you and members of your filmmaking team directly interact with your fans and audience members. For more reserved filmmakers, this direct contact may be difficult, but it's essential to establish this habit and to encourage other members of the cast and crew to do the same.

Each willing member of your cast and crew should identify the most important twenty-five to fifty people in their networks, from a promotional point of view, and place them on rotation for personal contact every three to four weeks. Many of these people will likely be influencers such as bloggers, podcast hosts, YouTube personalities and others. But remember to include – and cultivate – a number of super-fans. Also, while you don't want to harass anyone, it's typically acceptable (and even desirable) if there is some limited overlap between one person's list with another's . . . just don't send duplicate messages or content to the same recipient.

Once you've assembled a list, the next step is to compile a simple database of these influencers and fans together with their contact information. This should include telephone numbers, email addresses and physical addresses whenever possible. Also, make notations of any mutual friends or other relationships each contact may have with you and other members on your list.

As a part of this new one-to-one marketing habit, set aside thirty minutes a day (ideally the same time each day) to reach out to your contact list by telephone, voicemail, text message, email and through personal hand-written notecards. As with other aspects of your marketing and promotion, it's often helpful to vary the method of contact (telephone, email, text message, postcards, etc.). If you have any upcoming special events, if you will be visiting the contact's area, or if the contact lives nearby, suggest that you get together during the event or at another convenient time for a quiet get together over coffee.

BUSINESS CARDS

Business cards are one of the most important and yet least appreciated pieces of marketing collateral in which you may ever invest. In fact, for their size and cost, they are one of the most powerful components of your marketing.

Business cards help establish an instant and lasting impression and can be used to support many of your marketing and promotional campaigns (including media relations, event marketing, networking and as enclosures within physical press kits and other professional mailings). Because of this, it's important that you give careful consideration to the attributes that make you, your studio and your films distinct. Be deliberate about the image you want your business cards to project.

With regard to design, there are several elements that should be considered: size and shape; material and "feel" (paper, finish, plastic, metal, etc.); color; graphics and other images; edges, folds, embossing, foil, etc. Also consider using both sides of the card, if printing traditional cards, or the use of fold-over cards to maximize the amount of information and detail the cards are able to convey.

As with all marketing efforts, the design of your business cards should complement the design elements of your other marketing materials.

When beginning the design process it can be very helpful to conduct an image search using Google or other web search service to identify one or two dozen business cards that you feel best reflect the design elements you'd like to incorporate within your own business cards. Send copies to your graphic designer and explain, specifically, what you like about each card design. This is one of the best approaches to obtaining a well-designed card quickly and with minimal effort.

Unfortunately, given the small size of business cards, space is quite limited so you'll need to choose your words and images carefully. Which information is absolutely essential? Equally important, what should you leave out? Too much information can dilute or obscure your message. Some of the most common kinds of information included on business cards are your name and title, studio name, studio logo, tagline or slogan (if any), physical address, website address, IMDb address, office telephone number, cellular telephone number, social media addresses and email address.

Given their importance and relatively low cost, it makes sense to make the limited investment in time and money required to get the best business cards possible.

COOPERATIVE & AFFINITY MARKETING

Cooperative marketing, in which you join forces with a marketing partner to promote your film and merchandise alongside the products and services of your partner, offers significant advantages. Most importantly, coop marketing allows both marketing partners to expand their reach and leverage one another's reputations with customers while sharing associated marketing costs.

This increased cost efficiency and promotional effectiveness largely reflects the benefits of mutual promotion across each partner's marketing database lists, websites, social media activity, publications (print and/or electronic), promotional events, joint public relations campaigns and adverts and inserts within partner invoices and other mailings, etc.

The benefits of coop marketing are increased considerably when you partner with a business or organization with whom you share the same – or similar – customer demographics and interests. The number of such potential marketing partners is almost limitless. Some of the most common partnerships include those with affiliated charities, associations, fan clubs, niche publications and the brands of any wardrobe, jewelry, props, vehicles or locations that may appear in your film (see the following section, "Product Placement").

When looking to identify potential marketing partners, it's crucial that the goals and market of potential partners are aligned with those of your studio and film. The marketing relationship should be mutually beneficial and with balanced responsibilities. Unfortunately, if not well-structured, uneven partnerships – in which one partner gets more out of the partnership than the other and/or one partner fails to live up to expectations – are relatively common.

PRODUCT PLACEMENT

Product placement often provides filmmakers with an important ancillary source of income. At the same time, product placement also helps filmmakers reduce production costs via donated product placement items such as branded clothing, jewelry, vehicles, electronics (laptops, phones, televisions, etc.), hotels and resorts and other products and services. As an example, consider the many brands associated with the various James Bond films over the past fifty years, such as Aston Martin, BMW, Omega, Rolex and Walther Arms.

From a marketing viewpoint, product placement can also provide the film with additional cachet and visibility due to the brand association formed between the movie and the branded products. This is particularly the case for films such as those in the

FIGURE 15.3 When properly paired, both the film and product placement partners benefit from the mutual brand association. When seeking potential product placement partners, in addition to any financial consideration, it's critically important that the brand of the film and partner are mutually beneficial.

(Ivanti; Editorial/Fair Use)

previously mentioned James Bond franchise in which the clothing, jewelry, locations, cars and weapons are as much a part of the movie as the main character.

On the other hand, from the product placement brand's point of view, the branded products company wants to associate its products and services with films, characters and stories that best portray their organization's and product's image. At the same time, they also want to be assured that the film's target audience is sufficiently large and representative of their own customer base to make their product placement investment worthwhile.

More specifically, when a company is considering donating or paying for product placement, the company and its product placement advisors will want to know the following:

1. Details on the film, including script, budget and distribution.
2. The specific product or service being considered for placement.
3. The usage of that product or service within the film's plot.
4. The visual placement of the product or service and the frequency and length of time in which it will appear on film.
5. The film character's attitude, if any, toward the product.
6. The audience's attitude toward that character (is the character the protagonist or antagonist?).
7. The strength of the character's association with the product (is the product or service an essential component of the character's identity and/or "look"? Is the product or service a critical plot point?).
8. In addition to visual placement, will the brand be mentioned within the dialogue?
9. What will the audience's attitude be toward the product placement?

When considering product placement, it's important that the film avoid looking like a commercial. There is a fine line between having your film focus too much or too little on a promotional product. However, when done right, product placement can have a notable effect on reducing production costs, increasing production values and strengthening marketing and promotional campaigns.

DISPLAY & BROADCAST ADVERTISING

Although they form the foundation of studio marketing campaigns, regional, national and international display and broadcast advertising (such as magazine ads, radio spots and cable television commercials) have among the lowest response rates of all mass-advertising channels.

For independent films, mass display and broadcast advertising are particularly costly and inefficient. Not only must an independent film fight for attention against larger and more sophisticated display and broadcast advertisers but the independent film's marketing budget is largely wasted on a mass audience comprised of relatively few members of the film's highly targeted niche audience.

Even the existence of remainder advertising (also known as remnant or last-minute advertising) is insufficient to lower the cost of mass advertising to profitable levels. Although remnant advertising offers print and broadcast advertisements at a considerable discount (25–90% off standard rates), these discounts are rarely – if ever – sufficient to make remnant advertising cost-efficient.

However, like other advertising mediums, the solution to these challenges is to restrict advertising to only the most highly targeted outlets. Some of the most effective and efficient display and broadcast advertising channels include niche media outlets such as print and e-publications, websites, popular genre-related blogs and forums, podcasts, vidcasts, YouTube channels and other social media channels and personalities.

The success of many of these niche media outlets reflects their ability to create trust, support, status and participation among their audience members. This fosters a close relationship with their audience and, the stronger the audience's connection to the website, publication or channel, the higher the level of endorsement that their film's advertising receives from their visitors, readers, listeners or viewers.

Naturally, the performance of the advertising largely depends upon the "fit" between the film and any of these specific advertising outlets. When advertising channels are properly chosen and adverting terms negotiated, such highly targeted display and broadcast channels benefit from (i) a greater population of target audience members, (ii) lower costs per impression and (iii) expanded audience awareness and conversion rates.

A possible exception: Despite the warnings with regard to the lack of efficiency and effectiveness of general advertising and promotional channels such as newspapers and cable television, these may also be worth pursuing when having a limited theatrical release (or four walling your own limited release). In such cases, you may want to consider placing broadcast advertisements with any local television news program, newspaper, regional magazine or radio channel that agrees to attend and cover the premier (particularly in the case of local radio). Unfortunately, many media outlets establish an "iron curtain" between their news or editorial departments and their advertising departments that prevent such "tit-for-tat" arrangements.

Display Advertising

While display advertising once referred exclusively to print adverts with national and regional newspaper, magazine and other traditional print channels, more recently,

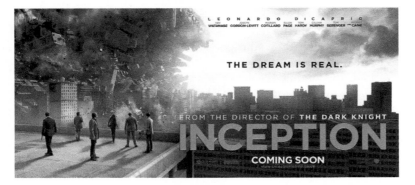

FIGURE 15.4 Banner display ads.

(Warner Bros Pictures)

display advertising is more commonly comprised of banner adverts within niche print and e-publications (magazines, newspapers, newsletters, etc.) and highly targeted websites.

In addition to the shift in display advertising channels, the static nature of display adverts themselves has changed. Online advertisements now incorporate different formats and contain items such as text, images, animation, video and audio; as well as overlays that appear over the top of page content (and can be closed by the click of a button); interstitials such as full-page inter-web page adverts; pop-ups and pop-unders; and other creative advertisements.

Regardless of the format and use of rich media features, the same design considerations apply to display advertisements as other forms of branding, marketing and promotion. This includes exciting and attention-grabbing titles, copy, colors and graphics; clear calls-to-action; the use of contrasting colors and shapes to accentuate buttons; and similar design considerations.

Unfortunately, although online advertisements have many benefits (they are relatively inexpensive, easily tracked, monitored, refined and adjusted), online banner ads suffer from relatively low click-through rates (typically 0.5% or less).

Fortunately, low click-through rates can be somewhat mitigated by (i) reducing the costs of advertising by leveraging advertising exchanges, coop marketing arrangements, product placement partners and encouraging fans to upload your adverts to their own websites and social media platforms and (ii) maximizing click-throughs as a result of crafting attention-getting advertising designs.

Another important consideration is placement: the specific sites, pages and locations on the page that your advertising appears. While it's important to carefully select the organizations and websites with which your advertising will appear, be careful not to place your display adverts on sites and/or pages that contain a number of competing banner ads or on sites with busy incoherent design/layouts.

Broadcast Advertising

With the evolution of display advertisements and their increasing use of rich media, it can be challenging to determine at which point an advertisement is a display advert and at which point it becomes a broadcast advertisement.

For the purposes of our discussion, broadcast advertising refers to video and audio adverts and sponsorships placed with cable television and online video channels (e.g. YouTube channels and vidcasts); celestial, satellite and internet-based radio programs (including podcasts); and websites using popular and/or proprietary media players.

The most common types of broadcast advertisements are video and audio film teasers and trailers. While we've dedicated a chapter to the creation and distribution of video trailers, audio-only teasers and trailers present unique challenges. Most obviously, without accompanying video images, audio trailers require attention-getting and emotionally evocative background music, sound effects and dialogue. Audio trailers also tend to be significantly shorter than video trailers . . . with running times of fifteen to thirty seconds having established themselves as de facto standards.

In addition to teasers and trailers, many films have met with success through sponsorship of websites, forums, e-publications, podcasts, YouTube channels and other organizations that are particularly popular with the film's target audience. Sponsorships are usually accompanied by online banner adverts, print adverts (if applicable) and video and/or audio sponsorship announcements that precede and follow podcast or vidcast episodes.

These short "pre-roll," "mid-roll" or "post-roll" ads are commonly brief three or four sentence mentions such as:

> This program is sponsored by the forthcoming feature film [title]. [Describe film.] To learn more about [title], visit [URL].com.

Notice that this short script omits the "html" and "www" from URL description. These extensions are unnecessary and their omission serves to shorten and clarify the message.

Again, the success of any display or broadcast advertising campaign reflects (i) a carefully selected highly targeted advertising channel; (ii) a well-crafted advert created to achieve a specific objective; and (iii) advertising agreements that demand little-to-no monetary expenses.

PROMOTIONAL MERCHANDISE

Unlike many of the advertising and promotional activities discussed within the chapter (and book), the value of promotional merchandise to your branding, advertising and promotional efforts is rarely direct.

Instead, promotional merchandise is most successful when used in combination with other promotional activities: (i) to establish brand recognition and identity of cast, crew members and other film representatives at film festivals and other events; (ii) to serve as an incentive, prize or gift in support of contests, sweepstakes, giveaways and other promotional campaigns; (iii) as a symbol of appreciation to cast and crew members, investors and super-fans; and (iv) as a form of ancillary income to be sold on your websites and at various events.

Promotional merchandise is available in an almost endless array of options, including: DVDs or electronic copies of the film; clothing such as T-shirts, sweatshirts, hoodies, jackets and baseball hats; backpacks, tote bags, drawstring bags, etc.; coffee mugs; action figures; laptop and cell phone skins/covers; screensavers and wallpaper images; script adaptations such as novels, ebooks, audiobooks and/or computer games; soundtracks; patches, decals and stickers; and gift cards.

Some of the most successful promotional merchandise is derived directly from the film's production, such as autographed scripts, wardrobe, props, film slates, posters, press kits, photographs, postcards and hardback picture books featuring behind-the-scenes photos, film stills and cast and crew portraits

Similarly, many filmmakers choose to select promotional merchandise that fits within a theme reflective of their film, such as: romance and beauty; food and drink; travel and leisure, including gambling, casinos, beach resorts, hotels; medicine and health; the military and law enforcement.

In addition to promotional merchandise from your own film(s), also consider unaffiliated, yet related, products of interest to the target audience. Items such as: DVDs or electronic copies of similar films, music/soundtracks, books, magazines and magazine subscriptions, branded clothing, admissions to genre-related events, and other related promotional merchandise.

For more ideas on the types of promotional merchandise available, be sure to visit such popular sites as Jakprints, Zazzle, Vistaprint and Branders.

VIRAL ("BUZZ") MARKETING CAMPAIGNS

Viral marketing, often referred to as buzz marketing, harnesses the network effect of word-of-mouth, the internet, social media and other new and emerging communications technologies. The power and effectiveness of viral marketing is a result of your audience members enthusiastically sharing your message with their own family, friends and fans. And, because your audience is responsible for spreading and amplifying your marketing message, the many benefits of viral marketing include its relatively low cost, its highly targeted nature and comparatively high and rapid response rates.

Your impression of viral marketing – probably similar to my own – has likely been shaped by the small handful of YouTube videos that have earned hundreds of thousands or millions of views. And let's be honest: if there were an easy recipe to viral marketing success, everyone would be making videos that receive millions of hits.

Fortunately, like the rest of our independent film branding, marketing and promotional activities, we aren't trying to appeal to a mass audience of tens of millions. As independent filmmakers, we are marketing our films to a smaller and much more specific audience. So, for our viral marketing campaigns to be successful, our promotional efforts need only become "viral" among those within our smaller more highly targeted market.

Unfortunately, it's impossible to know which piece of viral content will really take off, so achieving success with a viral campaign is as much a numbers game as anything else. You have to keep creating and delivering content. Once one or two videos or other content goes viral, many people will "rediscover" your earlier content . . . giving it a second chance at viral popularity.

To increase the chance of achieving viral marketing success, here are some of the more important factors:

1. *Study other successful viral campaigns . . . particularly viral campaigns created to promote feature films:* Is there anything you can learn from these campaigns that can be replicated in your own viral campaign efforts? With regard to your target audience, what types of viral content do they most enjoy sharing?

2. *Make it is easy on yourself and your audience:* Generally, shorter content, such as photographs and brief videos, are easier to create, consume and share. Also be mindful of creating content using popular media formats and file sizes that are easily shared via email, social media, messaging services and other platforms.

3. *Create buzzworthy content:* Buzzworthy content is typically distinctive with a compelling title, descriptions and an attention-getting image or thumbnail. Ask yourself what type of content would your audience find particularly interesting? What type of content would they be excited to share with their friends, family and fans?

4. *Include your cast, locations, wardrobe, props and film clips:* Don't lose track of your ultimate goal: to promote your own film. In addition to creating promotional-specific content that highlights the people, locations and assets from your film, also consider viral campaigns that feature bloopers, out-takes and film excerpts.

5. *"Seed" your campaign:* Once you've created your content, make sure to post and distribute it to as many of the "right" channels as possible (social media, forums, websites, blogs, etc.). Support your campaigns with paid advertising placement using Facebook and other social media pay-per-click programs.

6. *Make your content shareable:* Create content and select distribution channels that make it easy for your audience to share. Are there convenient email or social sharing

buttons? If you're posting video content, can viewers embed the video on their own sites and social media pages?

Of course the most important determinant of a viral campaign's success is the content itself. In addition to the bloopers, out-takes and BTS content already discussed, consider sharing videos of practical effects, explosions, gun shots or car crashes that may appear in your film; videos that demonstrate how creature effects, makeup effects or CGI shots were created; photographs, graphics or other visuals tied to interesting facts or quotes related to the film and/or the film's subject matter; and, perhaps, a free computer game based on the film (aka "advergame").

Other common viral content includes parodies of celebrities and cultural icons, current events, newspaper and magazine covers, music videos, movie trailers and of scenes and characters from popular movies and television programs. Other viral campaigns have met with success by recycling and/or riding the popularity of past memes and viral content; focusing on accidents with little-or-no serious injuries (car crashes, people falling, men getting hit in the groin, etc.); successful and failed attempts at extreme sports; and useful content such as how-to videos of interest to members of your target audience.

As I admitted earlier: there is no secret to viral marketing. Everything we've discussed up to this point has been advice, hints and suggestions meant to increase your chances of viral success. The more viral material you create, the more creative your ideas and the closer you adhere to these suggestions, the better chances you have of achieving viral success with your branding, marketing and promotional campaigns.

16

DISTRIBUTION

Today's independent filmmakers face a continually evolving, and occasionally frightening, environment in which to sell and distribute their films. In addition to rapidly changing distribution channels, an explosion in feature film production has resulted in intense competition among films and a significant shift in negotiating power from filmmakers and independent studios to distributors and other film buyers.

To overcome these challenges, it's critical to identify and understand your main objectives with regard to your film and its distribution. And, while the objective of the majority of independent films is to generate and maximize a financial profit, the goals of other films may not be strictly monetary.

For instance, many films and documentaries are produced with the ultimate objective to have an impact on a particular cause or situation. In this case, spotlighting the cause, educating an audience on its importance and generating action and/or financial support may be more important to the filmmakers than a financial profit.

Similarly, many short and low-budget feature films are produced to showcase the talents of the filmmakers and their cast and crew. For such films festival awards and industry recognition might likewise be more important to the long-term success of the filmmaker than a modest financial profit. The principal distribution strategy for these filmmakers is to assure that the film is seen by the greatest number of professionals and organizations in a position to finance, hire and/or promote the filmmakers and their future film projects.

Bottom Line: The ultimate objective(s) of your film is critical in determining how best to pursue distribution and in how aggressively you negotiate distribution terms.

That said, I think it's safe to assume that the objective of most filmmakers is to achieve and maximize financial profitability for themselves and their investors. And, despite the seemingly overwhelming challenges, successful distribution ensures that your film reaches the largest number of potential viewers while properly rewarding investors (which, in turn, affords filmmakers the opportunity to continue to make successive films).

Fortunately, filmmakers have never been afforded greater access to – or a greater number of – distribution channels. At the same time, the number and variety of distribution channels and technologies also continues to increase and evolve. Currently, the vast majority of commercially oriented independent films are distributed across the following channels:

Film festivals
Theatrical release
Cable, satellite and digital pay-per-view (PPV)
Subscription cable and satellite television
Digital distribution (Netflix, iTunes, Amazon, Hulu, etc.)
Additional ancillary:

(a) Airlines, cruise ships, hotels and resorts, etc.
(b) Military: Army, Navy, Air Force, Marines, Coast Guard, etc.
(c) Educational: schools, universities and/or libraries
(d) Four walled theatrical and road shows
(e) Merchandise and cross- or trans-media products: video games, soundtracks, audiobooks, print books and ebooks, apparel, toys, smart phone and tablet apps, etc.

These individual segments can be further broken down by North American domestic (for those of us in the United States or Canada) and foreign markets broadly comprised of Europe, Asia-Pacific and Latin America. Currently, the North American market represents approximately one-third of the total revenues and profits of globally distributed independent films. The remaining two-thirds of revenues and profits are generated by foreign (non-North American) markets.

While foreign markets generate the majority of total revenues and profit, foreign distribution – in all its various forms . . . not just theatrical – introduces increased complication and higher relative expenses than domestic North American distribution. As Richard Berger, Senior Vice President of Global Digital Strategy and Operations at Sony Pictures Home Entertainment, explains:

> The global market adds a significant amount of complexity. As services expand into different territories, you can't always just replicate what you did in one territory for another . . . Aside from language differences, there are many different rules and regulations for content ratings, privacy policies, and content protection standards that are challenging. Piracy is more problematic in some regions, which makes certain business models and offerings more difficult to establish.
>
> (Curtin et al., 2014)

As mentioned, distribution encompasses far more than just theatrical release. These multiple distribution channels and the schedule in which the film is released within each channel is termed the "film window." And properly managing the window is one of the most important ingredients to the film's ultimate success or failure.

Historically, the theatrical release of an independent film typically occurred within twelve months of its film festival premier; DVD, VOD and pay-per-view sales and rentals were generally released within ninety days of the film's theatrical "run"; and television and cable broadcast were scheduled to occur four to six months following the DVD, VOD and PPV releases.

Currently, particularly as it applies to low-budget film projects, the standard release window has largely been abandoned. Many low-budget films have scheduled their theatrical and VOD releases concurrently. Other films are released on VOD platforms first and, should the films perform well, are later released theatrically. Still other windows are structured around the demands, preferences or requirements of a single channel (such as iTunes).

FIGURE 16.1 The world's largest film markets by country as measured by total box office receipts.

(Motion Picture Association of America's annual *Theatrical Market Statistics*)

At the same time, the velocity at which movies move across platforms has also accelerated dramatically. As a result, unless a movie is truly an "event," many audience members will wait for the film to become available online.

> *If you really want to watch a movie when it first comes out, you can go to the theater and pay to see it on the big screen. If you want to watch it when it first becomes available in your home, you can rent it or buy it. If you want to wait a little longer and not pay separately for it, you can receive it as part of a subscription package. Eventually, if you wait long enough, you can watch it for free with ads.*
>
> (Richard Berger, Senior Vice President Global Digital Strategy and Operations, Sony Pictures Home Entertainment, quoted in Curtin et al., 2014)

DISTRIBUTION MODELS: TRADITIONAL, SELF & HYBRID

How filmmakers choose to pursue the sales and licensing of their films is as important to their film's popular and commercial success as are the choices they make around specific distribution channels and schedules. Essentially, each filmmaker has a choice from three distribution models: (i) the traditional model; (ii) the self-distribution model; or (iii) the hybrid model.

The critical component of the *Traditional Distribution Model* is that the distributor(s) are purchasing the global rights to the film and are then responsible for all domestic and/or foreign distribution. These large global distributors are able to offer comprehensive distribution across virtually every distribution platform (theatrical; DVD sales and rentals; cable, satellite and digital PPV and VOD, etc.).

These global distributors have often included several well-recognized studios and their subsidiaries, including Focus Features (Universal Pictures), Fox Searchlight (Twentieth Century Fox), IFC Films (AMC Networks), Lionsgate, Lionsgate Premiere, Paramount Vantage (Paramount Pictures), Screen Gems (Sony), Summit Entertainment (Lionsgate), Touchstone Pictures (Walt Disney Studios Motion Pictures) and The Weinstein Company.

Unfortunately, not only are such global rights distribution agreements increasingly rare, they commonly require filmmakers to surrender significant control over their final films and the marketing of them. Distributors will want the rights to re-cut the film and its trailers, and the right to redesign the film's key art among other rights that could fundamentally change the nature of both the film and the way it is presented to its audience.

In contrast to the traditional model in which the filmmaker and producers seek to sell the film's global rights, both the self-distribution and hybrid distribution models are based upon "split rights" – the sale of domestic and foreign rights to individual regional, national and, often, channel-specific distributors. The sale of split rights commonly results in a stronger negotiating position for the filmmaker and correspondingly higher financial returns.

To further maximize their financial return and control over the distribution process, a small group of filmmakers have adopted a do-it-yourself approach commonly referred to as the *Self-Distribution Model*. These filmmakers represent themselves and negotiate terms directly with each domestic and foreign distributor.

Regrettably, very few filmmakers have the knowledge or established relationships necessary to successfully represent their own films. In addition to the considerable time and effort involved in identifying, contacting and pitching appropriate distributors, filmmakers must also negotiate unfamiliar contract terms. Naturally, over the course of these negotiations, filmmakers often find themselves at a distinct disadvantage.

Obviously there are also significant monetary costs associated with marketing a film to distributors. While agents and reps (discussed shortly) can spread these costs over a portfolio of several films, a self-distributed film doesn't have this opportunity. Instead, self-distributed films must absorb the entirety of all associated costs, including: film market fees, costs of private screenings, travel and lodging and other marketing and promotional fees. Depending upon how aggressively a filmmaker chooses to market their film, such costs could easily add a hundred thousand dollars or more to their film's budget.

Because of the challenges associated with a pure self-distribution strategy, most independent filmmakers have now adopted a *Hybrid Distribution Model* in which the filmmaker retains electronic rights (including VOD) to the film while employing producer's reps and sales agents to license domestic and foreign theatrical, cable broadcast and other ancillary distribution rights.

While the hybrid distribution model is most appropriate for the vast majority of low-budget independent filmmakers, the key to its success is in the producers and filmmakers being able to secure the "right" sales agents and producer's representatives. Unfortunately, not only are the number of such talented professionals limited, but they also tend to be highly selective with regard to the films and filmmakers they represent.

SALES AGENTS & PRODUCER'S REPRESENTATIVES

As we've discussed, an independent film and its filmmakers face several challenges along the path to successful sales and distribution. Fortunately, there are a number of professionals and service providers to help filmmakers to navigate these challenges. Among the most important professionals are the sales agent and producer's representative.

Sales agents (aka "foreign sales agents") represent your film to foreign distributors in various countries and regions. Like the distributors and distribution channels themselves, there are a variety of sales agents with a number of differing specialties. However, fundamentally, the sales agent is responsible for representing an independent film and helping to (i) target regional and foreign distributors, (ii) submit the film for the distributors' consideration and (iii) assist in negotiating and closing distribution agreements. Sales agents are the essential component of the hybrid distribution strategy.

Some of the most experienced and successful sales agencies include:

- Arclight Films
- Aspect Films
- eOne Entertainment
- Epic Pictures
- The Exchange
- Focus Features
- Kathy Morgan International
- Lakeshore International
- Magnolia Pictures International
- Nu Image/Millennium
- Pathé International
- Spotlight Pictures
- The Works
- XYZ Films

In contrast, producer's representatives, also known as producer's reps, primarily assist in selling or licensing films to domestic (North American) distributors and networks (depending on the representative's experience, a producer's rep may also consult and advise filmmakers on each phase of production, including the development, financing, production, marketing and distribution process of a film). Given the almost overwhelming number of films available in the current market, domestic acquisition executives are increasingly focused on those films submitted by well-respected producers or producer's reps. Such producer's reps are particularly useful in assisting the filmmaker in selling the film's domestic broadcast rights to television stations, cable television networks and satellite systems/networks. Producer's reps can also be a great help with developing a film festival release strategy, choosing the appropriate festival at which to premier the film and making certain that the "right" people attend the festival screenings.

However, although the need for producer's representatives has never been greater, filmmakers have learned to become very selective in terms of which professionals and organizations they choose to serve as their producer's representative. Unfortunately, an alarming number of producer's reps will represent a great number of films, each of which they charge a large upfront fee, and then provide little promotional or distribution support to individual titles.

Fortunately, finding talented sales agents and producer's representatives is relatively straightforward. First, many independent film organizations (such as Film Independent) and most film markets publish directories that include legitimate sales agents and producers representatives. Second, books focused on film distribution (of which there are half a dozen or more currently on the market) often contain appendices listing the leading sales agents and producer's reps. Finally, and perhaps the best method, is to consult with entertainment attorneys, distribution consultants and other filmmakers for recommendations and referrals.

Some of the most trusted and accomplished names you are likely to discover include: Roeg Sutherland at Creative Artists (CAA), John Sloss and Erin Heidenreich of Cinetic Media, Jonathan Dana at Code Management, Ronna Wallace of Eastgate Pictures, Jeff Silver and Brian Kavanaugh-Jones at Grandview Management, Josh Braun of Submarine Entertainment, David Flynn at UTA and Jermone Duboz of William Morris Endeavor.

As you conduct your research and assemble a list of prospective agents and reps, you'll want to pay particular attention to the types and titles of films they've represented over the past three to five years. *How many years of experience does the agent or rep have? What types of films and genres have they successfully represented? What types of films and genres (and how many) are they currently representing? Which markets do they attend? Does the agent or rep work for a company or with other professionals with complementary experience, skills and relationships?*

Before selecting an agent or rep, you also need to contact past and present filmmakers who the agent or rep has represented. *What were their experiences? How many agents and reps has the filmmaker worked with? How does this agent or rep compare? How contentious – if at all – was the negotiation process? Was the agent or rep thorough in exploring distribution alternatives (countries, regions, channels, etc.)? How timely were payments made to the filmmaker? What about the quality and timeliness of any distribution and/or financial reporting?*

Finally, try to get a sense for how well-connected the agents and representatives are in the industry. As a general rule, there are very few sales agents and producer's reps who are able to successfully represent you and your film within both the domestic and foreign markets. However, well-networked agents and reps are in a position to make recommendations and referrals to complementary firms and professionals.

Note: As mentioned previously, the number of talented sales agents and producer's representatives are limited. In large part, their reputations reflect the fact that they are highly selective with regard to the films and filmmakers they represent. Therefore, it's imperative that you brand, market, promote and package your film – and yourself – as well as possible prior to contacting industry-leading agents and reps. Although a cliché, it's true: You only get one chance to make a first impression.

ATTORNEYS, ACCOUNTANTS, PUBLICISTS AND OTHER PROFESSIONALS & ORGANIZATIONS

Relative to other industries, the business of film can be exceedingly complex. Without the proper knowledge, experience, skills and guidance, a filmmaker can easily waste years of effort and lose hundreds of thousands of dollars – or more – of their producers' investment. To reduce such risks, and increase the opportunity for success, filmmakers and their producers should work to retain the most highly qualified support professionals possible. In addition to those professionals already discussed, the filmmaker should also add the following members to the team:

Attorneys: One of the first hires the filmmaker should make during development and pre-production is a qualified entertainment attorney. The attorney is instrumental in preparing and/or reviewing investment memorandum, cast and crew contracts, location agreements, music releases and other rights, clearances and chain-of-title documents. However, perhaps the most critical role of the entertainment attorney is in the review and negotiation of sales agent, producer's representative and distribution agreements (discussed shortly).

In addition to the attorney's role with regard to contracting and negotiations, an experienced and well-networked entertainment attorney should also be in a position to make recommendations and referrals to other talented industry professionals – particularly sales agents and producer's representatives. The value of this network, particularly if you're relatively new to the industry, is difficult to overstate.

Accountants: Another early hire should be a certified or chartered accountant who specializes in the film industry. Such accountants can prepare or review and improve the filmmaker's financial projections, production budget, monthly or quarterly investor reports, applications and submission for any governmental film incentives and tax filings.

Unfortunately, horror stories abound from scriptwriters, filmmakers and investors who were essentially defrauded of any financial return due to dubious "Hollywood accounting" practices. To reduce or eliminate such risks, the accountant, working closely with the entertainment attorney, should review sales agent, producer's rep and distribution agreements with regard to the definition of financial and accounting terms – and particularly the definition of such terms as "net receipts," "net proceeds" and/or "net profits."

Publicists: There are a number of publicists who specialize in supporting independent films and filmmakers. Although the principal role of the publicist is to generate publicity and promote the film and its filmmakers, specialized publicists increase the strength of film festival submissions and can correspondingly improve the chances for acceptance. Once acceptance to a leading festival has been secured, the publicist can be particularly helpful in assisting filmmakers gain admissions to some of the most exclusive festival parties and events and/or to help them arrange their own parties and events.

However, due to the expenses involved in retaining a talented publicist, most filmmakers choose to hire a publicist only after they've been accepted to one or more of the leading global festivals or if their production budget justifies such an investment.

Distribution Consultants and Organizations: Many early career independent filmmakers will find it difficult to network and meet with distribution professionals prior to – and during – the development process. For those committed to a career in independent film production and distribution, it is strongly advisable to join one or two organizations to gain the requisite knowledge, insights, support and professional network.

Three of the most respected are the Independent Film Project, Film Independent and The Film Collaborative. These organizations offer various membership benefits, including online resources, educational programs, conferences, networking events, film festivals and awards. The Independent Film Project, for instance, hosts IFP Film Week in New York City while Film Independent hosts the LA Film Festival and Independent Spirit Awards.

With regard to distribution, organizations such as The Film Collaborative can be particularly helpful in offering independent filmmakers a full range of education about distribution, distribution services and marketing services including sales representation, service theatrical releases, hybrid distribution, grassroots marketing, traditional marketing, digital aggregation, distribution consultation and contract consultation.

However, if you're looking for more personal support, consider hiring a distribution consultant such as Stacey Parks, a former sales agent and author of *The Guide to Independent Film Distribution*. In addition to individual and small group consultation, Stacey also offers a membership site, Film Specific, established to provide filmmakers with information, tools, training and personal consulting on low-budget film distribution. Although

Stacey is one of the most well-known, filmmakers are fortunate to be able to choose from several qualified distribution advisors and consultants.

Digital Aggregators: While there are a number of VOD channels through which filmmakers can post their films directly (such as Amazon's CreateSpace and Vimeo On Demand), most VOD distribution requires the use of a low-cost digital aggregator to properly encode, format and submit the film to various VOD channels. Some of the most well-respected aggregators include: bitMAX, Distrify, Distribber, The Film Collaborative, Gravitas Ventures, Indie Rights, Juice Productions, Premiere Digital and Zoo Digital.

When choosing a digital aggregator it's important to decide what level of service you require. At the very minimum, the aggregator serves to encode and format the film and then submit it to various VOD channels. At the other end of the spectrum, some aggregators (such as Gravitas Ventures) have relationships at national and global television, cable and pay-per-view networks and are, therefore, able to serve as quasi-sales agents or producer's reps.

THEATRICAL RELEASES

Unless your film receives an award from Sundance, Cannes or another leading first-tier festival, your film is highly unlikely to get a theatrical release. On the other hand, a theatrical release is increasingly possible *once* your film becomes popular via digital VOD.

Unfortunately, independent filmmakers (and the film industry more generally) have become fixated on theatrical releases and box office performance. And this fixation is,

FIGURE 16.2 Although highly regarded by filmmakers and audiences, the theatrical release is a particularly expensive distribution channel and, as a result, rarely profitable.

(AMC Theaters/Wanda Group)

in part, based on a crucial misunderstanding of box office receipts. What many people fail to realize is that box office performance reflects the total amount of tickets purchased at the theater ... *not* the amount of money earned by, or paid to, the studio or filmmakers.

Instead, the owners of the theater or theater chain keep 50–65% of ticket sales while the remaining 35–50% are paid to the theatrical distributor. *Assuming that the theatrical run is sufficiently popular for the distributor to recover its fees and expenses (including marketing and promotional costs), independent filmmakers are commonly left with no more than 5–10% of the gross from domestic and foreign theatrical release.*

Although theatrical releases are rarely profitable (including those films produced and distributed by the major studios themselves), theatrical releases often have considerable marketing and promotion value as film distribution shifts to more profitable channels. With the benefit of global audience recognition afforded by a theatrical release, the overwhelming majority of profitable independent and major studio films do so through subsequent cable and televised broadcast rights, video-on-demand (VOD), pay-per-view (PPV) and ancillary markets (as well as from non-distribution related sources such as product placement and sponsorship transactions, music and soundtracks, and film-based books, magazines, comics and video games, and the sale and licensing of apparel, toys and other merchandise or services).

NETWORK & CABLE TELEVISION RIGHTS

Reflecting the high promotional costs and the correspondingly low- or no-profit nature of theatrical releases, studio and independent producers must rely upon higher-margined non-theatrical releases to achieve profitability. For studio films, in particular, licensed films to broadcast networks, subscription cable television (including satellite) and pay-per-view channels continue to remain particularly lucrative.

With an ever-expanding number of domestic and foreign channels, studio films benefit from considerable broadcast distribution options, including broadcast networks such as ABC, BBC, CBS, ITV, NBC, NHK and Sky; subscription channels such as A&E, AXN, BT, Cinemax, Deutsche Telekom, Discovery, Hallmark, Lifetime, Showtime, SKY, SyFy, Star TV, Switch, TBS and USA; and pay-per-view programming from such providers as BSkyB, Digital+, Cinemax, HBO, HBO Europe, Premiere, Orange Cinema, Starz/Encore and Sky Box Office.

Despite the large and growing number of channels, lower-budget films are finding it increasingly difficult to secure network and cable distribution. As mentioned repeatedly, independent films are confronted with an almost overwhelming number of films competing for distribution. At the same time, broadcast and cable networks are being consolidated with large entertainment corporations that prefer to broadcast their own studio's films, particularly within North America. Other broadcasters have established long-term contractual relationships with one or more studios and/or have begun developing and producing their own content. While more "indie-friendly" channels have also emerged, such as IFC and Sundance in North America, these channels prefer to acquire acclaimed films from such festivals as Cannes, Sundance, Toronto and SXSW.

Fortunately, your sales agent and producer's reps will be instrumental in properly navigating this evolving landscape and in successfully targeting those domestic and foreign broadcasters most interested in acquiring your film. This industry insight is yet another reason why hiring qualified and well-networked agents and reps is so important to successful distribution.

VIDEO-ON-DEMAND ("VOD") DISTRIBUTION

Emerging technologies and their impact on the fundamentals of the film industry, as well as marketing and promotion, have been a consistent theme throughout this book. And perhaps there has been no greater force for change than the emerging dominance of video-on-demand as a distribution platform.

VOD allows viewers to watch movies at their own time on whatever device they like best, including large screen televisions, laptops, desktops, tablets, mobile phones and other devices. In fact, television manufacturers have all incorporated online capability and audience members can now view iTunes, Amazon, Hulu Plus, Netflix, YouTube Rentals and others directly on their televisions. As a result, an increasing number of people are cancelling their cable subscriptions in favor of lower- or no-cost online alternatives.

For filmmakers, the benefits are just as dramatic. VOD offers filmmakers and distributors significant control over the release date, marketing and promotion and the number and specific channels on which the film will appear as well as the individual countries and regions. For those filmmakers who retain VOD rights, they are afforded direct access to their target audience and viewers, global distribution and typically receive direct revenues and cash flows.

This shift to VOD had been difficult for many major studios . . . upsetting traditional distribution strategies and their financial performance.

> If you look only at the last couple of years, consumer spending on home entertainment products has remained fairly constant. But what we're finding from an industry perspective is the percentage of those revenues that come back to the studio is less than what it was before. That's because there's a trend toward more subscription and video on demand and a movement away from ownership.
>
> (Mitch Singer, Chief Digital Strategy Officer, Sony Pictures Entertainment, quoted in Curtin et al., 2014)

Compounding the confusion around VOD distribution is the fact that the performance of any given film can be so different from one VOD channel to another.

> Some platforms attract different customers than others, and that results in different content preferences across those platforms. We have a whole team here that figures out how to best promote titles, especially if we think they are great fits for certain platforms. In some cases, it's not one-size-fits-all. Take the PlayStation and Xbox services, for example. Both are gaming platforms. People who use them to watch movies are different than people who use iTunes or Amazon. This is apparent when we notice certain titles performing better on certain platforms.
>
> (Richard Berger, Senior Vice President Global Digital Strategy and Operations, Sony Pictures Home Entertainment, quoted in Curtin et al., 2014)

However, despite these challenges, studios are beginning to adapt. As early as 2014, the film *Snowpiercer* recorded ~$4 million during the first two weeks of its VOD release. With little to no promotion, the film entered VOD with strong word-of-mouth from film festivals and a brief eight theater limited release. Because of the success of *Snowpiercer* and similar films, many films are now achieving success by scheduling limited theatrical and VOD releases concurrently. As Tom Quinn, RADiUS-TWC co-president, explains:

FIGURE 16.3 The increased popularity of video-on-demand (VOD) channels, such as iTunes, offers independent filmmakers access to a vast global audience. At the same time, VOD is often the most highly profitable distribution channel available to independent production companies.

(Apple)

"Because of VOD first-window exploitation, more times than not our films have entered into profitability . . . [and] they've gone on to success in additional windows" (Lang, 2014)

Unfortunately, it's difficult to determine how many other films have met with similar success in the years since *Snowpiercer*. Unlike box office performance, there are no reliable sources of consolidated data on VOD sales and revenues. Instead, the video-on-demand performances of films are only occasionally self-reported and those that are tend to be for the most successful releases. Understandably, unsuccessful VOD releases are rarely publicized by their distributors. As a result, be mindful that these numbers have a strong upward bias relative to the performance of typical unreported VOD releases.

In contrast to the potential profitability of other VOD releases which pay filmmakers or their distributors 50–90% of gross rental and sales revenues, subscription VOD ("SVOD") such as Netflix, Amazon Prime and Hulu Plus typically offer little financial incentive to low-budget filmmakers and their distributors. For instance, many SVOD channels, such as Amazon Prime, pay filmmakers as little as $0.05–$0.10 USD per view. Netflix, the 1,000lb gorilla of SVOD, commonly enters into a one to two year licensing agreement for a flat licensing fee regardless of the amount of times the film is viewed. For low-budget independent films, these licensing agreements reportedly rarely exceed $5,000–$10,000 over the term of the agreement.

Unfortunately, in addition to low direct financial returns, when available to SVOD subscribers essentially for free, audience members will understandably be reluctant to rent or purchase the film from other channels – cannibalizing the performance of more profitable distribution channels. The bottom line? Low-budget filmmakers should be highly cautious of distributing their films through SVOD channels.

In fact, there are only three instances in which SVOD distribution *may* make financial sense. First, after the film's revenues have declined significantly three to five years (or more) following the film's initial release; second, in the six to twelve months leading up to the release of the film's sequel; and, third, when the filmmakers' objectives are not purely financial and, instead, want the film to be seen by the largest audience possible (e.g. films produced to drive social change).

Beyond higher profitability (SVOD notwithstanding), VOD channels also offer filmmakers and distributors considerable control over how the film is promoted on each channel. In addition to publishing meta data such as the film's title, key art, MPAA or film commission rating, run time, release date, genre classification, cast and crew list and a brief description, many channels will allow filmmakers and their distributors to optimize their film's listings with such promotional materials as:

- Trailer, teasers, featurettes, etc.
- Film stills and BTS photographs
- IMDb Rating (on a ten point scale)
- Rotten Tomatoes reviews with Tomato Meter
- "Top Critic's Reviews"
- Customer ratings and reviews.

To further maximize the promotion of their film libraries, most VOD channels have also developed specialized algorithms designed to recommend your film to audience members whose viewing history suggest that they would be most interested in your film. These recommendations often appear as such phrases as *"Viewers Also Bought . . . "* and *"Customers Who Watched This Also Watched . . . "* and are also promoted within such categorical listings as *"More by These Actors," "More by This Director"* and *"Top Movies in [Genre]."*

Many VOD channels have also added "Add to" functions ("Watch Later," "Favorites," "Create New Playlist," etc.) as well as email and "Share" functions (e.g. social media buttons). And some also include a comments section which often serve as a mini-forum for fans of the film.

Fortunately, relatively few films take full advantage of the many low- or no-cost promotional opportunities afforded by VOD channels. This creates an enormous source of competitive advantage for filmmakers, and their PMDs, who are able to incorporate these opportunities into their own launch team activities and within their social media and other marketing platforms.

ALTERNATIVE MARKETS

Alternative markets may include a number of non-traditional distribution channels such as airlines, cruise ships, vacation resorts, universities and colleges, military bases and others. Your sales agent and producer's rep will explore these opportunities, and others, directly with specialized distributors and at a variety of film markets.

However, for filmmakers themselves, the two most common alternative markets are four walled theatrical releases and road shows.

Four Walling: Four walling entails the filmmakers renting a movie theater (or theaters) for a period of time and in which the filmmakers receive all the box office receipts. Four walling allows the filmmakers to determine how many, and in which, cities the films will be released and how long the theatrical run will be available in theaters. Four walling also classifies as a theatrical release with the box office receipts correspondingly recognized by the industry. Further, four walled films can also qualify for Academy Awards nomination. Unfortunately, the cost of four walling, particularly the associated print and advertising expenses, is normally quite prohibitive. So, unless you are targeting an Academy Awards nomination or have other promotional or marketing objectives, four walling rarely makes financial sense as a distribution channel.

Road Shows/Film Tours: In contrast to four walling, road shows are typically held by hosting organizations that do not charge fees such as theater rentals. These organizations may include marketing partners, universities and film schools, public parks, community centers, museums, historical sites, special interest groups and "house parties" in which individuals host the film in their homes.

Road shows are much less expensive than four walling and allow the filmmakers to better target members of their core and secondary markets. Road shows also drive greater engagement between the audience and film since these events typically include personal appearances by the filmmaker, members of the cast and/or crew and, occasionally, a personal appearance by other celebrities.

Unfortunately, however, unlike four walling, road shows cannot be included in official "box office" receipts and cannot be used to qualify for Academy Award nominations. And, despite the lower costs, road shows (and four walling) rarely provide sufficient financial return or promotional value to make the effort worthwhile.

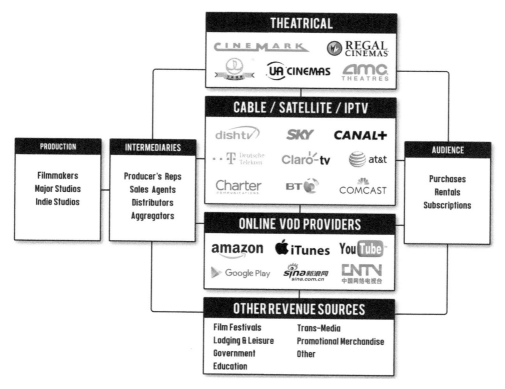

FIGURE 16.4 Independent film distribution channels including representative brands of some of the world's largest distribution companies/outlets.

(Robert G. Barnwell/Sandy O. Cagnan)

CONTRACTS & AGREEMENTS

Regardless of the distribution outlet or model a filmmaker may choose, it's an unfortunate reality that many filmmakers unknowingly give up much of their film's profits and control over final cut, marketing and promotion as well as sequel, ancillary and merchandising rights. What's perhaps even more disturbing is how relatively common this has become.

To prevent such challenges, independent filmmakers should work closely with entertainment attorneys throughout the production and distribution process. Mark Litwak, an entertainment attorney based in Los Angeles and author of *Dealmaking in the Film and Television Industry*, explains his role:

> *Ideally, I would get involved from the very beginning, before the filmmaker hires anyone, when they're still raising money. I would help create the legal entity – such as such as a corporation or limited liability corporation – and draft an investment memorandum and contract. So I should be meeting with the filmmakers at the script stage, when they're packaging their movies. Then, when the movie's finished, I can handle all negotiation and contracts related to the distribution of the movie, so I often work with the filmmaker and his representatives to decide which distributors are appropriate for the movie.*

While a comprehensive discussion of the legal issues involved in distribution contracts and agreements are beyond the scope of this book, Mark explains that there are several issues that entertainment attorneys and their clients should pay particular attention to:

- First and foremost, the agreement must identify the specific rights and the term or duration of those rights being licensed or purchased. In many instances, it is just as important that the agreement specify the rights *not* granted (and, which are instead, reserved to the filmmaker).
- It's also important that the licensing contract restrict distributors from fundamentally altering the character of the film or its marketing in a manner unacceptable to the filmmaker and the film's producers.
- Negotiate a limit, or cap, on expenses with each agent, rep and distributor. The filmmaker's attorney should also carefully define allowable expenses and the manner in which revenues, expenses, profitability and other financial metrics are calculated.
- To further protect the filmmaker and investor's interests, the filmmaker's attorney should negotiate (i) the right to audit the distributors books and records; and (ii) a several year period of time (known as "limitation on action") during which the filmmakers can contest any accounting or statement irregularities.
- Should the distributor default on any of its contractual obligations, the agreement must grant the filmmaker the right to terminate the contract ("termination clause"), regain rights to the film ("reversion rights") and the ability to relicense/distribute the film while reserving the right to seek damages for any breaches by the distributor.

Not surprisingly, these are only a few of the many "headline" issues on which filmmakers and their attorney's must concentrate. There are literally dozens, if not hundreds, of other issues of varying complexity that must be addressed during the negotiation process. Many of which – if ignored or improperly addressed – could significantly impair your film, its distribution and its ultimate profitability.

Fortunately, your sales agent, producer's representative and attorney will work together to limit sales and licensing agreements to legitimate distributors who will readily agree to appropriate filmmaker protections. However, even when dealing with such distributors, the responsibility of protecting the filmmaker's interests ultimately falls to the filmmaker and his or her attorney.

DISTRIBUTION DELIVERABLES

As a component of each of your distribution agreements, your distributors will provide you with a list of required deliverables. Although most of these deliverables will remain relatively consistent from one distributor to another, some items will be specific to the individual distributor and the country or region in which your film will be distributed. Any delay in furnishing these deliverables will likewise delay your film's distribution and the receipt of any distribution proceeds.

Although not exhaustive, required film deliverables commonly include:

1. Master, or "Universal," Digital HD copy of film with certified quality check
2. Master stereo sound mix
3. M&E (music and effects less dialogue) mix
4. Music cue sheet
5. Transcript/dialogue script (for closed captioning) and song lyrics
6. Credit list
7. A chain-of-title to include a registered copyright of the movie as well as copies of properly executed rights and clearances, letters of agreement, contracts, licensing, etc.
8. Distribution restrictions (such as agreements in the manner and order members of the cast and crew are credited)
9. Errors and omission insurance (E&O insurance which can often be covered by the aggregator's or distributor's policies upon request for a small fee)
10. Advertising materials (particularly key art, teasers and trailers, electronic press kits, behind-the-scenes stills, movie stills and supporting promotional materials).

The expenses associated with these deliverables can be quite high – often ranging from $25k to $35k or more. However, most of these expenses can be drastically reduced if the creation of deliverables is incorporated into the production and post-production process (as opposed to created later). Other expenses, such as E&O insurance, can be postponed until after distribution agreements have been executed. Some distributors and licensees may also agree to prepare some of these deliverables on your behalf with the associated costs added to their incurred expenses.

GETTING A HEADSTART ON SUCCESSFUL DISTRIBUTION

As with marketing and promotion, the sales and distribution process should begin well before the film's principal photography. Ideally, the filmmakers should begin to formulate a sales and distribution strategy during the film's initial development and prior to fundraising. The following are some of the many considerations and actions filmmakers should contemplate throughout development and preproduction.

Join industry organizations and familiarize yourself with the industry, marketplace and distribution trends: Join organizations such as The Film Collaborative and Film Specific which focus on assisting low-budget independent filmmakers to master the knowledge and practices required to successfully distribute their films. Keep abreast of market conditions by subscribing to and regularly reading publications and sites such as Deadline.com, Hollywoodreporter.com and Variety.com as well as attending various industry events (such as workshops and conferences).

Attend film markets and research market: Identify trends with regard to popular genres, storylines and distribution strategies. Meet and network with others well-positioned within the industry (including agents, reps, distributors, producers and other filmmakers) – particularly those who have recently distributed a film similar to yours in terms of both genre and budget. If and when possible, begin compiling information on comparable films, including: the film's genre, storyline and film "quality" (how the film plays as well as critical and popular acclaim), production budget, print and advertising (aka "p&a") budget and any other details with regard to the relative success or failure or each film's distribution and financial performance.

Contact sales agents and distributors for informal feedback: If you haven't done so already – once you've selected a genre, completed the treatment and developed a budding relationship with a few agents and reps – seek out opinions and suggestions with regard to the storyline, budget, prospective cast members and the market more generally. Be sure to thank each agent, rep or distributor for their input and update them periodically on your film's progress.

Produce pre-production trailers, key art and pitch sheets: Once you have developed a treatment, begin work on pre-production trailers and key art. The trailers and key art will help you to keep your script "on-point" as well as serving to promote the film to investors, agents, distributors and potential cast and crew members while building an audience. This is also a good time to consider hiring a distribution consultant.

Complete the script, budget, financial projects and production schedule: This information and material is necessary to raise investor funding and to attach popular actors. In fact, who is attached to star in your forthcoming film is one of the most common questions and important determinants of the film's marketability and distribution success. Although it may prove challenging, if you can attach a well-known actor during development or early in pre-production, fundraising efforts will likewise prove more successful.

As discussed in Chapter 4, by far, the most important determinant in achieving successful distribution is the quality of the film itself. In turn, the quality of the film (marketability and playability) will largely be determined by the work done during development and pre-production ... specifically by the (i) quality of the script, (ii) available financial resources and (iii) the skill, experience and creativity of the cast and crew (including the director, executive producers and the producer of marketing and distribution).

Finally, it's important that you remember: branding, marketing and promotion don't stop when the film is released. Depending upon your film's storyline and audience reception, your film can – and should – continue to generate revenues for years to come. However, it's up to you and your team to commit to the continued pursuit of consistent branding, marketing and promotional opportunities to make it happen.

BRANDING, MARKETING AND PROMOTIONAL AUDIT

MARKET RESEARCH

1. Have you instituted a process of regularly identifying and tracking trends with regard to the film industry, marketing and promotion, emerging business models, technology, the audience's entertainment options, etc.?
2. What industry periodicals do you regularly read or subscribe to? What industry associations or guilds are you a member and do you regularly attend meetings or other events? Which formal and informal film markets do you attend? Who are the industry professionals with whom you maintain regular contact?
3. Given the state of the film industry and emerging trends, what are the implications for your career, production company and future film projects? Do you have a clear vision of how you can best position your career and films relative to the needs and desires of the industry and marketplace?
4. Are you able to clearly define your target customer or market? What are the key demographic characteristics of audience members for your films and within your film genre? Have you segmented customers into different groups that share similar characteristics? Have you created an audience persona based upon an understanding of these characteristics?
5. What factors have influenced audience members to purchase or rent your past films? Are these the same factors that will influence future film purchases and rentals?
6. Over the past ten to twenty years, what are the titles of the leading, or most popular, films within your genre and budget range? What are the most critical audience expectations and characteristics of films within your genre and budget range?
7. Does your target audience feel that the films you produce are unique and differentiated within their genre and from other films in the broader market? Specifically, what elements within your films are unique or differentiated? Do you have objective research and information that supports this response?
8. Do you regularly collect audience and critical feedback, opinions and testimonials? How is this audience feedback incorporated into your marketing plans and activities?
9. Have you compiled a list and carefully studied competing filmmakers, production companies and films within your genre and budget? What are the key branding messages and elements contained within their marketing and promotional outlets?

How do they manage their brands on social media, their websites, IMDb profiles, electronic press kits, public releases and other outlets and materials?

10. What are the marketing strategies employed by these competitors? In which ways do their marketing strategies compare and contrast with your own? Have you established an archive or collection of the marketing materials of competing filmmakers within your genre and budget range?

MARKETING STRATEGY & ACTIVITIES

1. Given the current state of the film industry and future trends, what are the greatest threats and opportunities facing your films and your filmmaking career? Access to financing? Access to distribution? Access to quality cast, crew, equipment, locations, other? What steps can you take to proactively mitigate the threats facing your films and career?

2. Do you have a written marketing strategy, calendar and budget aligning your branding, marketing and promotional activities (and associated marketing and promotional materials) with each stage of production and the AIDA process? Does this marketing strategy and plan contain quantifiable objectives and performance measures?

3. How do you and your team approach market planning? How often is the plan revisited and revised? Who is involved in the planning process? What external sources of information are used on which to align your marketing plan with existing and emerging market realities? Once the plan is completed, who is ultimately responsible for its proper execution? A Producer of Marketing and Distribution (PMD)? Other?

4. What is the nature and status of your current film slate? Number of projects? Are these projects genre- and/or audience-consistent? What is the current stage of production of each of the films in the slate? To what extent, if any, have branding and marketing considerations played a part in the selection of film projects, titles and script development?

5. Have you extended your brand(s) via cross-media, promotional merchandising or other such opportunities? If not, is it appropriate to do so at this stage in your production company's lifecycle?

6. Are your branding, marketing and promotional efforts based on inbound (content marketing via websites and social media, search engine optimization and other digital campaigns) rather than outbound marketing (paid advertising)? Do you adhere to an integrated marketing approach in which the entire branding, marketing and promotional campaign appears uniform and seamless, utilizing consistent brand messaging, colors, graphics and other elements?

7. Are you, or have you considered, exploring efforts to maximize the effectiveness and efficiency of your marketing campaigns using cooperative marketing, affinity marketing and/or production placement opportunities?

8. Have you explored opportunities with audience-relevant traditional and/or new media channels in which you can regularly serve as a guest or contributor?

9. Who is ultimately responsible for the day-to-day branding, marketing and promotional activities for the film and production company? A Producer of Marketing and Distribution (PMD)? The filmmaker? Other? If the filmmaker, does the filmmaker have sufficient knowledge and resources to both produce and direct the film while adequately performing all marketing and distribution responsibilities?

10. How often do you review and reassess your actual marketing performance relative to original expectations? How often do you use these findings to revise and improve your branding, marketing and promotional activities and materials?

BRAND IDENTITY

(Note: At a minimum, you will likely have two distinct brands. The first is the brand image projected by yourself, your production company and your films to the viewing audience. The second is the brand image projected to industry professionals such as current and prospective investors, sales agents and others. Each of these brands must be actively and carefully managed.)

1. Are you conscious of the many images and perceptions (i.e. brand image) others form of you depending upon your various roles and relationships as filmmaker, business partner, colleague, friend and family member? If so, in what ways do you (or will you) plan to actively manage these various images or perceptions?

2. How do other colleagues, industry professionals and audience members currently view you, your production company and your films? On what basis do you know this to be true? Are you and your production company's brand image consistent with both the nature of your films and your target audience?

3. Does your current brand identity portray the correct image given your past, present and future film projects and targeted audience(s)? Is your brand properly aligned with your filmmaking objective(s)? Do your brands need to evolve or mature? Describe the desired brand for yourself, your production company and your films. What actions and materials do you plan to implement in order to bridge the gap between your current brand and desired brand?

4. Is your current and/or desired brand image supported by credible proof-points? Existing film education and experience? Past film festival or industry nominations and awards? History of industry and critical acclaim? Archive of favorable media coverage?

5. Have you clearly defined the genre and market segments you want to focus your films and filmmaking career on ? Does your current and desired brand identity – together with supporting branding elements – accurately reflect expectations within this genre and/or market segment?

6. Is your brand clearly differentiated from these competing filmmakers, production companies and films? If so, what is the primary point of difference on which your brand is focused? Are these points of differentiation clearly communicated to the industry and market throughout your marketing materials and channels? How do you know that these points of differentiation are valued and sought after by the marketplace?

7. Is your personal offline branding consistent with your current and/or proposed brand image? General appearance and physical condition? Brand and style of clothing? Vocabulary and manner of speech? Neighborhood(s) in which you live and work? Type of vehicle you drive? The brand and quality of your filmmaking equipment? Other elements?

8. Do you regularly perform an audit or review of your various brand touch-points? What impressions do audience members and industry professionals form when receiving an email from you? Reaching your voicemail? Meeting with you in person? Viewing your website and social media accounts? Other?

9. Which of the following brand identity elements have you incorporated within your filmmaking, production company and film brands: name, title logo, icon, taglines, type styles, colors, shapes, symbols, visual style, words and phrases, music, animation, etc.?

10. Are your marketing and promotional materials consistent with your brand identity? Are your brand elements consistently communicated and integrated within each of your branding, marketing and promotional activities and materials? Websites? Social media platforms? IMDb profiles? Electronic press kits? Public releases? Other?

VISUAL IDENTITY & BRAND IMAGE

1. Have you and your team established a consistent brand image and visual identity incorporating logos, color palette, typography/fonts, key art and imagery and other stylistic elements? Are these elements described within a style sheet or other visual branding guideline?

2. Do your visual materials accurately represent the atmosphere, emotion, mood and visuals of the film itself? When creating marketing and promotional materials, do you actively and purposely explore your films' scripts, storyboards and footage to identify and emphasize the most marketable elements? Do you develop and create films with marketing and promotional elements as inherent components of the scripts?

3. Are the film's marketing and promotional materials reflective of the film's genre? Do they include common elements, iconic imagery, colors and similar elements from the genre? Which elements of your visual identity differentiate your marketing and promotional materials from others within the genre?

4. Do you and your team maintain an archive of visual marketing materials from competing filmmakers, production companies and films? Do you and your team collect particularly interesting marketing visuals from outside of your genre and outside of the film industry? Do you use these materials as creative inspiration and on which to benchmark the quality of your own marketing and promotional materials?

5. Are the marketing visuals consistent and integrated across all marketing and promotional channels? Do the visuals remain relatively consistent and reflective of the filmmaker and production company's past and future films? Regularly assessing marketing materials and activities against an established style sheet or visual guideline is an important step in eliminating inconsistency.

6. What information must the film's visual marketing material communicate? Title? Tagline? Key art? Stars? Credit list or credit block? Release date? Website and social media URLs? Production company logos? Other?

7. Do you and your team create multiple versions of your visual marketing materials to meet the varying demands of different audiences and to serve different objectives?

8. Does BTS content illustrate and emphasize the film's most exciting shots and scenes? Does it include coverage of special and visual effects? Creature effects or special effects makeup? Particularly interesting wardrobe and props? Coverage of any specialty film equipment and/or techniques?

9. Do you extend your visual marketing and brand imagery to business cards, email signatures, portraits/headshots and other less obvious digital and offline marketing and promotional elements?

10. Do your film sets, equipment and location or stage signage properly reflect your brand and level of professionalism? When viewed by passers-by and visitors, what image do your film sets present? Base camp? Video village? Do producers, director, department heads and cast and crew members present themselves professionally?

PROFESSIONAL NETWORK

1. Are you and your team committed to expanding and cultivating a supporting network of investors, filmmaking colleagues, casting directors, sales agents, producer's representatives and other industry professionals? Note that each additional member of your professional network serves to increase the amplification rate in which your network is expanded by the reach of the other member's network (and so on).

2. Take an inventory and assess your current network as well as the production stage of your current film project. What is the nature of your existing professional network in terms of both quantity and quality? Who do you know and how would you best describe them? Fellow filmmakers? Film school alumni, faculty and administrators? Investors? Sales agents? Distributors? Cast? Crew? Other?

3. Given the current production stage of your film project or film slate, what types of professionals do you most need to add to your professional network? In addition to categories of professionals (investors, sales agents, etc.), are you able to assemble a list of names of such professionals, including contact details?

4. Among your list of current and targeted relationships, are there "super-connectors" who are well-positioned within the industry and able to make high-profile introductions? Such super-connectors typically include leading talent agents and managers, entertainment attorneys and accountants, sales agents and producer's representatives, entertainment publicists, film industry trade reporters, etc.

5. What value do you offer to members of your network? In other words: Why would someone want to have a relationship with you and your production company? Do you work to regularly provide contact and reciprocal value to members of your network? The greater the perceived value you offer members of your network, the greater the desire of others to join your network.

6. Are you well-known among those in your genre and/or filmmaking community? The greater your visibility among members of your genre and filmmaking community, the easier it will be to connect with and attract others to your professional network.

7. Have you scripted an interesting, yet brief, introduction to yourself and your production company? Is this introduction limited to twenty-five words or fewer? Similarly, what is the nature and availability of any networking or pitch materials and "leave behinds" such as pitch books, look books, pitch trailers, EPKs, etc.?

8. Have you created a library of various networking materials, including outreach and follow-up emails, letters and related materials? Do you use these materials to reach out to, or follow up with, a specific number of individuals per day, week or month?

9. Do you maintain an active "social calendar" or schedule of forthcoming events you plan to attend? Do these events include film festivals, film markets, associations, guild meetings and other industry events? Likewise, do you schedule regular calls and/or meet-ups (over coffee, lunch, etc.) with key members of your personal and professional network?

10. Do you have access to, and regularly use, a dedicated contact database with important details (name, title, company, address, telephone, email address, URL, birth dates,

name of colleagues, name of family members, etc.) of members of your network? Does this contact database allow for an automated system, or reminders, for regular follow-up and contact?

IMDB PROFILE(S)

1. What is the length (in terms of word count and number of paragraphs) of your IMDb filmmaker's biography and what type of information does it convey?
2. Does the biography contain information on why and/or how you became interested in filmmaking and your particular genre?
3. Does the biography contain information to which visitors/readers can relate on a personal basis? Where you grew up? Schools you attended? Experiences you've had? Other?
4. Is there a recognizable brand image or message contained within your biography? Do you lay claim to and advance a unique selling proposition?
5. What types of "proof-points" does your biography contain that establish or support your credibility as a filmmaker?
6. How many photographs does your IMDb profile contain? Do the photos show you on set behind the camera? Directing the actors? Alongside other luminaries/famous personalities? At awards ceremonies? Film premiers? Others? Do these images directly support any brand image or USP which you may claim within your bio?
7. Have you posted any videos or a reel to your IMDb profile? How many? What are the subjects of the videos? Behind-the-scenes? Film clips? Interviews? Awards? Premiers? Other? Again, in what ways do these videos advance your brand or USP, if at all?
8. What is the nature of your first several entries into your "Filmologies"? What are the roles/titles? Nature of the films (low-budget, studio, etc.)?
9. Does the "regular" (not Pro version) version of your IMDb profile mention the name and/or website address for your production company or any other ways in which visitors can contact you or follow you on other sites or social media accounts?
10. If you were a studio producer "short-listing" filmmakers for future film projects, for which types of films would you consider hiring you as a filmmaker? What overall impression do you believe your IMDb profile leaves with various industry professionals? Specifically, agents, managers, investors, actors and actresses and department heads and crew?

SOCIAL MEDIA MARKETING

1. Do you have a social media presence? If so, with which SM platforms? Do the colors, design and voice of your social media pages match that of your other marketing and promotional outlets? Are the differences and/or similarities appropriate for the demands of social media relative to your other marketing and promotional outlets?
2. Do your social media platforms and activity maintain continuity/integrity with the brand messages and stories portrayed on your website(s) and IMDb profile? Do your social media platforms and messages regularly reference your other website(s) and encourage other forms of communication both within and outside of social media?

3. What quantifiable objectives do you have for your social media marketing campaigns for the coming month? Quarter? Year? How successful have you been in achieving your social media objectives in the past month? Quarter? Year? To what do you attribute your success or failure in achieving these objectives?

4. Are your social media activities aligned with the social media platforms and topics most popular with your target audience? In addition to your target audience, how do your social media platforms and activities compare with those of other low-budget filmmakers, competing production companies and similar films?

5. How active have you been on your social media platforms? Consider the total number of posts, rate of posts (daily, weekly, monthly, other?), etc. What types of information and messages have you been sharing on your social media platforms?

6. How successful have you been in encouraging audience engagement with you on your social media platforms? What do you do to encourage direct engagement and active communication with audience members? Do you interact with social media participants by replying to audience or fan posts or comments? What social interaction campaigns, if any, have you performed (games, sweepstakes, polls quizzes, etc.)?

7. In addition to your own social media platforms, do you also engage and share relevant content on other platforms and/or sites where your target audience is active?

8. Do you leverage the social media platforms and marketability of each member of cast and crew prior to attachment? Have you leveraged the social media platforms of other associated people and organizations (such as coop partners)? Do you seek opportunities to serve as a guest on the social media sites and blogs of influencers, podcasters, vidcasters and other social media and new media personalities?

9. Do you purposely employ a variety of media and content types (blog posts, social media posts, pictures, videos, articles, news releases, etc.) within your social media activity? How are they aligned with your strategic goals? Are they aligned with any of your films' particular stages of production? Are they aligned with specific demands of the AIDA framework?

10. Do you monitor your social media activity and engagement to determine which topics and varieties of content are particularly popular? The greatest number of views, likes, shares, comments, etc.? Do you use this information to plan and create additional content?

WEBSITE MARKETING

1. Does the design of your website(s) reflect your brand message and appropriate level of professionalism? Consider issues such as your website's page layout, logo, tagline, banner, menu/navigation bar, images, colors, fonts, headings, etc.

2. Does the website have a mobile version or responsive design? Do you regularly test your site to see how it loads and looks on the most popular browsers, including desktop applications and mobile browsers?

3. Is there an immediately identifiable and obvious brand message conveyed consistently on each and every page? What would website visitors say makes you unique from other competing filmmakers? Why would they buy (either as a film distributor or audience member) your movies from the hundreds of others offered by competing filmmakers?

4. Is the content consistent across your website(s) with that which appears on your social media platforms, IMDb profiles and other marketing materials? Does your

website include social media buttons on all pages? Where are these buttons located? Alongside the navigation bar? Footer? Both? Similarly, does your website content contain social media and email sharing buttons?

5. Does your website feature "proof-points" to establish your filmmaking credibility and support your brand message? Proof-points such as: Studio experience? Awards? Financial and critical success of past film projects? Media quotes? Quotes from respected industry insiders? Film school degrees? Other "proof-points"?

6. What information, if any, is available for download from your website(s)? Your filmmaker biography? Resume or curriculum vitae? List of credits? Short films? Film clips? Trailers? Wallpaper of film key art? Storyboards? Behind-the-scenes pictures? Media interviews? Press releases? Electronic press kits? Other?

7. Does your website contain a video of you speaking directly to the website visitor and/or a video interview in which you discuss your background and passion for filmmaking?

8. Does your website provide any *compelling* reasons why a visitor would want to bookmark and/or return to your site? A career or film project diary? Cast and crew interviews? Fan comments? Fan photo albums? Ongoing portfolio/reel additions? List of favorite films or filmmakers? Confessions/lessons learned? Genre resources page? Interviews with genre personalities? Genre news archives with links? Invitations to ask questions/seek advice?

9. Do you regularly use web analytics to determine which of your pages are the most popular? Those pages with the highest number of visitors? Those pages on which visitors spend the most time? Pages with the highest conversion rates? Are you able to use this information to identify important topics and subjects on which to base additional website and social media content?

10. Does your website have a strong "call-to-action" on each and every page? Calls-to-action may include: (i) a request to contact you directly using email, telephone and/or a contact form; (ii) an invitation for visitors to interact with you via other digital platforms (social media, YouTube, Vimeo, related websites, etc.); (iii) encouraging the website visitor to respond within the comments section of a given page on a specific subject; (iv) an invitation to watch your latest film via an online service or at a local theater (or a coming premier); (v) an invitation to join a mailing or subscription list to receive periodic updates on various projects/subjects; and (vi) Including sharing, print or email links on each page among many other possible calls-to-action.

11. Does the site incorporate short URLs of 115 characters or fewer? Are the URLs descriptive and include keywords or phrases? Good URLs include keywords (but they are not keyword stuffed), include hyphens ("-") to separate the keywords, are unique for each page and comprise fewer than 115 characters (including the domain name).

12. Is each page properly optimized with a title tag, meta tags and ALT text for each image? Does each page have a unique title? Can the user tell from the title what the page is all about and is the description an accurate representation of what the page has to offer? Is the primary keyword or key phrase contained at the beginning of the title tag? Are page titles limited to fifty to sixty-five characters in length? If the title is longer than this, the entirety will not be displayed in the search engine results (SERPs)? Are image filenames descriptive in terms of the subjects of the images? Do the images use keywords in the filename? Do all images have the ALT tag defined?

13. Is your content well-formatted and easy to read quickly? Is the text broken down into easy-to-read paragraphs? Scannable? Are your page titles, headlines and subheads well-written? Do they generate attention, interest and anticipation? Does text include bold, italics, bullet-pointed lists, quotes, etc. to make the content more easily read and/or scanned? Is the text/content sufficiently brief? Does each page incorporate supporting pictures or graphics?

14. Does each page and form of content contain powerful internal anchor text? Does each page contain the primary keywords, phrases and secondary keywords and phrases as appropriate? Are meta keyword tags and meta descriptions used? Does each page have a unique meta description? Is each description tag between 150 and 160 characters? Are the meta descriptions representative of the actual content and do the descriptions entice users?

15. Does the website have a clear content structure? Does the website have a consistent interface across all pages? Is the content grouped into relevant categories and pages? Are the most important pages and/or content linked from the home page and placed higher in the pagination or navigation? Is the most important and interesting content located above the fold? Does each web page have between two and ten internal links? Are visitors able to reach desired content within no more than three or four clicks?

MEDIA RELATIONS

1. Have you established relationships with local and regional members of the media? Relationships with international, national and regional trade associations, guilds, unions, trade publications and other industry organizations?

2. Do you maintain a list of fifteen to twenty-five targeted media outlets? Do you have a media relationship development plan that includes regular contact, story idea pitches and public release submissions?

3. In addition to traditional media outlets, have you identified potential new media outlets such as blogs? Podcasts? Vidcasts? Other?

4. Have you collected and studied samples of past articles, newsletters, magazines and other content published by each targeted media outlet?

5. Do you have materials, such as press books and EPKs, which adequately support your media outreach activities?

6. Do you maintain a schedule of regular public releases? Are your public releases, and other media activity, aligned with your film's production calendar and the film's scheduled release date?

7. Do your public releases (and other branding, marketing and promotional content) adhere to the inverted pyramid? Do your public releases adhere to the writing style or guidelines used by most of your targeted media outlets?

8. Do you use dedicated public release distribution services? Are your public releases posted to your website's press room? Do you distribute public releases on your social media accounts and to those registered to your email database? Do you follow up any public release submissions to specific media professionals with email *and* brief telephone calls?

9. Do you maintain an archive or library of past media coverage on your website? Does this archive or library include coverage of your film? Yourself as filmmaker? Your production company? Members of your cast? Crew?

10. Are your media outreach and other public relations activities coordinated with your film's production status and release schedule? Likewise, are public releases, article submissions and pitches coordinated with the lead time required of each targeted media outlet? While some websites and forums may only require twenty-four to forty-eight hours to publish new material, trade publications, general interest publications and broadcasters may require thirty to sixty days or more.

FILM MARKETS, FESTIVALS & EVENT MARKETING

1. Do you maintain a budget and calendar of active meetings and events where you are able to interact with other industry professionals and members of your target audience?
2. Does this event or meeting calendar include events hosted by you and your team? Do these self-hosted events have clear marketing and promotional objectives?
3. Do you recognize and leverage the marketing and promotional value of launch parties, wrap parties, set visits and test screenings?
4. Do you have a list of targeted professionals (by name and/or profession) that you hope to connect with at specific events? In addition to external events, do you use self-hosted events to invite and meet such targeted professionals?
5. When attending external events such as film festivals and film markets, do you take the opportunity to collect marketing and promotional materials from other films within your genre and budget range?
6. When targeting film festivals, do you first consider your marketing and promotional objectives? The individual characteristics and composition of each festival? The appropriateness of your film, its genre, production value and reputation relative to each prospective festival? Have you allocated sufficient funds within your marketing budget to support your festival strategy?
7. Once accepted, have you coordinated with the film festival's marketing and media relations professionals? Are your film marketing and marketing materials appropriate (and of sufficient quality) for the festival? Are you able to enlist an adequate number of staff members to promote your film's screening while at the festival?
8. In addition to traditional film-related events, have you considered attending highly focused events that cater specifically to your target audience? Cosplay or Comi-Con events? Auto or boat shows? Vacation and travel conferences (if your film features a particularly attractive and exotic location)? Other appropriate conventions, conferences or events?
9. Do you regularly update your marketing and promotional materials with testimonials, industry awards, film festival laurels and critical reviews?
10. Do you actively market and promote the events you will be attending? Do you follow up with commentary, photos, videos and other content after the conclusion of the event? In addition to details of the event itself, do you share photos and stories of the people you had the opportunity to meet at these events?

LOW-COST ADVERTISING & PROMOTIONAL CAMPAIGNS

1. Do you restrict your paid advertising and promotional campaigns to only those opportunities in which you are able to *both* (i) reach the film's target audience at the lowest possible expense and (ii) ensure an acceptable rate of response from those audience members?

2. Have you identified and studied the various types of content most popular with your target audience? Have you incorporated the results and findings of this research into low-cost targeted buzz or viral marketing campaigns?

3. Do you have email database registration banners on each page of your website? Are the registration banners strategically placed among the most highly visible segments of the web page? Are only the most important banner ads placed above the fold of your website? Although banner ads placed above the fold receive greater attention and response, Google penalizes websites that, in its view, have too many ads above the fold.

4. Do you schedule and budget for pay-per-click and selective banner advertising campaigns to coincide with your film's release date? Have you created specific landing pages for those PPC and banner ad campaigns?

5. Do you use contests, sweepstakes and giveaways to (i) build your email database; (ii) conduct market research; (iii) obtain user-generated content (via photo, video and key art); (iv) enhance "buzz"; and (v) strengthen relationships and enhance audience engagement?

6. Have you selected a customer relationship management or database marketing system that (i) provides support for the various types of campaigns (email, text message, telephone, snail mail, social media, etc.) you expect to run; (ii) is compatible with any specific online apps or any file types you are likely to use and may be provided by list brokers and/or marketing partners; and (iii) for which one-time set-up and regular ongoing expenses are reasonable given the system's capabilities?

7. When conducting email and text message marketing, are you sure to: (i) create a welcome email and an auto-responder series comprised of ten to twenty automated and pre-scheduled emails for new subscribers; (ii) match the message and content to the audience; (iii) make the email and email return address familiar; (iv) utilize interesting subject lines; and (v) keep your email and text message marketing simple and repeatable?

8. Have you tested postcard marketing with highly targeted audiences such as super-fans, influencers, friends and family of cast and crew members, media professionals, sales agents, producer's representatives and other influential professionals and personalities?

9. Do you use promotional merchandise as a secondary revenue source and as a way to incentivize sweepstakes contestants, cast and crew members, super-fans, influencers and film festival attendees?

10. Have you pursued coop marketing and product placement opportunities to extend your market reach and increase target market access? Are the brands of your coop marketing and product placement partners consistent with the brand of your film and production company?

FILM SALES & DISTRIBUTION

1. Have you joined industry organizations, attended film markets and networked with sales agents, producer's representatives and distributors to conduct market research on recent and emerging industry, marketplace and distribution trends?

2. Do you restrict yourself and your production company to developing film projects based upon objective market research and proven market demand? If so, how do you leverage audience preferences and market research into you film's development, pre-production, production, marketing, promotion and distribution?

3. Are there aspects of your film or its production that may have particular appeal to other territories, nations or markets outside your own? Story elements? Film locations? Featured cast members? Other?

4. Do you have any objectives for your film beyond financial return? Perhaps to bring attention to a social issue? Showcase the talents of the filmmaker, director and cast and crew members? Other objective(s)? Have these secondary objectives been factored into your film's distribution strategy?

5. If accepted to a leading first-tier film festival, have you maintained sufficient budget to employ a publicist and, perhaps, a producer's representative? Have you met with these professionals beforehand to agree on a clear set of expectations and responsibilities for each?

6. Have you leveraged the use of marketing and distribution consultants and advisors to glean greater insights into the marketing, promotional and distribution process? To better "package" your film to prospective sales agents and producer's representatives? Are these consultants and advisors able and willing to refer you to other respected and well-positioned industry professionals?

7. Do you vet professional service providers such as sales agents and producer's reps with trusted members of your professional network? Particularly those who have worked with specific sales agents and reps in the past? If your sales agent or producer's representative are licensed attorneys, do you have your agreements with such agents and representatives reviewed by another objective outside independent entertainment attorney?

8. Do you have distribution agreements reviewed by a qualified and highly experienced entertainment attorney and accountant? Does your attorney (or prospective attorney) have a reputation for aggressively protecting the rights of the filmmakers he/she represents? Restricting the level of distribution and other fees that may unreasonably limit the filmmaker's income/profitability?

9. Have you budgeted sufficient funds to assemble and provide all required deliverables to distributors? Are there any deliverables or related expenses, such as errors and omissions insurance, that may be cheaper to obtain from a sales agent or distributor? Do you maintain a list of, and compile, distribution deliverables throughout development, production and post-production?

10. Do you recognize the importance of the launch team in driving initial sales through positive word-of-mouth, ratings and reviews and in generating early sales momentum? What plans, if any, have you developed for the recruitment and guidance of a launch team? Are you prepared to provide members of the launch team with examples of the types of ratings, reviews and other promotional activities most supportive of the film's release?

PERFORMANCE MEASURES & METRICS

1. What are the primary and secondary objectives for yourself as a filmmaker, for your production company and your films? Critical acclaim and awards? Number of views? Investor returns? How do you objectively quantify, monitor and evaluate your progress against these objectives?

2. Using these performance measures, how does your recent performance compare with the prior year and/or with your prior films? How does your recent performance compare with the expectations and/or estimates contained within your business or marketing plan?

3. Do you track and benchmark your film's performance against similar measures from competing filmmakers and similar genre films? What do these comparisons reveal with regard to your own films' performance? Are competing films outperforming you and your films? If so, how? What, if anything, can you do to close the gap and/or surpass these competing films?

4. From a financial point of view, have your past films generated sufficient revenues to cover distribution fees, marketing and promotional expenses, production costs and other expenses? What was the extent of the financial return earned by investors? How quickly have you been able to achieve break-even? How quickly have you been able to generate an acceptable return to investors? Are your current film projects on track with historical and projected expectations to meet or exceed break-even and profitability?

5. With regard to your social media activity, what are your total numbers of friends, fans, followers, subscribers, views, etc.? How much time do you allocate to social media and how does this time translate into the average number of posts, comments, etc.? Daily? Weekly? Monthly? What is the relative level of engagement as measured by shares, likes, comments, etc.? Specifically, by name whenever possible, who are your most engaged social media fans and friends?

6. With regard to your website, how many individual pages does your website comprise? What is the site's total number of visitors? Daily? Weekly? Monthly? Rate of repeat visitors? Rate of new visits? Average site visit duration? Bounce rate (rate at which visitors click away from the site after having arrived at and viewed only one page)?

7. How do your sites rank on the most popular search engines? How many external links are directed to your home page? How many links are directed to your internal pages? Which of website pages have the highest number of incoming links? Assuming that the pages with the most external links reflect those that are most popular with your visitors (double-check against your site's analytics), are you able to produce additional website and social media content with similar subjects or topics?

8. What is the conversion rate in terms of the percentage of visitors who complete a call-to-action? Conversion rates can be measured based on the total number of visitors to the site, new visitors, repeat visitors, visitors to specific pages or of specific calls-to-action located anywhere on the site.

9. What is the total number of current email database subscribers? How many, on average, are added each week? Each month? Have you automated a welcome email and series of auto-responders? On average how many emails do you send to your subscribers each month? (Two to four per month is considered ideal depending upon the stage of your film's production and scheduled release date.)

10. What impact, if any, have your branding, marketing and promotional activities had on such external measures as the IMDb STARmeter, Klout Score (klout.com), Hubspot Website grader (www.website.grader.com) and similar performance and measurement grading tools? How does your marketing and promotion compare to prior periods? Compare to competing filmmakers, films and production companies?

MARKETING PLAN

1. Summary

Founded by Robert G. Barnwell, Subic Bay Films is an independent film studio formed to produce and distribute intense low-budget (production budgets ranging from $500 thousand to $2.5 million USD) political-military action films. Subic Bay films highlight the world's lesser-known armed conflicts and provide audience members with a greater understanding of and insight into their underlying causes and effects. The films focus on special operations forces, domestic and foreign intelligence agencies, national and international government agencies, and local citizens and their adversaries. The films are further characterized by rapid pacing, strong story elements, multifaceted characters and carefully choreographed action scenes.

2. Key Success Factors

1. Stable and ready access to funding/financing
2. High production values achieved at relatively low cost
3. Expanding community of engaged fans

3. Marketing Objectives

1. Increase professional credibility (proof-points) and strength of professional brand
2. Expand investor, professional and referral network
3. Significant number of email database registrants

4. Marketing Performance Measures

1. Quantity and quality of professional network (and database registrations)
2. Frequency of audience engagement
3. Quantity and quality of media coverage
4. Number of social media views, likes, shares, friends, fans, subscribers, etc.
5. Number of active launch team members

5. Target Audience Description

The core audience is primarily comprised of males between the ages of 15 and 35. Target audience members tend to spend a considerable amount of discretionary income and time on cable and online video and film-based entertainment, particularly action-adventure films. Such audience members have high standards and expectations with regard to video and film-based entertainment (and associated marketing and promotion). Many have prior military experience while those without such experience tend to have a better-than-average knowledge of the military, weapons and tactics (and a correspondingly low tolerance for a lack of authenticity). Much of the core audience are also electronic gamers who regularly play such single and multi-player first-person shooters as *Battlefield*, *Call of Duty*, *Counter-Strike*, *Halo* and *Tom Clancy's Rainbow Six*. Members of the audience tend to own several mobile devices through which they are actively engaged online with a highly valued community of friends and acquaintances on such sites as YouTube, Vimeo, Facebook, Twitter, Instragram, Snapchat and special interest forums and sites.

6. Genre-Defining Films (Director)

[This list should be comprised of twenty to thirty films that represent a combination of: (i) those films most critically acclaimed within the genre, regardless of release date; (ii) those released within the past ten years and that are, therefore, most likely to have the greatest effect on current genre audience expectations; and (iii) those within the genre most reflective of your own film projects.]

1. *13 Hours* (Michael Bay)
2. *American Sniper* (Clint Eastwood)
3. *Apocalypse Now* (Francis Ford Coppola)
4. *Argo* (Ben Affleck)
5. *Blackhawk Down* (Ridley Scott)
6. *Braveheart* (Mel Gibson)
7. *The Deer Hunter* (Michael Cimino)
8. *Dunkirk* (Christopher Nolan)
9. *Full Metal Jacket* (Stanley Kubrick)
10. *Fury* (David Ayer)
11. *Hacksaw Ridge* (Mel Gibson)
12. *Hurt Locker* (Kathryn Bigelow)
13. *The Kingdom* (Peter Berg)
14. *Letters from Iwo Jima* (Clint Eastwood)
15. *Lone Survivor* (Peter Berg)
16. *The Patriot* (Roland Emmerich)
17. *Platoon* (Oliver Stone)
18. *Saving Private Ryan* (Steven Spielberg)
19. *The Thin Red Line* (Terrence Malick)
20. *Zero Dark Thirty* (Kathryn Bigelow)

7. Audience Viewing Criteria

Once made aware of a film, most potential audience members will base their viewing, rental or purchase decision on the following key criteria:

1. Genre
2. Title and key art
3. Reviews, ratings and word-of-mouth
4. Teasers and trailers

8. Marketing & Promotional Materials

1. Business cards and stationery
2. Key art
3. Script treatment and film summaries
4. Filmmaker, cast and crew biographies
5. Director's statement and producer's notes
6. FAQ sheet
7. Storyboards and concept artwork
8. Promotional reel
9. Pitch book and look book
10. Investment memorandum
11. Social media platforms
12. Website(s)
13. IMDb profiles
14. Electronic press kits (EPK)
15. BTS materials
16. Teasers and trailers
17. Public releases and press book
18. Promotional merchandise
19. Contact management database
20. Email marketing system

9. Marketing & Promotional Activities

Social media posts (3x/week)
Email database (2x/month)
Website updates (2–3x/month)
Networking events (2x/month)

Contact w/media or influencers (2x/week)
Public release distribution (1x/month)
Revise marketing materials (2 hours/day)
Review marketing analytics (1x/week)

10. Supplemental Documents/Information

1. Marketing budget: $XXX,XXX
   (Line-item budget with specific allocations attached)
2. Marketing calendar
3. Production schedule
4. Library of standard emails, auto-responders and Other Documents

TEST SCREENING QUESTIONNAIRE

Test Screening Questionnaire

Please take a moment to let us know how you feel about the movie. Thank you.

1. What was your reaction to the movie overall?

EXCELLENT ☐   VERY GOOD ☐   GOOD ☐   FAIR ☐   POOR ☐

2. Would you recommend this movie to your friends?

YES, DEFINITELY ☐   YES, PROBABLY ☐   NO, PROBABLY NOT ☐   NO, DEFINITELY NOT ☐

3. What would you tell your friends about this movie?
Not just whether you liked it or not, but how would you describe it to them?
(Please be as complete as possible.)

4. Please list what scenes you liked most and liked least, if any.
(Please be as specific as possible in your description of the scenes.)

SCENES LIKED MOST   SCENES LIKED LEAST

5. How would you rate each of the following elements of the movie?
(Please mark one answer for each performance and element)

	EXCELLENT	VERY GOOD	GOOD	FAIR	POOR
CHARACTER #1	☐	☐	☐	☐	☐
CHARACTER #2	☐	☐	☐	☐	☐
CHARACTER #3	☐	☐	☐	☐	☐
CHARACTER #4	☐	☐	☐	☐	☐
CHARACTER #5	☐	☐	☐	☐	☐
CHARACTER #6	☐	☐	☐	☐	☐
CHARACTER #7	☐	☐	☐	☐	☐
THE STORY	☐	☐	☐	☐	☐
THE ACTION	☐	☐	☐	☐	☐
THE SUSPENSE	☐	☐	☐	☐	☐
THE SCARINESS	☐	☐	☐	☐	☐
THE SETTINGS	☐	☐	☐	☐	☐
THE PACE	☐	☐	☐	☐	☐
THE MUSIC	☐	☐	☐	☐	☐
THE ENDING	☐	☐	☐	☐	☐

6. Which of the following words or phrases best describe the movie?
(Please mark as many as apply.)

ENTERTAINING	☐	INTENSE	☐	EMOTIONALLY SATISFYING	☐
BORING/DULL	☐	CONFUSING	☐	DIFFERENT/ORIGINAL	☐
DRAMATIC	☐	HAS A GOOD STORY	☐	WELL PACED	☐
POWERFUL	☐	NOT MY TYPE OF MOVIE	☐	TOO SLOW IN SPOTS	☐
FUN	☐	TOO PREDICTABLE	☐	TOO FAST IN SPOTS	☐
SCARY	☐	INTERESTING CHARACTERS	☐	GOOD MUSIC	☐
INTERESTING	☐	LACKS COMPELLING CHARACTERS	☐		☐
UPLIFTING	☐	SYMPATHETIC CHARACTERS	☐		☐
INNOVATIVE	☐	THOUGHT-PROVOKING	☐		☐
DONE BEFORE	☐	GRIPPING	☐		☐

6a. Who was your favorite character?

6b. Why do you feel that way?
(Please be as specific as possible.)

7a. Were there any other characters you particularly liked?

7b. Why?
(Please be as specific as possible.)

8a. Who was your least favorite character?

8b. Why?
(Please be as specific as possible.)

9a. Were there any other characters you disliked?

9b. Why?
(Please be as specific as possible.)

10. What were your feelings about [*Element of the Film*]?
(Please be as specific as possible.)

11. What, if anything, did you find confusing about the movie that was not cleared up by the end? (Please be as specific as possible.)

12. Did you feel that any part of the movie moved slowly? If yes, please list which scene or scenes moved slowly.
(Please be as specific as possible.)

13. Please indicate your gender:

MALE ⬜   FEMALE ⬜

14. Please indicate your age group:

UNDER 12	⬜	30 TO 34	⬜
12 TO 14	⬜	35 TO 39	⬜
15 TO 17	⬜	40 TO 44	⬜
18 TO 20	⬜	45 TO 49	⬜
21 TO 24	⬜	50 TO 59	⬜
25 TO 29	⬜	60 & OVER	⬜

GLOSSARY

Action – The fourth and final step of the AIDA model in which an audience member takes action, typically in the form of a film or merchandise rental, purchase or other brand engagement.

Advertising – The process of using paid announcements to increase an audience's awareness and interest in a particular film, filmmaker or cross- or trans-media product. These announcements are commonly in the form of print ads, banner ads, teaser and trailer campaigns and other paid messages via traditional and/or new media channels.

Advertising Medium – Any communication channel which is used as a vehicle for advertisements, including direct mail, email, websites, social media, television, radio and periodicals (newspapers and magazines), etc.

Affinity Marketing – A marketing strategy in which a partnership between two companies or organizations is formed to promote their collective products or services to a group of people who share the same interests (known as an affinity group) to reach a greater number of prospective customers on a more cost-efficient basis than either party could do on their own.

AIDA – An acronym that stands for Attention, Interest, Desire and Action. The AIDA model is widely used in marketing and advertising to describe the steps or stages that occur from the time when an audience member first becomes aware of a film or brand through the final rental or purchase decision.

Attachment – The process of "attaching," or securing, specific actors and/or department heads during the development and pre-production stages. The attachment of respected professionals is a critical component of fundraising and potential pre-sales.

Attention – The first step in the AIDA model in which an audience member first becomes aware of a film, product or brand, commonly through word-of-mouth, publicity, pay-per-click advert, social media post or similar channel.

Audience Profile – A description of an audience member or set of audience members that includes demographic, geographic and psychographic characteristics as well as common viewing and entertainment habits.

Audience Research – Research and analysis of the composition, attitudes, knowledge, interests, preferences, behaviors and other aspects of a particular audience or audience subsegment.

Awareness – The state in which an audience member is conscious, or aware, of the existence of a film, product or brand, commonly through word-of-mouth, social media, publicity or advertisement. Creating awareness is the greatest challenge facing low-budget independent filmmakers. (See also "Attention.")

Banner Ad – A form of online advertising, the web banner (or banner ad) entails embedding an advertisement into a targeted website or web page. It is intended to attract traffic to a website by encouraging viewers to click a link on the banner ad to visit the website, landing page or registration form of the advertiser.

Behind-the-Scenes (BTS) Content – Audio, photographic, video and other multimedia materials that describe or illustrate the individuals, equipment, techniques and other aspects of filmmaking utilized in the production of a given film project.

Blockbuster – A film that generates a financial return significantly greater than its production, marketing and promotional budget. The actual financial threshold required to qualify as a "blockbuster" is subjective.

Bounce Rate – The percentage of visitors who enter the site and then leave ("bounce") rather than continuing to view other pages within the same site.

Brand Image (aka **"Brand Identity"**) – The impression in the audience's mind of a film or filmmaker based on the audience's collective experience with associated marketing and promotional campaigns, social media and websites and other points of contact. Components of the brand image may include name or titles, taglines, typefaces and graphics.

Bugs – Graphic logos that appear beneath a credit block of production companies, distribution companies, ratings agencies and other pertinent organizations.

Buying Criteria – The information that audience members use on which to base their decisions on which films to rent or purchase, including genre, title, cast, reviews and ratings.

Buzz Marketing – Buzz marketing is a viral marketing technique that is focused on maximizing the word-of-mouth of a particular campaign, film or trans-media product, whether that is through conversations among audience members' family and friends or larger-scale discussions on social media platforms.

Call-to-Action – A directive – often in the form of copy, a graphic or other medium – to induce a viewer, reader or listener to perform a specific act, such as to make a purchase or join an email database.

Campaign – A series of coordinated activities designed to help market and promote a film or other cross- or trans-media product.

Channel – A means of communication or information dissemination. In the case of film distribution channels, the means may include theaters, video-on-demand or cable broadcasting. In the case of marketing channels, the means of communications may include email, live events, texts, direct mail, social media posts and website content.

Community – Collective group of individuals, often with common characteristics and interests, who engage with one another online and offline. Such communities often form around a shared interest in a particular personality, profession, film, hobby or other interest.

Composition – The manner in which text and graphics are arranged on a page, poster, website, advertisement or other work. Common elements of composition include alignment, grouping, placement, space and visual flow of body copy, colors, head-lines and illustrations. It establishes the overall appearance, relative importance and relationships between the graphic elements to achieve a smooth flow of information (message) and eye movement for maximum effectiveness. (See also "Layout.")

Conversion Rate – The percentage of site or page visitors who complete a call-to-action.

Cooperative Marketing – A marketing strategy in which two or more organizations agree to promote one another's products or services alongside their own. Such cooperative marketing arrangements allow each organization to benefit from lower marketing and promotional expenses, access to an otherwise difficult or impossible to reach audience, and the credibility the partner organization has established with their customer or audience base.

Credibility – A quality incorporating expertise, believability and trustworthiness. These attributes have both objective and subjective components. Expertise is primarily based upon relatively objective characteristics such as education, certification and experience. In contrast, believability and trustworthiness are based more on subjective factors such as perceived personality and character traits.

Credit Block – Also known as the billing block, the credit block is an abbreviated version of the credit list containing the film's stars, director, producers, crew heads and the logos of the production companies and distributors. The credit block traditionally appears at the bottom of film posters As with end credits, the order in which titles and individuals appear, as well as many official titles, are often determined by contractual agreement and/or union, guild or association requirements.

Credits – A list containing the film's actors, the directors, producers, the companies producing and distributing the movie (by name and/or logo) and the artistic and technical crew. The order in which titles and individuals appear, as well as many official titles, are often determined by contractual agreement and/or union, guild or association requirements.

Cross-media – The use of multiple media forms to communicate a story or extend a brand. Cross-media projects commonly combine many different types of communications channels (copy, print, graphics, animation, video, etc.) and are distributed across multiple platforms, such as films, books, magazines, comic books, television, social media, interactive websites and other outlets. Cross-media differs from trans-media in that different communication channels and platforms are used as alternate forms of distribution of the film's underlying storyline. Trans-media, on the other hand, uses these multiple channels and platforms to advance or continue the story-line.

Database Marketing – A form of direct marketing using databases of fans and audience members to generate personalized marketing and promotional outreach. The method of communication can be any addressable medium, as in direct marketing. Depending upon the level of detail contained within the database, such marketing may be highly personalized, incorporating such details as name, address, birth date, telephone number and other information.

Demographics – The characteristics of a particular population, such as a target audience, as classified by age, sex, education, income, political preference, etc., for market research purposes.

Desire – The third step in the AIDA model in which an audience member develops a favorable disposition toward the film, often the result of viewing teasers, trailers, reviews and ratings.

Development – The first stage in film production in which the market demand is studied, primary audience selected, genre chosen, the ideas for the film are created, the screenplay is written, investment documentation prepared and financing sought and obtained.

Differentiation – Result of efforts to make a film or brand attractive by contrasting its unique qualities relative to completing films or brands. For instance, films are often differentiated by integrating unique story elements to an existing genre, utilizing creative filmmaking techniques, incorporating popular fiction or non-fiction characters and other elements.

Direct Marketing – A targeted form of marketing that involves presenting information about your film or brand directly to your target customer. Common forms of direct marketing include postcard mailings and personalized emails.

Distribution Channel – A link in the chain of intermediaries through which a film or information is distributed to audience members. For films, common distribution channels include: theatrical release, subscription and pay-per-view cable, video on demand and broadcast television. For information, including marketing and promotional communications, distribution channels may include social media, websites, forums, podcasts, vidcasts, trade publications, popular magazines, newspapers, radio and television.

Editorial Calendar (see "**Publishing Calendar.**")

Electronic Press Kit (EPK) – A pre-packaged set of digital promotional materials distributed to members of the media and other organizations and professionals for promotional use. The contents of an EPK media kit are similar to other types of media kits, but, due to their digital nature, are likely to include a range of audio-visual materials, including photographs, audio clips and video. EPKs are commonly posted to websites and social media platforms and are easily distributed using email, DVDs and other digital media.

Email Marketing – The use of email to develop relationships with and communicate important marketing and promotional messages to audience members and other subscribers. In the broadest sense, every email sent to a potential or current audience member should be considered email marketing given email's impact on branding and relationship-building.

Engagement – The relative amount, or lack, of interaction and connection an audience has with a film or other brand. This connection can be a reaction, interaction, effect or overall customer experience, which takes place online and offline. Online customer engagement is qualitatively different from offline engagement as the nature of the customer's interactions with a brand differs significantly on the internet. Engagement can take many forms, including visiting a website, interacting with a social media account, watching teasers or trailers and posting reviews and ratings.

Film Festival – An event organized to present several films, typically selected by committee, from those films produced within the past year and with a similar focus or genre (feature films, documentaries, short films, animation, foreign, domestic, etc.). Film festivals are typically annual events and are commonly held in the same venue or city.

Film Market – An industry marketplace for the purpose of selling, financing and acquiring films. Participants typically include acquisition and development executives, agents, attorneys, directors, distributors, festival directors, financiers, film commissioners, producers and writers. Like film festivals, film markets are typically annual events and are commonly held in the same venue or city.

Forum – An online discussion website, or subsite, where people gather to hold conversations in the form of posted messages on particular topics of interest.

Four walling – A process through which a studio or distributor rents movie theaters for a period of time and receives all of the box office revenue. The four walls of a movie theater give the term its name.

Genre – A particular category or subset of film classified by similarities in form, style and subject matter. Popular film genres include action, comedy, drama, horror, romance and science fiction.

Google AdWords – An advertising service by Google for businesses wanting to display ads on Google and its advertising network (including YouTube). The AdWords program enables businesses to set a budget for advertising and only pay when people click links. The Adwords service is largely focused on keywords.

Guerrilla Marketing – The use of highly creative, innovative and low-cost marketing techniques aimed at obtaining maximum exposure for a film or brand with a targeted audience.

Impression – In the context of marketing, an impression is the number of times an advertisement, teaser or trailer, website page, social media post or other promotional material has been viewed. Ideally, each potential audience member is exposed to multiple impressions over the course of a marketing campaign.

Inbound Marketing – Form of marketing strategy in which a filmmaker or studio attempts to have potential audience members actively seek out and engage in the marketing and promotional activities of the film or brand via content marketing, social media marketing, search engine optimization, etc. (See also "Pull Marketing.")

Influencer – An individual that has above-average impact on a specific niche market or group. Common influencers include industry association leaders, trade magazine or newsletter editors, social media personalities, podcast and vidcast hosts, etc. Influencers are important gatekeepers who are able to provide credible access to their niche market or group. However, such individuals are not simply marketing tools, but also valued social relationship assets.

Integrated Marketing – An approach to creating a unified and seamless experience for consumers who interact with the studio or film's brand. Integrated marketing attempts to meld all aspects of marketing communication such as advertising, sales promotion, public relations, direct marketing and social media, through their respective mix of tactics, methods, channels, media and activities, so that all work together as a unified force. It is a process designed to ensure that all messaging and communications strategies are consistent across all channels.

Interactive Marketing – A marketing strategy that uses two-way communication channels to encourage audience members to engage with a studio, filmmaker or brand directly. Interactive marketing commonly utilizes email, social media posts, text messaging, blogs, forums and events.

Interest – The second step in the AIDA model in which the audience member becomes interested in learning more about the film or brand and how it may compare with other films or entertainment choices.

Investment Memorandum – A legal document that discloses the terms, conditions, risks and other information regarding a private placement. Because it is a legal document subject to specific legal and regulatory requirements, the investment memorandum should be reviewed by a qualified corporate attorney before being circulated to potential investors.

Investor Relations – The communications and interactions of the filmmaker or studio with existing and potential investors. Investor relations involves a full explanation of the investment; the intended (and actual) uses of investor funds; an estimate of projected revenues, income and cash flow; and the timing of any anticipated disbursements to investors, among other details. Ideally, investor relations should be viewed as a component of the film's, studio's or filmmaker's ongoing marketing and promotional activities rather than merely a legal and fiscal responsibility.

Key Art – The primary artwork used in the marketing and promotion for a motion picture, including: images, title fonts, credit blocks and bugs.

Keyword – A commonly used word to describe a person, place or thing (such as an audience segment, genre or film). Keywords are used by search engines to locate specific subjects and, therefore, are important components of film descriptions, websites, social media posts, public releases and other marketing and promotional materials.

Launch Team – A group of people (typically comprised of 100 or fewer friends and fans) who work collectively to promote the launch or release of a new film or other entertainment product. Members of the launch team promote the release to their circle of social media and offline friends and family; post favorable ratings and reviews to numerous websites; and perform related promotional activities designed to increase attention and interest. These activities are traditionally timed to peak during the days immediately before and after the film's broad release.

Layout – The manner in which graphics and copy are arranged or "laid out" on a particular promotional graphic, website or other promotional work. The arrangement of the individual visual elements and the relationship – or visual hierarchy – formed between them determines the relative visual appeal of the composition and the extent to which a viewer's attention is directed to the most important elements.

Look Book – A book, binder or electronic collection of photographs and graphics used to illustrate the producer's and director's vision for the completed film. The look book contains carefully selected photographs and graphics to quickly illustrate the proposed film's storyline, characters, key scenes, locations, wardrobe and props as well as color grading, lighting and other elements of the film's intended visual style.

Market Niche – A small market segment, or subset, of the larger market on which a film and its marketing are focused. The choice of market niche plays a significant factor in the film's production budget, choice of story elements and numerous other factors that affect the film's ultimate production value, marketability and playability. Some look books also contain key art, a film summary, character descriptions, director's or producer's statement, biographies of the cast and crew and similar information. In such cases, the look book is also able to serve is a "pitch book."

Market Research – Research and analysis of the market, or subset of a market, to determine the demand for a specific type of film, or genre, and the preferences of those within the market. Such research includes audience analysis as well as market trends and demand for films and/or other cross- or trans-media products of a particular genre, historical performance of similar films, identification of any competing films currently in development, the market effectiveness and preference for various distribution channels and similar information.

Marketability – The ability, or lack thereof, of a film to attract an audience. The marketability of a film includes numerous elements, the most common of which are there presence of recognizable actors, a script based on a popular literary or other media property, familiar characters, a popular genre and exciting marketing and promotional materials, such key art and trailers.

Marketing – The individual and collective activities used to support the branding and promotion of a film, slate of films, cross- and trans-media products or a filmmaker to an audience. Such marketing activities commonly include market research, digital promotion, media relations, database marketing and advertising.

Marketing Calendar – A schedule used to define and control the marketing and promotional process. The marketing calendar determines the types of marketing and promotional activities and materials required, where such activities and materials should take place or be distributed, and when these activities and materials should be completed or be made available. In the case of marketing and promoting films, marketing and promotional activities and associated materials are typically scheduled to align with the film's production and certain production milestones, such as fundraising or the film's general release.

Marketing Mix – The individual actions, or tactics, selected from all available alternatives, or options, to brand, market and promote a product or service such as a filmmaker, production company or studio. These actions and tactics may include social media, websites, networking, public relations, event marketing and advertising.

Marketing Plan – A comprehensive document or blueprint that outlines the marketing and promotional activities and objectives in support of a film, studio or brand over the course of a set timeframe. A marketing plan typically includes an analysis of the marketplace, customer profiles, tactical and strategic objectives, schedule of promotional activities and marketing budget.

Media Kit (see "**Press Kit.**")

Media Plan – A document describing the best combination of media activities to achieve the marketing campaign's objectives, including details on strategy, tactics, budget, schedule and the media mix.

Media Relations – Activities that involve communicating and coordinating directly with media professionals with the objective of maximizing positive coverage within the traditional and new media.

Networking – The process of meeting and interacting with other people to exchange information with other people, groups and institutions to develop mutually beneficial relationships.

Niche Marketing – A strategy whereby a film is developed and marketed for a narrowly defined and specific segment of the viewing population.

Outbound Marketing – Form of marketing through which a film, studio or filmmaker attempts to reach potential audience members who have expressed no prior interest in the film or brand, including such advertising mediums as television commercials, brochures, print ads and billboards. (See also "Push Marketing.")

Outsourcing – The process of using unaffiliated freelancers, independent professionals and companies to provide services that the filmmaker and his or her team could otherwise not do, or not do adequately, on their own. Such independent professionals are often sourced using services such as Upwork, Freelancer, Guru and Fiverr to complete tasks such as graphic design, website design and development, investment memorandum preparation and editing and post-production projects.

Pay-Per-Click ("PPC") – An internet advertising model used to direct traffic to websites, in which an advertiser pays a publisher (typically a website or search engine) whenever a hotlinked ad is clicked. Search engine advertising is one of the most popular forms of PPC. It allows advertisers to bid for ad placement at or near the top of the search engine's results when someone searches on a related keyword.

Pitch – A formal or informal discussion meant to persuade. The formality, complexity and sophistication of the pitch is determined by the nature, significance and/or value of the request or objective.

Pitch Book – A brief presentation used to provide its readers with a quick overview of a film and/or film investment opportunity. The pitch book is used during face-to-face or online meetings with potential investors, sales agents, cast and crew members and others. The pitch book is often a hybrid between a look book and a traditional investment or business presentation.

Playability – The extent to which the audience enjoys the film and how that film performs relative to the audience's original expectations. Playability is commonly attributed to the strength of the film's story, production value and its rhythm and pacing.

Positioning – A marketing strategy crafted to uniquely position a brand, relative to competing brands, in the mind of current and potential audience members. Production companies and filmmakers apply this strategy by emphasizing the distinguishing features and characteristics of their brand and seeking to communicate this image through marketing and promotion.

Post-Production – The fourth stage of film production, following principal photography. The post-production phase commonly takes place over several months and includes complete editing, visual effects, color correction and the addition of music and sound.

Pre-Production – The second step of film production, following development, during which the financing and script are finalized, cast and crew recruited, production budgeted, locations secured, principal photography scheduled, shot lists and storyboards prepared, and sets, wardrobe and props designed and assembled.

Press Book – A small book or brochure designed to publicize a motion picture. Press books are especially useful in promoting a particular film for the purposes of industry award nominations and to solicit awards votes from awards committees and voting members of particular associations, guilds, unions and other awards-granting organizations.

Press Kit – Often referred to as a media kit, a press kit is a pre-packaged set of promotional materials that provide members of the media information about a film, studio and/or filmmaker. Contents typically include a director's statement, producer's notes, key art, credit list, cast and crew biographies, BTS content, FAQ sheet, teasers and trailers and selective copies of past media coverage and critical reviews.

Press Mentions – Instances in which the traditional or new media mention, quote or otherwise refer to a film, studio or filmmaker.

Press Release (see "**Public Release.**")

Primary Audience – The target core audience to which the film production and its branding, marketing and promotional activities are focused. While a film may have broad audience appeal, there is typically a primary audience whose composition and demographics are particularly well-suited to the film, its storyline and its marketing and promotion.

Principal Photography – The third step of film production, following pre-production. In the strictest sense, principal photography refers only to the main unit's act of recording the film production (excluding filming of secondary units as well as any pickup or insert shots filmed later during the post-production stage). However, many professionals also use the term to refer more broadly to the filming stage of the production process and, in this context, it includes any filming by any unit that takes place during this stage or the production process.

Prints and Advertising (p&a) – Refers to the copies of the film ("prints") which cinemas run in their projectors (either physical film or digital files) and "advertising" refers to all the promotional activity designed to inform the public about the movie and encourage them to purchase or rent it. Although p&a implies there are only two categories of expenses, p&a encompasses all the costs associated with branding, marketing and branding.

Producer of Marketing and Distribution (PMD) – The senior-most producer charged with the oversight of the film's marketing and distribution activities. Responsibilities include assisting in the identification of the most commercially attractive target audience(s), markets, film genres, audience-oriented scripts and distribution channels. The PMD is also responsible for recruiting, supervising and coordinating with marketing and distribution professionals such as graphic designers, website developers, trailer editors, publicists and sales agents.

Producer's Representative – An individual or firm with deep connections to domestic distributors (such as studios and networks) and who sells and licenses films on behalf of filmmakers. Depending on the representative's experience, a producer's rep may consult and advise filmmakers on each phase of production, including the development, financing, production, marketing and distribution process of a film.

Product Placement – The practice in which manufacturers of branded goods or providers of a service gain exposure for their products and services by paying for them to be featured in films. In addition to the payment received from these companies, filmmakers often benefit from association with the company's brand as well as possible co-marketing opportunities.

Production Company – A company that coordinates the financial, technical and organizational management required to produce a feature film. In a broad sense, the production company is responsible for the overall creation of the work but may or may not own the physical studios in which the films are produced. (See also "Studio.")

Production Value – The combined technical qualities of the methods, materials or stagecraft skills used in the production of a motion picture or artistic performance. Ultimately, the production value is determined by the audience's overall impression of the film's lighting, sound, locations, set design, wardrobe, props, cast performance, direction and other associated production methods, materials and techniques.

Promotion – The individual and collective activities, efforts and materials designed to present the brand in a way that creates audience attention, interest, desire and action (AIDA) in regard to the filmmaker and their films. Promotion helps to establish and solidify the brand and, ultimately, either directly or indirectly, to increase demand for the filmmaker's movies and promotional products.

Public Release – A press release, news release, media release, press statement or video release is a written or multi-media communication directed at members of the traditional or new media for the purpose of generating coverage for the film, studio or filmmaker's brand.

Publishing Calendar (aka "**Editorial Calendar**") – A schedule used to define and control the process of creating content, from idea through writing and publication. The publishing calendar determines what subjects and types of content to publish, where such content should be published (website, social media, new media and/or traditional media outlets) and when such content should be published. In the case of marketing and promoting films, the publishing calendar is typically aligned with the film's production and certain production milestones, such as fundraising or the film's general release.

Pull Marketing – A promotional strategy in which a filmmaker or studio attempts to have potential audience members actively seek out and engage in the marketing and promotional activities of the film or brand, including email registration, social media engagement, visiting film and studio websites, attending events, participating in online contests and sweepstakes, etc.

Push Marketing – A promotional strategy in which a filmmaker or studio attempts to reach potential audience members who have expressed no prior interest in the film or brand, including such advertising mediums as television commercials, print ads, billboards, etc.

Relationship Marketing – A marketing strategy focused on long-term customer loyalty, engagement and value rather than the exclusive pursuit of shorter-term goals such as the sale or rental of a single film or product.

Sales Agent – An individual or firm with deep connections to international distributors and who sells and licenses films on behalf of filmmakers. Sales agents specialize in segmenting and selling rights to individual territories. Effective film sales agents must be able to negotiate, draw up contracts and deal with international client and distributor demands.

Search Engine Optimization (SEO) – The process of maximizing the number of visitors to a particular website by ensuring that the site appears high on the list of results returned by a search engine for specific key words or phrases.

Social Media Marketing (SMM) – A form of internet marketing that utilizes social networking websites as a marketing tool. The goal of SMM is to produce content that users will share with their social network to help a company increase brand exposure and broaden customer reach.

STARMeter – A ranking provided by IMDb that measures the relative popularity of the professionals (such as cast, crew and producers) who work in the entertainment industry. The rankings are based upon proprietary IMDb algorithms that take into account several measures of popularity.

Studio – A production company that has its own privately owned studio facility or facilities that are used to make films and other entertainment properties.

Target Marketing – The process of breaking a market into segments and then concentrating marketing efforts on those few key segments consisting of the customers whose needs and desires most closely match your film and/or trans-media product offerings. Target marketing commonly increases both the effectiveness and efficiency of marketing activities.

Teaser – A short-form trailer, often thirty seconds or less, for an upcoming film commonly released long in advance of the film and longer-form trailers. (See also "Trailer.")

Theatrical Release – The process of distributing a film within theaters for public viewing. A theatrical release may be limited, appearing in only a few theaters for a limited time, or wide, in which the film is made available within a large number of theaters for a duration subject principally to audience demand.

Trailer – Also known as a preview or coming attraction, a trailer is essentially a 30–180 second video promotion for a forthcoming film. Trailers consist of a series of selected shots from the film being advertised. Since the purpose of the trailer is to attract an audience to the film, these excerpts are usually drawn from the most exciting, funny or otherwise noteworthy parts of the film but in abbreviated form.

Trans-media – The use of multiple media forms to communicate a story or extend a brand. Trans-media projects commonly combine many different types of communications channels (copy, print, graphics, animation, video, etc.) and are distributed across multiple platforms, such as films, books, magazines, comic books, television, social media, interactive websites and other outlets. Trans-media differs from cross-media in that different communication channels and platforms are used to advance or continue the storyline; whereas cross-media uses these multiple channels and platforms as alternate forms of distribution of the film's underlying story.

User Experience (UX) – In the context of marketing, refers primarily to a potential audience member's attitudes with regard to their experience with interactive marketing materials and channels, particularly websites. In the case of websites, UX is optimized when visitors are able to quickly and easily navigate the site to achieve their own objectives with the greatest efficiency. Elements of website UX include efficient navigation, intuitive page layout, scannable page text (use of bullets, lists, quotes, short paragraphs, etc.) and access to a wide variety of relevant, high-value and entertaining short-form content.

Video-on-Demand (VOD) – Technology and systems which allow users to select and view video content of their choice on any one of a range of devices, including television, laptop computers, cell phones and/or other devices. Unlike broadcast services, VOD users are not constrained by a broadcast schedule and can – typically through subscription, purchase or rental – view content at any place or time.

Viral Marketing – A marketing technique that induces a great number of users to pass along a marketing message to other sites or users resulting in exponential growth of the message's visibility and effect.

WORKS CITED

Aint it Cool News. 2011. http://www.aintitcool.com/node/48036, January 12.

Christopher Booker. 2004. *The Seven Basic Plots: Why We Tell Stories*. New York: Bloomsbury Academic.

Robert Caldini. 2006. *Influence: The Psychology of Persuasion*. New York: Harper Business.

Rob Cowan. 2013. "R is for Reshoots." *Hollywood Journal*, http://hollywoodjournal.com/industry-impressions/r-is-for-reshoots/20131119/, November 19.

Michael Curtin, Jennifer Holt and Kevin Samson, editors. 2014. *Distribution Revolution: Conversations about the Digital Future of Film and Television*. Oakland, CA: University of California Press.

Gene Del Vecchio. 2012. *Creating Blockbusters! How to Generate and Market Hit Entertainment for TV, Movies, Video Games, and Books*. Gretna, LA: Pelican Publishing Company Inc.

Mike Flanagan. 2008. "How to Edit a Trailer that Will Get Your Film Noticed." Micro-Filmmaker Magazine Tips & Tricks, http://www.microfilmmaker.com/tipstrick/Issue14/EditTrl3.html.

Stephen Garrett. 2012. "The Art of First Impressions: How to Cut a Movie Trailer." Filmmaker Magazine, http://filmmakermagazine.com/37093-first-impressions/, January 13.

Ali Gray. 2014. "How Twitter Killed the Official Movie Website." The Guardian, June 16.

Jim Hemphill. 2015. "'Looking for False Performance Beats': Editor Fred Raskin on *The Hateful Eight*." Filmmaker Magazine, http://filmmakermagazine.com/96749-looking-for-false-performance-beats-editor-fred-raskin-on-the-hateful-eight/#.Vp5gmzaTFZw, December 28.

David Howard and Edward Mabley. 1993. *The Tools of Screenwriting: A Writer's Guide to The Craft and The Elements of a Screenplay*. New York: St. Martin's Press.

Matt Kapko. 2014. "Social Media Still Has Little Marketing Impact in Hollywood." CIO Magazine, October 9.

Jason Kehe and Katie M. Palmer. 2013. "Secrets of a Trailer Guru: How This Guy Gets You to The Movies." *WIRED*, www.wired.com/2013/06/online-trailers-mark-woollen/, June 8.

Brent Lang. 2014. "'Snowpiercer' Hits $3.8 Million on VOD as Weinstein Co Shakes Up Distribution." *Variety*, July 29.

Mark Litwak. 2017. *Dealmaking in the Film and Television Industry*, 4th edition. W. Hollywood, CA: Silman James Press.

Stacey Parks. 2017. *The Guide to Independent Film Distribution*. Oxford: Focal Press.

Robert Marich. 2013. *Marketing to Moviegoers: A Handbook of Strategies and Tactics*, 3rd edition. Carbondale, IL: Southern Illinois University Press.

Steven Jay Rubin. 2008. "Creating Your (Increasingly Critical) BTS Footage." Producers Guild of America, http://www.producersguild.org/?page=other_side.

Dov S-S Simens. 2003. *From Reel to Deal: Everything You Need to Create a Successful Independent Film*. New York: Warner Books.

Anne Thompson. 2014. "IMDb Launches New Casting Service: EXCLUSIVE." IndieWire http://www.indiewire.com/2014/03/imdb-launches-new-casting-service-exclusive-193242. March 11.

Ronald Tobias. 1993. *20 Master Plots*. Cincinnati, OH: Writer's Digest Books.

Robert G. Barnwell is the founder and creative director of Subic Bay Films – a specialty film production company established to reduce the risks and increase the profitability of low-budget film projects on behalf of its investors. Prior to establishing Subic Bay Films, Robert worked as a strategy consultant and corporate banker providing advice and financing for such studios as 20th Century Fox, Columbia Pictures, Disney, MGM, Paramount Pictures, Universal and Warner Brothers.

Robert has served as an adjunct professor at Ringling College of Art & Design and as a speaker and guest lecturer at several leading film schools, seminars and workshops. In addition to *Guerrilla Film Marketing: The Ultimate Guide to the Branding, Marketing and Promotion of Independent Films & Filmmakers* (Routledge, 2018), he is the author of the forthcoming book, *The Entrepreneurial Filmmaker: The Ultimate Guide to the Production and Distribution of Highly-Profitable Independent Films*. Robert completed his undergraduate degree at Georgetown University and received his graduate degree from New York University.

In addition to his own film projects, on a limited basis, Robert also works with other filmmakers to provide branding, marketing, promotional, distribution and production support.

INDEX

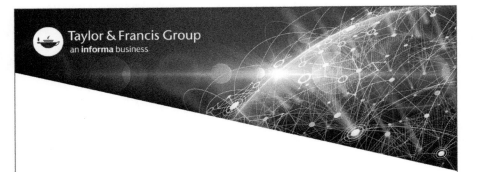